# The Durable Dominion

## A Survey of Virginia History

### Second Edition

## Peter Stewart

*Old Dominion University*

Cover image © Matej Krajcovic

**Kendall Hunt**
publishing company

www.kendallhunt.com
*Send all inquiries to*:
4050 Westmark Drive
Dubuque, IA  52004-1840

# CONTENTS

# THE SETTING

Resembling a rough pyramid with a wide base at the bottom and a narrow top, the current state of Virginia covers roughly three degrees of latitude, from just above 36 degrees 30' to about 39 degrees and six degrees longitude at the widest. A detached portion known as the Eastern Shore of Virginia serves as an eastern boundary for the Chesapeake Bay.

Save for the meteor or part of a comet that struck on the lower part of the Eastern Shore some 35 million years ago and radically changed Virginia's coastal area, nature took a long time to develop the landscape. Yet, since this major episode, Virginia's appearance changed drastically as the entire world experienced several major shifts in temperature and alignment. Until the last few hundred years, humans had only a marginal impact on nature's handiwork, but in the recent past with far more humans and increasingly sophisticated ways to tap nature's resources, the pace of change accelerated.

The collision of two continents produced tall and rugged mountains in today's western Virginia. Then as the earth's single continent began to pull apart, inland seas and swamps covered much of today's eastern part of North America. The existing mountains, formed by the previous movement of masses of land, maintained their height despite erosion from water and wind. The eastern portion of these mountains came to be called the Blue Ridge. The western part took the name Alleghenies. The Valley of Virginia rested in between the two components of the Appalachian Mountain chain. Wind and water created gaps and sent sediment down the rivers to meet the oceans, which rose and fell in response to various ice ages. Eastern Virginia eventually contained a thin layer of soil near its foothills and greater amounts of comparatively loose material above bedrock nearer the ocean. At the Fall Line, where the Piedmont and its undulating land meets the Tidewater (Coastal Plain), rocks and sudden descents made navigation of the rivers almost impossible.

The process also left vast amounts of coal underground in the Appalachian Mountains and smaller quantities in the Piedmont immediately southwest of the Fall Line on the James River. The area west of the Blue Ridge contains a wide variety of soils, minerals, and other potentially useful resources such as a pocket of arsenic in Floyd County and natural deposits of salt along the Kanawha River (modern-day West Virginia) and in what is now Smyth County, Virginia. The valley and its surrounding hills had small deposits of low-grade iron ore, gypsum, lead, bauxite, some manganese and other minerals to accompany its limestone-fed soils. In addition to its coal and at least one major deposit of iron ore on the Rapidan River, the Piedmont has trace amounts of titanium, gold, plus some less precious holdings, along with its reddish soil. The Tidewater has deposits of bog iron and marl (decayed marine life) and a wide variety of sandy soils. Its Dismal Swamp, a comparatively new phenomenon, contained piles of peat and the tannic-laced waters of Lake Drummond, one of Virginia's two natural freshwater lakes.

At the time the English first settled in the colony, a wide variety of trees covered the surface in most areas. Cedar and cypress predominated in the Dismal. Fire-resistant longleaf pine prevailed outside the swamp on sandy soils, along with occasional live oak in the southeastern part of Tidewater. In the interior, magnificent stands of chestnuts, known for the quality of its wood and its edible seeds, ranged across the landscape to accompany several other types of vegetation. Grasslands covered parts of the Valley of Virginia.

Except for the times of "little ice ages," the coastline has been moving westward since the end of the last Ice Age, roughly 10,000 years ago. Ice from that particular age did not cover modern Virginia, but the frozen water to the north reduced the oceans, thus creating a coastline considerably east of its current location. Warming of the climate also changed both flora and fauna.

Several rivers and the Chesapeake Bay emerged and over thousands of years. The oldest waterway, the New River, moves north and west from its origins in western North Carolina through the mountains to the Kanawha and the Ohio rivers. Most other major rivers, bearing native tribal names, flow southeasterly. The Roanoke forms on the eastern slopes of the far set of mountains and flows across the Valley, through the Blue Ridge, and into North Carolina, where it reaches the coast near the site of the first English attempt at settlement in the New World. The James, a blend of several small rivers, also starts in the distant mountains. After crossing the Valley of Virginia and the Blue Ridge it meanders across the Piedmont, where the Rivanna adds to its size. Like several other rivers it traverses a fall line as it passes from the Piedmont into the Tidewater. In the Coastal Plain the Appomattox and the Chickahominy add their waters. Near the coast the Nansemond and the Elizabeth, two tidal estuaries, join the James just before the water meets the Chesapeake Bay at Hampton Roads. The Mattaponi, itself a product of four small streams, and the Pamunkey create the short but deep York River at West Point in the Tidewater. Other smaller waterways, including the Rapidan, form the Rappahannock, which passes through Fredericksburg near the Fall Line, long before it exits into the bay. The Potomac, aided by the Shenandoah flowing north in the Lower Valley (northern part) makes its way to its fall line near the District of Columbia and then on to the bay. No matter where they were located, these rivers provided resources both for transportation as well as hydroelectric power. They also at times proved to be obstacles in the movement of people and goods.

The bay results from the waters of a huge system of rivers, including those previously described plus the Susquehanna that enters the bay in Maryland. The rivers, especially the Susquehanna and those in Virginia, contribute much water, but the width of the bay and the wide mouths of these rivers are also due to the advancing ocean, which flooded what was once a large valley. Nature stocked the bay and its rivers with an abundance and variety of marine life, some of which is currently on the brink of extinction due to parasites and other factors.

The eastern portion of the coastal plain contains several peninsulas, starting with the Eastern Shore of Virginia, between the Atlantic and the Chesapeake Bay. The Potomac and Rappahannock rivers create the Northern Neck, the northernmost peninsula on the west side of the bay. The Rappanhannock and York rivers form the Middle Peninsula partially divided by the Piankitank River, an estuary of the bay. The area between the York and James rivers bears the title "the Peninsula."

Although no consensus exists about the name for the area south of the Peninsula, it contains numerous inlets and river branches, much marshland, and many morasses, including the Dismal Swamp, a huge bog that crosses into North Carolina. A more inviting grassy place a few thousand years ago before it became more densely forested, the Dismal allowed natives to use bolas, but as it became more impenetrable, native paths skirted around its edges.

Virginia's natural setting and attributes are keys to understand the state's history. The beauty and other assets of her mountains and shoreline inspired land speculators, industrialists, artists, and poets. Coal and other deposits greatly influenced the commonwealth, bringing both positive and negative contributions, including industrial development, acid rain, and poor air quality. A combination of soil and climate, along with international markets, encouraged tobacco growing, which in turn, set the stage for the introduction of slavery. The area usually averages about 44 inches of rain annually, but the amount varies considerably. Two or three years of drought or near drought, such as the time when the English first settled along the James River, may be followed by a year of two of well-above average moisture. The four seasons of the year provide a pattern quite noticeable even to the inveterate indoor person, but on several occasions, as in 1816, during the last stage of a little ice age, at least part of the state went without any summer weather, a phenomenon that played havoc with crop production. Although the overall climate is quite temperate, nature sometimes throws a 16-inch snowstorm at Tidewater. On several occasions in the 19th century, the waters of the Elizabeth River iced up to permit residents to walk or skate across it. The most severe winter weather in modern times in eastern Virginia occurred in 1857, when a blizzard and below-zero temperatures over several days froze the waters of Hampton Roads, as well as the rivers and much of the Chesapeake Bay. Although the blizzard killed numerous residents and stopped steamboats and other watercraft from operating, the storm temporarily transformed the coastal landscape into a veritable winter wonderland, causing at least one editor to comment on its beauty. Every few years a major hurricane threatens the coast, but only in 1933 did a 20th-century hurricane cause major damage. A 1749 storm carried so much earth away from Point Comfort that the walls of Fort George collapsed. Possibly that particular storm, but more likely two others that struck in the early 19th century, formed Willoughby Spit on the opposite side of the Hampton Roads. Usually the sounds of North Carolina serve as a buffer, protecting southeastern Virginia. Heavy rains in winter or spring, however, occasionally move inland and flood river valleys. Such a storm caused destruction and death in 1969, especially in Nelson County. Major storms inundated inland rivers in 1667 and 1769. Although weather is vitally important to people's lives, the residents of Virginia, like those in other places, recovered from natural disasters, such as droughts and floods.

Nature often provides people with challenges to which they must adapt, but humans also affect nature. Human activity changes weather patterns, even raising the temperature and thereby elevating ocean water levels. It has long been known that humans' presence affected most living things, including the landscape.

Historians of the late 19th and early 20th centuries tended to emphasize material forces in man's past, stressing evolution and the importance of economic classes. Both Marxists and proponents of freewheeling capitalism emphasized the material nature of the past. That generation also benefited more than any previous people from advances in technology, yet they also noted the negative consequences of progress.

# PART ONE: THE COLONIAL ERA

The colonial era officially lasted from the time Europeans settled in what became the Old Dominion until 1775, when Virginia and twelve other colonies rebelled against Great Britain. This section examines Algonquian culture, the Spanish attempt to establish a base, English failed efforts at Roanoke Island, and the creation of an English outpost at Jamestown in 1607. Under the auspices of a joint-stock company chartered by James I, the English beachhead became a permanent settlement following a struggle with the natives. During this cultural clash, settlers introduced a religious structure and a set of cultural beliefs known as Anglicanism, first grew commercially viable tobacco, started a representative government, and brought in African slaves. In 1624 King Charles I revoked the company charter, thus making Virginia a royal colony.

As residents adapted to the environment, they continued to be influenced by events in England, such as a civil war in the 1640s as well as characteristics of English culture, including religion. Chapter 2 provides a political narrative of the era, starting in 1625 and ending in 1688, with the Glorious Revolution in England. It includes information on Bacon's Rebellion in 1676, a major landmark in a "Time of Troubles," an era marked by numerous economic and social problems. The turmoil continued both in England and in Virginia until the English turned to less volatile monarchs. The next chapter covers the gradual maturation of the colony as residents blended elements of English culture with necessary adaptations to the changing environment. The rise of slavery and the proportional decline of indentured servitude was a trend of considerable long-range significance.

Although personal disputes troubled the political landscape over for the next generation, the colony grew in population as settlers moved onto ever-changing frontiers. Chapter 4 deals with an era when an Anglican parson, James Blair, played a rather unusual political role that spanned about fifty years. Chapter 5 covers a "golden age," which commenced around 1730, at least those with wealth, as prices for tobacco stabilized and the number of slaves grew rapidly. This era produced great estates and mansions, many of which have been preserved to this day. Scots-Irish and Germans came into the colony, mostly by way of Pennsylvania, and settled much of the interior, especially the Valley of Virginia. In the next section, we follow the events that led to the American Revolution and the end of the Colonial Era.

# Chapter 1

# The Clash of Cultures

About 15,000 years ago, when the most recent ice age still gripped the region, the first Virginians came. These New Stone Age (Neolithic) people were primarily hunters and gatherers, but they also became adept at farming and fishing as they adapted to the environment. They used dugout canoes along the rivers and in the bay. Skilled at pottery making, they made spear and arrow points from materials at hand or obtained from native tribes located outside the area. By the time the Europeans came, the indigenous people operating within modern Virginia formed several different societies, rather arbitrarily described by anthropologists by language. Algonquians dominated the coastal habitat. Siouans, distantly related to the people later associated with the Great Plains, resided west of the Fall Line in the Piedmont. Iroquoians controlled an area well north of Virginia and another region south of the James River stretching into modern-day Kentucky. Several tribes used the Valley to travel to their favored hunting grounds. The Cherokee, an Iroquoian people, controlled what became Kentucky and the Shawnee and others held sway over the future West Virginia.

In 1600, Algonquians of the Tidewater were under the chiefdom of Powhatan (Wahunsonacock), whose recently enlarged realm Tsenacommacah consisted of roughly 15,000 residents scattered among over 30 tribes residing in about 160 villages. In earlier times, they had probably been more numerous, but droughts in the late 16th century and European diseases, such as smallpox, which came to the New World in the Caribbean in the 1490s, reduced their numbers. By 1600 some tribes had but a handful of members, but others had a few hundred fighting men. The comparatively numerous Chickahominy (crushed corn) were not officially tributary to Powhatan, but they normally supported him. Powhatan, starting out with six core tribes, including the Powhatan (his home tribe), the Pamunkey, the Appomattocs, and three other tribes located near the Fall Line, extended his jurisdiction to the east and north.

Powhatan made no concerted effort to wipe out the new colony of Europeans, as he did not see the threat the intruders posed and even considered allying with them against his adversaries to the west. But even later, after finding out about English intentions of creating a permanent colony, he did not mount a full offensive. Native warfare rarely included full-scale attacks on fortified positions. Using short bows, warriors attacked at close quarters in one-on-one combat. Lacking a written language, the Powhatans, like other natives, relied on spoken words for communication and preserving their knowledge about the past. They complained that the English did not take time to consider what was said. Many problems doubtless resulted from either the substance or style of language, but other problems stemmed from vast cultural differences in manners and morals, differing concepts of land ownership, and the role of deities.

The list of complaints about each other's cultures was quite lengthy. The English found the native habit of stealing irksome, but the Algonquians felt cheated in many of their transactions with the whites. Some English observers commented on the native lack of clothing in warm seasons, the paint on native bodies or the piercing of the same, the male practice of shaving one side of the head, and any number of other superficial differences. More seriously, the English considered red men especially barbaric for scalping and otherwise desecrating the dead. Whites found the native habit of torturing captives by stripping off pieces of skin and burning people alive especially repulsive.

In condemning native lifestyles, the English forgot their jaded culture, where unarmed prisoners taken in battle, along with their women and children, were executed. The Algonquian macho sometimes called for personal military valor, but victory usually included taking women and children prisoners. The English, in their subjugation of the Irish acted more brutally than native Virginians. Moreover, in England as well as throughout Europe, winners beheaded losers and hanged others of lower stature. Neither natives nor Europeans were submissive people or had a monopoly on humane conduct.

Religious differences proved difficult to overcome or even for each side to understand. Algonquians believed in manitou, a supernatural force that controlled nature. A polytheistic people, they worshiped several gods, including one called Okeus, who had power over undesirable happenings. They had ceremonial centers such as Orapax, located in Powhatan's home area not far from the Fall Line on the James. Priests had special status among the natives as healers and prognosticators. The first English settlers thought the natives were a witty, but pagan people, who looked like they could be converted to Christianity and take on the main features of English culture. The English had no idea of exterminating the natives, but they understood from the outset that many aspects of native life had to change. Anglicans considered the natives culturally backward, possibly even the work of the devil. If natives perished in the fight to wrest Virginia away from the devil, Europeans believed it was but the will of God.

Native males certainly had a lifestyle different from the English. The males at puberty usually went through a rite (the husquenaw) that required mental and physical endurance, during which they presumably became men. They then rowed dugouts, fished the rivers near the villages often located near waterways, traded, hunted, and made war, often far from home.

Although Powhatan's people could not be fully classed as a matriarchal society like some other North American societies, women had a more important role in Algonquian culture than found in Europe. Like men, they went through a rite in recognition of their womanhood. Unlike young men, they grew and cooked maize, tobacco, pumpkins, beans, and other crops in plots near the family hut. A woman could become the commander of the tribe (werowance or weroance) through family connections. Among Native Americans, men married into the wife's family. On occasion the wife told the husband return to his original family, a sort of no-fault divorce. On the patriarchal side, although lower level natives usually had but one spouse, tribal leaders often had more than one wife. The English criticized Powhatan for having about a hundred wives, forgetting that their own King Henry VIII had married on six different occasions, disposing of some wives violently.

Natives lived in villages, often on two sides of a stream, and farmed without title to the land (lack of written language made deeds impossible). They moved their villages over the years and even seasonally. The outlying woodlands supplied fuel and small game. Like the river, it belonged to the tribe. The English were moving toward a restrictive form of private ownership at the time, but in some ways the medieval manor, then on the wane in much of Europe, was similar to the more temporary Indian village, for it possessed shared domains. Although the English had not yet fully developed the idea of individual ownership of small plots of land, many of the early settlers aspired to possess property under "free and common socage," a system that allowed greater personal control than the prevailing practice in England. Natives accepted neither this practice nor the notion that "wastelands" (land not fully and permanently occupied) were subject to exploitation by outsiders.

In possessing sailing craft, canons, small arms, armor, and a written language, the English, like other Europeans, had a decided edge in their efforts to take over native lands. The English also had an advantage of being supported by a more advanced political system with a large population, one that could send armed forces across an ocean. Although diseases and a tendency not to adapt swiftly enough to the environment took a toll on the invaders, the natives faced even greater dangers in the form of Old World diseases.

The Spanish made the first attempt to establish a colony in what became Virginia in what they called Ajacan. After meeting with a local tribe in a reconnoitering voyage, the Spaniards took the son of a chief to Spain. In 1570 the renamed Don Luis de Valesco returned to his home as what the Jesuits, his sponsors, thought was a converted Christian. The young man, however, soon reverted to his former lifestyle. The natives destroyed the Spanish mission and slaughtered the fathers, allowing only a boy to survive. Unable to locate Luis, a returning Spanish officer ordered the hanging of several members of a nearby tribe, after which the Spanish departed. The episode did not bode well for future relations between Europeans and natives.

Meanwhile, the English did little in the way of exploration or colonization. They had paid scant attention to the potential of the New World after the 1490s, when the English sent an explorer into the periphery of North America. King Henry VIII busied himself defending the pope from the German monk

Martin Luther, breaking with the pope over Henry's efforts to end his marriage to the daughter of the king of Spain, eliminating a series of wives, and confiscating lands owned by the Catholics. After Henry's death, England remained in turmoil until Elizabeth became Queen in 1558 and established the Church of England (Anglican).

With the internal political situation stabilized and her nation revived, Elizabeth faced down the Spanish, who were not pleased that Protestantism prevailed or that Elizabeth was queen in England. In the 1570s Elizabeth unleashed her "Sea Dogs," among them Sir Francis Drake, who circumnavigated the globe and made a career out of capturing Spanish galleons loaded with precious metals. Elizabeth knighted him for his efforts. Other knights explored the coasts and planned colonies in North America. Walter Raleigh (he spelled it Ralegh), a favored courtier of the queen, established a community on Roanoke Island on the coast of what is now North Carolina. The English called the place, Virginia, for the "Virgin Queen." Elizabeth financed one of the ships and gave her blessing to the enterprise.

The establishment of this colony followed the ideas of clergyman Richard Hakluyt, who in 1582 advised the queen to embrace English colonization of the coast of North America to prevent the Spanish from taking it. Hakluyt's ideas were in large measure a response to the circumstances of the late 16th century. The nation needed to build up its merchant marine, find precious metals and baser materials, locate a more direct passage to Asia, find employment for idle countrymen, and last but not least, convert the natives to the Queen's kind of Christianity.

The effort to create this colony proved unrewarding. Two explorers reached the area in 1584 and found the native Algonquians gentle, good looking, and cooperative. They returned to England with two natives. Manteo became a friend to the English while Wanchese became an enemy. The following year over a hundred Englishmen came under Sir Richard Grenville, who soon left to bring back more colonists and supplies. Ralph Lane, the military commander of the operation, attacked the natives when they retaliated after an Englishman killed a native for stealing a silver cup. Short of supplies, the remaining settlers accepted an offer to be taken home from Sir Francis Drake. Somewhere in the Atlantic, they passed Grenville returning to the island.

Sir Walter Raleigh (knighted for his earlier efforts on Roanoke Island), still convinced of the feasibility of colonization, organized a company that sent about a hundred settlers, this time including some families. The governor of this colony, John White, had gone to Roanoke with the first adventurers. White's watercolors of the local Algonquians still serve as a guide to understanding the interplay of man and nature in the Roanoke area. The settlers were supposed to land at Roanoke and pick up Grenville's survivors and then establish a new colony near Chesapeake Bay in an area Lane had explored two years earlier. Finding no English on the island and with a navigator unwilling to relocate, White reestablished the old colony. With supplies running low, he headed for England, leaving most of the colonists, including his daughter, son-in-law, and recently born granddaughter, Virginia Dare, the first English child born in the New World. Reaching England in the fall of 1587, he could not return for nearly three years because a Spanish fleet (the Armada) then threatened England. The Armada finally met destruction at the hands of Sea Dogs and a storm, but White could not get to Roanoke until late summer 1590, and then only as a passenger. He found a settlement completely abandoned and a sign ACRO carved in a post and a lengthier inscription in a tree, neither being the prearranged symbol of distress. That suggested the settlers had followed Manteo to his home on Croatoan near Hatteras. White could not follow up on this lead and died at his Irish home some three years later, still wondering about the fate of his loved ones. Had the natives wiped out the colony? Had the Spanish carried out their planned attack? Had they gone to the Chesapeake Bay as originally planned? Had they gone west, or more likely south to mix with natives there? White did not know and neither do we.

In 1606, with the death of Elizabeth in 1603 and the war with Spain officially over, King James issued a charter for two joint-stock companies to establish colonies on the North American coast. With overlapping areas for potential settlement, the Plymouth and London companies, under the umbrella of the Virginia Company, created two communities. The efforts of the former came to naught in present-day Maine in 1608. The work of the later produced the Jamestown settlement in Virginia in 1607. In December 1606, three ships set sail from England. The 105 potential settlers on board the *Susan Constant*, *Godspeed*, and *Discovery* consisted of gentlemen and a few men that might be familiar with hard work. Under the command of Captain Christopher Newport, with Bartholomew Gosnold and John Ratcliffe in charge of the two smaller ships, the little fleet reached Virginia in April 1607. The settlers came ashore inside a cape they named Henry for the king's son. They prayed with Reverend Richard Hunt, drove off an attack from some natives, boarded their ships, and made their way to the site selected for a permanent settlement. Once at the island on the north side of the James River they built a fort and several huts. The directors of the company had named three ship captains to the ruling council plus several others including untitled John Smith, who during the voyage over had been put in chains because of an argument with another passenger.

That first year diseases almost ruined the colony. Dysentery and other diseases spawned by tainted water and possibly typhoid, brought by the sick minister, killed about half the settlers. The storehouse burned, and the winter proved unusually cold. The water was too salty, the land too low lying. Smith, captured and released by the native leader Powhatan, possibly at the urging of his favorite daughter, became the natural leader in a scenario similar to a modern television series, as the council members formed temporary alliances and conspired against each other. After Newport left for England after exploring the colony to the fall line of the James River, the council dismissed Ratcliffe as an imposter. The remaining members replaced another leader and military veteran, Edward Wingfield, supposedly for being insufficiently Protestant. The Council tried and executed Councilman George Kendall as an alleged Spanish spy (some scholars think an unknown agent put arsenic in the food to cause an even higher rate of death). Gosnold, the only peacemaker on the council, died from illness. By default and clever maneuvering, Smith ended up as the leader.

As Smith explored the Chickahominy River, Indians killed his men and captured him. In the end he secured his release and returned to the colony after meeting with Powhatan at Werowocomoco on the York River. When Newport returned with company instructions that the paramount chief of the local Algonquians had to accept being a vassal of King James by wearing a copper crown, Smith reluctantly arranged for a ceremony during which Newport placed the crown on Powhatan's head. The latter likely thought the ceremony was the English way of recognizing him as their ruler.

On his return from England, Captain Newport also brought supplies along with people to replace those who perished. Newport then left with the disgruntled Wingfield in tow to bring back even more supplies and several Dutch and Polish glassmakers. This experiment, like so many others to find products that would give the company revenues, never worked out. Another effort to make glass in the early 1620s also came up empty.

The colonists limped through the next winter with Smith presiding. The stored corn decayed, but poultry and pork kept the settlers alive as they spread out looking for sustenance, a step that also reduced the death rate. Pocahontas saved Smith again, this time, by informing him of a probable native attack. But in the early autumn of 1609, Smith had to leave the colony, having been wounded in a gunpowder explosion and possibly facing his own internal rebellion.

Faced with the failure of the Plymouth Company in 1608 and problems in Jamestown, the investors petitioned the king for a new charter. The first charter had divided the American coast between the two groups and allowed ownership 100 miles inland. The second charter created one organization, the Virginia Company, which now had jurisdiction over four hundred miles of coastline, 100 miles into the Atlantic, and all the land north westward to the Pacific Ocean. Earls, lords, squires, knights, doctors, and captains headed the list of nine hundred or so investors. Many merchants from London and the smaller ports joined with guilds of tradesmen in investing in the company. The government also gave exemptions from tariffs on both imports and exports. It repaired a defect in the previous charter by allowing the council (board of directors) in England to pick a governor to lead the colony and provide him with written instructions. The settlers, many of whom went as indentured servants, were supposed to carry the traditional rights of Englishmen with them, but the charter permitted martial law in emergencies. Because the colony endured a constant state of emergency for the next several years, rights really mattered little.

The winter of 1609–10 proved to be "the Starving Time," but the settlers knew little about the new charter, as the governor Sir Thomas Gates and Captain Newport, driven off course by a storm, spent the winter in Bermuda trying to arrange transportation to Jamestown. Some of the convoy reached Jamestown, and these colonists, with the settlers already there, faced a hard winter. Late that summer, with these reinforcements, Captain George Percy led a preemptive strike against the Nansemonds, thus commencing a war that would carry on sporadically for several years. That winter most of the colonists took refuge in Jamestown. The natives attacked frequently enough to prevent foraging and refused to trade any maize. Disease and death stalked Jamestown. One man, accused of cannibalizing his dead wife, was executed. When a man cursed God for putting him in such dire circumstances, Percy, the leader of this motley group, thought the creator meted out justice by having natives kill the man. The natives killed a few that wandered outside the stockade, but those inside the fort were dying from disease and other internal causes. Settlers had a constant battle with summer pestilence, and now, even in the winter, they died possibly because of a limited supply of good water.

When Gates finally arrived in the spring, only a handful still lived, though the garrison at Fort Algernourne (near modern Fort Monroe) fared much better. Short on supplies, Gates evacuated the settlement, but Lord De la Warr appeared with several English ships and several hundred new settlers. Not knowing the fate of Gates, the company had sent a new governor to the colony. With a new commission and instructions, De la Warr ordered everybody back to Jamestown. During a brief stay, the governor organized a full-scale assault against the nearby Paspaheghs that virtually destroyed the native village. The colonists at Jamestown then withstood an Indian attack on the garrison at Jamestown. At this point De la Warr became ill and returned to England, being replaced by Sir Thomas Dale, who took some time to reach the scene. Armed with detailed company instructions called the *Lawes, Divine, Morall and Martiall*, Marshall Dale closely controlled every aspect of life in the fragile colony. The detailed rules on morality and religion listed in Dale's book dominated virtually every waking moment of the residents of the outpost. Even though De la Warr carried out elaborate Anglican services in 1610, Dale and the religious leaders favored a less ostentatious ritual. Reverend Richard Buck, the minister De la Warr brought with him, had puritan proclivities, and the minister assigned to Henrico, Alexander Whitaker, was the son of a prominent English Puritan.

Those who failed to attend church twice a day went without food. They could suffer death if they persisted in swearing or not attending church or for any number of things. Dale stopped people from bowling, had a pin thrust through a miscreant's tongue, and ordered hangings and torture. Because complaints about his methods did not surface until well after their occurrence, what happened is not entirely clear, but regarding such acts as necessary seems questionable. Dale, Gates, and others, mostly veterans of the English campaigns in the Low Countries to help Protestants against Catholic Spain, or in Ireland to suppress rebellion, ran a strict military venture. With experienced military men available, Dale continued the offense against the natives. Following company instructions, he carried the war directly into Powhatan's original chiefdom, not far from the current city of Richmond. As part of what might be called a "Second Front," the settlers built Henrico, named for Prince Henry, the king's eldest son, who died about the same time. Well armed and armored, the English soldiers proved too much for the natives to hold back, although their leader, the famed Jack of the Feathers (Nemattanew), used a form of psychological warfare. After setting up the fort at Henrico, the English finished 1611 by virtually wiping out the villages of the Appomattocs.

Samuel Argall came to the colony in 1612 as a captain of one of the supply ships. While Dale adopted the role of the "bad cop" in aggressively pursuing natives, Argall acted as a "good cop" in trading with the natives. Although he practiced no little skill in diplomacy, he once attacked a native village over a minor disagreement. Eager to make money, Argall learned that a favorite daughter of Powhatan had taken refuge among the Potomacs, away from the prying English. In 1613 he exchanged a copper kettle for her and brought Pocahontas (a.k.a. Amonute and Matoax) to Henrico to ransom her, but colonial authorities used the princess to elicit improved behavior from her father. John Rolfe, who the previous year had introduced West Indies tobacco to Virginia, fell in love with her. The marriage sacrament was performed after Pocahontas accepted Christianity and took the name Rebecca. They soon had a child, Powhatan's grandson, and the two peoples stopped attacking each other.

An important era in the company's history ended in 1616, when Dale left the colony with Pocahontas and Rolfe. As his ship approached the English coast Dale hanged an English spy for the Spanish. On shore he arranged an exchange of a Spanish spy for an Englishman kidnapped by the Spanish. Pocahontas, after an exciting social whirl in England, died as she prepared to return to Virginia, another victim of the cultural exchange.

By this time the directors of the company had exerted extraordinary efforts to settle the colony, but the settlement remained frail. In 1616 the colony only had a small fraction of the immigrants, as hundreds had died. Many of the 350 survivors would soon have their classification changed from indentured servants to renters. The company would continue to make money, but in time these settlers would own their own lands. In addition, supply ships cost money and government officials had to be paid. No gold or other precious metals or a passage to Asia had been found, despite Captain Newport's best efforts. Tobacco provided possibilities, but some company leaders thought its growth diverted attention from more important matters. King James considered it "a nasty weed/ which from the devil doth proceed." The company made some money selling lottery tickets in England and cut losses by turning over distributing supplies to private interests. It retained certain lands on which it placed indentured servants whose efforts supported the governor. The directors had more land to give away, but they were uncertain how the company could make money.

In 1612 directors had formed a successful subsidiary stock company to control Bermuda, the island Gates had accidentally found. In 1616 following this model, the Virginia Company formed "particular plantations" or what became known as "hundreds"—a name taken from a political jurisdiction in England. Investors obtained grants of thousands of acres along the James River. Clustered in villages, indentured servants under contract to investors toiled on land grants. The river, from several miles east of Jamestown to Henrico, soon had these plantations, along with others that contained a few people who had invested in the company and had their own land. Others rented land from the company. The decline of the native menace permitted the settlements to spread out. With population dispersal, the death rate subsided. One of the hundreds, Berkeley, became renowned for having the first Thanksgiving in the New World, in 1619. Others had quaint titles, like Flowerdew, named for the wife of George Yeardley, one of its owners. Another called Martin-Brandon (not to be confused with Martin's Hundred) had virtual autonomy from the company. This approach brought a few hundred settlers, but the company did not derive much income from the experiment.

Around the time that King James approved a revised charter in 1618, Sir Edwin Sandys, a thorn in the side of King James I in Parliament, emerged as the company treasurer. Sandys sent a new governor, "Sir" George Yeardley. Despite objections that standards for knighthood were becoming too lax, King James knighted the one-time apprentice to Gates. Four corporations (later known as counties) and seven particular and regular plantations sent delegates to confer with the governor and the council in the summer of 1619. The governor accepted the credentials of twenty of these "burgesses," delaying recognition of one of the hundreds until it recognized the full authority of the Virginia Company. The Assembly drew up a number of acts dealing with land disbursement, labor relations, crop production, and native relations. The burgesses were to meet with the governor and council annually. This system of representative government, with some modifications, eventually became a fixture in Virginia. Sandys, an active member of the Virginia Company since 1609 also took other steps in 1619 to build up the colony. He negotiated with Separatists (Pilgrims), then in exile in the Netherlands, to start a new colony under the jurisdiction of the Virginia Company, a plan that went awry when their ship landed too far north. The Virginia Company sent out a boatload of women to add to the relatively small number of that sex with the hope that families would take root. Someone other than Sandys arranged for slaves from Africa to come to Virginia.

One of the first actions of the assembled burgesses was to approve the already-existing headright system, whereby the company gave fifty acres to anyone that paid passage to the colony. The passage-for-land idea was not new, but the scope proved broad, for thousands of people came as indentured servants to individuals that paid passage for them. Those who worked off their indentures got a suit of clothes and the chance to rent land. They could then own land by paying the passage for still others. The Africans (Angolans) who came in 1619 and others that arrived over the next several years were treated much the same as indentured servants, even though they never volunteered. Yeardley informed the delegation that the company expected them to plant certain crops, agree to prices for tobacco, abide by standards of behavior that would make ministers content, and keep their powder and shot handy. Sandys and his colleagues also warmly endorsed building a college at Henrico and the work of George Thorpe, the religious leader of Berkeley Hundred, and others to convert and educate natives.

Relations with the natives stayed on a positive note even after Powhatan's death in 1618, when his brother, Opitchapam, headed the natives. Eventually Opechancanough came to power and plotted a massive assault against the white settlers that killed over 350 whites. Not all Algonquians participated, and legend credits a native for warning the settlers at Jamestown. Thomas Savage, one of the fur traders, learned about a possible threat from an outlying tribe, but colonial authorities questioned the report's reliability. Almost all of Martin's Hundred and Berkeley were wiped out. Natives burned the iron works on the upper James along with the college and other buildings. Another college did not come into existence for over seventy years, while iron making would not resume for over a hundred years. The whites pulled back into fortified areas and carried out forays to destroy supplies of maize. Because the whites were confined for protection, diseases killed more people than the Indians had. A year after the incident, the colony contained some 1,300 residents, mostly servants, but despite the continued loss of life, mostly to disease, the number rose to near 3,000 in the mid-1620s, as immigrants streamed into the colony.

At the time of these events, negative reports coming from the colony's critics convinced James to cancel the charter. The slaughter, along with Sandys's former association with the company (the Earl of Southampton had replaced him as company treasurer), persuaded a king's commission to recommend the end of the company. By this point, the company could no longer conduct lotteries, the principal source of its revenue. It was, therefore, only a matter of time before the company would be bankrupt. James died before acting to withdraw the charter. Charles, his successor, annulled the old charter but did not end the role of the burgesses. Charles appointed a royal governor, and Virginia now became the property of the crown.

The Virginians, who had not cooperated in the commission's inquiry, worried about the consequences of the decision to kill the company, but their fears gradually evaporated when former company leaders became the new royal governors. The governors routinely met with designated councilmen and, after a brief hiatus, with the burgesses. The new government eventually ratified previous land transactions including preservation of the head right system, and local affairs remained the same. For a time the king gave Virginia tobacco a sheltered market, something Sandys had been requesting for years, but English merchants proved so dominant that some Virginians hoped the king would take over the entire business.

For the Algonquians, the uprising proved to be the beginning of the end. Already severely damaged by various European diseases (small pox and measles) against which they had but limited immunity, the tribes gradually grew weaker. As their numbers diminished and they intermarried with whites, they retained some their culture, but they also acquired English guns and implements, along with horses, pigs, and sheep. The descendants of the Nansemond, Chickahominy, Pamunkey, Mattaponi, and Monacans (the only non-Algonquian people) still live in Virginia. Many of them have preserved or restored elements of their heritage.

English settlers learned a few methods of hunting, farming, and fishing from the natives. They came to appreciate native plants. George Thorpe even discovered how to produce corn liquor. A few English such as Thomas Savage, Henry Spelman, Robert Poole, and Henry Fleet, lived among the natives, served as middlemen and interpreters, and took up native lifestyles, but they also retained their Englishness. The settlers brought with them much of English culture. Medieval serfdom (a form of slavery where people were affixed to certain lands) no longer pervaded Western Europe, and so never came to the colony. Guilds (trade unions), which still had some influence in the home country, did not secure a foothold in the New World. But the colonies did have room for apprentices (those learning a trade) and indentured servants (contracted laborers). Today's political institutions, the methods of conducting business, language, and modes of thinking, all were built on a foundation brought over from the homeland. And England continued to influence the area's development for centuries.

The climate, more favorable for growing tobacco and less so for producing traditional English products like barley, made the colony less reliant on England, but the English brought seeds for wheat and other cereals as well as horses, oxen, cattle, cows, pigs, the latter running wild and consuming the seeds of the longleaf pine, which in time nearly erased that valuable tree from Virginia's landscape. They built shelters that resembled structures in the homeland. Although the colonists learned some things from the natives, inefficient medieval farm practices took root in Virginia to accompany the production of tobacco. The availability of large amounts of fertile land in the New World and the low density of population reduced the need to improve agricultural practices. In addition, the English imported honeybees and thereby changed the flora.

Some scholars contend that the first Virginians lived in harmony with nature, their religion supposedly encouraging an ecology friendly lifestyle, but the reason the natives did not have a major impact on the environment was their relatively small population. With less than one person per square mile and a Stone Age technology, they did only so much damage. Even so, their practice of burning large areas to trap game may well have changed the landscape.

The Europeans who came to live in Virginia brought with them a different cultural heritage, which they adapted to new circumstances. That heritage, of course, rose in part from a constant interaction with the European physical environment as well as other factors, such as a recent experience with a great religious reformation. Thus both cultural heritage and environment played roles in forming the Virginia of today.

# Chapter 2

## Troubled Colony, 1625–1689

Difficulties did not end with the demise of the company in 1625, for settlers faced a series of disturbances almost to the end of the 17th century. These tumults and troubles were spread out enough to allow the population to grow, so that the colony with but 1,250 people in 1625 had nearly 60,000 by 1689. During this era, colonial leaders tried to regulate the commercial activities of the residents to make them more self-sufficient, but the lure of making money from agricultural resources made it a nearly impossible goal.

As the colony recovered from its struggles with natives and disease, a series of former company governors eased the colony's transition into royal status. When one of these men died, the council appointed Dr. John Pott, a physician, to lead them in the interim as they awaited the arrival of Sir John Harvey. Some years before, an unwelcome Harvey had visited the colony to conduct a census and gather evidence against the company. With his reappearance, the council and many residents contrasted the congenial doctor with the abrasive and recently knighted Harvey. In 1629, before Harvey arrived, the council gave Lord Baltimore (George Calvert) the cold shoulder in his efforts to establish a Catholic colony in the southern part of Virginia. When the perceived intruder refused to take an Oath of Supremacy, the council ordered him to leave. But Lord Baltimore's son (Cecil Calvert) received a charter to all Virginia north and east of the Potomac River, a royal decision that annoyed many Virginians. When the newcomers, some of whom were Catholics, stopped by Jamestown in 1634 on their way to Maryland, Harvey assisted them as the crown instructed him, to the annoyance of several Virginians, among them Councilman William Claiborne.

Claiborne started out in the colony as a surveyor and then participated in the fight of outnumbered militia against several hundred Pamunkeys in 1624, which temporarily broke the back of native resistance. Afterward he acquired a ranch in Elizabeth City County, a trading post on Kent Island, and a network of fur trading operations that reached into modern Pennsylvania. When Lord Baltimore and his settlers arrived, Claiborne, a Puritan, argued with him about the latter's authority. The religious difference between the two possibly played a role in their dispute, but Claiborne's unwillingness to recognize Calvert's authority caused the rift. After Lord Baltimore persuaded some white fur traders to take his side in the struggle, each side armed their ships, and a pitched battle ensued near Pocomoke Creek on the Eastern Shore. Lord Baltimore's forces finally captured Kent Island and hanged several of Claiborne's men. Claiborne went to England, where he failed to change the Maryland charter. There he took part in the English Civil War, and although his side won that contest, he never did regain ownership of Kent Island. Returning to the colony, he participated in colonial politics and lived out his life in New Kent County, named for his English home shire.

As Claiborne was squaring off against Lord Baltimore, the council in Virginia scuffled with Harvey. The governor jailed John Pott, the colony's only physician for rustling, a charge forcing Pott's wife to go to England to obtain a pardon for her husband. The governor physically attacked councilmen and ordered their arrest, but in 1635 his enemies turned the tables and captured him. Accompanied by Pott, he sailed to England to present his case to the crown. Having convinced the authorities that he deserved a second chance, the governor returned to Virginia. On his return Harvey assured the settlers that they retained their rights to land and traditional English liberties. But he, the council, and their allies went through another round of seizures, exiles into the wilderness, and fisticuffs until 1639, when the English government fired Harvey and sent Sir Francis Wyatt, an earlier royal governor, back to the colony. Harvey fled in disgrace.

The new permanent governor that eventually replaced Harvey turned out to be the most powerful and impressive Englishman to lead the colony in the 17th century. The witty and urbane Sir William Berkeley, knighted for his battlefield efforts on behalf of King Charles I, arrived in 1642 at a time of rebellion in the homeland. Puritanism and problems with the Parliament were proving troublesome to the king. The new governor came to Virginia as a Cavalier (supporter of the king) from the area west of London.

Following instructions from the king, the new governor ordered some Puritan ministers that had recently moved to two eastern counties to leave the colony. When Berkeley's own chaplain proved to be a Puritan, the governor exiled him. But then Berkeley softened his approach and persuaded the Assembly to moderate the use of the oath of allegiance for dissenting clergy. Vestries could withhold payments to clergymen that failed to use the *Book of Common Prayer*, but in practice a Puritan-minded minister could function in the colony. A few years later, some Puritans from the lower counties left the area, a number, curiously enough, going to Maryland, which offered a degree of toleration because Lord Baltimore feared the intolerance of others and, moreover, offered money to Puritans to help him control his colony.

Also in the mid-1640s, Berkeley convinced the General Assembly to continue to allow Dutch ships in Virginia. By supporting this policy Berkeley opposed the Claiborne faction, which wanted to restrict competition from fellow Calvinists. When England discouraged the Dutch carrying trade, Berkeley challenged Parliament's power to restrict commerce in the colony. Because Parliament was at the time preoccupied with the war against the king, it did not immediately react to this challenge.

In his first term as governor, Berkeley developed his home estate at Green Springs (the Assembly gave him the land) as a model by experimenting with several crops, including mulberry trees for silk production. Berkeley knew about similar efforts in England and earlier attempts to encourage, if not coerce, Virginians to produce silk. He also introduced a wide variety of English fruits from apples to pears and even oranges and lemons. His vineyards produced grapes and raisins as well as low-quality wines. His fields had numerous flocks of birds and livestock. He also tried to grow rice as well as sugar. Berkeley's agricultural program dovetailed very closely with the aim of the English government to diversity Virginia's agriculture.

Having resolved the Puritan question, Berkeley dealt with Indians that had carried out a massacre in the spring of 1644 on the Thursday before Easter. Nearly 500 settlers died in an eerie episode similar to the uprising 22 years earlier. The governor took time from full retaliation to go to England to help Charles. In his absence, Secretary of State Claiborne tried unsuccessfully to persuade Virginians to raid Kent Island. On his return, the governor led the troops against the Indians. No pitched battles occurred, but the capture and death of Chief Opechancanough (killed by one of his jailers) and destruction of crops forced nearly all Tidewater tribes to accept tributary status in 1646

Berkeley, like many Virginians, retained a longstanding interest in the frontier and in the possibility of finding a waterway to the Pacific Ocean. Abraham Wood, who came to Virginia in 1620 as a young indentured servant, came to possess a small plantation on the Appomattox River and represented Henrico County in the Assembly, while still in his twenties. When the Indians attacked in 1644, Wood captained the local militia and supervised the construction of one of four forts ordered by the Assembly. After the war ended, Wood used the fort for trade and as a base for exploration. In 1650 he and Edward Bland led five others south of Fort Henry (Petersburg) into Nottoway country, where the local tribe, which had no guns, strongly advised Wood and his party to go no farther, arguing that local natives had killed over 200 Pamunkey warriors for the garroting of a Chowan chief. Taking that comment as a threat, Wood expressed pessimism about future exploration, when his party returned to Fort Henry.

The news from England also proved disconcerting to Berkeley and most Virginians. The Roundheads, under Oliver Cromwell, captured the king, and after searching their souls, beheaded him in 1649. For the next three years Berkeley's governorship in Virginia stood in peril, as the governor, though never having had a high regard for Charles, refused to accept the right of Parliament or its Council of State to rule in Virginia. In 1650, when the council forbade all foreign vessels from trading in the colony, the Virginia assembly condemned the measure, word of which reached England just as Cromwell's forces crushed the remnants of the king's army. In England, William Claiborne and other Virginia Puritans called for force to bend the Virginians to their ways. Arriving in 1652, the English navy compelled acceptance of Puritan rule. Berkeley initially called out the militia but soon determined that resistance would be futile. The two sides arranged a compromise whereby the Assembly would stop insulting Parliament, and Berkeley would step down as governor. Several designated Puritans such as Claiborne took top government positions. The Anglican ministers and parishioners could still use their prayer book, with references to the crown deleted. Berkeley did not have to take an oath to the Commonwealth of England and could even privately pray for the king. Berkeley spent most of the next eight years at his Green Springs plantation.

During the Interregnum, when Puritans dominated England, Virginia had a commonwealth. The burgesses elected a succession of governors, two of whom—Richard Bennett and Samuel Matthews Jr.—were Puritans. Edward Digges, who served between the other two, was an Anglican acceptable to the English. When Cromwell became a dictator in England, Virginia remained a republic. The Puritan presence did increase enforcement of religious rules especially in Lower Norfolk County, which instituted a ducking stool to dissuade residents from slandering their neighbors, a common habit made worse by the acrid tongues of Quakers (also known as Friends). Through most of the 17th century, local courts fined people for not attending church or for working on the Sabbath (Sunday). People did penance in public and were occasionally whipped for fornication and other unacceptable behavior. Public drunkenness occasionally produced penalties through the whole era both in New England and Virginia. Lower Norfolk County, noting that the absence of a competent minister discouraged church attendance, sent an agent to New England to find a qualified person.

During this era, the government retained Berkeley's policy toward the natives. When a tribe in the Piedmont threatened, the militia attacked with the aid of some of Berkeley's tributary tribes. Unfortunately for the Algonquians, the white army proved untrustworthy, leading to the deaths of many Mattaponis and Pamunkeys, including Chief Totopotomy. In 1652 Secretary of State Claiborne arranged a treaty with his one-time fur suppliers, the Susquehannas. His efforts produced a treaty that ensured good relations with the largest tribe immediately north of Virginia.

Virginia grew rapidly during these years of turmoil in England. By 1660 the colony contained about 33,000 as compared to 8,000 some twenty years earlier. At the time of Charles's beheading, Governor Berkeley invited defeated loyalists to join him in Virginia. Hundreds accepted the call, especially from the West Country. Many of those represented families with title and money, both of which were being threatened. Because the Puritan leaders did nothing to deter the flow of Cavaliers into the colony, Virginia became a haven for royalist ideas and ways of life. The same sorts of people continued to come even after Puritan dominance in England ended. Few people with Puritan sympathies or connections made their way into the colony during these years, for mainline Puritans preferred New England.

In 1660 the Restoration brought Charles II to the English throne, Berkeley back as governor of Virginia, and a decidedly West English style to life in Virginia. On learning about this impending event, along with the death of Governor Matthews, the Virginia burgesses, tendered the vacant governor's post to Berkeley. Once in power, Charles II approved the selection, supposedly praising Virginia as his loyal "Old Dominion." Berkeley resumed his policies, seeking to diversity crops, raise the price of tobacco, protect against native incursions, and explore the wilderness. He also undoubtedly hoped his kind of English culture would prevail in the colony. Immigrants from the West Country into Virginia brought with them a culture that made Virginians even more different from New Englanders in a host of ways including dialect and methods of burying the dead. Berkeley's praise for Virginians for having no newspapers or schools reflected part of that culture. In the case of public education, many West Country residents saw no urgency to educate anyone below the gentry. Despite Berkeley's advice, private benefactors such as Benjamin Syms and Thomas Eaton in Elizabeth City County financed schools. The former provided for the first free school in the English colonies. Before coming to Virginia, Berkeley produced a play. Yet he made no effort to develop such interests in Virginia. In 1665, some residents of the Eastern Shore put on "Ye Bear and Ye Cub." Hauled before the court, the cast had to perform the play verbatim. The court pronounced the actors not guilty of making seditious comments and made the complainant pay court costs. That was the extent of stagecraft in Virginia until after the turn of the century.

Neither Anglicans nor Puritans liked Quakers. When Elizabeth Harris entered the colony in the 1650s to convert Virginians, authorities ordered her to leave. The colony fined ship captains for knowingly bringing such troublemakers into Virginia. When Quakers persisted in yelling about "Episcopal knaves" and "anti-Christs," they were taken to Jamestown for punishment, though whipping could be avoided if the criminal agreed to leave or change such behavior. Virginians never went to the extreme as in Massachusetts, where the authorities executed several Quakers, including a woman, but Virginia Quakers may have had less desire to be martyrs. Under the restored Berkeley, the burgesses took steps against the Quakers similar to those employed by the Puritans. In his second term in office, Governor Berkeley, noting the number of Quaker women, ordered the imprisonment of all women who refused to take appropriate oaths. The governor was especially aggrieved when Mary Chisman of York County persisted in secretly meeting with other Quakers, including her slaves. Despite these efforts, Quakers survived. In the early 1670s George Fox, England's leading Quaker, found dozens of people of like mind in the less-settled parts of southern Virginia. Anglicans, whether Puritan or not, could neither make these people be quiet nor stop them from being Quakers.

In 1669 and 1670 the German, John Lederer, explored the Piedmont and the back part of Carolina. Wood waited for eleven years after Berkeley's return to power before resuming his explorations. Based on Lederer's work, Wood privately sponsored Thomas Batte and Robert Hallam (various spellings), both of whom crossed the Blue Ridge in 1671 and worked their way up the mountains to villages along the Roanoke and the New River (one possibly located at what is now Radford's city park). They then headed west to a spot, beyond the crest of the Appalachians. On their return to civilization they reported they had seen the other side of the mountains and a river that looked like it flowed directly to the Pacific. And they had seen no Spaniards, which pleased Governor Berkeley as he did not care to damage Anglo-Spanish relations.

In the years immediately following the Restoration, the governor tried to solve the problem of low tobacco prices. From prior failed experiments Berkeley and most Virginians knew many of his experimental crops did not do well in the Old Dominion, but the governor constantly urged the colony to vary its agricultural production and focus less on producing tobacco. When the price of tobacco dropped to less than a penny a pound, the Assembly considered stopping all tobacco growing for a year. Virginians agreed to the policy but although Maryland's leaders seemingly agreed, they reneged on the deal. Berkeley went to England to try unsuccessfully to convince the Privy Council to modify the Navigation Acts, which in the 1660s gave American growers a sheltered market in England but prevented them from selling directly outside the empire, thus lowering returns on the sale of tobacco. In addition almost all imports into the colony had to come from the mother country on English or colonial ships with crews largely from those places. Berkeley had been actively encouraging Dutch shipping into and out of Virginia via a trade pact with the New Netherlands, so his policies conflicted with those of the crown. In the colony the situation worsened, when the English went to war with the Dutch largely over the effort to stop the latter's trade in the colonies. During three maritime Anglo-Dutch wars (the first one occurred during the Interregnum), a Dutch fleet captured several Virginia tobacco ships in Hampton Roads in 1667, despite the governor's efforts to organize resistance. Many planters lost their annual income, but the price remained low as the tobacco made its way to European markets. Six years later, when a smaller Dutch fleet tried to repeat the action, the governor mustered enough ships and militia to patrol the shores to provide warning.

The colony grew despite a series of natural and man-made disasters in the 1660s. A flood took out hundreds of buildings in 1667, including the tobacco sheds in the river valleys. Servant unrest rose in the early 1660s. In York County the authorities discovered that several indentured servants, possibly veterans from Cromwell's army, plotted a rebellion, when they realized the futility of seeking redress for their complaints about food. Other Cromwell veterans and felons sent to Virginia as servants plotted a rebellion in Gloucester, for which several were hung in 1663. A few years later, Virginia banned felons from being sent to the colony. The problem of rebellious servants, however, continued. The courts often failed to act in cases of mistreatment, and numerous servants thought their rights under English law had disappeared. In increasing numbers they ran away.

Under Berkeley, a clique of men loyal to the governor received rewards, usually in the form of land grants, some of which far exceeded the size allowed under the headright system. In 1649, an exiled Charles II promised proprietorships to some of his supporters. Twenty years later he turned over the Northern Neck to loyalists, and in 1673 he created another proprietorship. The governor and his followers were dismayed to find out that the crown named a proprietor to receive Virginia quit rents. To protect the interests of the councilmen and other prominent investors, Berkeley's government sent Philip Ludwell to England to beg the crown to reverse its action or permit the colonial agent to buy out the proprietors with money from Virginia taxpayers. Ludwell was still in England trying to negotiate the matter when rebellion broke out in Virginia, having been preceded by local outbreaks as early as 1674 in New Kent County. Poll taxes, already quite high, simply kept going up. Colonial and local tax revenues in the form of tobacco tended to go to the governor's clique. Councilmen paid no taxes. The licensing system created in 1661 for the fur trade favored a few. At least one government official also questioned the disposition of customs receipts. In addition, the governor's personality underwent a change after his marriage in 1670 to a much younger woman. His spurts of anger, so characteristic of his class, became more frequent, and his wife could be less than charming. Those who had grievances against the governor, but who did not care to challenge him directly, generally blamed the governor's wife for their troubles.

Nothing of great consequence might have come from these circumstances save for a spark that ignited flammable materials. In an incident fairly typical in the relations between natives and whites, a tiny but troublesome tribe located near the Potomac killed a fur trader. Militia units from Maryland and Virginia shot up a cabin full of Susquehanna chiefs in the mistaken impression that these were the killers. With their leaders assassinated, the Susquehannas (Susquehannocks) attacked the Virginia settlers along the Fall Line. The normally resolute Berkeley, knowing that not all natives were involved in the uprising, hesitated in retaliating with a full-scale war, and called for arming forts along the frontier that would provide settler's protection, but he did not want to send a "flying army" because he knew its presence might excite peaceful natives or the militia might again confuse friends and enemies. Nevertheless, he called out the county militias and outfitted an army of 1,000 men.

Nathaniel Bacon, the only son of a prominent member of the Suffolk gentry, had come to Virginia largely to escape from the wild oats sown as a young man. Soon after Bacon's arrival, Berkeley appointed him to the council, but the newcomer rarely, if ever, attended meetings. With Berkeley's help, he obtained property on the bend of the James a few miles below the Fall Line. A year later the Indians struck, killing his overseer. The settlers in his neighborhood appealed to Bacon to lead them in attacking the natives. Without the governor's permission and no military experience, the newcomer led a large force into the southwestern interior to destroy the enemy. Meanwhile, the governor brought his troops into the area just after Bacon had left. Bacon's forces reached a spot on the Roanoke River (now Clarksville), where the Occoneechees had a base on an island. The Occoneechees and Bacon's men collaborated to defeat some nearby Susquehannas (or possibly another tribe). As the victorious natives tortured the prisoners, the nervous frontiersmen and the Occoneechees turned on each other, and Bacon's troops slaughtered men, women, and children. Bacon and his men returned to "civilization" in triumph.

Now a declared outlaw, Bacon was captured in Jamestown and came before the governor, who remarked, "Now I behold the greatest rebel that ever was in Virginia," Berkeley then released Bacon on parole, but Bacon returned to his troops and marched on the capital. With wonderful theatrics, the governor shouted at the rebels as they pointed their guns at him. "Here, shoot me, fore God, fair mark, shoot!" Neither Bacon nor his men had any intention of hurting the old man, but with guns pointed toward them, the burgesses and council urged the governor to give Bacon a commission to kill more Indians, which the governor grudgingly granted. Soon after Bacon departed, the governor withdrew the commission and reissued the charge of treason against Bacon and other leaders. The rebels assembled at Middle Plantation (Williamsburg) and at Green Springs to plan strategy. They agreed not to surrender to English troops, expected soon, until they could secure a hearing from the crown. Moving on to Gloucester County, they pursued Pamunkeys allied to Berkeley into swamps.

When the governor returned to the capitol, the rebels once again moved on Jamestown. They captured it, this time after a battle during which Berkeley's men attacked in the open outside the fort, where they were routed. As Berkeley again fled to the Eastern Shore, the rebels burned Jamestown and returned to Gloucester County to pursue some supposed Berkeley men. Facing almost no resistance, Bacon confiscated property and imprisoned those opposing the rebellion, but made ill by his exertions in the swamps, Bacon died of the "bloody flux"(dysentery), and his supporters buried his remains in an unknown grave. With the tide now turning to the governor's favor, Berkeley's people on the Eastern Shore captured Bacon's ship and its captain, William Carver, of Lower Norfolk County. Rebels held out for a time in Surry County at a seized fortified house (known as Bacon's Castle, even though the rebel leader never went there), one of the few remaining examples of Jacobean style architecture in Virginia. As Berkeley regained control, he confiscated land and hanged major rebels. William Carver and Giles Bland, a customs collector died on the gallows. Berkeley's men found Scotsman William Drummond (for whom a lake in the Dismal Swamp is named) hiding in another swamp. Berkeley welcomed Drummond and informed him that he would be "hanged in half an hour." It took a day, but Berkeley had his way.

In January 1677, the arrival of English troops helped quiet the remnants of the rebellion. The commander of these forces prevented the execution of an aged royalist that had supported King Charles I. After a few more hangings, the commander finally followed his instructions and removed Berkeley as governor. Sir William and Lady Berkeley returned to the homeland to present their case to King Charles II, who did not care to hear it. Berkeley soon died.

Most historians agree that Indian problems sparked Bacon's Rebellion. But they disagree on the nature of the complaints about Berkeley and the reasons for temporary reforms. After new elections for the burgesses in 1662, no general election took place for 14 years (the Long Assembly). The first full election produced the Virginia Assembly of June 1676. It included Bacon as one of the representatives, but he never attended the session. Only one or two of these laws dealt directly with the current crisis with the Indians. An equal number seemed aimed at Bacon and his followers by giving the governor special powers to subdue unauthorized meetings or not allowing newcomers special status in the colony. This body in June gave freemen the right to vote for the burgesses, a right restricted to certain property holders six years earlier. The June Laws, sometimes mistakenly called "Bacon's Laws," (better called June Laws) also gave freemen the right to send representatives to meetings of the county justices when the tax rate would be set. Vestries would no longer be self-perpetuating. Council members had to pay taxes like anyone else and were no longer to hold local posts. Some positions now had term limits. The burgesses also tried to restrict the sale of alcoholic beverages. These reforms, which tended to increase local power at the expense of the colonial government and were clearly designed to reduce the tax burden, seem to be aimed against Berkeley and his cronies, but at the same time they reduced the burdens of office for the governor. Bacon's people, however, were not necessarily the beneficiary of these changes. Demanding and receiving his commission from a reluctant group of burgesses at gunpoint, Bacon and his fellow rebels did not seem very concerned about basic reforms in June 1676, when most of the legislation passed. Only the matter of a monopoly over the fur trade struck a chord with these people. One can scarcely imagine such folk being concerned about drinking. One may well wonder why Berkeley opened up the floodgates by allowing the election in the first place and then approving the resulting legislation. Most of the reforms were soon repealed after the English took direct control.

During the rebellion, many indentured servants and some blacks sided with Bacon. In the rebellion's last stages a band of white servants and blacks held out against Royalists. Their fate is unknown, but that Bacon attracted the support of the underclass, along with the approval of laws that temporarily broadened influence for the freemen, suggests that the rebellion may have been a crossroads, the path not taken being the one toward a more equal and just society.

Women played active roles during the struggle. Lady Berkeley proved quite forceful. During Bacon's siege of Jamestown, his men used a number of wives of the supporters of the governor as shields. Berkeley demanded the queen of the Pamunkey aid him. Cockacoeske continually reminded him of the fate of her husband who had died trying to help the English twenty years earlier. She nearly suffered the same fate, but managed to escape into the swamps. The wives of several rebel leaders rallied the troops. Sarah Drummond urged Bacon's men at the rebel headquarters at Green Springs to take on England. A daughter-in-law of a troublesome Quaker told the governor that she urged her husband to rebel. One of Berkeley's men, whose pregnant wife had been hurt by the Baconites, took vengeance on rebel women. Many women on both sides became destitute at least temporarily. Sarah Drummond and others were able to recover property when the commission took power. The commission refused to accept Berkeley's assertion that women played a major role in the events on the rebel side. Women, however, had played major roles, and not always behind the scenes. Women would have less public influence in ensuing generations.

The era that followed the rebellion also had its difficulties. The new governor, Lord Culpeper, the proprietor of the Northern Neck, took his time reaching the colony because he preferred life in London with his mistress. He came only because the king threatened to take away his commission. Culpeper arrived in 1680 but stayed only for a few months. He generated goodwill by ending all acts of indemnity related to the recent rebellion, regulating slave meetings, and naturalizing citizens. After receiving a nice bonus from the Assembly, he left. An annoyed Charles II chastised him for taking money and thereby undermining his authority over the Virginians, particularly egregious as Culpeper already received three times Berkeley's salary. He sent him back to the colony with instructions to assert authority over the colonists. In his absence Virginia experienced a rebellion when farmers tried to raise the price of tobacco by cutting their neighbors' crops. A death sentence or two, whippings, seizures, and the like restored order. Culpeper was chiefly concerned with increasing the power and revenues of the crown and his own properties. He demanded higher tobacco taxes to give more income to the crown and followed the king's instructions by drafting laws without benefit of the council or burgesses. After claiming control over the speaker of the house, he dissolved the burgesses, and left the colony. On his arrival in England the king charged him with bribery and treason. To accommodate the court, Culpeper gave up all quit rents in Virginia to a relative. He also ceded rights to the Northern Neck for a lump sum and an annual payment for 21 years.

In 1684 Lord Howard of Effingham replaced him. This lord, who looked down on the lower orders even more so than the usual members of the English aristocracy, became embroiled with both the council and the burgesses as he followed royal instructions. Under both Culpeper and Howard, the crown hoped to stop the tendency toward autonomy as part of a policy applied to most colonies. Howard, picking up where Culpeper left off, took control over the dispersal of offices, ending the practice of allowing local justices of the peace to appoint sheriffs. He removed an offending clerk and gave out the best jobs for his supporters. The house lost the ability to review decisions of the general court. He negotiated a treaty with the Iroquois in 1685, reorganized the militia, and carried out other activities without much input from the council or the house, which he dissolved. Philip Ludwell, who had married the widow Berkeley, led the Green Springs Faction, which plotted against the governor. Ludwell, in bringing a case before the crown, charged that Howard had, among other things, charged fees improperly. In addition, a notorious and often drunk English naval officer, who ran roughshod over Virginia merchants, brought charges against Lord Howard, whom the Privy Council exonerated.

Also at this time, most Virginians did not want to accept an edict of King James II to allow a degree of religious freedom. Both Culpeper and Howard tried to ease attacks on Quakers to little effect, as most Virginians had a negative attitude toward them. That view was perhaps best expressed by a Lower Norfolk County resident in 1687, who said it "would be better for that Quaker dog to go stark naked into a red hot oven than put his foot on my plantation." Attitudes toward Catholics (Papists) were no better. When a priest carried out a marriage ceremony in Norfolk County in 1687, he was brought before the colonial court. Many residents of the Northern Neck, a frontier at the time, feared the French, possibly with the aid of Maryland Catholics and the Quakers in Pennsylvania, were inciting the Indians to attack.

During these years, Virginians and Lord Howard welcomed Protestant (Huguenot) refugees from France with support from Virginia Anglicans. In 1685 Louis XIV revoked the Edict of Nantes, which had allowed Protestants to live in France. Plans fell through for a colony of Huguenots near the coast, and the French settled in Manakin Town, an abandoned Monacan village, located some 20 miles up the James River from the Fall Line. They soon spread out and resided on plantations. They belonged to the Anglican Church with services conducted in French. They acquired slaves and were eventually absorbed into the Anglican culture.

During much of Howard's term in office, England was in the throes of its own turmoil. James II, who replaced his deceased brother as king in 1685, consolidated the northern colonies, seizing their charters that permitted representative governments. When his Catholic wife bore a son who would be raised in that religion the predominantly Protestant Parliamentarians removed James from office in what came to be called "the Glorious Revolution," and as he fled to France in 1688, they invited Mary, the daughter of James, and William, her Dutch husband, to become queen and king of England. An era came to an end that year both in

Virginia and in England. Lord Howard probably could have returned to his old job, but his heart was not in it. The reorganization of the colonies would not be sustained. The new government soon issued an Act of Toleration, which allowed people to practice several versions of Protestantism. Virginians still faced difficulties, but better times beckoned.

# Chapter 3

# A Culture in Transition

Virginia differed from the homeland in physical appearance, but for much of the colonial era it remained essentially English. Although many settlers, even those born in the colony and who remained their entire lives, still thought of England as home, environmental circumstances meant that Virginia could never be an English clone. The colony's culture came mostly from the area to the west of London, where an Anglican subculture dominated, with a unique dialect, different attitudes toward everything from sex to death, and a skewed distribution of wealth, to go along with religious differences. Because so many of the settlers that came to Virginia around the middle to the 17th century originated in the West Country, Virginia acquired many of that area's folkways.

Although cultural differences existed in the homeland, a common political system prevailed in the mother country, and Virginians tended more than most colonists to copy these political features. In 1618, while still under company control, the directors ordered the creation of local governments. Patterned on similar institutions in England, various corporations (later known as counties) such as Elizabeth City, James City, and Charles City came into being. Each jurisdiction had the proceeds from 1,500 acres of land to run local courts and additional acreage called glebes to support a minister. The governor and council handled major criminal and civil cases.

In 1634, the Grand Assembly, consisting of the vitriolic Governor Harvey, the council, and the burgesses, organized eight counties with the same role as shires in England. Each had justices of the peace (commissioners) to try cases and adopt local ordinances. They eventually became self-perpetuating bodies, whose recommendations for replacements were nearly always accepted. Only prestigious planters that expected the lower classes to defer to their wishes could serve as justices. Sheriffs (usually former justices) brought cases to the court, the same as in England. Parishes, religious subdivisions of counties, had vestries (occasionally elected) that supervised church policy, recommended ministers, and appointed wardens, who carried out a variety of religious and political duties such as caring for the poor and prosecuting sinners (drunks, adulterers, fornicators, slanderers, etc.). A 1642 law required ministers to be ordained by a particular English bishop and approved by the governor before taking his post in the colony. In 1662, under Berkeley, the Assembly reaffirmed, as the king's instructions bade, the *Book of Common Prayer* and required ministers to have certification from the Bishop of London. Eventually the Presbyterians found a way around these restrictions, but for years Lutherans often sent their ministers to England for approval.

Virginia, however, was not a precise replica of England in religion. For almost the entire colonial era, Virginia contended with a shortage of qualified Anglican ministers, forcing some to serve vast areas and several congregations. Also, the absence of bishops meant the power of the church remained unfocused. It also meant that no religious figure controlled any part of local government, including keeping records and implementing wills. Recent scholarship points out that the Anglican religion remained an essential element in the lives of white Virginians throughout the 17th and far into the 18th century. Although a few clergymen had less than exemplary morals, the majority behaved prudently as did most of their parishioners. Both believed in following traditional Anglican services, making some attempt to read scripture, and striving to live an upright life.

During the company phase, and for some time after, leaders treated residents as if they were a drunken rabble, even though company charters often spoke of the rights of Englishmen, but the Assembly, once it established its right to exist, tried to replicate English common law. Virginia soon had grand juries required to meet annually in every county. Trial by jury (petty jury) existed possibly as early as 1623, for civil cases, if desired by either plaintiff or defendant. In the 1640s, the colony wrote the right into the law. Another law pointed out that Virginians could not exactly replicate the English jury system due to the remote distances people lived from the courts, but the sheriff had to have six men meet for duty at the most convenient place.

Colonists frequently mention the need to retain English practices, and a law in 1662 demanded the use of English common law, but because few people with exalted titles ever permanently resided in Virginia, the colony developed a system of government that, in a sense, better fulfilled the English ideal than what existed in the homeland. This kind of local government, with a few modifications, followed the pioneers as they crossed the mountains and competed with the town type of local government more popular in the North.

In its essential political features Virginia looked like mother England, with some differences. The crown-appointed governor had an advisory council, something like the English Privy Council. Its members and the governor met with burgesses, who started meeting separately in 1643, with Governor Berkeley's encouragement. They soon asserted their right to make laws with approval from the council and governor, subject to the possible disallowance from the crown. The Speaker of the House emerged as a position of power. During the time of Puritan domination, the colony had a vague idea that government should, at least to some degree, represent the wishes of the governed. In 1652 Northampton, an Eastern Shore county, complained about paying poll taxes without having real representation in the Assembly. The House then encouraged elections and lowered the poll tax by more than half.

Each county elected two burgesses, but unlike the situation in the mother country all freemen were entitled to vote (indeed they had to) by voice for representatives as of 1646, the servants and slaves being exempted from this requirement and right. In 1670 Governor Berkeley and the Assembly allowed only freeholders (those who owned property) to vote to reduce the disturbances at the polls and to be more in conformity with English practices. The June Laws of 1676 expanded the electorate, but the crown repealed the measures for being out of step with English practices. Unlike in England, Virginia law required representatives to live in the counties they represented. Local magistrates, following English traditions, wielded considerable power over county residents. Wardens and sheriffs charged numerous people with all sorts of petty crimes. In addition to the ones already mentioned concerning the violation of the Sabbath and illicit sex, local officials prosecuted cases for drunkenness, profanity, reveling, alleged witchcraft, gambling above one's status, and others too numerous to mention.

Freedom of the press, speech, and religion did not exist. These future rights had greater reality in the homeland and in some other colonies. No one tried to print a newspaper in Virginia until 1692, and at the time officials told the editor to desist. One had to attend the prescribed church and only that church. In this regard, Virginia's Anglicans were a bit sterner than their counterparts in the homeland. The colony and the local courts were always on the alert for loose tongues. In the wake of Bacon's Rebellion, the Grand Assembly passed a measure that penalized people for using terms like "traitorous rebel" in arguments with their neighbors. One could avoid the fine only if the person so criticized had provoked the encounter, in which case he or she paid the fine. In the aftermath of Bacon's Rebellion, order was far more important than freedom of speech.

It would be folly to insult one of the leaders, but accusing anyone of witchcraft had mixed results. Of the several cases involving such accusations, only one, that in a court in Princess Anne County, produced a guilty verdict. When Grace Sherwood survived the ducking stool there, the court deemed her a witch, thus allowing the charge to stand. But unlike in Massachusetts, this alleged witch endured only her ducking and a brief imprisonment. The Anglican philosophy of the late 17th century, with its milder reactions to this particular deviation, might be responsible for the difference between New England and Virginia, but Virginians were more tolerant of witches than the home country but less tolerant of religious dissenters.

Many colonial laws had little to do with events in the home country, though English precedents permitted the local and colony government to pass such legislation. The reliance on tobacco compelled the company and later the crown, with the help of the Assembly, to control production and prices. In the 1630s rules mandated the number of pounds of tobacco the planter could produce, the number of leaves on his plants, even when he had to plant and harvest. The colony required the production of a certain amount of corn or other foodstuffs. A law in 1632 prohibited the indiscriminate killing of swine and encouraged killing wolves. At various times the government tried to encourage—through subsidy or monopoly—the production of goods that the colony lacked. In 1630, the master of a plantation had to save urine in casks to facilitate nitrate production. In Berkeley's time every planter had to grow a number of mulberry trees per acre to make the colony proficient in silk production. A law to encourage the settlement in the colony of textile workers suggests that well into the 17th century ordinary farmers must not have had spinning wheels and looms in their homes. None of these laws had any measurable impact on the colony.

In the 18th century Virginia continued to pass legislation to encourage certain behaviors and discourage others. One was not supposed to strike fish in the rivers or use the native method of killing deer called "fire hunting," for the practice not only reduced the deer, but also played havoc with the environment. A 1738 act noted that previous laws to protect deer had not had the desired effect and residents continued to kill merely for skins and left carcasses that attracted wolves. Thus the Assembly imposed a fine on anyone who killed a buck between 1 December and the end of July and a fawn or a doe between 1 January and the last of September.

Over the years, the colonial Assembly passing legislation on a wide variety of matters, reaffirmed the requirement to attend church on Sunday, but it toned down belligerent views about Quakers and other Protestant sects. Any "lewd woman," who bore an illegitimate child, was still subject to whipping or fines. Midwives were required to report such occurrences to wardens or justices of the peace. The 1705 Code restricted the availability of tippling houses. The Assembly outlawed a rate of interest above 6%, later lowered to 5%. It prohibited anyone from winning any more than ten pounds from "gaming, or playing at cards, dice, tables, tennis, bowls, or other game or games," thus banning professional gambling. Many of these and other laws were selectively enforced, but their passage indicates that a modified form of the Puritan ethic survived in Virginia.

Family life was difficult to export to the colony. In the early 17th century, the company sent mostly men. Anne Burras, a servant girl who came in 1608, married carpenter John Layden, who had come with the original colonists the year before. They had the first child born in Jamestown. By 1623 the Laydens were living in Elizabeth City County with their four daughters. John was likely the only original resident still residing in the colony. And his family, with its several children, was a rarity. About 10% of those who lived in Virginia at that time were children, most of them still babies. Wives accounted for a slightly greater percentage. Women and girls constituted but about one-sixth of Virginia's total population of around 1,300 people. The number of adult unmarried females was minimal, although a number of widows, some with small children, lived in the colony. Several married couples were caring for children with different last names, a result of the high rate of death. One community had forty men, 31 of them indentured servants, and no women. The limited number of women, along with the death rate, prevented the appearance of normal English family life. Men outnumbered women by at least two to one into the next century. Although the situation improved, hundreds of people continued to die from disease over the years. Numerous men and women had several spouses in the course of their lives due to the high rate of death. That meant that many half-brothers and sisters lived in the same household. The nuclear family had a hard time becoming established. Deep into the 18th century, distant kinship often meant as much to people as their immediate family, as was also the case in parts of England, where cousins sometimes counted as much as sisters or brothers.

Virginia inherited English practices regarding women. Women, with essentially the same rights they had in England, had a dower right to one-third of their husband's estates at his death. They could not own property after marriage except under peculiar circumstances, nor could they hold public office or minister to a church. They assisted magistrates in carrying out the law only in unusual circumstances (i.e., determining pregnancy in the case of a woman subject to the death sentence). Both women and men faced stiff penalties for sexual relations outside marriage; those with insufficient funds absorbed whippings. Indentured servants were especially vulnerable to prosecution. Late in the 17th century, the common penalty for producing an illicit offspring was to have one's time of service extended. English law said and did all these things, but the shortage of women in Virginia may have given some females slightly better conditions than in England. The absence of village life in Virginia, however, often meant lack of contact with friends and acquaintances.

As in England, status bore more weight than sex. Sarah Offley, the daughter of the mayor of London, came to the colony as the bride of Adam Thoroughgood. They established a plantation in Lower Norfolk

County and prospered. Adam died and Sarah remarried. The second husband died, and she remarried again, this time to a much younger man. The county justices kept asking for an accounting regarding her several children, a statement she steadfastly refused to give them. Such magistrates might cow lesser folk, but they simply did not have enough status to control one of a higher class, regardless of sex.

As was true throughout much of the world, physical punishment was used to promote order. Pig stealing, a common problem, could result for the first offense in whippings with different numbers of stripes for free and slave. For a second offense the criminal would have each ear nailed to a pillory alternately, followed by more whipping. In an early version of "three strikes and you're out," the third offense produced death. Few were executed in those times for such petty acts, but the law had many crimes short of murder for which one could suffer death. Such a penalty, however, was reserved for the poorer classes, because one could avoid death by reading from the Bible.

The nature of the environment did make the settlers' sports different from those popular in England. Robert Beverley, a resident of Virginia around 1700, described how Virginians modified the English favorites of hunting, fishing, and fowling. The colonists used stalking horses and swift dogs to hunt deer. Both on foot and horse, they chased raccoons and opossums in forest and field. The game sometimes sought refuge in a tree; then the settlers sent "a nimble fellow up after it, who must have a scuffle with the Beast, before he can throw it down to the Dogs." Settlers hunted wolves with traps and guns. Beverley himself rode horse bareback after wolves, took them live from traps, and dragged them for sport. Turkey hunting without guns was a special favorite. In fishing, some employed the Indian tactic of staking out a long line with numerous hooks on short strings, which yielded "an abundance of diversion." "I have sat in the shade, at the Heads of the Rivers Angling, and spent as much time in taking the fish off the Hook, as in waiting for them taking it," Beverley informs us. Young people hunted wild horses, a very dangerous avocation.

In the late 17th and 18th centuries Virginia had its share of naturalists. John Banister, the son of a commoner, an Anglican divine, an M.A. recipient from Oxford, and a friend of the Bishop of London traveled extensively in Virginia, sending back about 300 samples of local flora to England and communicating with members of a botany club. In 1692, with William Byrd I as a guide, he was accidentally killed, exploring the Roanoke River. John Mitchell, who attended a Scottish medical school, sent numerous samples of Virginia plants to members of scientific societies in England, being an authority on opossums, yellow fever, and numerous other matters. Two John Claytons became authorities on plant life. One was a Virginia lawyer and the colony's attorney general. Late in life, the son, after collecting many examples of Virginia flora, helped found a society for promoting useful knowledge. Like Mitchell, he belonged to an English royal society. The reputations of these naturalists live on in the names of plants. We know a great deal more about the natural environment of the time thanks to their efforts. The College of William and Mary opened a chair of natural philosophy and math in 1711, but the recipient fell victim to "an idle hussy" and strong drink.

Crown officials and colonial leaders constantly lamented the lack of communities. In 1655, while the Puritans held sway, the lack of "orderly villages" convinced some of the need for controlling commerce and creating ports and markets. Churches, courthouses, jails, and taverns would all be encouraged to take root in these new communities, but the Assembly repealed the measure the next year. In 1660, just after Berkeley returned to power, the legislature, at the governor's urging, demanded that the seventeen county governments each establish a substantial building in Jamestown to accompany a new capitol. Nothing much came of this plan. In 1680, under Lord Culpeper, the Assembly called for each county to purchase fifty acres of land to encourage trade and manufacturing. Commerce had to enter and exit through these places. The officials of Lower Norfolk County bought and surveyed the prescribed acreage and divided it into lots by late summer that year. Within a few years a handful of families took up residence despite the fact that Charles II rescinded the act. Norfolk and a few other designated spots matured into villages, largely because the locations so chosen had natural advantages. In 1691 the Assembly passed another act to promote ports, this time encouraging potential residents with the possibility of avoiding customs duties. That same year a progress report indicated that about half the counties had any buildings in their designated towns. In 1705 the Assembly once again tried to establish towns. This law required each county to create one. At that time, all imports except slaves and salt and all exports save coal, corn, and timber had to enter or exit through these communities. Each burgh would have an annual fair and two market days per week, during which time nothing could be bought or sold within several miles except at the prescribed location. Residents potentially would have their own court and council to be elected by the freemen. When these communities acquired at least thirty families, the voters residing there could pick a burgess for the assembly. Many English towns at the time had these same features.

Despite all these efforts, few counties ended up with towns of any size. The act itself seems to have been followed only up to a point, and then the English government disallowed part of the act. Norfolk became a town under the act, but not until 1736, when the king made it a borough, did it have a bicameral council, an unelected self-perpetuating body much like the magistrates on the county level. Its qualified voters could elect a burgess. Williamsburg, the capital of the colony created at the end of the century, secured its bicameral council and court of hustings several years earlier than Norfolk, but neither community, the biggest towns in the colony at the time, had even 1,000 people in the 1730s. Considerable growth ensued, and the borough had about 6,000 in 1775, at which time Williamsburg had over a 1,000, and Hampton, Yorktown, Winchester, and a few others had a few hundred each.

By mid-century the Assembly authorized residents to organize the Fall Line towns of Richmond and Petersburg. The concentration of tobacco inspection houses in these localities encouraged Scottish traders to settle there. Several other towns materialized. Most of those survived, but others disappeared. Late in the colonial era, several towns came into being in the Valley of Virginia. The growing trade in grain and other factors contributed to the appearance of Winchester and several smaller communities in the Lower Valley. The Assembly's favorite way of encouraging the growth was to outlaw wooden chimneys and prevent goats and pigs from roaming the streets. Some towns were allowed to conduct fairs and operate marketplaces. The legislature also clamped down on retailers that sold hard liquor in small quantities and sometimes watered down their product. Despite the colony's efforts, a traveler in 1759 reported that although the assembly had created 44 towns, not but half of them had more than five houses, most being little more than "inconsiderable villages." The English government allowed them to have fairs and markets, but disallowed attempts by the Assembly to prevent the arrest of debtors during such times.

Late 17th-century Virginians tended to live in comparative rural isolation because Tidewater, with its numerous inlets and marshes, provided few unbroken stretches of arable land. Roads remained little more than twisting paths through near wilderness conditions. Even older counties exhibited an ephemeral atmosphere because farmers built temporary shelters. Wooden posts sunk in the ground held siding and roofs that could not possibly last but a few years because residents planned to produce as much tobacco as they could and move on to another location. The typical grower had only a handful of acres in production at any one time. The standard agricultural practices of the time took a short-term toll on the environment as well as accentuated class differences. Within a comparatively short time, soil exposed to excessive tobacco growing weakened in fertility. Lands away from the rivers were especially wanting in durability. Thus those in possession of river bottomlands did better than those with thinner soil. Proximity to rivers also permitted settlers to supplement their diet with fish. Despite a pervasive attitude that stressed immediate exploitation or resources, residents did little overall permanent damage to the environment because of limited number and density.

No governor or any authority in England did anything to discourage the development of slavery in the colony. During a time when English authorities cracked down on colonial commercial actions, they did nothing in any mainland or Caribbean colony to stop the rise of slavery, an institution unknown in England. Virginia and Maryland shifted from using English indentured servants as their main source of workers to Africans. Contracted indentured servants had to be released after working for a specified time. Some planters connived to force extensions of these indentures, but the courts sometimes protected the workers from excessive beatings and violations of their contractual rights. Conditions in England were improving, and the ordinary resident had little desire to emigrate, which encouraged those in the business of supplying servants to the colony to kidnap people, especially poor young men and women. As the value of English labor rose, the cost of running a plantation also increased, while the price of tobacco stayed the same. In Berkeley's time

Africans came to be considered chattel. In 1670 the governor estimated that Virginia contained some 2,000 black slaves out of a total of 40,000, but the shift to African labor had just started.

Virginia became increasingly different from England as slavery evolved. The institution developed slowly until the 1690s. One British company had a monopoly up until 1698 and supplied several hundred slaves, but before then most slaves came into Virginia from the West Indies. Then the English government opened up the trade, and thousands endured the torturous Middle Passage from Africa to reach the tobacco colony. The climate and soil of Virginia helped the colonists produce a commercial crop. That in turn gave them sufficient income to buy slaves. The slaves made planters more productive, permitting them to buy even more slaves. Many growers continued to contract with white indentured servants, but planters turned increasingly to African slave labor.

Defenders of slavery later argued that planters had little conscious control over the institution and were simply responding to environmental circumstances. But the acceptance of the slave trade and of slavery was due in part to the predominant Anglican attitude. In neighboring Pennsylvania, where the soil was as fertile as that in Virginia and which grew a wide variety of crops that could have employed slave labor, most of the new settlers were English Quakers or Germans, many quite pious. Their religious views often did not accept holding fellow humans in permanent bondage. Slavery, therefore, did not grow firm roots there. By the time Virginia churchmen decided that something might be wrong with enslaving people, the institution had already secured a foothold. Historians tend to blame tobacco, a labor-intensive crop, for the rise of slavery. Yet many of the first Africans worked as slaves in a variety of jobs. Around 1630 the biggest slave owner on the lowest peninsula did not produce tobacco. In time, however, the parts of Virginia that grew the best and most tobacco ended up with the highest percentage of slaves.

The English made more of racial differences than southern Europeans, but the relative absence of Africans in Briton itself left the homeland with only a minimal legacy of legal racism. Even so, bias showed up in the first generation of Virginians, who denounced the comingling of the races. Over the years the colonists intensified their racial attitudes and refined their racial laws. In the 1640s black indentured servants received harsher punishments than whites of the same class. It soon became common to keep only Africans and those of African dissent in slavery. In the early 1660s a child of a slave mother automatically became a slave at birth. These laws became a slave code, designed to control those under the institution. Many features of this code came from English colonies in the Caribbean, particularly Barbados.

Slavery, in turn, intensified racial views. In time, a body of law reflected and sanctified slavery and racism. In 1705 the assembly defined a child of a union of a white woman and a slave as a servant who served until age 31, at which time he or she was to be free. That practice persisted for several generations. In 1705 the colony also made it clear that no nonwhite had the right to vote. In 1723 the legislature outlawed any assembly of five slaves or more, unless under the supervision of an owner or overseer, at a public mill, or church on Sunday. Owners and overseers were expected to give passes (licenses) to their slaves that went off the plantation. An earlier law demanded that citizens allow slaves visiting their farms to stay no more than four hours. Free black housekeepers and slaves on the frontier that obtained a license could keep a gun and powder, but no nonwhites could carry guns in the militia. They could, however, be compelled to beat drums, blow bugles, or do servile labor. In 1742 the Assembly affirmed that no Negro, Mulatto, or Indian, either slave or free, could testify in court except at a trial of a slave charged with a capital offence. A black Christian could, however, testify in a debt case involving people of color.

No great planters could have acquired their large estates and status without slaves. Whites holding few or no slaves had little chance of success in a tobacco economy. Moving into the Piedmont did little to provide new opportunities, because planters secured land from a government that distributed it on the basis of the number of slaves one owned.

One of the few Virginians that opposed aspects of slavery, William Byrd II urged the crown to end the slave trade, saying it was turning Virginia into Africa. The owner of Westover found that among the results of increasing slaves was that white pride grew and slavery ruined work habits of whites, who "seeing a rash of poor creatures below them, detest work for fear it will make them look like slaves." The institution also forced owners to punish slaves to prevent insolence, and "foul means must do what fair will not." The master had to keep a tight rein or slaves would throw the rider. In addition, whites lived in constant fear of a slave uprising, and punishment for alleged plots was swift and harsh. Planters worried about Africans wandering loose in the colony. Byrd believed a desperate and courageous slave might make wide rivers flow "red with blood," and so implored the government not to cave in to slave traders and "put an end to this un-Christian traffic, of making merchandise of our fellow creatures," but Virginia's efforts to tax the slave trade out of existence failed.

As part of a policy to control the Africans, masters controlled the process of cultural assimilation, usually giving them names from scripture, English places, or Classical references. For several generations, slaves had no last names. Church registries refer to them by a first name or no name at all. African names commemorated an event or denoted a trait. Africans tracked their children's births through notable events such as a natural disaster or political occurrence. Children, therefore, had only a rough idea of their actual age as they grew up. Masters paid little attention to African tastes in food or much else. In South Carolina slaves came from the Caribbean in numbers that exceeded those of whites. They were, therefore, able to retain more of their culture. In Virginia, slaves had less chance to influence aspects of the overall lifestyle. Despite all this, slave women kept African methods of cooking, which concentrated on vegetables. Africans used the peanut, of South American origins, like they did a similar nut in the home country. Sweet potatoes and other items, including tobacco, went to Africa from South America in the century following Columbus's voyages to the New World. Several African plants, including okra, made their way into Virginia. Slaves found ways of adapting their cooking methods to the materials at hand. Eventually the resulting combination worked its way into Southern cuisine and appeared in cook books in the 1830s.

Some of the first slaves in Virginia had been seasoned in the West Indies, but most of those who entered the colony toward the middle of the 18th century came directly from West Africa. Although in certain years more slaves came from the Caribbean and more ships came into Virginia from that locale, the direct importation from Africa accounted for a larger percentage of the immigrants because ships from West Africa tended to carry larger numbers of slaves. Whether from Africa or the West Indies, by 1750 almost 70,000 had entered Virginia. They continued to be brought into the colony until their importation became illegal in 1778. Many died on the trip from Africa and more died in the first winter in the colony. Africans developed some immunity against some diseases such as smallpox, but they had to adjust to an alien climate. Many planters hoped for the time when no more immigrants would come from Africa and they could depend on their native-born slaves, because they were thought to be more pliant and less susceptible to disease. The next generation was a little bigger than their parents, having been fed a diet of pork supplemented by Virginia's wild game.

Although most of African culture disappeared in Virginia, some aspects were retained. The exalted status of the male elder could not survive. African males of status sometimes had two wives, but women committing adultery or men who took another man's wife might be executed. In Africa marriage united two families. In Virginia marriage among slaves mattered little, as planters might sell one or both spouses to different parties. Some Virginia masters urged African men to have sexual relations with "wenches" in the hope of selling off the children. A few white masters forced themselves on their female slaves and sold the children. Africans knew how to grow crops such as tobacco, cotton, and even corn before they arrived, so they needed to learn very little except how to work the animals. Africans knew how to smoke a pipe; make ironware, shoot guns; and use hoes, axes, and shovels. Women knew how to spin and weave. In Africa both men and women worked in fields some distance from their place of residence. In Virginia, a few slaves stayed near or in the main house, but the tobacco plantation required a lot of outdoor work some distance from shelter.

Although Virginia homes for big planters were more substantial than the more simple African abodes with grass roofs and raised floors, the homes for slaves in Virginia usually fell below the African standard. On frontier plantations, slaves had little more than brush to cover pens held up by pine poles. Slaves on established plantations usually had cabins, which had roofs and some of which had wooden floors. The larger farms often looked like villages with dozens of structures to accompany the main house. The "big house," except for a few, would be small by today's standards, running perhaps a little over 1,000 square feet. Homes for some slaves and for most white families usually occupied about 300 square feet. Some slaves resided in crude lofts. Although parts of Africa had conjurers or witches, those accused of witchcraft in 17th-century Virginia were whites. Africans believed in a single creator but had lesser gods, and they tended not to differentiate between the spiritual and the material. Islam had made inroads in West Africa, especially among the elite, but the typical African retained local religions. The custom of dusting or sprinkling the ground with food and drink to honor one's ancestors did not survive long in Virginia, but the majority of slaves preserved African beliefs. Forms of witchcraft and various superstitions could be found among blacks and whites for generations.

Even though Olaudah Equiano did not tarry in Virginia, his experiences tell us a lot about slavery. Born around 1745, he was captured as a boy and taken to the African coast, after which he endured the Middle Passage to the West Indies and thence to Virginia. During the second leg he ate better meals than provided on the voyage from Africa. In Virginia he worked in the fields weeding and then fanning an ill master. Seeing a clock and an iron muzzle attached to a slave, he had no idea of the purpose of the first but quickly figured out the utility of the second. As luck would have it, a visiting mariner purchased him, which started a chain of events that eventually led to his manumission in the West Indies. The former slave knew how to farm the land and work iron before he left Africa, but now he could pilot a ship. As soon as possible, he resumed his African name. Some years later he described his African life to the English-speaking world. In comparing African slavery to that in the New World, Equiano noted that some Africans had slaves, often taken prisoner in battle, but in no cases were they treated as badly as the English treated their slaves in the West Indies.

At about the time Equiano visited Virginia, some ministers began to take a deeper interest in the slaves. In the 1750s and especially in the years just before the Revolution, evangelical ministers accelerated efforts to Christianize blacks. Equiano expressed interest in George Whitefield and the Society of Friends. The Presbyterian divine Samuel Davis enjoyed success in the Hanover area among both blacks and whites. Another minister noticed that Africans "above all the human species…have an ear for music" and loved to sing psalms. He urged their recruitment to the cause of Christianity. In a "compassionate address to Virginia blacks," he begged the converts not to be dissuaded by the poor behavior of Christian Caucasians. The creator, he suggested, must have planned their tribulations to bring them out of African paganism and away from the influence of Islam.

If some slaves and ministers found the religious revivals of the mid-18th century, to be quite exciting, the masters were of a divided mind about whether the slaves should be subject to the emotionalism associated with religious revivals. Some thought agitating slaves could harm their work. Others felt it might improve their behavior. By the end of the century the link between evangelism and Africans created churches whose ministers incorporated religious customs from Africa.

African and English attitudes toward work were also similar. Many propertied Englishmen complained about the slothfulness of their poorer countrymen and the Africans. They both came from cultures that had yet to shift to a modern industrial society that required rigorous routines. Africans traditionally were active at night and moved slowly during the day. Virginia planters constantly complained about these perceived failings, but outsiders often remarked that white Virginians possessed the same traits.

**Sampler on Slavery, Servitude, and Race**

| | |
|---|---|
| 1630s | Hugh Davis whipped before Negroes and others for "defiling his body in lying with a Negro."<br>Black servants excluded from militia duty and bearing guns. |
| 1640s | White man whipped for getting a Negro woman pregnant.<br>If white servant runs away with black slave, white servant must make up black's time and own.<br>John Punch serves master or assignees for the rest of life. |

32

Six white servants and one black stole guns; whites had service extended; black, serving life, whipped.

Black servant owned daughter of Negro woman; could sell child.

Indian freed of life servitude; he spoke English and wanted baptism.

The status of a Christian mulatto changed to servant (later freed).

1650s    Elizabeth Key, a Christian, mother slave and father white, jury returned her to slavery.

In another case, child of freeman and slave mother given freedom

1660s    Slave, freed by will, given clothes, two cows, house, etc

English runaways serve double penalties for slave time.

White servants should have certificates.

No trading with servants, too much stealing.

Rebellious servants sent out of colony.

Fornication by servants, extra 6 months penalty; bastard resulting, add 5 years

Children got by any Englishman upon a Negro woman, all children born in this country shall be held bond or free only according to the condition of the mother. Any Christian fornicating with a Negro man or woman, he or she shall pay a double fine.

Conferring of baptism does not alter the condition of the one in bondage.

Negro women set free not to be admitted to a full fruition of the rights of the English and still had to pay tithe, although white women did not.

Exempts white master or overseer from felony should death result from punishing slave. "If a slave resists his master (or others by his master's order correcting him) and by the extremity of the correction should chance to die," his death shall not be considered a felony.

1670s    Killing a runaway slave not penalized; colony compensates master at 450 pounds of tobacco.

1680s    Thirty lashes for any Negro slave raising hand against whites

Slaves penalized for carrying weapons, especially to meetings (feasts and burials)

1682    Repealed 1670 act making Indians slaves.

1691    Those who free their slaves must pay transport costs out of colony.

1705    Codification of Virginia Law repeats many earlier laws on slavery

Child of union of white woman and slave a servant until age 31.

# Chapter 4

## Three Governors and a Commissary

A new era commenced when William and Mary assumed the throne in 1688. England, soon to be Great Britain with the union with Scotland in 1707, enjoyed a more relaxed domestic atmosphere. War with France erupted in 1691 and lasted for six years, followed by five years of peace, then another twelve years of war. Colonists called the first King William's War and the second, Queen Anne's War. After Queen Anne's War, Great Britain enjoyed 25 years of not being officially at war.

As Virginia felt the effects of the two wars only marginally, the half-century from 1690 to about 1740 proved peaceful and prosperous. The colonists subdued most of the natives in the Piedmont in the last half of the 17th century. Although possible perils still lurked, constant attacks became a thing of the past east of the Blue Ridge. Religious turmoil also eased as crown and Parliament called for a new age of toleration for all Protestants. The price of tobacco remained high enough that the use of slave labor allowed substantial returns for many producers. Most important, the crown no longer insisted that the colonies, including Virginia, give up their representative assemblies. In Virginia, elected delegates usually bowed to the wishes of the appointed council, which consisted of the most powerful and prosperous planters.

Although the political situation was less acrimonious, the new era had its own controversies. Not a governor, nor a prominent planter, nor even a heroic military leader, James Blair, an Anglican minister, dominated the era. That such could occur says something about the political culture of the time, but Virginians were not even especially interested in disputing religious matters. Blair, a Scotsman, arrived in the colony in the mid-1680s newly ordained in his homeland but with ties to the Bishop of London. Blair took up the duties near the site of old Henricus. Several things made him different from other clergymen. The Bishop of London gave him his blessing and the position of commissary in 1689, a post that made him the chief Anglican in the colony. Blair also had access to the Archbishop of Canterbury, the top religious position under the king or queen. Then in 1687 Blair married into the powerful Harrison family, his wife Sarah (she refused to use the word "obey" during the marriage ceremony even though asked three times) providing him with access to a large estate, the most powerful people in the colony, and a disputed seat on the prestigious council. The key to Blair's power rested on his connections, his understanding of English politics, and knowing the mood of Virginia's planters. The current planter class appreciated monarchs properly restrained by representatives of the English rural elite. Blair himself had renounced James II and thereby lost a religious post in England before he came to the colony, so his credentials as a supporter of William and Mary could not be doubted and he fit right into the prevailing political and religious mood.

Blair combined idealism and pragmatism. When he first became commissary, he introduced the idea of establishing special courts to try ministers that drank to excess or otherwise ruined their reputations. Whether he made any headway in this regard is unclear, for the small number of English clergy may not have been quite as immoral as some thought. He also hoped to help convert the slaves to Christianity by imposing a special tax on those who owned slaves between the ages of fourteen and eighteen to educate the youngsters in the commandments. When this idea met resistance, Blair simply joined with the council and wealthy planters, sometimes against the interests of the clergy, and enjoyed Virginia's social life. He officiated at horse races, handed out prizes, and traveled through the colony and often to England. His sermons were a model of simplicity as he encouraged low-church Anglicanism. In 1739 he welcomed the famed revivalist George Whitefield, who delivered his sermon "What think ye of Christ" at his church in Williamsburg to a small audience at Bruton Parish Church, even though he sometimes attracted thousands in other places. Virginia planters had little interest in his emotional approach to saving souls. Blair usually talked in general terms about sin and what constituted proper behavior, unlike a later Anglican minister who lectured one of his wealthy parishioners about excessive pride only to find his church boarded up the next day.

In dealing with religious dissidents Blair and the Virginia government reluctantly agreed to abide by England's Act of Toleration (1688). When Francis Makamie started preaching in Accomac County in 1696, the local officials arrested him and then allowed him to preach so long as he secured a license. The Virginia government put Blair in charge of keeping track of dissidents. In 1699 Virginia ratified the English act, but made it clear that radicals would be regulated. In an unusual burst of toleration, Virginia allowed Quakers to assume political duties with an affirmation rather than an oath. Later they were exempted from militia duties. Atheists, agnostics, and Catholics (Papists) had no rights under the English or Virginia acts of toleration. An Arminian (named for a Dutch theologian who rejected Calvin's idea of predestination), Blair believed that Christ had died for all people, not just a select few. Not too deep in their minds, the Tidewater planters doubtless thought they had been destined to receive God's goodness. But on the surface, they, like Blair, adhered to the prevailing Anglican view and rejected Calvin's "doctrine of the elect."

A few years before the Glorious Revolution, Charles II sent Edmund Andros, a courtier and veteran of the wars against the Dutch, to New York, recently acquired from the Dutch. When James II established the Dominion of New England (a super colony that controlled all New York and New England as a dictatorship), he assigned Sir Edmund (knighted by Charles II in 1678) to govern it from Boston. At the same time, Francis Nicholson, another military officer, received an appointment to run affairs in New York under Andros. When word of the impending removal of James II reached Boston, Puritans seized the governor, after he returned from fighting Indians, and sent him to England. Having failed to find Connecticut's charter hidden in an oak tree during his time in New York, Nicholson also returned to England, leaving the colony in a condition of chaos.

With two unemployed governors, William and Mary sent Nicholson to Virginia as a lieutenant governor and temporary replacement for Lord Howard. In 1690, Virginians welcomed Nicholson mostly because he was not Lord Howard. The new governor followed the advice given him in England to be tactful. He met with the council and allowed the House of Burgesses to function. In 1692 he went to Maryland as governor, when William and Mary sent the more experienced Andros.

As governor, Nicholson had a good relationship with James Blair, even encouraging the minister in creating a college. In 1693, in order to encourage the study of the ministry, Blair went to England to solicit support. Even though one potential patron suggested Virginians should busy themselves growing tobacco, Blair obtained the necessary support, including money from the will of Robert Boyle, a famous chemist, and from some chastened pirates, who had to make amends for their misdeeds by donating part of their booty. Two years later the College of William and Mary opened its doors, having been chartered by the crown. As the first and only president for nearly fifty years, Blair had a marked impact on the little college's career. Through its grammar school for Indians, Blair tried to help the colony's policy of preserving peace with the natives.

The experienced Andros looked like he could govern the Old Dominion, as Virginians did not have the ill repute of the Puritans or the Yorkers, but James Blair alone was more than a match. During a war between the French in Canada and the English in the colonies, Andros required revenues and a unified militia. Residents complained that only recent English immigrants or those born in England got all the colonial and county posts. After initially meeting with the burgesses, Andros tended to ignore or bully them. Blair complained about the arbitrary use of power, and also vied with the governor over funds from rents. In the ensuing struggle, Andros removed Blair three times from the council, but he was twice overturned by higher ups in England. An irritated Blair worked with former governor Nicholson to undermine Andros. Daniel Parke, a wealthy planter with a less than savory reputation, tried to help the governor by enticing the visiting Nicholson into a fencing duel. When that failed, he beat him over the head with a horsewhip, and the veteran Nicholson responded with his fists. Governor Andros even had his Maryland counterpart detained by a local sheriff. Parke later grabbed Sarah Blair by the wrist and forced her from her favorite pew at Bruton Parish Church.

In 1697 Blair took his case to the Board of Trade in England. The political philosopher John Locke, a member of the board, told Blair to write a report and list grievances. In his report Blair observed that the governor had too much unchecked power, which allowed him to select a few favorite planters that kept ministers under their thumbs. Blair argued that the governor undermined efforts to raise money for the college. The end of the war with France in 1697 meant the Old Dominion's help for its northern neighbors was no longer needed and thus Andros had no excuse for diverting money from Commissary Blair's projects. A fall from a horse, a bout with malaria, and Blair's efforts brought Andros down. Young William Byrd II tried to defend the governor by pointing out that Blair had filled the Virginia church with Scots in hopes of forming a party spirit, but the Bishop of London and the Archbishop of Canterbury dismissed the charge, and the Board of Trade recalled Andros.

Blair's next victim turned out to be Francis Nicholson, sent to replace the one who had replaced him as governor. This time, Nicholson failed to be tactful as governor. Indeed, his first tirade erupted when Blair brought a letter to him from the Archbishop of Canterbury, warning Nicholson to control his anger. The 46-year-old bachelor fell in love with 18-year-old Lucy Burwell, a member of one of the leading families in the colony. So infatuated did the governor become that he wrote love poems ("Virtuous pretty charming innocent dove, the only center of my constant love.") and constantly found excuses to visit the Burwell home. At one point, on learning of the possibility that Lucy might be marrying someone else and on seeing a minister near the Burwell estate, the governor threatened with bodily harm any minister who performed such a marriage as well as to the prospective bridegroom. The minister, one of Blair's aides, evaded the agents sent by Nicholson to prevent him from reaching England. At one point Nicholson thought Blair's brother was pursuing Lucy.

Even before Blair regained his seat on the council, that body was already at odds with Nicholson. The governor talked about not allowing the colonists to produce their own clothes, uniting all the colonies as one, preventing the councilmen from holding lucrative posts, and stopping abuses in the distribution of land. The minister later reported on Nicholson's controversial efforts to change the county courts and appoint sheriffs and military commanders without consulting the council. In 1703 six councilors petitioned the queen for Nicholson's removal. The next year Blair presented his case against the governor to the Board of Trade. The minister stressed the governor's constant cursing, and cited quotations attributed to Nicholson that called the planters "rich and haughty" criminals, "tainted with republican notions" and almost ready to separate from England. Their wives were flighty in the extreme, a comment that, given Nicholson's behavior, provided considerable irony. Blair informed the officials that Nicholson expressed contempt for English laws, even cursed the Magna Carta, and accused members of the Virginia clergy of being "rogues, rascals, villains, and Jesuits." Blair sought to convince the board that the governor was behind an incident at the grammar school, where some of the students nailed shut a door to force an early Christmas vacation, a custom among English schoolboys. As Blair and a couple of servants were breaking down the door, the students fired guns after warning the intruders. Blair decided that the shooting and injury to one of the servants was accidental and exonerated the students for their behavior, but he traced the guns to the governor.

Nicholson, through his agent, responded that Blair was no saint, being known for lying, pushing servants down stairs, and not properly represented the clergy's interests. When he first became commissary, Blair favored letting the governor induct ministers for life when the vestries failed to act, but he later agreed with the planters that annual contracts between the vestries and the ministers best served the colony. At least a score of clergy disagreed with Blair and sided with the governor on this issue. Blair also had recently done little to raise the traditional annual ministerial pay of 16,000 pounds of tobacco. Although most of the burgesses also sided with the governor against the complaining councilmen, the board granted Blair's request for removing the governor.

Aside from his peculiar deficiencies, Nicholson did quite well as governor. In 1698, the House of Burgesses, in accord with the council and governor, called for the rebuilding of the burned capitol building near the college at Middle Plantation, suitably renamed Williamsburg. Nicholson drew up the street plan as he had for Annapolis, but this time he did not use a circular scheme. Some thought he might shape the streets into a "W" and an "M," but he stuck to straight lines and right angles, although one map hints at the possibility that these letters would appear within the parameters of the new city. He also helped subdue the piracy problem that had plagued the coast for some time, as he led a contingent of Virginians on board an English warship in Chesapeake Bay to beat a French pirate with a crew of nearly 200 into submission and rescued several hostages. Some of the pirates were hanged locally; the leaders went to England for special prosecution and a delayed execution.

Before Blair could dispose of his next victim, Lieutenant Governor Alexander Spotswood became the most noteworthy royal governor since Berkeley. Spotswood, who arrived in 1710, understood that dictatorial actions were no longer acceptable in Great Britain as well as in the colonies. Unlike previous governors, he had not served the Stuart monarchy and thus had no poor reputation to live down. His exemplary military record in Europe made him a natural candidate as a colonial leader. Under his direction the colony rebuilt its Governor's Palace, despite serious complaints from the burgesses, and the college replaced its burned-out building. He even helped in the building of a new Bruton Parish Church, in which Blair served as minister for years. Spotswood helped quiet the southern frontier in the aftermath of a Tuscarora uprising in 1711 in nearby Carolina. After being subdued, the Tuscarora, along with remnants of the Nottoway, moved to New York to become the sixth nation of the Iroquois Confederation.

Spotswood also gained favor for attacking the problem of piracy. Right after Queen Anne's war, pirates again replaced privateers (legal piracy), and Edward Teach (Blackbeard) ravaged the coast and hid out in the Outer Banks of North Carolina, supposedly aided by the governor of that colony. Spotswood dispatched sloops and men under Lieutenant Robert Maynard. Despite lacking serviceable cannons— unlike Blackbeard—they tracked down the illusive pirate and in hand-to-hand combat killed the pirate leader, chopped off his head, and brought body parts to Hampton for public display.

The governor of North Carolina complained that Virginians had not informed him of their plans to invade his colony. Like Berkeley, the new governor promoted westward exploration. To help offset the French in the interior of North America, the governor called for the settlement of the Rapidan River and the hill country beyond. In 1716 he led an expedition from the Mattaponi River up the Rapidan and across the Blue Ridge. They drank to King George's health at the summit. Then they rode to the valley below, where they ate and drank ample quantities of wine, brandy, and cider, consumed as they fired guns. They toasted nearly everyone in the royal family and the governor. After completing an excursion of 400 miles, Spotswood gave mementos to his "Knights of the Golden Horseshoe."

Although Spotswood had marked success in these matters, failures undercut his administration. Early in his term in office, he nixed a bill to put a high tax on all imported African slaves, largely because he had instructions not to approve such legislation. The British government later disallowed a similar measure because of complaints from slave traders and some Virginians. Spotswood also encouraged and approved the Virginia Indian Act of 1714 that concentrated the fur trade south of the James River to the community of Christanna, on the Meherrin River. All trading had to be carried out in this outpost, which included a fort as well as a school for Indians. Tribes sent their children as hostages to be educated at the site. The project encountered numerous problems, not the least of which was the killing of unarmed natives supposedly under English protection, by a band of roving Iroquois. After operating for a few years, the community closed down.

The governor's program to raise tobacco prices became a fixture after he left office and thus may be considered a partial success. The tobacco inspection system went into operation in 1713, but the representatives repealed the measure, only to return to it in 1730, long after Spotswood's removal. Under it, exported tobacco had to pass through privately owned and government designated warehouses for grading. The program eliminated trash tobacco from export and use as currency. The clustering of warehouses eventually promoted urban growth and the certificates distributed provided an acceptable currency. Because the colony lacked both towns and money, the program proved beneficial on many counts. Spotswood persuaded the burgesses to back his program by offering members lucrative positions as inspectors. Over half the burgesses secured posts of inspector. The governor's scheme came to a bad end, when new elections threw many inspectors out of the House of Burgesses. Spotswood vetoed a repeal of the measure in 1715, but in 1717, abiding by the wishes of merchants and producers, the Board of Trade canceled the program.

Spotswood also tried to reform the land system, under which members of the council and a few others amassed staggering amounts of acreage. The governor had special problems with Councilman Philip Ludwell, whose father had acquired Berkeley's Green Springs by virtue of marrying the widow Berkeley. In one deal, Ludwell added several hundred acres of government land to his possession without paying for it. Ludwell also only paid for 2,000 acres but acquired 20,000 (a judicious use of a zero). Spotswood considered Ludwell "uncouth" and decried the inaction of the jury in the Green Springs case.

Other councilmen were nearly as bad in this great land grab. Robert "King" Carter served as the agent of the heiress to the proprietor in the Northern Neck. He paid a few hundred pounds to Lady Fairfax each year, and then made what he could on the quit rents and loose change. Normally the colonial or county governments would pick up forfeitures of felons, but Carter arranged it so that he obtained these funds. Fellow councilmen rarely blocked his efforts. On one occasion, they stopped him when he tried to take the estate of a suicide on the grounds that the person had committed a felony, but he added almost 4,000,000 acres to the Fairfax estate in the Piedmont and the Valley, from which he secured several hundred thousand acres for himself.

Failing to curb excesses in land distribution, the governor participated in the practice, with Carter rendering Spotswood assistance. The governor brought in several dozen German families to develop iron ore in the upper part of the Rappahannock River. The council approved his avoidance of paying the usual duties for this land by claiming these workers were "rangers" sent into the area to protect it. After arranging for the construction of Fort Germanna, Spotswood focused on the production of iron and land acquisition. His holdings grew from 8,000 acres in 1716 to some 85,000 by 1730, several years after his removal as governor. When the Germans quit, Spotswood sent slaves and indentured servants to turn out numerous pots, pans, and other hardware to make the colony more self-sufficient. English restraints on this line of work did not take effect until 1750, some ten years after Spotswood's death.

William Byrd II, another councilman and adversary to Blair and Spotswood, wandered all over Virginia looking over the land he owned and surveying the boundary line between North Carolina and Virginia. He rarely had anything good to say about the settlers he encountered. And when the work looked like something a gentleman should not do, he made sure others did it. He sent a work party through the Dismal Swamp and waited for their exit at the home of a woman who lived near the western edge of the morass. An enemy of the governor, Byrd had to watch that Spotswood did not have him removed from the council for his frequent and lengthy absences.

About midway in Spotswood's term in office, the governor angered the council by attempting to add judges from outside the council to the General Court. The oyer and terminer (hear and determine) court in the colony, the council met too infrequently to handle its business, and William Byrd II rarely attended. In attempting to pack the court, Spotswood, the council contended, violated an "ancient custom," adopted but a few years before of only having councilmen serve as colonial judges. If Spotswood had his way they would have to sit with "inferiors." English custom usually ensured a trial before judges of a class at least equal to the defendant. The governor sent the issue to the Board of Trade for resolution. That body agreed with the governor but advised him to impose his policy judiciously. At the peak of the controversy in 1716, Spotswood, in trying to ease matters by having a party to celebrate George II's birthday, inviting musicians and attending a play in the new theater across the street from his "palace." Instead of attending, the "oligarches" went to a bonfire and enjoyed alcoholic beverages. After months of wrangling, Spotswood proposed that if the council would agree that he had the right to appoint judges that were not on the council, he would not do so. They grudgingly agreed, but it was simply a question of time before the governor would be removed.

Although James Blair refrained from criticizing anyone for amassing land, the commissary and the governor argued over inducting ministers, an issue Blair and other governors had skirmished over. Spotswood even questioned Blair's role as the minister of Bruton Parish Church. The governor's clergy allies demanded to see proof of the Scotsman's ordination by an English bishop, a requirement that Blair could not or would not meet. The commissary journeyed to England in 1722, and he soon returned to Virginia with a replacement in tow. They greeted Spotswood as the later came back from a successful meeting in New York, whereby the Iroquois agreed to pass west, rather than east, of the Blue Ridge, and a smaller tribe withdrew from south of the Potomac River. As the governor basked in the glow of a diplomatic victory, Blair notified him of his dismissal.

In 1727 Sir William Gooch took over as governor. Perhaps because Gooch's brother was an English bishop but mostly because the governor had been forewarned and had sharp political instincts, he managed to avoid the wrath of the "vile old fellow." When Gooch had to leave the colony to conduct a military campaign in 1740, Blair became the interim governor despite Gooch's secret efforts to derail that possibility. Blair died at age 87 in 1743. By then Virginians had entered a new era, and the elite was thoroughly enjoying the fruits of a "golden age."

# Chapter 5

## The Golden Age of the Elite

By 1750 the Old Dominion was growing at a rapid rate. From about 70,000 residents (10% slave) in 1700, the number grew to 285,000 (over 33% slaves) about a half-century later. During Sir William Gooch's time as lieutenant governor (1730–1751) the population nearly doubled from about 144,000, when he first arrived in the colony. African slaves entered at the rate of nearly a thousand each year, indentured servants came in much smaller numbers, and the death rate declined, as those that survived childhood developed immunity from diseases. During this era, the environment and the British heritage continued to exert considerable influence.

The Assembly created counties and subdivided existing counties to make the local government more convenient. By 1700 the colony was organizing counties near the Fall Line as the colony also reorganized local governments in the east. Only a portion of the southwestern Tidewater remained frontier. By 1750 all the Piedmont and much of the Valley had county governments. Almost all these took names of English royalty, nobility, or royal governors. Spotswood had his name enshrined over the territory containing his ironworks. Chesterfield honored a famous lord. Prince William, Princess Louisa, daughter of George I, Princess Amelia, daughter of George II, among others, all remain etched in Virginia culture to this day, though none of those so honored ever set foot in the colony. Places like Brunswick and Lunenburg counties recognized the German origins and holdings of King George I. The earls of Albemarle and Loudoun, successive titular governors who never came to the colony were honored with names of counties in the western Piedmont.

Scots-Irishman Sir William Gooch served as the lieutenant governor during most of the "golden age." Appointed in 1727 and reaching the colony in 1730, he remained a popular figure in Virginia until his death in 1751. Gooch served with the military in Queen Anne's war and in the suppression of a Scottish uprising in 1715 and moved on to civil duties in England before coming to the Old Dominion. Once here, he established himself as a friend to the colonists, managing to avoid hot button issues with the council and working closely with the burgesses.

After rising for a time, tobacco prices once again fell. The governor convinced the House of Burgesses to impose restrictions on trash tobacco without offering any potential jobs to the burgesses. Commissioners in charge of customs in Britain opposed the measure because it would reduce tariff revenues. The Board of Trade, however, agreed with the governor that most merchants would benefit from the higher quality of tobacco. With the board's recommendation, the Privy Council and the king concurred in 1731. In implementing the program Gooch encountered opposition in the colony. Small growers even went so far as to burn warehouses. In response, Gooch published a fictional dialogue between Thomas Sweet Scented and William Orinoco (two planters who represented the two types of tobacco produced in Virginia) and "Justice Love-Country." Gooch, the fictional justice, argued that the new policy would promote prosperity for all. Small growers continued to oppose the plan. Indeed, the burgesses repealed the act in 1736, but the council supported Gooch. In time, opposition disappeared as higher prices for tobacco prevailed.

In 1739, England went to war with Spain over maritime rights. The Spanish insisted on the right to inspect British ships operating in Spanish colonial waters. The English, noting the case of a captain whose ear had been cut off by a supposed Spanish official, declared war. During the War of Jenkin's Ear, the government asked the colonies to assist in an assault on Cartagena in South America. Virginia contributed several hundred men, mostly felons recently sent to the colony. In 1738, so many vagabonds wandered about the colony that the General Assembly told the sheriffs that they no longer needed to scour the countryside for 12 men of property to serve on juries to try recent arrivals. Because the accused had already been found guilty of a crime in Great Britain or Ireland, the sheriff simply collected a jury from the courthouse crowd and carried out a quick trial. When war with Spain broke out, the Assembly had the sheriffs round up those that had been troubling the colony and mustered them into the army. Alexander Spotswood was supposed to lead Virginia's troops but died before the expedition left, so Gooch led the force. During the failed attempt to capture a fort, a cannon ball damaged the governor's ankle. The handicapped governor returned to Virginia even more honored than before. Many conscripts died of fever or injury and did not return at all.

Gooch's relationship with the burgesses always remained on a positive note as he consistently supported "heir ancient rights and privileges." His administration coincided with the time Robert Walpole served as Britain's first Prime Minister. That masterful, if corrupt, politician gave the colonies considerable latitude in running their economies under a policy called "Salutary Neglect." Gooch knew how to deal with the numerous and lengthy instructions sent to him. In 1732, for example, he allowed the home manufacture of linen, a decision that ran counter to the idea that the colonies ought to be buying British goods.

The governor continued the policy of previous leaders to open up the frontier as quickly as possible. In 1744, he obtained a treaty with the Six Nations (Iroquois) that protected the settlers already in the Valley and for a price opened up settlement possibilities farther west. Although Gooch usually refused to allow land distribution in areas that directly conflicted with the holdings of the French, he endeared himself to numerous speculators, when in 1749 he authorized the dispersal of about a million acres of land along and beyond the Alleghenies. That land included much of what became Kentucky and West Virginia.

In Gooch's time and with his approval settlers, mostly from Pennsylvania, entered the lower (northern) part of the Valley of Virginia. Predominantly of German and Scots-Irish origins, these people mixed with some English moving west. By 1750 Augusta, in the south, and Frederick, the northernmost county, had almost 10,000 people each, with another 2,000 residing in Hampshire County. This flow of people and the environment produced a unique culture west of the Blue Ridge. Some Germans built solid stone homes and ran well-stocked farms equipped with big barns, the prototype for which came from Pennsylvania. Adam Miller (Mueller), Joist Hite, and Jacob Stover pioneered in the area, starting in 1726. They acquired generous grants of land, and did tolerably well as speculators and planters. Joist Hite brought more Germans into what became the Winchester area in 1732. The Hites and others eventually acquired some slaves, but they never competed with planters east of the mountains in finery or fashion. The Germans, many from the Rhineland, were usually a quiet, peaceful people. Although many were Lutheran, some belonged to other religious sects, such as the Mennonites. The Germans continued to speak their language for generations. Although they often had farms next door to those of the Scots-Irish, the two tended not to intermarry, but they did carry on business activities with each other. Scots-Irishman John Lewis opened up the area around what became Staunton as his people made their way along the Great Wagon Road out of Pennsylvania. Noted for their emotionalism, individualism, aggressiveness, hard drinking, and occasional indolence, they contrasted rather sharply with the Germans. They were usually Calvinistic Presbyterians and their ancestors helped England subdue Northern Ireland. Their culture closely resembled that in lowland Scotland and northern England. Some people used the term North Briton to describe an entire cultural subset of British culture. Whatever their differences, Germans and Scots-Irish fared well in the Valley and in other parts of western Virginia. Some of them passed through the gaps in the Blue Ridge and settled in the western part of the Piedmont. Because the Scots-Irish and Germans tended to be self-sufficient, they developed a lifestyle that did not resemble that which prevailed east of the Blue Ridge. Although the area soon had its own elite or gentry class, few possessed plantations and great wealth at least compared to that of the Tidewater dandies. An English prisoner of war during the Revolution claimed that no "gentlemen" existed within forty miles of Staunton, but some settlers accumulated tidy fortunes and some settlers in the Valley brought in elements of English culture. And, of course, English law and government dominated the scene.

In the 17th century, prevailing English practices produced an irregular architectural style, befitting that tumultuous time. Bacon's Castle in Surry County gives us a surviving example of this Jacobean (Stuart) style in Virginia. Some followers of Nathaniel Bacon once occupied this famous home. With the exception of Bacon's Castle, few 17th-century homes survived to the present. Berkeley's sprawling mansion at Green Springs doubtless was the most imposing residence of the time. Most settlers, however, lived in rather modest wooden homes, which often exhibited a medieval style and depended on four wooden posts (sometimes of cypress and thus less susceptible to termites) for their primary structural support. Virtually none of these lasted for any sustained time largely because those who exploited the land had no intentions of remaining on it permanently.

The golden age brought the well-born planters to a cultural plateau in architecture. Starting in the 1720s, the second and third generation constructed beautiful homes, many of which remain to this day. Built in the symmetrical style then popular in England, they were usually two-storied brick (often in Flemish bond) with a door in the middle with an equal number of windows on each side. Windows on the second floor matched those on the floor below except the one directly over the door. Single-story wings jutted out an equal distance on each side. Matching chimneys were usually located at each end of the first floor. The pitch of the roof varied a bit as styles changed, but what became known as the Georgian (for the kings of England) reflected balance and control. The gardens that accompanied these structures demonstrated man's ability to control nature. Examples of 18th-century Georgian architecture in Virginia include William Byrd's Westover, the Burwell family's Carter's Grove, west and east of Williamsburg, respectively. Governor Spotswood built the prototype in the capitol or "palace" in Williamsburg. Berkeley, property of the Harrisons, also can be found along the James River. Gloucester County contained Rosewell, the Page family mansion. The Northern Neck had, and still has in some cases, the homes of various Carters and Lees: Robert "King" Carter built Corotoman, an early and small version of the "big house." Landon Carter built Sabine Hall, which still survives, and Robert Carter, "King" Carter's grandson, built Nomini Hall. The Lees constructed Stratford and other homes. The generation of the Revolution built or inherited Gunstan Hall (Mason), Montpelier (Madison), and Monticello (Jefferson). At Monticello, Thomas Jefferson added Roman features like the dome, though classical references can be found in other buildings or even in place names. Jefferson developed a unique architecture, which in turn provided the basis for the next generation of "big houses" in Virginia. The interiors followed English traditions and styles. High-ceilinged rooms and large entryways met cultural standards and also made these homes especially inviting in the warm Virginia summers. Many of those who owned these domiciles kept libraries. Both William Byrd II at the onset of the golden age and Jefferson at its end were avid readers and writers, though with different tastes. Kitchens, of course, were separated from the main building for comfort and safety but not for the convenience of slaves who had to carry the utensils and food, sometimes through underground passageways.

Despite the presence of some well-built and well-known structures, most Virginia houses, even in the middle of the 18th century, were not solidly constructed. Virginians developed a variety of architectural styles, some of which they took into the Piedmont and farther west. Homes of middling planters usually had two wings, each twice as wide as a hall in the middle. The simply constructed "dogtrot" had two rooms, with each room functioning independently. In newly occupied areas, the homes were even less pretentious among the first settlers, but the Shenandoah Valley soon had stone homes alongside wooden ones as the farm economy evolved. By the 1780s the most prevalent type of house there was a thin two-story one of Georgian style.

During this era, Tidewater Virginians moved their transformed culture into the Piedmont. For a time it looked like the newer area would differ from the old. Residents spoke of "Tuckahoes" in the Tidewater and "Cohees" in the Piedmont, meaning two types of people, the second less aristocratic. The Tidewater grandees gave way to leaders less pretentious as English culture moved west, but the fundamentals of the elite culture based on racial slavery and English West Country traditions moved west as well. After the Revolution the area would have more slaves than the Tidewater. Yet for the much of the 18th century the elite considered much of the Piedmont, including all of the Southside, a cultural backwater. The elite concentrated near the Fall Line, in Northern Virginia, and on various necks or peninsulas, but few of them were located on the Eastern Shore of Virginia or in the Norfolk area. By 1800 observers considered all Eastern Virginians "Tuckahoes" whereas Cohee culture became associated with the Blue Ridge and beyond.

William Byrd II's decoded diaries, written in London and at Westover, remain one of the best sources for understanding Colonial Virginia. He also published a *History of the Dividing Line, Journey to the Land of Eden*, and *Journey to the Mines*, quite a record for the colony, which had a very small nonpolitical literary output. In his recounting of his leadership in surveying the boundary between Virginia and North Carolina, he commented, usually negatively, about the residents of the region. His detailed account of the land and other resources of the area describe the flora and fauna as well as the manner in which the frontier residents tackled the environment. Like most of the planter class, Byrd saw the land and its resources as something to be exploited. He called for the draining of the Dismal Swamp to turn the area into productive farms. A generation or so later, George Washington surveyed the perimeter of the swamp and, with a group of investors, took steps to follow Byrd's advice. The company tried to grow rice in the supposedly watery environment, but when such farming proved unrewarding, the capitalists turned to cutting timber, including staves and shingles. In time lumbermen pretty much cut down most of the natural forest. In his social life, Byrd bowled and played billiards and cricket, picking up the rudiments of the latter game when he resided in London. Lacking sufficient numbers of men of proper station and race, Byrd played with white neighbors, who belonged to the upper class but whose number fell considerably short of two full teams. The absence of villages explains the failure of cricket to become commonplace in the Anglican colony. Byrd played English sports and did not engage in the rougher sports that reflected the tastes of the less wealthy in Virginia. Like many Anglicans, Byrd went to church and prayed almost every evening, but he indulged in what even he considered sinful behavior.

The sparseness of population and poor roads also explains the widespread availability of horses. Most Virginia elite males rode horses and owned large carriages (usually made in England) so their families could ride in style, but even elite women sometimes rode horses. As people today have developed a lifestyle that largely revolves around automobiles, Virginians rode horses even at times when it would have been more sensible to walk. Only the slaves and the very poor did not ride.

Horse racing and gambling became fixtures. By the late 17th century, Virginians routinely raced and bet on the results. A local court fined a resident who had the temerity to win money from someone of higher station, but over time all classes participated in one way or another in quarter horse racing. This Virginia style consisted of races of a quarter mile where the jockeys, who often owned the horses, whipped each other as they raced. In the 1730s the elite turned to English-style racing, which had recently become popular in the home country. Requiring a horse that could run several heats of three or four miles each, these organized races featured much publicity and large crowds. They took place mostly near towns or at ferry crossings. Many of the elite planters owned stud farms as they sought to upgrade the quality of horses originally imported from abroad at considerable cost. They trained some of their smaller slaves as jockeys. Backcountry people, whether in the area below the James River or in the western Piedmont, preferred the older type of racing.

Virginians also enjoyed other sports, based to some extent on class preferences. Cockfighting, a blood sport that supposedly originated in the West Country of England, was such a popular diversion that some counties had competing teams. People of all classes attended. Sometimes the events were well publicized and organized, but they also took place in barns on individual plantations and remained a popular diversion among slaves. Boxing, as we now know it, was a rarity, but folks of the backcountry engaged in "no-holds-barred" contests in which they more than occasionally gouged out their opponents' eye. Billiards had a large following, especially as the century progressed. All these activities involved gambling and often drinking. The restraints of Puritanism or Quakerism remained quite weak. So-called "blood sports," where animals tore each other to pieces or had humans do the same, were more prevalent in the Anglican colonies of the South and in New York, less so in New England or in Pennsylvania.

Of the great political leaders that emerged out of this milieu, only George Washington may be considered a proponent of sports, and he had only mild interest in cockfights and no interest in gouging. Washington and George Mason frequented horse races, but Washington's diary focuses on hunting. Sometimes he hunted foxes in organized forays, but he usually rode across the countryside with one or two human companions and his dogs. Thomas Jefferson and James Madison, two great political theorists, had little interest in sports. Jefferson could ride a horse fairly well and thought outdoor activities of value compared to village games. But he was no athlete and only on rare occasions do we find him playing at quoits, a forerunner of horseshoes. Both Jefferson and Washington enjoyed the theater. They attended numerous performances in Williamsburg, Petersburg, or Fredericksburg put on by troupes of English actors and actresses.

Life for these planters was not a continuous round of parties and other pleasures. Landon Carter's diary provides numerous references to his plantation's struggle against diseases, especially in the mid-1750s, when the colony was in the midst of a war against the French and natives. In September 1756, a time of hot foggy mornings, he found the plantation besieged with an "obstinate, irregular fever." Dozens of his people were "laid up," getting well and then relapsing. One daughter had convulsions and appeared to have but a 50/50 chance of survival. The daughter was still sick in October, when Carter himself caught the disease. The symptoms included throwing up and night sweats. The epidemic finally eased, helped along by Carter's numerous concoctions. He gave the slaves rattlesnake powder and something less heroic for his immediate family. Hearing that one of his other farms had smallpox and that one of his workers at the main plantation developed symptoms of the dreaded disease, he followed a familiar protocol to put the victim in isolation and provide doses of natural drugs. In January 1757, during a cold spell, his cattle and horses died from some mysterious ailment. Both people and tobacco plants suffered from a variety of worms. At least four types struck the plants, while the slaves endured a form of tapeworm. Carter gives elaborate details on how to deal with human victims. The only way to combat the vegetable kind was to make sure each tobacco plant was free of the predators.

An English traveler in 1759 found Virginia planters, with some notable exceptions, to be indolent, good natured, and fond of convivial pleasures. They were, he thought, generally ignorant, believing "numerous errors and prejudices regarding Indians and Negroes, whom they scarcely considered human." They were also "haughty and jealous of their liberties," and they could "scarcely bear the thought of being controlled by a superior power."

According to travelers, Virginia women, while making tolerable wives and mothers, could not compare with women in England as they had few advantages and consequently were seldom accomplished as conversationalists or in much else. This assessment typified English comments well into the 19th century. French travelers usually disagreed with this sentiment. One Frenchman praised the young women of the Nelson family in Hanover County. Whatever foreign travelers thought, elite women indulged in a great many social activities that carried them outside their own homes. They also supervised the home, educated the young, went to church on Sundays, and entertained. Dancing proved the favorite form of entertainment, though card playing and musical performances rated high.

Most travelers agreed that eastern Virginia in the 18th century had distinct classes, each with certain traits. The elite, who numbered a few hundred, consisted of gentlemen and their families, many of them descended from Cavaliers that came in the middle of the 17th century. Although many were the younger children of English aristocracy and, in rare cases, lesser members of the nobility, they did not bring great wealth with them. Their background, however, gave them status and advantages in acquiring material wealth. By the middle of the 18th century, they owned large estates and hundreds of slaves. They were often well educated (sometimes in England) and refined. A very hospitable people, they welcomed travelers as long as they were of a high enough station. They invariably owned the most expensive English carriages and possessed tea sets made of silver plate. A second group, numbering perhaps a few thousand, owned smaller estates and a few dozen slaves. Some ministers might be found at this level, but as they ordinarily owned farms and slaves, their status depended on a mix of property and occupation. This class had some luxuries and all the necessities. Occasionally one of their number rose to political power. Below them, one found a mixed lot, comprising most whites. A much larger group than their counterparts in Europe, they owned or had lifetime leases on farms and might have a few slaves. These yeomen to a considerable extent descended from the class of indentured servants that had come in the previous century. Their behavior varied from affability to rudeness. Although education was not a high priority in the colony as compared to places to the north, some of this class could read and write. At the bottom resided poor whites. They rarely owned land or slaves or much in the way of material goods. They were unbelievably crude and backward. Many were addicted to liquor, but heavy drinking and coarse behavior prevailed in the other classes as well.

The slaves had their own class system, with house servants holding a higher station in the hierarchy than field servants. Big planters often gave coachmen and butlers tips as well as used clothes and special livery. The slaves and free blacks of the towns dressed quite fashionably by the end of the colonial era. Such

44

privileged slaves looked down on the lowest class of whites. But typical field hands wore the coarsest and least costly cloth available, and young slaves in the summer often wore no clothes at all.

Virginia's class system had flexibility for whites. Although virtually no one rose from the lowest station to the highest, many moved from one class to the next. Kinship or a marriage helped. Merchants and some tradesmen often possessed a considerable estate putting them in the second rank. Many started out as factors for foreign merchants or even as indentured servants. Some skilled workmen, coming directly from Great Britain, acquired a small plantation after a short stay due to the comparatively high rate of pay for their work.

Women gained few rights during this era. Some leeway for love existed, but certainly no one could drop too far down the social scale and expect one's parents to accept the result. Laws gave widows limited protection. Moral persuasion might be employed against those who mistreated wives. Heavy drinking among males was so pervasive that women of all classes must have suffered. In addition, many males were far from faithful. William Byrd II fondled women even in the presence of his wife. His wife's father, a notorious rake, left her mother to live with a mistress. In his will, the mistress and her children acquired much of his estate. Some men pursued female slaves. Such behavior did not usually violate an unwritten code nor did most planters see it as a breach of honor, unless one's own female family members became the object. A religious revival before the American Revolution raised standards among the lower and middle classes.

A comparatively few families constituted almost half the membership in the House of Burgesses during this era. Planters often had five or six male children, who then had a similar number of male children in the next generation. Not all amassed great wealth, but many had kinship with the most powerful people. Under primogeniture, the eldest male inherited the lion's share of an estate. "Entail" allowed an owner, through a deed or will, to prevent heirs from breaking up estates. Had these two systems prevailed in Virginia, they doubtless would have contributed to the retention of huge estates, but English law used primogeniture only when someone died without leaving a will. And even then the widow was entitled to one-third of an estate. The Virginia legislature also modified the system of entail. Great estates came into being and remained so largely because of the way the colony administered the distribution of land and the existence of slavery, not because of medieval customs.

Voting depended on property holdings for adult white males. As of 1736 one had to own at least a farm of 100 acres and a home to qualify to vote for the burgesses. The Assembly reduced the qualifications in 1762, but that action was rescinded. Many people could qualify, but an undetermined number of white males could not meet the qualification of ownership, but sheriffs may have allowed those who held long-term leases to vote. Many county elections brought out well over 50% of the adult white males. Despite a comparatively high participation percentage in some places, a number of influential gentry dominated colonial Virginia. Even in the area west of the Blue Ridge a few wealthy families controlled politics. Even though this "elite" had not near the number of slaves or value in land holdings of those in the same class in the east, they certainly had far more material possessions than their neighbors. The skewed distribution of land came about even though the colonial government, under Gooch, encouraged settlement by families rather than speculators.

Some of the races were hotly contested. Almost invariably a planter of some stature ran for office. George Washington had an agent supply the electorate with hard liquor. After a drink or so, the voter stood up and announced his choice. Although on rare occasions a candidate might say something about tobacco inspection or some other topic, candidates usually did not campaign, at least in the modern sense. Political parties did not exist. The most prominent candidate and incumbents usually won, but in the turbulent times of the Revolution many incumbents lost elections.

Politics and sports interested the planters, but what most excited them was the quality and price of their tobacco. The big planters took great pride in the quality of their crops and took criticism of it, from whatever source, as an insult. Differences in soil, weather, and growing techniques meant that grades of tobacco varied, but the great planters thought they only grew the highest quality.

Even though a number of these planters acted as middlemen in the tobacco trade, they considered themselves planters and not businessmen. Some of them looked down on merchants, even though their fathers or grandfathers often made their initial fortunes in the fur trade or some other commercial way. They saw their speculation in land as a way to carry on their plantation life for their children. European aristocrats, who had sinecures, considered the Virginians opportunistic money-grubbers, an insult not taken lightly by the planters. Through much of the 18th century planters carried on a love/hate relationship with English merchants. Their relations reveal a lot of tension, as growers sent their tobacco and occasionally other products at great risk only to have the merchant often find the quality suspect or the market weaker than expected. Merchants, who supplied the growers with imports, often gave advances or credit. They filled orders on the prospect that the future sale of tobacco would cover the debt. Often it did not, and many planters found themselves several years in arrears. Usually planters stuck with one merchant as they understood the risks involved in owing money to many creditors.

Scottish merchants, appearing in numbers about midway in the 18th century, brought a new way of doing business. They had the same legal status as English merchants in terms of trading in the empire, but they lacked prestige. The big planters did not do business with them because they were of a lower rank than the English merchants. The Scottish firms sent junior partners at best, sometimes merely agents. They often bought tobacco directly from the producer, though at a price less than available in Great Britain. They also usually refrained from extending loans to the predominantly middle-income customers that used their services. They also were less picky about quality, more flexible in finding markets, and could cut transportation costs. They set up stores near the inspection warehouses and did business with the smaller growers and those who were opening up the Piedmont. Dozens of them showed up in places like Port Royal, along the Fall Line, and even in the Norfolk area, where little tobacco came through. The Scots adapted themselves to the West Indies trade, which relied on the exchange of Indian corn for molasses or rum. Some of them ran several stores in the interior, a forerunner of the chain store concept.

They succeeded, but many Virginians hated them both for being Scots and running capitalistic enterprises. Negative comments often appeared in the newsprint and in correspondence. "A North Briton is something like the stinking and troublesome weed we call in Virginia wild onion. Whenever one is permitted to fix, the number soon increases so fast; that it is extremely difficult to eradicate them and they poison the ground so that no wholesome plant can thrive," opined one writer. Another complained about Scottish companies, which like a cancer spread "to the villages and court houses, and…consumed the substance of all that came within their grasp." James Blair had encountered criticism (for not having proof of English ordination), but nothing to the extent endured by later Scots. This negative view was due to changed commercial circumstances plus the rebellion of the Scots in 1746 against Great Britain.

# PART TWO: REVOLUTION AND REPUBLICAN GOVERNMENT

As the 18th century passed the midpoint, Virginia, like most of the Western world, developed new ways of thinking about religion and the role of government. These new attitudes played a major role in promoting ideas of revolution and republican government. In the mid-1760s, just after the French and Indian War, Virginians, like the other twelve mainland British colonists, wanted to handle their own affairs. At the same time the mother country decided to exert greater control over the colonies, especially with respect to raising revenue from them. Chapter 6 covers the countdown to rebellion went through several stages, with each one worsening relations between the colonies and the mother country.

Although the Revolution, treated in chapter 7, started in April of 1775 in Massachusetts, organized conflict did not commence in Virginia until the following fall. In the early stages of that conflict, the colony became a state, following the implementation of a provisional government. A convention in June 1776 approved a Declaration of Rights, soon followed by the Declaration of Independence in July by the Continental Congress in Philadelphia and the commencement of a state government under a written constitution based on republican principles. The American Revolution produced a loose band of republics, whose citizen soldiers fought for independence under the Continental Congress and later under a written constitution known as the Articles of Confederation. However one interprets its causes, the war and the revolutionary era as a whole produced profound change in the institution of slavery, the relationship of church and state, the role of state government, and finally, the relationship of the state to a new federal government that began in 1789.

Chapter 8 discusses Republican politics and federal-state relations dominated the next five decades, including the era of the "Virginia Dynasty," when three Virginia Republicans held the presidency for two terms each. The argument over the rights of the states, including opposition to the expanded powers of the Supreme Court, proved to be critical issues during this era. Virginia's political role became less influential after 1825.

Chapter 9 describes internal affairs in the state between the American Revolution and the Civil War, a time that included two reworked constitutions, one in 1829–30 and another in 1850–51. The state also expanded its role in public works and assisted in a limited way in promoting public higher education, both higher and lower. These changes occurred despite of prevailing conservative viewpoint in eastern Virginia. The middle period of American history included a prolonged agricultural and general economic decline in eastern Virginia followed by some recovery in the 1850s and the rise of industries and related urban growth, all part of the traditional way Virginians operated and studied in Chapter 10.

# Chapter 6

## Road to Revolution

The Colonial Era came to an end in 1775 with the Revolutionary War, the seeds for which were planted when the English first landed at Cape Henry. But throughout the 17th no one, even Bacon and his followers, considered the possibility of separation from the mother country. Starting in the 1750s, a combination of events and ideas within and outside Virginia directed the colonists toward rebellion and eventually independence, but roots of the rebellion rested on fundamental changes in political and moral philosophy.

Throughout Western civilization a new way of viewing the world took hold in the late 17th and early 18th centuries as scientists gained more understanding of the nature of the universe. Sir Isaac Newton discovered the law of gravity, Robert Boyle made breakthroughs in chemistry, and still others added to knowledge about the solar system and mathematics. A parallel development in political thought brought John Locke to the forefront. In the late 17th century, England developed a balanced political system that included a monarchy, nobility, and representatives of the propertied and commercial interests. An opponent of the Stuart monarchy, Locke rationalized rebellion against a monarch who broke his compact (contract) with the people. Grounds for removal included taking away essential rights, including life, liberty, and property. By 1750 most learned Virginians accepted the notion that the universe operated on fixed laws that humans had the ability to understand. Human affairs, moreover, were susceptible to rational thought. English kings no longer contended that God gave them a right to rule. Their power had to be balanced against that of representatives of the better class of people. Personal and property rights could not be arbitrarily ended. In Britain and its colonies a balanced system gave at least a part of the population some role in governing. Scholars of this enlightened time puzzled over the nature of man and reality. Locke, the English philosopher, argued that children's minds were blank slates at birth, thinking that experience through physical sensations and the innate ability to reason produced ideas and allowed humans to make ethical decisions. The mass of humanity was not naturally depraved, as some philosophers and theologians thought. Even though Locke believed in Christianity, he thought people could be molded into moral beings even though not exposed to Christian teachings. Locke looked to the empirical, even though he knew humans had limitations. Although Locke wrote extensively, his works did not circulate widely. His ideas, however, showed up nearly everywhere in Western civilization, including Virginia.

As the 18th century progressed, the Scots developed a somewhat different view about human nature. Placing less emphasis on rational laws and man's ability to reason, several Scotsmen, some of them ministers, argued that just as humans developed physical characteristics and refined their senses as they matured, so, too, did they possess intrinsic mental qualities that naturally led to virtues such as benevolence. Exposure to Christianity and the scriptures were helpful, but most humans were born with a predisposition toward goodness. By their very nature humans perceived the differences between right and wrong and were not depraved from birth. Humans had reason and moral sentiment, a view not too different from the Quaker idea of an "inner light."

Many moralists in the 18th century believed that God endowed mankind with natural reason and intuition to make choices. People could achieve happiness through knowledge and proper choices. Some Scotsmen of the Common Sense School lived in Virginia prior to the Revolution, serving as teachers in various academies. William Small, who taught math and moral philosophy at the College of William and Mary, influenced Thomas Jefferson.

Another influential Scotsman, Adam Smith, was close to but usually not considered a member of the Common Sense School. Smith's *Theory of Moral Sentiments*, published first in 1759 and reworked several times, talked about natural rights and higher virtues, such as reason, conscience, principle, honor, and justice. In Smith's most famous work, *The Wealth of Nations*, which appeared in 1776, he discussed self-interest, certainly not a higher virtue, but something God embedded in mankind. Life and liberty were natural rights, while the right to property had a somewhat lower station. Great Britain, he thought, should do less regulating between workers and employers, apprenticeships, trade, and the exchange of property. Only when private interests could clearly not attain some socially desirable goal, such as a major public work, should government assume responsibility. Smith, therefore, embraced the idea of *laissez faire* (let alone), already popular among French theorists and the antitheses of mercantilism (the regulation of the economy for the benefit of the business interests of the mother country). Smith contended that the navigation rules, as applied to the American colonies, did not profit residents of Britain, for the system cost more to operate than it yielded in returns, but he criticized colonists for owning slaves and opposed the American rebellion.

Some of Smith's ideas came too late to influence American thinkers at the time of the rebellion. Yet, both Jefferson's views as expressed in the Declaration of Independence and those of Adam Smith drew on the same intellectual atmosphere that the Enlightenment brought into being.

A more pessimistic strain of political thought, harking back to the English Civil War and Cromwell's failures, worried about corruption in government, a related loss of liberty or independence, and threats to the rural gentry. These thinkers did not trust human nature, especially as found among businessmen and politicians. Although neither of these ideas belonged to the mainstream of British thinking, some Virginia planters adopted elements of this attitude.

Jefferson and Madison, two of the most important leaders in Virginia, were more optimistic about human nature. They both enjoyed full exposure to the most advanced scientific and political thoughts of their time. Madison attended a school run by a Scottish scholar for several years and then went on to the College of New Jersey (Princeton), an institution affiliated with Presbyterians from Scotland. Like most members of their social class, both Madison and Jefferson knew Latin and some Greek and also were fully acquainted with ancient history, including the democracy of 5th century BC Greece and Rome's over 500- year record as a republic often marred by dictatorship.

The political ideas of the time also were also linked to architecture. A Roman temple in France that seemed to date from the time of republican Rome inspired Jefferson in designing the new Virginia capitol in Richmond. The federal buildings of the District of Columbia, whose stones came from a nearby quarry on Aquia Creek, also reflected Roman references. Madison and Jefferson called the political party in the 1790s they created Republican because of concerns about the word "democracy." At the time, the style of architecture that predominated in home construction, which retained some classical references, came to be called Federalist, the name of the political party that opposed the party of Jefferson and Madison. In the early 19th century Americans shifted to Greek examples, as the idea of democracy became more acceptable.

The last half of the 18th century experienced sweeping religious changes. By 1775 Jefferson suggested that most Virginians were no longer active in the established Anglican Church. Presbyterians and other denominations were growing in the colony on the eve of the Revolution. The former obtained the right to switch tithe payments to their own ministers, but a large number of Virginians paid taxes to support a church they no longer attended. The Great Awakening put a personal God in control of human affairs. Its apostles reacted against the emphasis on rational thought and, to a lesser extent, the ideas of the Scottish moralists, but like those philosophers, evangelical preachers thought the ability to know the creator crossed class lines. Called New Lights, (not to be confused with the Quaker "inner light") they brought back the faith of the forefathers without the idea that God, through grace, had chosen only a few for salvation. New Light Presbyterians found numerous recruits in Hanover County and in parts of the Piedmont and western Tidewater. Early in the Revolution, other Presbyterians, with help from local Anglicans, founded Hampden-Sydney College in honor of two 17th-century Englishmen who died fighting against the monarchy, one in battle and the other on the gallows. Virginians in the 17th century did not consider these men heroic, but in the next century both established planters and religious dissenters admired them.

A radical group known as Separate Baptists concentrated in lower Virginia; the earlier Regular Baptists frequented the Northern Neck and areas to its immediate west. In some areas prosperous planters sometimes greeted the especially loud and persistent Separate Baptists with whips, as the evangelicals spoke of the dissipation of the gentry. Those with little property seemed especially enamored with those new preachers who expressed concern for their souls. Slaves, finding support among these evangelicals, converted. Although deference for the gentry did not disappear overnight and only a few thousand were converted during this time, these religious people brought a new factor into Virginia's cultural mix. Jefferson, Madison, and Patrick Henry, at one time or another, defended their religious freedom. In 1774, for instance, Madison spoke out against the imprisonment of unlicensed Baptist preachers in Culpeper County. In the early 1770s Methodists (Anglicans who followed John Wesley) came to the colony. When these revivalists hit Norfolk in 1771, no one had ever heard preaching on its streets before. Residents flocked to the playhouse to hear more.

The movement toward rebellion began under Scotsman Robert Dinwiddie, who replaced Lieutenant Governor Gooch following interim replacements. The goodwill generated by the popular Gooch soon evaporated under Dinwiddie, a former customs collector in the colony. Knowing that his share of the customs receipts for tobacco exported from the colony, plus the customary bonus given by the Assembly at the start of any new administrator's term, would not allow him to cover the contract he had made with the royal governor, Dinwiddie demanded a pistole (a Spanish name for a coin minted in Scotland) as a tax on land transactions that had transpired before his arrival. After a lengthy controversy, the Board of Trade finally forced a compromise whereby Dinwiddie could not collect for previous sales or for future transactions involving small amounts of acreage.

Before the resolution of this issue, another matter concerning land took precedence. Ever interested in the well-being of speculators and settlers, and his own financial gain, the new governor promoted westward expansion. In 1749, before Dinwiddie took office, Gooch allowed the Ohio Co. a grant of land in the Ohio Valley, an area later claimed by the French. In 1753 Dinwiddie sent Joshua Fry, a veteran frontiersman and mapmaker, with a guide, an interpreter, and a young officer named George Washington to inform the French of their trespassing. After returning to Williamsburg in the middle of winter, Washington reported that the French rejection of English claims. Making Washington a lieutenant colonel, Dinwiddie ordered him to oust the French from the disputed territory. Despite the absence of Fry, a victim of a fall from a horse, Washington's troops routed a French and Indian force at Great Meadows. The young commander found "something charming in the sound" of bullets whistling, but he soon discovered that a much larger body of French and Indians surrounded his hastily erected Fort Necessity and forced his capitulation. After he signed a humiliating document, the French released him. Returning to the colonial capitol in disgrace, Washington resigned his commission, and Dinwiddie appealed to British officialdom for help. A few months later, General Edward Braddock arrived with over 1,000 professional soldiers. Dinwiddie met with Braddock but failed to deliver necessary supplies to the army, which, with a reinstated Washington and other colonials acting as auxiliaries, made its way overland toward Fort Duquesne. Before reaching their objective, the French and their allies drove them back in disorder. Heroic acts by Washington and others prevented a complete slaughter, but Braddock and many others died.

Virginia's War soon became a general conflict between the British colonies and the French in Canada, usually called The French and Indian War. The Shawnees attacked, scalped, and captured settlers deep in the Virginia frontier. Mary Draper Ingles survived an attack at what is now Blacksburg. With two young sons, she was taken over the mountains to near the Ohio River, where she and a German woman escaped. They somehow made their way back across the mountains. The French and their native allies swept across the northern frontier. They captured outposts through upper New York and threatened the Valley of Virginia. Colonial authorities ordered the construction of several forts, including Fort Loudoun, to defend recently-settled Winchester. The garrison not only provided protection for the area, it also contributed much-needed currency to the community's businessmen, especially its tavern keepers. In becoming a full war between France and Great Britain and their various European allies, this conflict affected Virginia in several ways in addition to creating fear about attacks on the frontier. The British ordered a temporary halt to exports that might fall into French hands, thus blocking the flow of goods to the West Indies. The colonial and British governments unleashed their privateers, as did the French. Also during this war, a band of refugees, forced out of French Acadia (renamed New Scotland or Nova Scotia) because they would not pledge their loyalty to Great Britain, wintered over in 1755–56 in Norfolk. The locals rendered aid to the Acadians and their Catholic priests, most all of whom went on to settle in Louisiana. After a string of setbacks, William Pitt reorganized the military and the British rebounded with a series of victories, including the taking of Fort Duquesne and the capture of Quebec. The Spanish entered the war on the side of the French, and the British captured the capital of Cuba. A storm drove a British ship that carried the Spanish governor of the island and his family into a Portsmouth shipyard, where the Norfolk militia saved the governor from an angry mob of British sailors and thus spared the British from a nasty international incident as they negotiated the Treaty of Paris with both Spain and France in 1763 by which the British received nearly all of Canada from the French and Florida from the Spanish for the return of Cuba.

Disquieting events took place during the struggle and more soon followed. Dinwiddie, who more than once sent the members of the House of Burgesses home without any legislative action, finally agreed to its demand to allow payment to Peyton Randolph for representing the Assembly in England in its argument against the fee on land sales. Only in this way would Virginians agree to support the military. The colony also printed paper money and made it acceptable for all debts. Virginia occasionally closed its courts and thereby stymied debt collectors. During the war, the British temporarily allowed these actions plus a cutback in the import of slaves. Also during the war, British generals ordered settlers not to go beyond a line along the crest of the Appalachians to prevent more fighting with the natives. In 1763 the government kept the Proclamation Line after the French withdrew, as Indians attacked along a broad front, including as far as east as Winchester. This policy did not sit well with Virginia planters deeply involved in land speculation.

Not connected to the war, in 1758 the Assembly passed a Two-Penny Act, by which the delegates set the rate parishes paid ministers. Each minister received a specified number of pounds of tobacco, which under the new legislation could yield a salary no higher than if it were worth two cents per pound. The going rate of tobacco had escalated, so the delegates were, in effect, cutting salaries. On the complaints of the ministers, the home government reprimanded Lieutenant Governor Francis Fauquier for not vetoing the legislation, disallowed the act both in the future as well as in the past, and prevented any legislation from taking effect until the government approved it. Encouraged by this decision, an Anglican minister took the matter before the Hanover County Court. No one questioned that he would win the case, but a young lawyer named Patrick Henry, whose oratorical skills emulated those of the revivalists of his county, persuaded the jury that the minister was only entitled to a penny in damages. Many Baptists and Presbyterians that opposed the special status given to Anglican ministers cheered the outcome of the case. After failing at running a plantation and barely getting by as a storekeeper, Henry, after reading a massive volume by an early 17th-century English jurist, went to Williamsburg for a brief interview with the colony's top legal expert, George Wythe, who gave the young man the papers he needed to secure his license to practice before the county courts.

After the French and Indian War, the British government changed its overall financial policy toward its colonies. Britain had acquired a debt in fighting a war that produced benefits to the colonists. The crown and Parliament felt it only proper that the colonies at least pay current expenses. Virginians agreed but argued that they no longer needed the Redcoats with the end of the French threat. The British, however, kept troops in the colonies. In addition, members of the colonial militia did not appreciate the condescending attitude of British military. Thus the recent war set the stage for a confrontation between the mother country and her colonies.

Virginians had long disliked aspects of the mercantile system. A few producers near the coast benefited from the subsidies on naval stores and some farmers in the Valley of Virginia received a subsidy to raise hemp, but Norfolk's merchants grumbled about the prohibitive tariff against molasses coming from the foreign West Indies. Although the policy gave tobacco growers a monopoly over the British market, most planters thought they would do better in open trade. Because over 80% of their tobacco ended up on the European continent but had to go through Britain first, they figured they lost thousands of pounds every year and also believed the huge private debts owed to British merchants were due to the navigation system.

Britain cracked down on illicit trade and did away with some trade restraints but did not open up direct trade for growers. It would now allow sugar products to come from the French West Indies, but a beefed-up customs force ensured collection of a small tariff. To man the ships needed to end smuggling, British captains forced local sailors into service. In Norfolk a mob led by the mayor prevented one particularly obnoxious English naval officer from grabbing unsuspecting seamen from the grog shops in 1767.

The government decided that paper issued by the colonial assemblies, including that of Virginia, during the recent war, could not be used to pay debts to British merchants. During the recent war, the Assembly temporarily closed the courts, but in peacetime creditors could once again take debtors to court. Tobacco certificates and bills-of-exchange were not considered legal tender, so Virginians had little with which to pay debts, as coins were in short supply. Treasurer John Robinson, who was also the Speaker of the House, bailed out some prominent planters by loaning them money he was supposed to be destroying. That saved them for the time being, but when Robinson died three years later, an audit uncovered the deception. The affair ruined several prominent men.

When delegates at a future convention to rewrite Virginia's state constitution discussed what the American Revolution was about, they concluded that two primary principles were at work—namely the idea that Britain tried to collect taxes in the colonies without securing permission from the legislative bodies in those colonies and secondly, attacking the civil liberties of the colonists. Either one of these issues might have led to a break with Britain. During the revolutionary epoch, those who supported the king and Parliament in their dispute with the colonists cited material concerns of the colonists. Many Britons pointed out that although Virginians talked a good bit about "freedom," they kept thousands of blacks in bondage. British efforts to control land speculators to prevent more conflict with Native Americans, disputes over taxation and trade regulation, an erratic tobacco market, heavy indebtedness, which Virginians hoped to escape from, ministerial pay, and British resistance to a reduction in the slave trade, among a host of factors, encouraged a breakdown of relations with the motherland. But Virginians thought their rights as Britons were at stake, and they presented their case based on the principles of governance in Great Britain. Thus the American Revolution in a sense was a product of the British political system.

In 1765 the policy of getting revenue out of the colonies reached a critical stage, when Parliament sent stamp distributors under the Stamp Act. Dozens of activities required stamps, with income going to the royal governors or other officials. The colonists pointed out that such a system, without approval of the assemblies, was unconstitutional, being a violation of the principle of "no taxation without representation." In reaction, the House of Burgesses passed several resolves, five of them introduced by Patrick Henry. As he introduced the fifth, he supposedly said, "Tarquin and Caesar had each his Brutus, Charles the First, his Cromwell, and George the Third..." followed by shouts of "treason" (John Robinson for one), whereupon he expressed the hope that George I "may profit by their example. If this be treason, make the most of it." The fifth resolution claimed that the General Assembly had the "only and exclusive right and power to lay taxes and impositions of this colony." Attempts to subvert that power would tend "to destroy British as well as American Freedom." The Burgesses passed the motion 20 to 19, but the next day, when Henry had gone, they rescinded the final resolution. Henry's resolutions, however, were widely circulated as the Virginia position on the matter. One version of the Virginia Resolves, now seven in number, claimed that Virginians did not have to obey any law regarding taxation except if mandated by the Assembly, and that anyone who said otherwise would be deemed an enemy to the colony. Delegates from several colonies met in New York. Virginia sent no official delegation, as Governor Francis Fauquier dissolved the legislature before it could act, but its leaders supported the position of the Stamp Act Congress. British leaders found colonial unity puzzling, as but a decade earlier efforts to unite the colonists against the French and Indians had been futile. They also could not accept the colonial argument against "taxation without representation" because in Great Britain few people had the right to vote and some people represented districts that had virtually no people. The Virginians and other colonists refused to use the stamps, prevented the courts from collecting debts, harassed the distributors, and otherwise went about their business as usual. Facing such unity, Parliament repealed its objectionable law. That body, however, in ominous fashion retained the right to rule over the colonies.

During the spat over stamps, Virginia planters and merchants in the colony united against Parliament's program. The two, however, broke apart during the next argument between the colonies and the mother country. The British treasurer persuaded Parliament to pass a series of duties on all sorts of goods entering the colonies. These low tariffs secured revenues without collecting them "within" the colonies. The actions were a violation of the principle of mercantilism because British goods would also bear the tax. Despite the arrival of Lord Botetourt, a titled aristocrat as governor, the House of Burgesses took a stand against the new duties. "I have heard your resolves," said he, "and I augur ill of their effects." Accordingly, he dissolved the Assembly, but the Virginians had authorized a program to compel merchants not to sell the taxed merchandise. Many planters talked about getting by with less, about their need for liberty and an independent lifestyle, but Virginians failed to sustain the boycott or Association (an agreement not to sell taxed goods). The economy had only recently recovered from a depression, and producers did not care to forgo good returns.

Scottish merchants, harried by local committees, became incensed that they took most of the heat for breaking the boycott. Many of them bore the brunt of criticism because of their origin and also for their role in colluding to set low prices for tobacco. In an unrelated matter of inoculating against smallpox, a mob attacked Scottish families in Norfolk. Jefferson served as a lawyer for the Scots in a court case, but no leaders of the mob were ever tried, and the underlings got off with a slap on the wrist. The smallpox riots coincided with the efforts to enforce the Association. Thus Scottish merchants were twice cursed. As relations with Britain deteriorated, the Scots, although they often favored the idea of representative government, nearly all became Loyalists. They did not have to decide for a few years, however, as Parliament repealed the duties, save the one on tea. Before the issue subsided a "massacre" took place in Boston. Governor Botetourt, much admired despite of the arguments over taxation, died, and his replacement, John Murray, the Earl of Dunmore, came in 1771. A Scotsman, whose family helped the rebels against King George in 1746, Dunmore had loyally served the crown as he rose through the military and subsequently served as governor of New York.

Dunmore promoted westward expansion as Britain officially stuck to the idea of not allowing settlement beyond an imaginary Appalachian line. In a delicate balancing act, agents strove to keep the Indians from forming alliances that could endanger the colonies. At the same time, they tried to keep the Indians from fighting each other. By 1768, with the various Indian tribes at peace, two British officials in charge of the frontier arranged treaties whereby, among other confusing aspects, the northern agent paid the Iroquois for Kentucky, which was not theirs to sell. The legislature granted vast amounts to various companies for Kentucky, the western slopes of the Appalachians, and the Ohio Valley. The British invariably rejected these proposals. Settlers moved onto these lands, but speculators could not charge "squatters" a cent. The government also negated land bounties dispersed for military service during the recent war. George Washington, in the belief that the government policy would change, had agents buying up these notes for a fraction of their value. Dunmore, like governors before him, an advocate of the land speculator and planter class, allowed the Loyal Co. to survey its holdings in Kentucky and other companies to take up land west of the Proclamation Line even putting in a claim of 100,000 acres for himself. With the governor's encouragement, George Mason reactivated the Ohio Co., whose charter had expired. British leaders, however, persisted in preventing bounties from being used and land companies from doing business. In 1774 the British decided that even land east of the Proclamation Line could not go to veterans but had to be sold to the highest bidder. That same year Parliament turned over the Ohio River Valley to the province of Quebec, which had no representative government.

In the spring that year, Dunmore, convinced by speculators to do something about the Mingoes and Shawnees in the Ohio area, had an agent goad them into attacking. In response, militiamen from the mountains and the Valley of Virginia marched under Andrew Lewis. The Shawnees, under Chief Cornstalk, attacked the "Long Knives," as the Indians called the frontiersmen, at Point Pleasant at the confluence of the Kanawha and Ohio rivers. After bitter fighting, the Virginians drove off the attackers. "Dunmore's War," as it was dubbed, ended with a treaty that removed the natives from the area east of the Ohio River, thus clearing the way for settlers, but legally not land companies, in what is now West Virginia. It left only Cherokees and the British government to deal with for the control of Kentucky. Another and bigger war would take care of both. Dunmore upset British authorities with his behavior in this episode, but the colonists would be the ones to remove him. In 1773 the British, determined to make the colonists pay some taxes and hoping to save investors facing bankruptcy due to a boycott of tea, gave the East India Co. a monopoly and allowed it to bring tea directly to America. Untaxed, smuggled Dutch East India tea now would have to compete against a product with a lower price even with a tax on it. Virginians forced several shipments of tea away from the colony, but in Massachusetts a mob destroyed a shipload of it. Almost a year later, in November 1774, Thomas Nelson and other Virginians dumped some imported tea in the harbor at Yorktown. By that point Parliament's Coercive Acts had closed the port of Boston in retaliation for the earlier action. It also reformed colonial and local governments in the Bay Colony.

All across Virginia opposition to the Coercive Acts mounted. Albemarle County freeholders even argued that Parliament had no authority over them, a position soon published by Jefferson in his *Summary View*. The burgesses, meeting in Williamsburg, did not go that far but did denounce the port closure as a "hostile invasion" and called for a day of fasting and prayer. Dunmore dissolved the Assembly, but the delegates met at the Raleigh Tavern and with Peyton Randolph still acting as the chair, resolved to resist arbitrary taxes. This provisional government directed its Committee of Correspondence to propose a meeting with the other colonies. Virginia sent delegates to Philadelphia in 1774, where the Continental Congress drew up a statement of rights and urged another boycott, this one on imports effective in December followed in September 1775 with an additional one on exports. The Virginians concurred in this approach, except that they exempted the ban on exports to the West Indies and changed the date to cut off future sales to August. A Second Association now set to work to boycott business with Great Britain. At the meeting of the next Continental Congress the following year, Patrick Henry, one of the delegates from Virginia, made his famous "I am not a Virginian, but an American" remark, indicating the degree to which the colonists were allying against the homeland.

As Dunmore left on his western adventure in 1774, relations between the colonies and the mother country were seriously strained. Just before going west, Dunmore dissolved the legislature for protesting the Coercive Acts. Having returned from the west to a public that admired him for his successful efforts against the natives, Dunmore now faced a crisis measurably worse than when he left.

# Chapter 7

# The Revolutionary Epoch

As relations with Great Britain deteriorated, Lord Dunmore planned to call the General Assembly into session in May, but representatives, without the governor's approval, met in March at St. John's Church in Richmond. In successfully urging the colony to prepare its defenses, Patrick Henry warned that "the next gale that sweeps from the North will bring to our ears the clash of resounding arms! Our brethren are already in the field! Why stand we here idle?…Is life so dear or peace so sweet as to be purchased at the price of chains and slavery? Forbid it, Almighty God! I know not what course others may take, but as for me, give me liberty, or give me death!" This meeting was one of five voter-elected "conventions" that first met in Richmond and then back in Williamsburg. These conventions approved steps taken by the Continental Congress and supervised the war effort in Virginia, especially after learning about the shots fired at Lexington and Concord in Massachusetts in April of 1775. Portly Peyton Randolph presided over the Second Continental Congress but soon returned to Virginia, and Thomas Jefferson replaced him as a delegate from the Old Dominion. Congress gave command of the new Continental Army to George Washington, who, though serving without pay and worrying about his reputation, headed to Boston.

In response to rising hostility in Williamsburg, Dunmore had British sailors remove the gunpowder from the magazine at Williamsburg. As Patrick Henry led the Hanover County militia toward the capital to reclaim the powder, the governor paid for the powder and declared Henry an outlaw. In arguing with one of his critics, the governor suggested that if the colonists did not behave themselves, he might call on the slaves for help. The situation improved temporarily but then worsened when Dunmore had the magazine booby-trapped. In May 1775 Dunmore, having moved his family to safety, boarded a British naval ship moored on the York River. At about the same time as Dunmore sailed to Norfolk, the House of Burgesses dissolved itself, having met without the governor's approval, and convened as a convention. Just as Dunmore reestablished his royal government at the Gosport Shipyard near Portsmouth on the Elizabeth River, the convention met, with Edmund Pendleton in the chair, and ordered out several regiments of militia and created a Committee of Safety to carry on the functions of government. The committee and its local counterparts jailed those accused of violating the boycott or otherwise befriending the enemy. Pendleton, who presided over the committee, could not stop Patrick Henry from taking charge of the First Regiment, but he blocked Henry's efforts to command troops in direct conflict with Dunmore.

An ensuing war of words soon gave way to more lethal actions. Mobs gave Loyalist sympathizers coats of tar and feathers. British naval forces made sorties on shore to procure food. Militia sniped at shore parties and ships offshore. The militia drove off a British attempt to land at Hampton in October, considered as the start of armed conflict. In accordance with instructions from Britain, Dunmore sent troops searching for rebel cannons, stands of arms, and ammunition. On two separate raids Dunmore's soldiers, including blacks and whites Loyalists, embarrassed the Princess Anne and Norfolk County militia at their training grounds at Kemp's Landing, not far from Norfolk.

After the second of these fiascos, in November 1775, Dunmore published a proclamation whereby he freed all rebel-owned servants, Negroes or others "able and willing to bear arms for his Majesty's crown and dignity." Residents who refused to pledge support would be considered rebels. The convention responded to this proclamation by warning slaves to put down their arms and return to their masters within ten days or face deportation to the West Indies. Also, after these defeats at Kemp's Landing, the convention government called for the Second Regiment to cross the James River and advance to Great Bridge, where British troops had taken over a partially built fort along the only wagon road access to Norfolk across the area's swamps.

At about this time word reached Virginia that Dunmore had earlier plotted to bring Indians from the west to his aid. The agent at Pittsburgh, who had concocted the crisis in 1774 that led to victory over the Indians at Point Pleasant, proposed a plan, accepted by the British general in Massachusetts, to form an alliance with Natives. Under this scheme, armed Natives would move east to rendezvous with Dunmore at Alexandria the following April. The plan became public with the arrest of Dunmore's agent in Maryland. The governor had, in effect, played two race cards. One card employed Natives and the other exploited slaves, but neither card won the game.

In December 1775, Dunmore's troops attacked rebels as they massed below Great Bridge, located on the southern branch of the Elizabeth River. A slave, acting as a double agent, convinced the governor that the Americans were too few in number to be able to repulse an attack. At the time the governor's forces included about 100 British professionals, some 400 members of the Ethiopian Regiment with the words "liberty to slaves" on cloth across their chests, and 400 white Loyalists, all facing about 1,500 Virginia and North Carolina militia. With troops stationed in the fort, the British controlled the approaches to the bridge, but Dunmore went on the offensive by crossing the bridge. Efforts to flank the rebels through the morass failed, and the charging British met a hail of lead, including that fired by blacksmith William Flora, a free black from Portsmouth. The British leader and several other redcoats fell with multiple wounds. With heavy losses, the British and Loyalists fell back to Norfolk in disorder. With no feasible way to defend the borough in the face of advancing rebels, Dunmore ordered his supporters into about 100 ships in the river, retaining but a small outpost on the Portsmouth side of the river.

On 1 January 1776 Dunmore's celebrated the New Year by cannonading Norfolk to cover a shore party that set fire to the buildings used by snipers. Cannonballs crushed into buildings, one killing three women, another shattering brick and wounding a rebel officer. The rebels took the occasion to break into the warehouses, loot them, drink as much of the rum as they could, and burn the lower part of the borough. A few weeks later, the convention ordered the destruction of the rest of the community, which included the church then being used as a hospital. Six thousand people were made homeless. Dunmore still occupied the river, and his forces remained in place until near summer.

During the ensuing standoff, fighting continued sporadically in lower Virginia between loyalists and rebels, with some families such as the Goodriches of Nansemond/Isle of Wight switching sides in the conflict. The most capable mariners in coastal Virginia, the family initially brought in gunpowder for the rebels, but upon being chastised by the Committee of Safety for bringing in linens in the same cargo and then being apprehended by Lord Dunmore, they agreed to help the British and attacked American shipping from Virginia to the West Indies. In May 1776, 500 Virginia militia occupied Portsmouth. They loaded up wagons with all the dry goods, rum, sugar, and molasses belonging to the "enemies of the American cause" and destroyed some of their houses, including that owned by John Goodrich.

By the summer of 1776 Dunmore enlisted over 800 blacks, but by August smallpox had killed more than half. Ravaged by disease, low on supplies, and with no additional Redcoats coming to help, Dunmore ordered his flotilla to leave the Elizabeth River. The fleet journeyed across Hampton Roads to an island in Gloucester (now Mathews) County, where the British established a base on an island, but they were soon attacked by elements of the Virginia militia under General Andrew Lewis, leading Dunmore to evacuate Virginia. A large entourage went to New York, others went to Bermuda and the West Indies, and still others were driven off course by a mid-July storm and ended up prisoners on the Eastern Shore. Many blacks, on reaching New York with Dunmore, were dismissed from the service as Sir William Howe reversed Dunmore's racial policy.

As Dunmore exited, the state of Virginia and the United States of America came into being. The move toward independence had been mounting through the previous winter and early spring. The destruction of Norfolk helped convince Americans of the need for such action, as Dunmore received most of the blame for the tragedy. Tom Paine's pamphlet published at about the same time as the burning of Norfolk also influenced rebel thinking. The earlier boycott had severely hurt many small farmers, who, finding it difficult to pay rent in hard money, insisted on paying in tobacco, which now had no market in Britain, or in paper money issued by the Assembly. Nearly everybody was in dire need of necessities such as salt. Poor and middling farmers grumbled about the high pay appointed officers received. Members of the provisional government thought that an independent state, based on republican principles, would go a long way in rallying the lower classes to aid the war effort.

The fifth convention assembled in May with Edmund Pendleton again presiding. This assembly included Patrick Henry, George Mason, Richard Bland, Archibald Cary, and young men like Edmund Randolph and James Madison. Pendleton and other conservatives reluctantly agreed to the move toward independence. A few leading conservatives disagreed and joined the Loyalists or dropped out of political affairs. In May, after a ceremony during which a handful of old burgesses formally disbanded their body, the convention unanimously directed its delegation at the Continental Congress to end any connection with the British crown. By this point many Americans concurred with Jefferson that they never had any connection with Parliament. By the late spring delegates in Philadelphia postponed acting on Richard Henry Lee's resolution for total separation from Great Britain, pending a written statement. Thomas Jefferson then wrote the Declaration of Independence, the rationale for severing the relationship with the crown. The document embodied the best of British and a bit of French political philosophy in its preamble. The rest of the Declaration indicted the king, pointing out specific grievances to a "candid" world. On 2 July 1776, Congress accepted Lee's resolution and declared independence. With some major changes in wording such as modifying Jefferson's condemnation of the slave trade, Congress approved the Declaration of Independence on the fourth, and the "United Colonies" now become the "United States." George Wythe, Thomas Jefferson, Richard Henry Lee, Francis Lightfoot Lee, Carter Braxton, Thomas Nelson, Jr., and Benjamin Harrison appended their names to the document as part of the Virginia delegation. Given the roles and knowledge of these men and those who stayed in Virginia to produce its new constitution, one may argue that no state ever amassed such political talent at any one time.

In the meantime, the Virginia convention that called for independence worked on the formation of a new and permanent state government to start once Congress declared independence. George Mason of Fairfax County wrote most of the key parts of the Declaration of Rights and also created the basic format for the plan of government. The preamble to the Virginia constitution contained criticism about the king. These complaints became the basis for the indictment against the king found in the Declaration of Independence, though Jefferson altered the order and wording.

Despite the differences between the Declaration of Rights, which became the foundation for the Bill of Rights, and the Declaration of Independence, they both assumed that the right to govern depended on the consent of the governed and that all people possessed essential rights. "All men are by nature free and independent and have certain inherent rights," which could not be taken away from posterity, stated the Declaration of Rights. In the Declaration of Independence, Jefferson talked about the "unalienable rights" of "life, liberty, and the pursuit of happiness." Mason wrote about "the enjoyment of life and liberty with the means of acquiring and possessing property, and pursuing and obtaining happiness and safety." His Declaration of Rights called for regular and free elections, impartial juries, no general warrants, no standing army in times of peace, a regulated militia, and freedom of press and religion (this clause greatly influenced by a young delegate, James Madison).

The Declaration of Rights predated the Declaration of Independence. Jefferson wrote to Mason about the former, but his comments did not arrive in time to influence the document and the convention pretty much ignored his advice on making the new state government more democratic.

The Constitution of 1776 was based on the concept of separation of powers with three distinct layers: legislative, executive, and judicial. The bi-chambered legislature had a House of Delegates with each county entitled to two delegates serving annual terms. The principal towns retained one representative. The convention divided the state into 24 senatorial districts with six members being elected every year. Those voting for these representatives had to meet the same property qualification as they had under the royal charter. Every year the two chambers jointly picked a governor, who could serve no more than three consecutive one-year terms. They also picked eight members of the Privy Council (Council of State), almost the same as the council that had long advised the royal governors. As before, the council itself would decide its presiding officer, who would also become the Lieutenant Governor, able to assume the role of chief executive in the absence of the governor. The two houses also picked judges for the state court of appeals and the general court, the attorney general, and other positions. The governor commanded the military and appointed justices of the peace and other county officers, but he had no veto power.

Many Virginians, especially from the northern area, served as officers in the Continental Army besides George Washington. Horatio Gates, a recent English immigrant to the northern part of the Valley and a veteran, commanded American troops at Saratoga (New York), probably the most critical victory in the war. There Daniel Morgan and his riflemen from the Lower Valley ably assisted him in defeating the British. Later Gates suffered a humiliating defeat at Camden in South Carolina, in the aftermath of which he rode over 180 miles in three days in an effort to regroup, but he lost his command. Morgan, who started his military career as a teamster during Braddock's campaign, led the attack at the Battle of Cowpens against the feared British cavalry officer Banastre Tarleton, "the Hunting Leopard," known best for the slaughter of wounded Americans in a previous battle. Using militia as a screen and cavalry sweeps, Morgan's men humiliated the vaunted Tarleton so badly that a Scottish regiment refused to serve under him in later encounters in Virginia. Charles Lee, a friend of Gates and also a recent English immigrant into the northern Valley and with far more military experience than Washington, commanded forces arrayed against Dunmore in the Norfolk area. Later during a battle in New Jersey in 1778, as the rebels pursued Lord Cornwallis back to New York, Washington removed Lee from his command for disobeying orders.

Brigadier General Peter Muhlenberg, another Valley man, ably served the cause. A Lutheran minister at the outset of the war with but limited military experience, he recruited a regiment of Germans in Dunmore County (the name was soon changed to Shenandoah) that first fought in defense of Charleston, South Carolina. Muhlenberg commanded the 8th Virginia in the Continental Army in the bitter fighting around Philadelphia and later in New Jersey and New York. Still later he directed troops against the British invasion of Virginia and participated in the capture of British redoubts at the Battle of Yorktown in 1781.

Virginia's Continental Lines, including over a hundred free blacks, excelled after receiving instruction from the Prussian veteran of the Seven Years' War, Baron von Steuben, at Valley Forge in the winter of 1777–78. The Virginia regulars also at times included the huge Portuguese-born Peter Francisco, who served heroically at several encounters. He supposedly killed over 20 redcoats in two separate incidents. Wounded at battle in North Carolina where Lord Cornwallis commanded the field at the end of the day but lost so many men that he gave up hope of ever controlling the Carolinas, Francisco recovered to take on the British in Virginia.

Western Virginians also played major military roles. The "Over the Mountain Boys," along with Carolina rebels, attacked over 1,000 British led Loyalists atop King's Mountain near Charlotte. Pushing their way up the mountain, they fell back but recovered. Unfortunately, the victors continued a murderous fire into the defeated Loyalists, apparently in retaliation for earlier British atrocities. This defeat effectively took the backcountry Loyalists out of the war in the Carolinas. Other westerners secured Kentucky and drove the British out of the Ohio Valley. Young George Rogers Clark, a native of Albemarle County, helped defeat the Cherokee in the "dark and bloody ground" of Kentucky. As one of the delegates to the Virginia Assembly, Clark came to the Virginia government with a plan to seize British outposts in the west. Secretly in 1780, with less than 200 men, Clark moved along the Ohio River to the falls at what became Louisville (recently confiscated from Dunmore's agent and now named for the king of France, a new American ally). Then they marched overland for six days to Kaskaskia, and a few weeks later to Cahokia and Vincennes. Clark left these forts in the hands of the French. The British recaptured Vincennes, but in the middle of the winter Clark drove his forces, virtually without food and through floods, to retake Vincennes and capture a British commander who had urged Indians to attack defenseless settlers. Years later the Assembly considered paying Clark and his men $15,000 but, failing proper documentation, delayed payment until after the leader's death, and so creditors seized the lands he was entitled to. As to the territory, Virginia, with Congressman James Madison playing the principal role, surrendered ownership to the new national government under the Articles of Confederation in 1781. That was done to convince smaller states to join the new government. The state did exempt about 150,000 acres designated for Clark's soldiers.

In the coastal parts of Virginia, the war went on as a series of guerilla actions. The swampy nature of the terrain allowed marauders, remnants of Dunmore's loyalists, to stalk the land. In November 1778, a petitioner asked to be repaid the cost of killing a Negro slave abetting Josiah Phillips, a laborer (possibly black) from the Lynnhaven part of Princess Anne County, in the "perpetuation of their wicked and traitorous actions." Phillips and his band of escaped slaves terrorized the inhabitants of Norfolk and Princess Anne counties so much that rewards were offered to anyone who killed any of the terrorists, thereby saving the expense of sending troops. Phillips himself was caught and executed in an act some consider a blot on Jefferson's record as governor, but the Assembly offered these men trials if they turned themselves in.

The Revolution also produced John Paul Jones, who came to Virginia as a fugitive before the war. A lieutenant in the fledgling U.S. Navy, he helped capture munitions for Washington, led a daring raid on the English coast, and then went to France, where, with the help of Benjamin Franklin, he obtained a ship the *Bonhomme Richard,* and a French crew. In hand-to-hand combat they captured the much larger British ship *Serapis,* as their own vessel sank.

In coastal Virginia the departure of Dunmore did not bring peace. British ships-of-the-line frequently came into Chesapeake Bay and privateers constantly menaced shipping. Loyalists also raided coastal communities, forcing Virginians to respond by finding novel ways to combat these incursions. At one point they erected a 50-foot pole at Cape Henry with signals to warn of approaching enemy ships. The state also authorized privateers and also built its own navy to supplement that of the United States. Sometimes it simply converted merchant ships, but it also built galleys, small, maneuverable craft that could tackle privateers but not big British ships.

Providing more vessels than any other state, Virginia purchased or paid for the conversion or building of the *Liberty,* often under the command of Captain (later Commodore) James Barron and the *Patriot,* under Captain Richard Barron. Other ships included *Norfolk Revenge,* and *Tartar,* among others. The biggest of these carried but 18 cannons. Caesar Tarant, a slave from Hampton, later received freed status for his heroic work as a navigator for the Virginia navy. Plans to build 36-gun ships at the Chickahominy River and Gosport public yards went awry. The Nansemond River, the Mattaponi River, and South Quay on the Nottoway River also had small private yards. South Quay developed overnight as a depot for smuggling Virginia goods through the Outer Banks.

During this phase of the war, the Continental Congress arranged for prisoners to be kept in the interior of Virginia. At the time the British occupied Philadelphia, refugees suspected of being Tories, were brought to Winchester. About the same time several hundred prisoners captured at Saratoga, a great many of them Hessians (Germans), were escorted into the Charlottesville area. German and British prisoners lived in the Barracks (the name for the community), though German and British officers, under parole but usually armed, roamed the countryside. Jefferson entertained the commanders, including General William Phillips. The latter, having been paroled and exchanged, later led a British expedition into Virginia, where he died from disease.

Along the Fall Line, British officers met a local planter who had some "curious mills and ironworks" on the James and Colonel Randolph, whose Tuckahoe estate impressed them. Randolph and his family, including refined young ladies, entertained their visitors in the high-ceilinged and one-story passageway between the two taller wings of the H-shaped home. Such pleasant treatment of the "enemy" did not please the local "peasantry," but the colonel persisted in traditional courtesies despite the "popular clamor." Jefferson and a Scottish "commonsense" philosopher friend agreed that this sort of improved treatment of prisoners indicated mankind's progress. Unfortunately, this humane treatment did not carry over to American privateers and others captured by the British

Entering northern Virginia in the winter of 1779, the Baroness Riedesel, traveling with her children with a light escort to reach her husband, a prisoner, sought food at a home. Even though offered money, the residents refused "with hard words, saying that there was nothing for dogs or Royalists." When she pointed to some hominy, the angry Virginian said, "No, that is for our Negroes, who work for us, but you have wished to kill us." The baroness, who did her best to maintain the behavior expected from one of her station, reported on

59

the construction of "the Barracks" near Charlottesville, where Hessian prisoners built their temporary homes in the style of their homeland, including garden plots and enclosures for fowl. "I saw a pretty little town spring up," she declared. Local blacks brought fowls, fruits, and a few vegetables while white farmers of the neighborhood sold them butter and eggs. The British government managed to send enough aid to allow the prisoners to live tolerably pleasant lives. After negotiations, the officers and the men were finally exchanged. A few of the noncommissioned prisoners, hired out as mercenaries by their prince, found a permanent home among the Germans of the Valley of Virginia. One of them became a successful Richmond businessman after the war, based mostly on his connections to German farmers.

War certainly affected women in different ways and presented unusual challenges. One woman's name appeared in the newspaper for being "inimical to American interests" so that people would shun her. A cannon ball wounded one woman as she was feeding her baby, when the British attacked Norfolk in January 1776. With the town destroyed, midwives, milliners, and teachers relocated to Richmond or other towns. One planned to "carry on her business as heretofore," including curing "inveterate ringworm, scaled heads, sore eyes…and many other disorders incident to both sexes." Her displaced daughter hoped to open a boarding school. A Loyalist sympathizers, in seclusion with their children on farms in Princess Anne County, sewed their own clothes "and did everything possible" to maintain themselves. The mother's chief concern, other than the high prices, was that the children could not improve themselves "by reading, writing, keeping polite company, etc." Despite their Loyalist leanings, the women suffered only the loss of some cattle during the war. But the "plundered" wife of an American soldier captured by the British "was greatly distressed." The British promised to release the husband if the wife of the young John Goodrich could be exchanged. Making sure her husband was properly attired in home spun, Martha Washington sewed and directed others who did the same. She also directed meal preparation for the general and his entourage, including at Valley Forge, where she also served as an aide, especially for women who wished to see the general. With so many men away from home, women directed slaves or worked in the fields themselves. They served as nurses in the hospital in Williamsburg or in their homes. Many women in the fighting against Indians in Kentucky participated directly as they had done in previous frontier battles. Virginians were more than a little irritated by the women that came with British troops during the invasion of 1781, because the soldiers confiscated private horses, carriages, and even clothes so that their women could ride in style.

In May 1779 a British flotilla under Sir George Collier entered Hampton Roads. The British quickly moved along the Elizabeth River. A landing party approached the rear of Fort Nelson (later the site of the U.S. Naval Hospital). As they advanced, the American troops fled to the eastern branch of the Elizabeth as the civilian population fled in terror. The British captured two large French ships loaded with 1,000 hogsheads of tobacco and two smaller tobacco ships, captured a 14-gun privateer, and destroyed two potential 36-gun ships the Americans were building at Gosport. They moved into Suffolk and burned its warehouse and other buildings and even destroyed a small farm owned by George Washington and some associates in the Dismal Swamp. Collier advised his superiors to make a permanent British base at Fort Nelson, but they had more important tasks for him in the Carolinas. Within a few days, Virginia lookouts reported that the enemy had "gone to sea."

The raid signaled a new British approach to the Revolution. Having failed to subdue the rebellion in the North, although they continued to occupy New York, they attacked the South. In May 1780, an army that surrendered to the British after the siege of Charleston included one of Virginia's Continental Lines. After subduing the Carolinas and Georgia under the overall field command of Lord Cornwallis, the British planned to move on to Virginia. As part of this campaign the British replayed Dunmore's race card to entice slaves to join the British. In June 1777, during a quiet phase of the war in Virginia, the legislature insisted that any black serving in the Virginia militia or the various Virginia Continental Lines had to prove they were free. When the British threatened Richmond in 1781 the council decided not to arm slaves. At the very end of the war the legislature permitted some planters to use their slaves as substitutes. After the war some of these planters tried to put the men back into slavery, but at least in some cases they were prevented from doing so. Also in 1781 the Assembly considered the possibility of making the wealthier slaveholders give up a few of their slaves to be distributed to poor men serving in the military.

In mid-1780, the British returned with 54 ships, captured Hampton, burned ships, and met local loyalists. But the Loyalist loss at King's Mountain in the Carolinas convinced Cornwallis he needed more forces at Charleston, and so this British expedition also moved on. A few months later, in January 1781, a small British force under turncoat General Benedict Arnold encamped near Portsmouth and then moved swiftly up the James, as Virginia scrambled to put militia into the field. Governor Jefferson could only watch as the British destroyed the foundry at Westham and other public structures in Richmond. Arnold then withdrew to the coast, but William Phillips, the general recently entertained at Monticello, brought in additional troops. The British once again attacked in force up the James River as far as Richmond, where a small army of New England Continentals under the Marquis de Lafayette blocked further advance, despite being outnumbered at least three to one. Virginia militia under Steuben could not prevent the British from capturing Petersburg and destroying the valuable tobacco warehouses there and burning barracks at Chesterfield Court House. They also temporarily occupied Williamsburg and destroyed the Chickahominy Shipyard, including a nearly completed 36-gun state ship. General Phillips died, but Tarleton and his cavalry came to pave the way for Cornwallis. Having given up on the Carolinas, Cornwallis marched through North Carolina, met with his other armies at Petersburg, and set about to subdue the Old Dominion.

When Arnold set up winter quarters at Portsmouth, Governor Jefferson hoped the French fleet would close the entrance to Chesapeake Bay and allow the rebels to bag Arnold's army. General Washington, who would doubtless have given his false teeth to capture the traitor, sent Lafayette for that purpose and also ordered General "Mad" Anthony Wayne and his Pennsylvania Line to rendezvous with Lafayette. He also asked that a French fleet plug the entrance to the bay. Wayne did as ordered, but the French, after inflicting damage to the British ships, withdrew. The chance to capture Arnold failed, but an even better scenario was about to play out.

Lord Cornwallis sent two armies west of Richmond, as Lafayette, far outnumbered, withdrew as far north as Spotsylvania Court House. Cavalry under Tarleton moved west across the Piedmont toward Charlottesville. A determined housewife delayed breakfast for Tarleton long enough to allow Jack Jouett, a militia cavalryman, to ride through the night to warn Jefferson, who barely escaped from Monticello. Tarleton destroyed some supplies gathered for two new "legions" of militia recently called out by the Assembly. That body, having escaped from Tarleton's clutches, reconvened in Staunton where, miffed at Jefferson, they named Thomas Nelson, Jr. the new governor. Another British detachment pursued Steuben and elements of the Virginia militia. Steuben and his men eluded the British but lost their much-needed supplies.

At about this point, regiments under Lafayette and Wayne met north of Richmond and cautiously pursued Cornwallis. Although Cornwallis outnumbered the Americans, Virginia's summer sun wore down his troops. After a series of skirmishes, Cornwallis enticed the Americans into believing he had left only a rear guard, as he put his troops on ships near Jamestown. Two days after the Americans celebrated their day of independence in 1781 "Mad" Anthony's men advanced into the British trap, but the Pennsylvanians realized their predicament just in time to avoid being snared by the British flanks. Lafayette, observing the main British force, held his men in reserve. Thus two Continental Lines remained a fighting force in the war against Cornwallis.

Cornwallis abandoned Portsmouth as his main base and moved to Yorktown. The Americans learned about Cornwallis's intended move from James, a slave belonging to the Armistead family, who later took Lafayette's name, serving as a double agent in British-occupied Portsmouth. The general sent Arnold to raid the New England coast, thus sparing him from possible capture in Virginia, but the Americans now trapped bigger game. French troops, formerly at Newport, and several thousand Continentals under Washington quietly and quickly moved overland from New York to Virginia. One French fleet brought additional men and materials and another came from the West Indies and prevented aid from reaching Cornwallis as a result of the Battle of the Capes. A large British fleet remained in the West Indies and Clinton stayed in New York as Franco-Americans forces besieged Yorktown. American continentals, French forces, and Virginia militia soon overspread the Peninsula. Muhlenberg, Lafayette, and Steuben joined Washington and the French for the kill (Wayne was temporarily out of action from friendly fire). The Americans and French built parallel trenches within a half-mile of Cornwallis. By 15 October, they had a second line some 250 yards from the

British. They were so close to Cornwallis that enemy artillery struck some Virginia militia in their sleep, for the "stupid wretches who are not acquainted with the life of a soldier" had camped too close to the British lines, according to a Pennsylvanian. The French captured Tarlatan as he roamed the area, thereby possibly saving his life. The British suffered from smallpox and a shortage of food. Weather intervened on the Franco-American side when a storm prevented Cornwallis from moving to the north side of the York River. As cannon fire penetrated his headquarters (the home of Governor Nelson, who possibly called for the attack on his own house) and Franco-American forces broke through the inner defenses, Cornwallis surrendered officially on 19 October 1781.

The loss of this army, the high cost of conducting the American campaign, and the desire to concentrate on fighting the French and Spanish persuaded the British of the need for peace with the Americans. It took several months to complete negotiations during which at least one Virginia line fought heroically in the Carolinas and Georgia along with the Pennsylvanians, who had served so well in Virginia. The British and Americans reached a preliminary agreement in November 1782, at about the same time as a "Battle of the Barges," won by Tory irregulars against the Virginia navy, took place near Tangier Island. The Treaty of Paris officially ended the war in 1783.

The Revolution, like most wars, had material ramifications, causing much disease and destruction. From the spread of smallpox to the total annihilation of Norfolk and the destruction of public warehouses in several places and shipyards near Portsmouth and on the Chickahominy, it exacted its toll on the people and the environment. It also left hallowed grounds, where patriots gave their lives for freedom, created a host of heroes, and ruined some reputations

The commonwealth recovered relatively quickly. Well before the end of the war, merchants were throwing up wooden warehouses amid charred, cannon-battered brick walls in Norfolk, which soon bore the appearance of a frontier town. The enemy carted off thousands of slaves and a great deal of livestock, but they rarely destroyed the private residences even of rebel leaders. Commerce resumed as soon as the threat of war lifted and soon reached a level exceeding what it had been before the Revolution. Prosperity proved to be ephemeral as the pent-up demand for Virginia tobacco ended. Even though Americans no longer needed to send their tobacco through Britain to reach European markets, they discovered that the only access to the French market went through an agency whose chief purpose was to pay as low a price as possible. Virginia farmers found they were in pretty much the same predicament they had been in before the war. To make matters worse, the British prevented Americans from trading directly in the British West Indies. British merchants smugly reminded everyone of the advantages of their empire as they dumped British goods on the Virginia market at sharply reduced prices. Overall the Virginia economy came through these tribulations in better shape than in other states. Income from tobacco and the generally strong economy immediately following the war allowed the state to pay off much of its public debt and reduce the amount of cheap paper money. Thus Virginians only experienced rumors of rebellion in contrast to Massachusetts, where veterans tried to prevent the courts from foreclosing on their farms in 1786.

The break from Britain allowed Virginians to take action regarding slavery. The state ended the international slave trade, legally at least, in 1778. In 1782 the state ended restrictions on masters freeing their slaves, thereby encouraging manumissions, because owners no longer had to pay to transport newly freed people out of the state. The legislature also paid for the freedom for several slaves who performed special services during the war. And it demanded freedom for anyone who had served as a substitute for the master to meet military requirements. The legislature also weakened provisions that exempted masters and overseers from prosecution should a slave die from excessive punishment. Although Virginia retained its policy against race mixing, it changed the definition of non-white to include anyone who had a grandparent of Indian or African ancestry rather than a great-grandparent as the act of 1705 had required. These moderate measures constituted the extent of reforms related to race. Virginia's politicians turned a deaf ear to the idea that all slaves should automatically be freed under the preamble to the Virginia Constitution of 1776, as one of the state's legal experts, George Wythe, suggested. The legislature did not even debate Jefferson's plan to start freeing slaves born in 1800 or thereafter. Despite some changes, the treatment of slaves remained as it had been before the war. The wife of a German officer believed that the landed proprietors in Virginia treated their slaves badly. Her stern, disciplined husband decried the lashings of the hard-hearted overseers. What most shocked the baroness was that masters permitted slaves up to age fifteen to run about with no clothes and after that age the dress given them was "scarcely worth wearing." Foreign travelers also commented on the amount of miscegenation in Albemarle County and about how particularly attractive women of mixed blood were mistreated by overseers.

The Revolutionary era wrought a major shift in religion. A traveler in the mid-1780s noted that Richmond had but one church for its population of nearly 2,000 and no one had any trouble finding a seat on Sunday. Historians have recently challenged this negative assessment of the vitality of the Anglican Church, maintaining that many planters took the religious instructions of their families quite seriously. Many ministers were often quite capable and moral people who did not try to answer theologically thorny questions. In any case, dissenters as well as those not interested in organized religion, sought change. Clause #16 of the Declaration of Rights, written at least in part by James Madison, who studied religion in college, called for religious freedom and urged everyone to "practice Christian forbearance, love and charity toward each other." One of the first pieces of legislation passed by the Virginia Assembly in 1776 ended all laws forcing attendance at church and exempted non-Anglicans (dissenters) from paying taxes to support the established church, but the same act left intact the rest of the colonial code on religion. For the next three years the Assembly annually suspended payments to Anglican clergy from public resources. Would-be ministers no longer needed credentials from London or special licenses to preach in Virginia. The Assembly devised a new system for taking care of the poor where Anglicans were not in sufficient number to form a vestry. The delegates called for the election of five secular Overseers of the Poor to assume the functions of the wardens (selected vestrymen) in those counties, mostly in the western areas, where Anglican parishes no longer operated.

In 1779 a representative from Albemarle County submitted Governor Jefferson's idea to end all connection between church and state. George Mason and other liberals persuaded the Assembly over considerable opposition to end public financial support to the Anglican clergy, but the Assembly delayed discussing a more complete separation of church and state until 1785, when James Madison prevented Patrick Henry from creating a general assessment to support religious educators. Madison soon thereafter resubmitted Jefferson's Statute for Religious Freedom. After some "mutilation" of the original bill, the statute assumed that "Almighty God hath created the mind free" and wanted mankind to develop religious thought without coercion. Future assemblies that sought to undermine this principle would be infringing on natural right. Most Baptists and many other religious people favored the idea, even though it also gave non-Christians and even atheists freedom from Christianity or any other religion. In 1786, the legislature overwhelmingly approved the measure, which effectively ended any major connection between church and state. People did not have to attend or support any church and would be "free to profess...their opinions in matters of religion." Legislation passed in 1776 gave the Anglican Church the right to keep title to its holdings, but the Episcopal Church, the successor to the Anglican Church, lost considerable property early in the 19th century, when the Virginia Court of Appeal turned over the glebe lands to the counties. In many instances, they were turned over to the overseers of the poor or used for some public purpose such as schools.

In the same year that Jefferson drew up his Statute for Religious Freedom (1779), he also worked on a plan for the greater "Diffusion of Knowledge." Under this scheme for universal education the man from Monticello wanted the Assembly to provide funding for a three-tiered system of education. All free children would attend neighborhood schools for three years. They would learn rudimentary reading, writing and math along with and some basics about morality and government sufficient to allow them to function in a republican society as independent producers. The best 10% of these would receive government help to attend, along with the more affluent, schools or academies that would instill more sophisticated science, math, foreign languages, Greek, and Latin. Another winnowing process would send a tiny number of these on to higher training at public expense. Despite the brilliance of the proposal and the great need for higher literacy in the state, the assembly never acted on Jefferson's plan.

Jefferson had better luck with his assault on privilege and artificial aristocracy. The constitution disallowed special ranks, titles, and emoluments. The old British practice of paying someone for his rank would not be permitted in the new republic. The first legislature also ended the practice of entail. Ten years later the Assembly ended primogeniture. To the extent that these medieval measures had affected the distribution of land, the reforms made Virginia less aristocratic.

Virginians became less deferential to aristocracy during this era. In visiting Randolph of Tuckahoe, a British officer saw three "peasants" come into a room where the colonel was entertaining guests, sit down near the fireplace, begin spitting, taking off their boots covered with mud, and then talking about having the colonel grind their wheat. After they left, the officer asked the colonel how such conduct could be tolerated, to which the colonel replied that the "spirit of independency" and "equality" made even the lowly think "himself upon a footing with his neighbors," and he doubted not that each of the men thought himself "in every respect my equal." Before the rebellion Virginians had been more deferential to "gentlemen."

Some minor changes regarding the right to vote took place. The qualifications for the right to vote for members of the Assembly in 1776 remained the same as they had been before the war, but in 1782 the Assembly reduced the amount of property one needed to own to 50 unimproved acres to qualify to vote. And in the 1780s residents in some of the towns secured the right to select their councilmen. The Assembly authorized charter changes for Richmond, Petersburg, and other communities, which called for the direct election for the common council. Conservatives in Norfolk sent a petition signed by many of the borough's leading citizens against this experiment, but the Assembly, seemingly more democratic in spirit than the merchants, compelled Norfolk to accept some direct voter input. At least one woman in Virginia thought members of her gender who owned sufficient property should have the right to vote, but this privately expressed opinion did not make its way into public discourse. Virginia was far too conservative to accept such a radical position, even though at least one northern state experimented with the idea.

Neither the war nor the revolutionary spirit substantially affected the distribution of landed estates, but the war created a fluid situation to allow some to benefit. Very few big planters chose the wrong side in the struggle and had their property sequestered or confiscated. At the end of the war, the governor allowed Loyalists to return. In 1783 the Assembly decided they could stay, and they even had the right to pursue old debts. Those Loyalists whose family members stayed in Virginia during the war rarely lost their property. After the war, those who aided the British faced civil suits, but the state took criminal action only in extreme cases.

In the mid-1780s the legislature appointed Thomas Jefferson, Edmund Pendleton, and George Wythe to revise colonial laws. They examined English common law, the development of the legal system, and the current situation. As a result Virginia ended up with a strong appeals court. Conscious about the right of property, Pendleton wanted to ensure creditors a fair chance of collecting debts to offset British complaints that Virginia planters had rebelled primarily to avoid paying debts to merchants. The Virginia legislature, however, insisted that Britain compensate for removing slaves before courts could act on debts owed to former enemies, but Pendleton convinced the people of the necessity of maintaining rights of property. Having an independent judiciary would help Virginia's reputation and its future development. Pendleton also wanted to keep the system of primogeniture as part of the rights of property, but the legislature rejected his idea. Later, as the head of the Appeals Court, he planned to disallow state confiscation of the glebe lands but died before casting his vote.

The creation of district courts in 1788 facilitated the legal system. A traveler in the mid-1780s noticed that Virginia had many laws that were not enforced. The German baroness heard about cases of incest and wife swapping with no legal action taken. Imprisonment remained uncommon despite a crime rate that probably exceeded that in many states. Part of the problem related to the fact that cases involving whites had to be brought to Richmond for prosecution. The new system helped alleviate that problem.

Jefferson hoped Virginia might make far greater changes than it did during these years. Indeed, he called for a convention in 1783 to rewrite the constitution along more liberal or democratic lines. That Virginia's voters had not directly approved the frame of government remained a cause for concern. In the end the "Sage of Monticello" went after reform piecemeal, a process that produced a few changes. Although Jefferson did persuade the legislature, through Madison, to end primogeniture, he was less successful in having the legislature rationalize the common law. The legislature waited for another decade to reduce the number of possibilities for the death sentence from the 200 felonies on the books, although authorities rarely imposed such sentences. By 1796 the legislature had sharply reduced the number of criminal offenses for which one could be executed. In the end, both human and property rights gained ground during the Revolutionary Era.

The concept of a strong state received a long-term boost as a result of the Revolution. Virginians assumed that the state government would take over many of the functions taken away from the British. British control of commerce ended, but the state government carried on a degree of mercantilism even after the war ended. Regulating the flow of goods through certain ports and collecting import duties provide two examples of this policy. During the war, the state subsidized a woolen mill at Williamsburg, a large iron foundry in Franklin County, a foundry at Westham, a forge in New Kent County, lead mines in Bedford County, salt works on the coast, gun manufacturing in Fredericksburg, and other war-related enterprises. They printed money to pay for the war and confiscated Loyalist properties to help defray some of the costs. When the war ended, however, almost all of these public enterprises ended. States, as sovereign republics, had embraced differing economic philosophies and legislation. Virginia employed a series of import duties and forced commerce through designated ports. It taxed goods coming from other states and from overseas at moderate rates. It also taxed exported tobacco, as had been the case before the war. Virginia feuded with Maryland over Potomac River oysters. The state supported several corporations for canal construction. Madison shepherded bills through the Assembly, at the behest of George Washington, for the formation of the James River Co. and the Potomac River Co. The state needed these semipublic ventures to improve transit around the various falls. During the war the state improved the waterway west of Richmond. In the 1780s it incorporated joint stock companies to make major navigational improvements. In 1787 Virginia and North Carolina both incorporated the Dismal Swamp Canal Co. to dig a ditch between the two states. The state of Virginia owned shares in the all these projects. The Assembly gave some shares from the Potomac and James River ventures to Washington, who in turn donated the James River shares to Liberty Hall Academy, soon called Washington College and later known as Washington and Lee. He also hoped the shares in the Potomac project might help develop a national university.

The war, however, slowed down public progress in education and treating the mentally ill. Just before the war the Assembly created and funded the Eastern State Lunatic Asylum, located at Williamsburg. Although the state continued to operate this agency, a traveler who visited the institution in 1796 found but 15 inmates, split between those with drinking problems and others bitten by excessive religious enthusiasm. What concerned him most was the lack of aggressive treatment of the patients. After the turn of the century, the facility would be reinvigorated as its patient load increased and a progressive doctor prescribed electric shocks and other up-to-date methods. It even admitted free blacks. The facility improved as the city, having lost its status as the state's capital and with its surrounding farms in trouble, declined. The state did little for the College of William and Mary. Jefferson, once a student there, tried to reform the curriculum, but the institution lost enrollment. A French traveler thought the state underfunded education and also complained that the school's leaders allowed the students to live off campus and thus lost control. By 1800 a number of free thinkers with long hair dominated the small student body. Although such folk did not disturb Jefferson, they likely did little to help the college.

A strong nationalist, Washington and other leaders realized the Confederation had numerous weaknesses, exacerbated by a downturn in the economy in the 1780s. Virginia's Assembly resolved to let the Congress impose a low uniform tariff for revenue but later repealed the measure. Having no direct way of raising taxes, Congress provided inadequate funding for its military or any domestic programs. Its navy ceased to exist, and its army proved incapable of suppressing Indians in the west. The ability of the Confederation to negotiate treaties was hamstrung by its overall weakness and by the fact that any state could stop the enforcement of treaties within its jurisdiction. Virginia, for example, refused to allow British agents to collect debts in the state for a number of years despite a clause in the Treaty of Paris (1783) that required it. Progress had been made in western lands. The Ordinance of 1784 set up a uniform way of distributing lands in the Northwest Territory and even provided future funding for education in the area. The Confederation

Congress agreed to Jefferson's proposal to stop slavery in the area with the Northwest Ordinance of 1787, a measure that established the procedure for creating states.

In 1786 Washington met delegates at Mount Vernon to suggest solutions, and five states, including Virginia, sent representatives to Annapolis to discuss the situation. James Madison played a major role during these negotiations. The next year Congress responded to complaints raised in these various meetings and asked all the states to send representatives to Philadelphia in May to revise the Articles of Confederation. At this convention, George Washington, as its chair, secured his desired stronger national government. The delegates quickly determined that a simple overhaul of the old frame of government would not suffice. The delegates took little time to determine the need to reduce the power of the states over commerce. Under the proposed constitution, only the new national government could tax commerce and coin currency. In a major concession to Virginians and other Southerners, the new national government could not put tariffs on exports, but it could collect revenue directly from the people without going through the states. Over the objections of George Mason, the constitution prevented any federal action against the international slave trade until 1808.

With Madison playing a critical role both in debate and keeping notes of the proceedings, the delegates determined that they needed a president who would not only be in charge of the military and foreign policy, but would also have the power to veto congressional action. By this point, nearly everyone agreed to a system of checks and balances based on three separate entities. All states, including Virginia, had an executive, a legislature, and a judiciary, but the role of each varied. The Confederation never had a judiciary. In addition, the relationship of the states to the new national government required checks and balances. For a time "the Father of the Constitution" considered giving Congress the power of disallowing state laws. Madison embodied many of his ideas in resolutions submitted by Governor Edmund Randolph. A portion of this "Virginia Plan" engendered prolonged debate. It proposed a bicameral Congress like Virginia's Assembly. The existing Congress had one chamber in which every state had but one vote, no matter the population. Population would determine representation to both bodies in the new legislature. Small states objected strenuously to this idea, and in the Great Compromise the delegates agreed to each state having two representatives in the Senate and a number in the House dependent on population. That necessitated the periodic collection of population data to determine the number of representatives from each state. In another compromise between Northerners and Southerners, five slaves would be counted as three free people. Even with but three-fifths of its slaves counted, Virginia would be the largest state in the new union, and would therefore be entitled to the greatest number of members in the House of Representatives. The delegates also agreed that the typical American was not informed or intelligent enough to vote directly for president. Under the new government, state legislatures controlled the right to vote for president. Virginia would permit its qualified voters to select electors. Those so chosen formed a college, presumably a group of upstanding citizens, who would then make independent decisions in voting for the president. Every state would have a number in the Electoral College consisting of two senators plus the number of representatives in the lower chamber.

The document needed to be ratified by nine states. Once ratified, the constitution provided for amendments through the action of Congress and three-fourths of the states. The Confederation required unanimous support from all states to change the frame of government. That defect had made it nearly impossible for the old government to change itself. Delegates at the convention knew from the outset of their session that the results of their work would have to go directly to the states for approval of their work.

By the time Virginia finished its ratification convention in Richmond in the summer of 1788 nine states had ratified the document. But had Virginia, the largest state not joined, the future of the federal government would certainly have been in doubt. A majority of Virginians opposed, or at the least had deep reservations about, the new constitution. Support for it could be found in the commercial towns and along the major rivers and generally throughout the northern parts of the state. Citizens of the coastal areas recognized the value of a strong navy and other positive effects of a stronger national government. Their representatives to the convention strongly favored the document. Delegates of the backcountry, including the Southside and Kentucky, opposed it. Frontiersmen worried that the new government would give away their right to trade on the Mississippi River to help eastern merchants expand opportunities to trade with Spain.

Federalists (those who favored the new constitution) triumphed. Their champion, George Washington, did not participate in the convention but urged support for the new constitution. He persuaded Randolph, who had refused to sign the document in Philadelphia, to help secure ratification. Pendleton, one of Virginia's most powerful politicians, chaired the session and favored the new government. War hero Henry "Light-Horse Harry" Lee and old George Wythe joined the advocates to help James Madison in the floor fight of his life. Madison, after serving as a delegate to the Confederation Congress, produced his part of the famous Federalist Papers, some of the greatest political philosophy ever written. One of Wythe's recent students, delegate John Marshall from Richmond, thought the creation of an independent federal judiciary would be a positive step. The anti-Federalists arrayed George Mason, Patrick Henry, George Grayson, and young James Monroe against the document. Mason, who had left the Philadelphia convention, totally dissatisfied, picked the proposed constitution to pieces. Henry roared for days at Richmond, through heat and thunderstorms. Despite the presence of reporters who took down his every word, Henry uttered nothing that stood the test of time. By instinct, Henry knew the new government had the potential to be as tyrannical as the monarchy had been. He twirled his wig with great vigor but could not convince his opponents that the document lacked sufficient checks on arbitrary power. Nevertheless, Madison had to promise that basic rights could be written into the document in the form of amendments. Some Baptists feared the new national government threatened their religious liberties recently obtained from the Virginia legislature and many delegates thought the instrument lacked sufficient guarantees for the rights of the states.

In the showdown the convention rejected Henry's idea that the constitution be renegotiated and approved the document by a vote of 89 to 79. Madison widened the margin when he persuaded three Kentuckians to support ratification, even though they had been instructed not to. Although the approval had a few strings attached regarding the rights of the states, these did not specifically allow for future secession, as some historians maintain. As a member of the first Congress, Madison made good on his promise to obtain amendments. Some, particularly the first, sound a great deal like Virginia's Declaration of Rights. The tenth reserved to the states, or to the people, powers not delegated to the national government by the Constitution nor prohibited by it to the states. Enough states approved these ten amendments to make them part of the Constitution in December 1791.

Patrick Henry, however, maneuvered to have Virginia send two anti-Federalists, William Grayson (later James Monroe) and Richard Henry Lee to the U.S. Senate, although Henry Lee, a supporter of the federal constitution, served as governor.

# Chapter 8

## Virginia and the New Federal Government

In 1789 the American people launched their new central government. The states that had ratified the document held elections in the fall of 1788. Washington received the unanimous support from the Electoral College for president. The new president and the duly elected members of the House and Senate met in New York to conduct the nation's business, but soon moved to Philadelphia. Jefferson became Washington's secretary of state and Edmund Randolph his attorney general, taking two of the five cabinet posts. Washington refused to accept any fancy title for the presidency.

Nearly everyone agreed to a federal import duty for revenue purposes, but the situation heated up in 1790, when New York's Alexander Hamilton, as the secretary of the treasury, proposed an ambitious program to pay off the old Confederation debt and assume the state debts. Madison argued against the first on the grounds that most of the people who had lent money to the national government no longer held the paper. Thus, when Hamilton proposed paying off the debts at face value, speculators, who had purchased the paper at considerably below face value, had a windfall. Hamilton hoped to help a particular class of businessmen with his plan. The treasurer's idea prevailed. Hamilton also got his way when the federal government assumed the state debts and paid them off at face value as well. Again Jefferson and Madison, who noted that Virginia had no debt for the federal government to pay, objected. Through a curious compromise that included the defection of some northern Virginians from Madison's camp, Congress approved the construction of the future capitol along the banks of the Potomac River and assumed the state debts. Hamilton's tax on whiskey also faced opposition when it passed in 1791. In that same year the federal government built the Cape Henry Lighthouse, the idea for which appeared almost sixty years earlier. The completion of this project not only provided an exceedingly practical device for mariners, but it also symbolized the success of the new federal government. Hamilton finished off his grand scheme with the establishment of the Bank of the United States. Taking the new notes of the refunded debt as collateral and some new federal coinage, Hamilton created a semipublic federal bank. Private shareholders and the federal government shared ownership and management of the new institution. The bank had the power to issue bank notes, well beyond the amount of gold and silver in its vaults, which could be used to pay federal taxes. It could also create branch banks with its parent bank being located in Philadelphia. Madison and Jefferson found numerous reasons to object to this enterprise. But Washington rejected Jefferson's assertion that the constitution did not expressly permit the federal government to create such a business and accepted Hamilton's doctrine of "implied powers" that rested on Article I, Section 8 that Congress had the power to provide for the general welfare of the nation and could make all laws "necessary and proper" to that end. Madison, railing against the threat of "consolidation," blocked Hamilton's proposal for a protective tariff, and joined with old anti-Federalists to creating a Republican Party. Their opponents soon became known as Federalists.

To worsen matters, Great Britain and France entered into another of their many wars. In the wake of that upheaval, Republicans in Virginia at first enthusiastically supported the French people in their efforts to throw off monarchy and strive for equality. Washington called for the United States to be neutral in the conflict, but many Virginians thought the United States had special obligations to France. Even when the French Revolution turned away from republicanism, most Virginia planters still favored the French. Pro-French mobs dominated the waterfront of Norfolk, even though Federalist merchants held political power in the borough.

Two events brought matters to a head in Washington's second term. Farmers in backcountry Pennsylvania rebelled against the whiskey tax in 1794. The president put down this uprising with the use of nationalized militiamen, bypassing the governor of the state in so doing. The rebels had all but disappeared by the time federalized forces arrived on the scene, but those who opposed federal power soon had another issue. The following year the president submitted the Jay Treaty to the Senate for ratification. In his negotiations with Great Britain, John Jay failed to obtain British recognition of neutral rights in the ongoing war with

France. He did secure a British promise to cease aiding the Indians and remove their forts in American territory below the Great Lakes, but American forces under General Anthony Wayne wiped out serious Native American resistance in the area at about the time Jay was obtaining this concession. Although the Senate approved the treaty, which incidentally contained the prospect that the federal government would pay some of the debts Virginians still owed British creditors, the House planned to prevent any funding for its initiation. Washington, however, put his entire prestige behind the document and saved the treaty.

By this point the Federalists and Republicans had grown from factions into political parties. Madison and Washington, one time close personal friends, were no longer on speaking terms. Washington ended his two terms in office with partisanship at high tide, even though he refused to join the Federalist camp. In 1796 Jefferson, as the leading Republican, ran against the heir apparent, Vice President John Adams, his old ally. The Federalist won narrowly. Virginia, of course, cast its electoral vote for its native son.

When the new president sent delegates to France to try to end the Revolutionary War alliance, representatives of that government demanded money to begin negotiations, leading to a quasi-war between the two countries. As ships of each nation attacked each other, the United States began to build its first navy. Fearing a French invasion, the nation paid for this arms buildup with a series of direct taxes, including a tax on property. Virginia planters, who had a penchant for fancy carriages, complained bitterly about a tax on such conveyances.

Worried about foreigners as well as critics of any sort, Congress and the president approved the Alien and Sedition Acts. The Alien Acts comprised several measures to allow the president to deport foreigners, differentiating these from nations deemed friendly or unfriendly. The Sedition Act made it a crime to make derogatory statements about the president and a number of federal officeholders, excluding Vice President Jefferson. Critics of the Adams administration were in danger wherever Federalists controlled the government. James Callender, a particularly avid critic, fled Philadelphia for the supposed safe haven of Republican Virginia, only to be nabbed in Richmond, where Federalists ran the courts. A Supreme Court Justice handpicked a Federalist jury who found Callender guilty. The justice fined him $200 in June 1800 and sent him to the Richmond penitentiary for six months. Republicans complained but had little recourse. An appeal of the verdict to the Federalist Supreme Court would avail nothing. Jefferson raised money to pay for Callender's fine, but later, when Jefferson had become president and refused the Scotsman a federal job, he published accounts of Jefferson's relationship with Sally Hemings, the mulatto half-sister of his wife.

In one of the odder aspects of the political situation, Patrick Henry came out in support of the federal government, likely the only old anti-Federalist to do so. In 1788 Patrick Henry had expressed profound fears about the potential use of the "necessary and proper" and "general welfare" clauses in the constitution. At the time Madison assured the convention that the new federal government would not exercise power not expressly granted to it, but in the ensuing years, the federal government added to its powers as it diminished those of the states. Virginia's legislature passed resolves against the various components of Hamilton's financial plan and the Virginia Doctrine consistently opposed consolidation of federal power. In 1798 Republican legislators of Virginia and Kentucky took action. John Taylor of Caroline submitted a resolution, drawn up by Madison, to the Virginia legislature that condemned the Alien and Sedition Acts. Citing the 1st and 10th Amendments, plus clauses in the original constitution, Virginians approved a ringing indictment, though it decided against calling for the possible nullification of the acts, as the Kentucky Resolve, secretly written by Jefferson, suggested. The Virginia and Kentucky Resolutions looked to the other states for redress. They also considered the possibility that Article 5 in the Constitution gave the states the right to review federal acts in lieu of a recalcitrant Supreme Court. The Federalists helped stop more extreme language in Virginia, but the overall measure passed over their objections 100 to 62 in the House and 14 to 3 in the Senate. The Virginia Republicans rejected the Federalist idea that Virginia's own laws regarding aliens and slander differed but little from the federal versions on the grounds that the First Amendment clearly stated that the federal government could not infringe on the rights of the people. Passed in December, the resolution became part of what Virginians called "the principles of 1798."

In 1800 Jefferson ran for president on his record as a champion of the rights of the states and the people. The Federalists argued that Jefferson was an atheist and an infidel. When the incumbent Adams negotiated an end of the treaty with France and thus terminated the quasi-war against that country, the Federalist-induced hysteria disappeared. When the Federalist coercive measures proved to have been unnecessary, the Republicans carried the election by a close margin. Jefferson's running mate, Aaron Burr, received as many electoral votes as Jefferson did, and thus the election went to the House of Representatives. Federalists, facing a choice between Burr and Jefferson, voted for the Virginian. With the peaceful Revolution of 1800, for the first time in American political history, one political party replaced another in control of Congress and the presidency.

The new century opened an unusual era for Virginia and the nation. Starting in 1801 a Republican from Virginia would occupy the presidency for the next 24 years. Thomas Jefferson, James Madison, and James Monroe, all born and raised in and residents of the Old Dominion, would serve two successive terms each. As the largest state, Virginia had the most electoral votes and the most congressmen. It seemed only natural for Republicans to look to the Old Dominion for leadership, especially because the state had a knack for producing such outstanding political leaders. So influential were the Virginians that some New England Federalists during the War of 1812 sought a constitutional amendment that to prevent two successive presidents from the same state.

The Republican Party depended on organizations spread across the country, including a group of Virginians commonly, but perhaps mistakenly, called the Richmond Junto. It included the editor of the *Richmond Enquirer*, Thomas Ritchie, the president of the Bank of Virginia, Dr. John Brockenbrough, and Judge Spencer Roane, all natives of Essex County. Ritchie's newspaper benefited from state printing contracts. Brockenbrough headed the state bank, chartered in 1803, to compete against the federal bank. Roane, head of the court of appeals, constantly advocated the rights of the states. Each party used a caucus system of congressmen and legislators to choose candidates for various posts. The regular Republicans eventually took the name "Democrat."

Jefferson opened his terms in office with a conciliatory message to the Federalists. Because Adams, through diplomacy, had ended the fracas with France, the new president and his political allies saw no need to spend additional money on new ships, even though the pirates of Tripoli posed a threat. The need for high excise and federal property taxes disappeared as the nation paid off its debt through revenue tariffs and land sales. The Alien and Sedition Acts required no action, as they had expired when Jefferson took office. Jefferson let the Bank of the United States run its course.

A disquieting note in Federalist-Republican relations arose in Jefferson's first term. Just before leaving office, John Adams appointed John Marshall as chief justice of the Supreme Court. He also named several lower-level judges. On taking power, the Republicans repealed the Judiciary Act under which the latter appointments were made. A disappointed office seeker sued Secretary of State James Madison for his commission as a justice in the District of Columbia. In the *Marbury v Madison* of 1803, the Marshall court decided that the act under which William Marbury received his appointment was unconstitutional. Although this decision seemed to be a victory for the administration, Jefferson and other Republicans fretted about Marshall's establishment of the principle of Judicial Review.

Jefferson enjoyed good fortune when Napoleon Bonaparte sold all of French Louisiana to the United States in 1803. The emperor had recently acquired a sizeable chunk of North America from Spain with the intention of reviving France's interests in the New World. But when the French failed to retake Haiti and, with renewed war in Europe pending, Napoleon sold the territory for $15,000,000. American diplomats had been instructed to buy only New Orleans and its adjacent territory so American goods could pass unobstructed to the Gulf of Mexico. Virginian James Monroe and another negotiator agreed to the much better offer of the entire territory. After some misgivings over the constitutionality of the deal, Jefferson accepted the purchase of Louisiana. In May 1804 he sent Virginians Meriwether Lewis and William Clark to reconnoiter the western rivers, find a path to the Pacific Ocean, and report on the people and other resources of the new territory.

Jefferson's second term was less successful than his first. Two embarrassing court cases went against him. In one, the administration failed to have an obnoxious judge, who had trampled over the rights of Republican newspaper editors, impeached by the Senate. John Randolph of Roanoke failed to make the prosecution's case. And in the infamous Burr Trial, John Marshall thwarted Jefferson's effort to have the former vice president found guilty of treason. Burr had become a loose cannon after the presidential election in 1800. After killing Hamilton in a duel, he conspired to form a new nation out of parts of New Spain and the United States. The commander of American troops in the affected area joined the conspiracy but then disclosed the plot. In 1807 Jefferson had Burr brought to trial in Richmond. John Marshall picked John Randolph, who had recently become antagonistic toward Jefferson, as foreman of the jury. After Marshall pointed out that the prosecution failed to produce two witnesses to each part of the indictment for treason against Burr and asking exactly what constituted "levying war" against the United States, the jury found Burr not guilty.

As the trial proceeded, the commander of the British ship *HMS Leopard* launched an unprovoked attack on the *USS Chesapeake*. Once war between France and Great Britain resumed in 1803, the British imposed severe restrictions on American trade and also regularly took American seamen from American ships (called impressments) in order to fill out their shorthanded crews. In June 1807, commodore James Barron, a native Virginian and resident of Norfolk, took charge of the refitted Chesapeake, then anchored near the old Gosport Shipyard, now owned by the federal government. One of the Federalist-financed frigates built during the quasi-war with France, the vessel went to sea, without a readiness check. A few miles off the Capes, the Leopard lay in wait. After a brief parley, during which Baron refused to turn over alleged deserters from the British vessel, the British opened fire, raking the deck and killing several crewmen of the unprepared American ship, which soon surrendered. The British boarded and carried off several crewmen, including at least one black, under the curious claim that anyone who had served in His Majesty's Navy was automatically British. The stricken ship limped back to Norfolk. Several thousand angry Norfolk residents attended the funeral of one of the victims.

Prior to this incident, when James Monroe failed in his efforts to modify the Jay Treaty, which expired in 1805, Congress drew up measures to cut off British imports into the United States. Knowing the country was unprepared for war (thanks to his own policies), Jefferson accepted a British half-hearted apology and called not for war but for peaceful coercion in the form of an embargo against all exports. Under this scheme, imports would also die a natural death. Some shippers avoided the restrictions, but it was sufficiently enforced so that several ports virtually shut down. With but limited coastal business, the borough of Norfolk hired dozens of unemployed seamen to sew cloth and its slaves to dig the Dismal Swamp canal. Idled workmen and ships predominated.

During the year of the embargo (1808) the nation elected Madison the next president. That "Little Jimmy" won the office so easily in the year of a depression caused directly by the party for which he served as secretary of state testifies to just how far the Federalists had fallen in their battle of ideas with the Republicans. Only coastal New England and a handful of localities still favored Federalists. Even the congressman from Norfolk now belonged to the Republican Party, although he considered himself a nationalist. The only real opposition to Madison could be found within the ranks of the Republicans, who led by John Randolph, wanted James Monroe to be president.

Madison's tenure in office proved less than sanguine. The great political philosopher lacked decisiveness, and both the British and the French played him for a fool. As he took office, Congress repealed the Embargo and replaced it with a Non-Intercourse Act, which opened trade with all nations except Britain and France. When that policy didn't produce the desired result, Congress turned to the brilliantly conceived but flawed in practice Macon's Bill #2 that reopened trade with everyone. It threatened, however, to close off commerce with either France or Britain should the other agree to American terms of neutrality. Napoleon indicated that he might allow American ships to enter France after they obeyed British rules by going through England. As Madison prepared to cut off commerce with Great Britain, the French seized dozens of Virginia ships.

71

Oddly enough, although the British belatedly rescinded the most obnoxious of their orders, Congress, led by "War Hawks," such as Virginia-born Henry Clay of Kentucky, declared war in June 1812. Supposedly upset that American soldiers found British weapons on the battlefield after a victory over the Indians in Indiana Territory in 1811, young congressmen called for war in order to acquire British Canada and Spanish Florida (Britain was an ally of Spain at the time). Complaining about the loss of maritime rights, Madison asked for a war declaration. Much of the maritime part of the country and John Randolph objected, but the measure passed. The Virginia legislature demanded and received Randolph's resignation, but he went to the House of Representatives. Madison won the presidential reelection over a fellow Republican in the fall as "Mr. Madison's War" got underway.

Because Americas were still unprepared for war, efforts to capture Canada fizzled, but the small U.S. Navy excelled as commerce raiders, and Britain's concerns about Napoleon saved the United States from total defeat. Even so, a British fleet drove the *USS Constellation* (a frigate) into Norfolk harbor in 1813. As the British established a blockade of the Chesapeake Bay, militiamen flocked to Norfolk under the command of Robert B. Taylor. Anchored at Lynnhaven Bay, the British skirmished with the militia as they sent parties ashore for provisions. The British then launched an attack similar to the one in 1779, planning to take control of the Elizabeth River and destroy the shipyard and the federal frigate. With Fort Norfolk (built in 1794) and Fort Nelson, a chain of gunboats, and a swampy terrain protecting Norfolk and Portsmouth, Taylor forced the British to try to conquer Craney Island. Hundreds of militia and sailors from the federal ship, adept in the use of canons, drove back a two-pronged attack on the island. Unable to bring their big guns into shallow water, the British tried an amphibious landing with some 1,500 troops, only to be repulsed, with heavy loss. When the captain's barge sank, the British withdrew and their enraged troops sacked Hampton.

Although the Virginia militia and the U.S. Navy won one of the few American victories during the war, the blockade forced Virginia trade through South Quay on a river that went to Albemarle Sound, where swift schooners did business with the West Indies. In June 1814, a 20-ton, double-decked vessel brought brandy and bacon from North Carolina to Norfolk to signify the opening of the Dismal Swamp Canal. Virginia now had a fairly secure inland water route. Unfortunately, seizures in the bay or on the ocean remained likely. To complicate matters the Madison administration passed another embargo late in 1813 and then curtailed the James River trade into Norfolk, to prevent the British from seizing it. Some merchants persisted in bucking the law and the British, but commercial activity virtually ceased for over a year. In early 1815 one could find "no rum puncheons, no…hogsheads, no bawling Negroes, no drays passing" in downtown Norfolk. Save for dram shops the place seemed deserted.

In early 1815 the second war against Great Britain officially ended. Word did not reach the British in time to prevent their biggest loss near New Orleans. That victory offset several defeats for the Americans, which included the loss of the *USS Chesapeake* off Boston and the burning of the public buildings in the District of Columbia, where Dolley Madison saved precious relics as she left the presidential mansion. In the aftermath of the war, Madison and the Republicans embarked on nationalist programs. With the rival Federalists virtually dead, the Republicans resurrected several of Hamilton's ideas about a national bank, protective tariffs, public works, state and national debts, and a strong military. Deciding the nation could use a national bank, whose charter had been allowed to expire in 1811 against Madison's protests, they now created a second bank, nearly identically to the first one. Madison also changed his mind about the assumption of state debts and the protective tariff, which even Hamilton had been unable to have Congress approve. It did so now with alacrity, as American producers of iron and textiles needed protection from an expected glut of British products. Virginia's congressional delegation opposed the move, but even some parts of the Old Dominion (the Valley, Wheeling, and Petersburg) favored protection. Both Madison and Jefferson, as early as 1807, believed federal public works programs had merit, but constitutional scruples prevented Madison and Monroe from favoring full funding.

In addition, under Madison, the nation started to improve its military defenses, planning to build a bigger navy in the belief that another war with Great Britain or another European power seemed likely. The Norfolk Navy Yard built the 74-gun *USS Delaware* in the years immediately following the war. It required the services of hundreds of workmen and took several years to complete. Hampton Roads also profited from the construction of Forts Monroe and Calhoun. The two forts would make it unlikely that any future foreign enemy could enter the Roads.

As Madison stepped out of office in March 1817, his replacement, James Monroe, the third consecutive Virginian to serve as president, took over. Known as the "last of the cocked hats" for being a bit old fashioned, Monroe inherited an "Era of Good Feelings," called such because only one political party existed, thus ending partisan strife. Like Madison, Monroe had doubts about additional federal funding for internal improvements, but he had pursued a long political road since being an anti-Federalist delegate at the Virginia ratification convention in 1788. Extensive work as a diplomat had made him think in more national terms or even international terms, but neither Madison nor Monroe sanctioned the work of the most extreme nationalist from Virginia—John Marshall.

As chief justice, Marshall's decisions conflicted directly with the prevailing political sentiment in Virginia. The Marshall court, absent the Chief Justice, who had a conflict of interest, took issue with a verdict of the Virginia Court of Appeals, *Martin v Hunter Lessee* (1816). A complicated matter, the case dealt with the disposition of the old Fairfax claims in Virginia. Spencer Roane and others resisted the national court's encroachment on the rights of the state. Thomas Ritchie wrote several letters under the alias "Hampden," reviewing Marshall's decisions and urging his fellow Virginians to adhere to the "principles of 1798." Virginia never did accept the verdict in the Hunter case. A few years later, members of the Cohen family sold tickets for a lottery set up by Congress to raise money for a municipal building in the District of Columbia. Virginia law allowed only lotteries authorized by the state. The Marshall court sustained the state court of appeals decision in *Cohens v Virginia* (1821), but the Virginia House of Delegates resolved 138 to 18 that the Supreme Court had no constitutional jurisdiction in the first place. During arguments over the case, lawyers debated Article III and the 11th Amendment, but the Supreme Court contended that Congress had not intended to create an interstate lottery. In 1819 the Marshall's court rendered the Bank of the United States constitutional (*McCulloch v Maryland*). Marshall argued that the "power to tax is the power to destroy," invalidating Maryland's efforts to tax the notes of the national bank, an institution that Congress wanted to function interstate. Many Virginians considered this decision simply one more attack on the rights of the states.

The Era of Good Feelings was also troubled by a major downturn in the economy as a result of the financial panic of 1819 and the rise of the issue of slavery. Many businessmen in the state's major cities went to jail for failure to pay debts. That same year, the question of slavery in Missouri arose. Following the second war against Britain, several thousand Virginians and others migrated into the Missouri territory, part of the original Louisiana Purchase. Congress resolved the problem by having Maine enter the union as a free state and ending slavery in the bulk of the rest of the Louisiana area. The Compromise of 1820 ended that particular crisis.

In that year Monroe won a second term without opposition, receiving all but one vote in the Electoral College. In 1823 Secretary of State John Quincy Adams wrote the Monroe Doctrine, which Monroe issued in the wake of rebellion in Spanish possessions in the New World. The United States recognized several new republics, and desiring to open up commerce, Monroe and Adams, with the support of the British navy, put the Western Hemisphere off limits to future European colonization efforts. This program became a cornerstone of American foreign policy. With Monroe's departure from the presidency in 1825, the era of the Virginia Dynasty ended. A symbolic end of the era occurred the next year (1826), when on July 4, fifty years to the day of the approval of the Declaration of Independence, both John Adams and Thomas Jefferson died.

In 1824 traditional politics returned, when Andrew Jackson, the hero of the Battle of New Orleans, received a plurality of the votes, both popular and electorally. Few people really knew where Old Hickory stood on the issues, but John Q. Adams and Henry Clay split the nationalist vote. The only states' rights candidate carried Virginia, but did not do well elsewhere. In the vote in the House, Adams won with the help of Clay, whom Adams appointed secretary of state. Jackson, thinking he had been cheated by a "corrupt bargain," prepared to run again. At about the time Jefferson died in 1826, New York politician Martin Van Buren circulated among the Jefferson Republicans to organize opposition against President John Quincy

Adams. He touched base with Thomas Ritchie to bring the Virginians on board. Called the Old Republicans, they launched their campaign to elect Andrew Jackson. Their rivals led by Adams, Clay, and Daniel Webster called themselves National Republicans. John Randolph of Roanoke did what he could as one of Virginia's senators for the Old Republicans. During a debate over sending representatives to a meeting in Panama where Americans might sit with black delegates from Haiti, the eccentric Randolph, having read the novel *Tom Jones*, claimed that the union of Adams and Clay reminded him of the alliance between "Blifill and Black George." In Fielding's story, Blifill was an effeminate scoundrel who cheated the hero out of his inheritance, and Black George was a poacher. The insulted Clay challenged Randolph to a duel. On the outskirts of Washington D.C., Clay's shot went into Randolph's coat, and Randolph shot into the air, as he later explained, so as not to make orphans of Clay's children.

In the bitterest election to date, Jackson defeated the incumbent Adams, the candidate of the National Republicans, in 1828. In Virginia the absurdly high protective tariff of that year and the president's propensity to fund federal public works were two primary issues. The administration also mishandled negotiations to reopen trade with the British West Indies, thus injuring Virginia's ports. The coastal residents voted for the nationalist ticket, but by a smaller margin than usual, and the state as a whole backed the challenger overwhelmingly. The Virginia legislature passed resolves opposing federal public works in 1826 and once again reminded everyone of the "principles of 1798." Downstate Virginians were especially troubled by the Chesapeake and Ohio Canal, which helped a few Virginians in the northern reaches of the state but tended to divert commerce out of the Old Dominion. The federal government had also invested in the Dismal Swamp Canal enlargement. The parts of Virginia that benefited from these projects had National Republicans as Congressmen. In the rest of the state Old Republicans prevailed. In 1826, 1827, and again in 1829 the Virginia legislature formally protested the protective tariff. Some western Virginians and the owners of the new textile mills in Petersburg appreciated the benefits of protection, but the state as a whole saw the northeastern United States, as it industrialized faster than the South, gaining the most from the nationalistic program. Thus Virginia stood to gain if they could remove the National Republican from office.

Jackson easily carried the state. In some southwestern counties the old war hero received hundreds of votes and Adams garnered numbers in the single digits. Officeholders such as Moses Myers, the customs collector in Norfolk who favored Adams, soon lost their federal jobs.

In two terms in office Jackson proved to be a strong exponent of states' rights. The new president beat back efforts to put federal money into canals and roads, worked to lower the tariff, fought and defeated the existing national bank and prevented the extension of its charter, and allowed the state of Georgia to have authority over the Cherokee Indians, though Chief Justice Marshall rendered an opposite opinion. Marshall could have his opinion, as far as Jackson was concerned, but he had no way to enforce it. Marshall declared the Bank of the United States constitutional, and Jackson said it was not. Having been elected by the people, Old Hickory had his way on both issues.

Although Jackson looked like a true champion of states' rights, the views of the man from Tennessee fell short of what some advocates for that policy wanted. Vice President John C. Calhoun argued that a state had the right to nullify federal acts. By the spring of 1830 Jackson made it clear that on this single issue he stood with nationalists, when, in his most famous toast, he said "Our Federal Union—it must be preserved." Calhoun and Jackson had already had a falling out over etiquette and now the South Carolinian resigned as the president purged his cabinet of malcontents. Jackson stood for reelection in 1832 opposed principally by Virginia-born Henry Clay, a National Republican from Kentucky. Knowing Old Hickory now stood for the union, South Carolina cast its electoral vote for Governor John Floyd of Virginia, recognizing him as sympathetic to their ideas.

In that same election, William Wirt, a former federal attorney general and a lawyer from Virginia, accepted the nomination of the Anti-Masons. The disappearance and subsequent cover up of the apparent killing of a critic of Freemasons in upstate New York (the victim was a Virginian) spawned a third political party in the presidential election. Jackson, at one time Grand Master of Tennessee, refused to drop his fraternal affiliation, and Clay, who had once led the Freemasons in Kentucky, claimed to have no current connection to them but refused to denounce the order. In hopes of later securing support from National Republicans, Wirt accepted the nomination tendered to him at a Baltimore meeting of Anti-Masons in the first political party convention ever held in the country. When the National Republicans nominated Clay, the anti-Jackson vote remained divided, thus dooming Wirt's scheme. But even if all of Jackson's enemies had presented a united front, they could not unseat the popular incumbent. Wirt took the electoral vote of Vermont and picked up a handful of popular votes in Rockbridge County, among a few Presbyterians worried about Freemasons. Virginians, on the whole, did not make religious and social matters political, and they enthusiastically supported the "Old Warrior."

Following the election, South Carolina set a date for nullifying the collection of any tariffs in the state, despite the fact that Jackson had approved a measure in 1832 to lower rates. A crisis loomed as Jackson called for Congress to give him the power to put down the potential insurrection. With Henry Clay's help, Congress approved both a Force Bill and another tariff bill to lower import duties gradually, both to take effect on the same day in 1833. The Compromise of 1833 succeeded, when South Carolina rescinded its ordinance of nullification, but the Palmetto State nullified the Force Act in a meaningless gesture.

Virginia's role during this crisis is instructive in trying to estimate how far the doctrine of states' rights could be carried. John Floyd, the governor of Virginia, supported Calhoun, but the legislature was divided over the issue. By a large majority the Assembly resolved that the Principles of '98 had little resemblance to South Carolina's doctrine of nullification. If nothing else, the former dealt with civil liberties, the latter with tariffs. Floyd seemed eager to take to the field against the federal authorities, but Jackson said that he would meet Governor Floyd at the head of his troops and arrest him. It is very doubtful that Floyd could have mustered any meaningful number of militiamen to fight Old Hickory. The legislature narrowly defeated a resolution to support the president's Force Act. Virginia's two senators split over the issue, with John Tyler casting one of the few votes against the measure. Virginians thought the South Carolinians were wrong but did not want to be put into a position to put down a rebellion. Some, like Tyler, thought Jackson was too headstrong. James Madison argued that neither nullification nor secession from the national government was possible. Although some Virginia legislators muttered that the aged Madison might be losing his grip, they really did not want to tackle the ticklish question of the validity of secession. While all this was going on, the Virginia legislature was debating the merits of adopting a program to end slavery in the Old Dominion, with the more democratic-minded westerners pushing reform. Eastern Virginians certainly recognized a connection between the issue of slavery and nullification or secession. If the federal government could block action against a tariff, could it not take action against domestic slavery?

A number of extreme states' rights Virginia politicians, most all of them in the eastern half of the state, broke with the Old Republicans over Nullification and the Force Act. A greater number of Virginia's leaders left the Old Hero over his handling of the banking question. In 1832 Jackson vetoed a plan to extend the charter of the national bank. Clay made that his central issue in his losing bid for the presidency that year. Not satisfied with leaving well enough alone with the bank charter due to expire in 1836, the reelected president went after the institution, largely because his rivals had used its money against him. In 1834 Jackson hired and fired two treasury secretaries before he found one (Roger Taney) who would remove federal deposits from the national bank and put them in approved "pet" state banks, such as the Bank of Virginia. That the Senate never confirmed Taney deterred neither Jackson nor Taney. The Senate, back in session, censured Jackson for his conduct.

Dozens of leading Republicans in Virginia left the party—John Tyler, Littleton Tazewell, and Thomas Gilmer, among others. They formed the Whig Party in opposition to "King" Andrew's dictatorial practices. For any other politician such defection would signal the end of power. But in Old Hickory's case it did not matter. The Jacksonians, now called Democrats, lost control of the House of Delegates in 1834, but regained it in 1835 and increased their hold through 1837. Gilmer lost his seat from Albemarle County, a position he won and lost several times over the next few years. John Tyler resigned as senator from Virginia. His replacement, with help from other senators, expunged the censure statement from the pages of the Senate journal. More importantly, Van Buren, Jackson's vice president and his handpicked successor, rolled to victory in Virginia and across the nation in 1836. Neither Henry Clay nor any Whig, individually or collectively, could match Thomas Ritchie, in getting out the vote for the Democratic Party. Nathaniel Beverley Tucker wrote *The Partisan Leader* that election year. In that novel he forecast a Virginia-led rebellion against the dictatorial Van Buren in 1849. The war would be fought in the mountains of the Old Dominion. The rebels, after a minimum of bloodshed, would emerge victorious. Virginia would then join an existing southern confederacy. Reality turned out to be quite different. The New Yorker took office in 1837 only to have commercial markets collapse. In the year before he left office Jackson stemmed the flow of state bank notes in an overheated economy by requiring that all federal land be bought with specie (gold and silver coins). Its charter having expired, the Bank of the United States, once a restraining influence on the state banks, no longer existed as a federal institution. Jackson's measure cut land sales almost immediately and fostered a panic.

Because the business cycle tended to produce a depression every 15 or 20 years, the economy might well have been due to enter hard times anyway, but Van Buren had neither the skills nor the inclination to deal with the crisis. Many Northern Whigs thought the federal government capable of intervening, but states' rights Democrats could not visualize any major government action on either state or federal levels. Van Buren's short-run solution was to separate the federal government from banking as much as possible. After extensive debate, he secured an Independent Treasury Act, which severed, at least theoretically, the federal government from the state banks.

Under the Virginia branch-banking scheme, the state had the Bank of Virginia, established in 1803, and the Farmers' Bank, formed in 1812 just after the first Bank of the United States went out of business. Headquartered in Richmond, they both had branches in places like Norfolk, Fredericksburg, and Petersburg. In 1816, facing numerous complaints from the west, the legislature authorized a Bank of the Valley, with its parent bank at Winchester, and another with headquarters in Wheeling. In the 1830s the state allowed Norfolk its own parent bank, belatedly responding to charges that the Richmond banking interests abused their power to keep Norfolk down. Each parent and branch had the capacity to issue paper money based on specie reserves. During the financial crisis, Virginia politicians debated whether to allow the state banks to distribute paper money without paying specie on demand. During the banking crisis of the late 1830s and early 1840s, the legislature kept passing and rescinding the right to issue paper. Although hard-money Democrats, called Locofocos, demanded specie payments, the House of Delegates, where Whigs now outnumbered Democrats, and in the almost evenly divided senate a number of conservative Democrats, gave the banks several exemptions to paying specie. They also cooperated with Whigs in opposing Van Buren's subtreasury and in picking a succession of Whigs to be governors.

In the "log cabin and hard cider" campaign, Van Buren faced William Henry Harrison, the onetime general known for his victory over natives at Tippecanoe. The Whigs emphasized his lowly origins and drinking habits even though he was born in a mansion on the James River. Balancing their ticket with a states' rights representative from Virginia, they campaigned as "Tippecanoe and Tyler, too." Doing everything possible to win, they even brought Daniel Webster to Richmond to speak to an audience composed largely of women. The ticket carried much of the nation but not Virginia, despite the fact that Harrison was a native son and Tyler a popular Virginian. Even amid a weakened economy, Virginia voted, albeit in a fairly close election, for the Democrat. They voted for the New Yorker, because, among other considerations, Van Buren was considered safe on the slavery issue. In the Amistad affair, he tried to have slaves who escaped from Spanish jurisdiction returned to their former owners. Such behavior endeared him to Virginia slaveholders, who tried to keep word about this incident from their slaves for fear that it might give them ideas. In 1848, long after his presidency, the Little Magician switched positions and campaigned against allowing any slaves in the territories.

During this time, Virginians argued with the state of New York over the latter's refusal to turn over three free blacks suspected of aiding a Virginia slave escape. Governor Gilmer sent one lengthy letter after another to New York's governor. Finally, in response, having heard all about the rights of states, that worthy claimed he was upholding the right of the state of New York. When New York refused to extradite the three fugitives, Gilmer retaliated by failing to send an accused forger to the northern state. Failing to receive full support from the Virginia legislature on the issue, Gilmer resigned and took a seat in Congress.

When Harrison died soon after his inaugural, Tyler became the first vice president to assume the presidency on the death of his predecessor, but "His Accidency" soon ran into trouble. Like many Virginia Whigs, Tyler advocated the rights of the states and opposed a national bank, protective tariffs, and federal internal improvements. Henry Clay, the leading Whig in the Senate, favored all three of these programs as part of his American System. Most nationalist Whigs, including the Virginian John Minor Botts, supported Clay's ideas. Although Tyler was willing to cancel Van Buren's Independent Treasury program, he opposed the recreation of the old Bank of the United States or anything that remotely resembled it. Nothing Clay constructed met Tyler's demands. Botts became so irritated with his fellow Virginian that he called for the president's impeachment. Tyler soothed feelings by agreeing to keep the last vestige of the protective tariff and permitting a distribution of funds to the states for public works. All of Tyler's cabinet resigned, save Daniel Webster, engaged with the British in delicate negotiations. As soon as those were completed, Webster handed in his resignation. Tyler found cabinet replacements from the ranks of independent Whigs like himself or Democrats.

Several states' rights Whigs from Virginia served his administration, including Abel Upshur as Secretary of the Navy. When Upshur became Secretary of State, Thomas Gilmer replaced him as Secretary of the Navy. A defective cannon exploding on the *USS Princeton* killed both men. Tyler escaped injury when he went below deck to tend to the needs of young Julia Gardiner. Tyler replaced Upshur with John C. Calhoun to continue negotiations to annex Texas. He later brought in John Y. Mason to replace Gilmer apparently determined to have a Virginian serve as Secretary of the Navy. Less than a year after the Princeton incident, Tyler married fair Julia.

Although Tyler could be admired for his romantic qualities, Whigs had no intention of supporting him in the election of 1844. Some Democrats thought of making him their candidate, but his earlier break from the Jacksonians made that an absurdity. In the end they chose James Polk, "Young Hickory" from Tennessee. As president, Polk renewed the Independent Treasury, lowered tariffs so that no one could find a bit of protection in them, and ended even the slightest possibility of federal funding for transportation. This anti-federal program remained in place until the eve of the Civil War, to the general satisfaction of most Virginians, especially the Democrats.

The voting habits of most Virginians were fairly predictable throughout this era, with location determining a great deal. Some counties were neatly divided in two, with those that possessed better croplands and, therefore, more slaves and higher incomes more likely to vote Whig. A religious or ethnic set of mind also helped determined the vote. Episcopalians and Presbyterians tended to be Whig, but they also tended to be wealthier, thus making it difficult to infer too much from the trend. Methodists usually voted Democrat, though that depended on location and occupation. German Lutherans in the Valley of Virginia were said to vote for Jackson long after his departure from the White House. Scots-Irish Presbyterians usually voted Whig. Whigs generally thought the law could upgrade human conduct; the Democrats tended to think improvement came from within the individual.

Democrats inherited the old Jeffersonian middle-class farmers. Most businessmen in Norfolk, Petersburg, Lynchburg, and Richmond voted Whig as did prosperous planters. Skilled workingmen tended to be Democrats. Whigs could not have functioned without the support of some middle-class producers, but in the division of that vote the Democrats usually emerged with a decided edge, particularly in more remote areas.

In the 1840s the electorate began to vote for parties more than for candidates and their personal reputations. Legislators learned to toe the line as their organizations took positions. Elections provided a great deal of excitement and much expertise. Party managers knew how votes were likely to turn out based on limited returns. That elections took place over several weeks often made these events even more exciting. The practice of voting by voice allowed campaign managers who paid voters to be sure of a return for their investment.

# Chapter 9

## The Role of State Government

From the time of the Revolution until the Civil War, Virginia conservatives, especially in the eastern part of the state, succeeded in slowing down political change. Thus Virginia fell behind most states in adapting to meet changing times. This trend can be observed in altering the state's constitution but curiously not in the matter of the role of the state in developing public works.

In both houses representation failed to keep up with demographic changes. Early on, Jefferson pointed out that Warwick County, with 100 fighting men, had the same number (two) of delegates to the lower house as Loudoun County did with 1,700 militiamen. In 1816 a gathering of dignitaries in Staunton also pointed out that the small Tidewater counties had a disproportionate share of representation. With greater representation, Westerners thought they could obtain a fairer distribution of state funding for public works such as canals and highways. Another meeting at Staunton in 1825 came to the same conclusion. John Tyler from tiny Charles City County in the Tidewater urged Westerners to subdivide their counties and thereby gain more representation, but nothing came from this idea.

Westerners and some people in the east also thought the property restrictions on the right to vote put Virginia out of step with the rest of the country. Virginia remained one of the few states that required property ownership to entitle one to vote for both branches of the legislature. The self-perpetuating and, therefore, undemocratic nature of the county court system also distressed reformers. In 1828 the Assembly submitted the matter of revising the state constitution to the qualified voters, who by a margin of 21,896 to 16,632 agreed to a convention. A large majority of Easterners voted in the negative whereas an even larger majority of Westerners favored the convention. Almost 90% of the Valley and nearly 80% of the Trans-Allegheny favored constitutional revision. In the East, the borough of Norfolk proved to be an exception, as it voted 144 to 102 for the convention. The East, with some exceptions, voted solidly for conservatives; the west generally voted in reformers.

In 1829 the two sides conflicted at what came to be called the "Last Gathering of Giants," as James Madison, James Monroe, and John Randolph made their last appearances at a public forum. John Marshall, another "giant," represented the Richmond district to add to the prestige of the event. The chief justice still wore knee breeches and his hair in a queue. Madison had given up his wig but still powdered his hair. Presumably Monroe took off his cocked hat as he entered the hall. In virtually everything he wore, rode, and said Randolph represented the England of before the American Revolution. It was also the "last hurrah" for William Branch Giles, the one-time ally of Jefferson and Madison, who helped found the Republican Party. Like Randolph he had broken with Jefferson for not attacking Federalists and their ideas vigorously enough. He had also opposed Madison over the war against Great Britain. Giles had recently served as governor of the state. Some conservatives and many reformers vied with each other in putting down Federalist ideas and claiming Jefferson as their champion. Marshall, Randolph, and several others found no need to be enthralled with the notions of the departed wise man from Monticello.

Madison and Monroe acted as moderates at the convention, but Marshall, Randolph, and a number of younger eastern politicians resisted change. Madison, barely audible, could no longer carry on a floor fight. Monroe served as chair for a time (but resigned due to illness) and figured out a reasonable compromise on the major issue, but neither Randolph nor any other conservative would accept it. Marshall, chair of the committee on local government, rejected any modifications of the current system, thereby keeping democracy at bay in Virginia local government for another generation.

Abel Upshur presented the eastern argument against a drastic change in representation. The Eastern Shore man saw "two kinds of majority, one of interest as well as a majority in numbers." If only numbers counted, he maintained, women, children, paupers, and slaves should have the right to vote. Randolph pierced the atmosphere with his opposition to the "tyranny of numbers" in a long tirade against western arguments. Randolph would not accept any Constitution that had "the monstrous, the tyrannous, the preposterous, and abominable principle, that numbers alone are to be regarded as a fit basis of representation in the House of Delegates...I nail my colours to the mast...I will never surrender to the principle of mere white population as a basis for the lower house."

John Cooke of Frederick, Philip Doddridge, Alexander Campbell of Brooke, and Chapman Johnson of Augusta carried the burden of the western argument for fairer representation. Two easterners Charles F. Mercer and Robert B. Taylor, the "Hero of Craney Island," favored the western idea. All but Johnson favored extending the right to vote to all adult white males. Cooke gave an extensive discourse on the origin of natural rights, John Locke's writings, the Virginia Declaration of Rights, and Jefferson's Declaration of Independence. The Westerners argued that the American Revolution had been fought over the question of "taxation without representation." A conservative responded that the war had to do with preserving rights of Englishmen. Indeed, many conservatives sounded like they would have been quite comfortable as landed gentry in 18th-century England.

Alexander Campbell best exemplified the western position. Both he and Philip Doddridge represented the panhandle part of northwestern Virginia. As ministers, neither was eligible to serve as members of the General Assembly either under the old or the new constitution. Campbell led a sect of Baptists named for him. Unlike many western delegates and radical ministers, he had a solid higher education, having attended college in Scotland, where he received instruction from members of the Common Sense School of moral philosophy. In a long soliloquy, Campbell spoke of creating basic principles before rewriting the constitution and of the importance of reason, observation, and experience to understand political economy. The leaders of 1776 based their government on natural rights. "That government ought to be instituted for the benefit of the governed" was as true as the axiom "that a straight line is the shortest possible distance between any two given points." In using the term "freeholders" in 1776 the founders did not mean "slaveholders," Campbell noted. Old-fashioned Virginia statesmen had an advantage in metaphysics and rhetoric. They also had their slaves to fan them after returning home from political battles. Western Virginians had to take off their coats and plow fields. Such work gave them bone and muscle along with republican principles "pure and uncontaminated." Contending that mankind came out of a natural state, Campbell went to some lengths to describe its possible features. As to Abel Upshur's idea that a wealthy man represented all sorts of people, Campbell asked what would happen should one so endowed purchase a couple of Virginia's counties and depopulate them. Should such a person be entitled to all the representation? Campbell saw Upshur's "men and interests" argument nothing more than one of "men and money."

In arguing for lowering the bar for voting, Westerners pointed to the sacrifices made by their neighbors during the recent war against Great Britain. One spoke of 1,200 Shenandoah County men coming to the aid of the coast. Another remembered men coursing the falls of the James to reach the coast. Over 160 westerners lay "in the sands" of Norfolk, mostly victims of disease. Now the convention refused to give fighting men the right to vote. A westerner pointed to Culpeper County, east of the mountains, which sent one militia unit with 74 men to defend against the British, only two having the right to vote. The argument carried weight with Robert Taylor, who commanded these men during the war, but few other Easterners found merit in the case. Taylor resigned halfway through the deliberations because he found himself at odds with his Norfolk constituency.

Conservatives noted the riots that accompanied voting in other states. In response, Doddridge pointed out the only riot he had ever seen at an election took place in Richmond, the district the delegate most concerned about the matter, one John Marshall, represented. Westerners grumbled about eastern serfs; Easterners mentioned the "peasants" of the backcountry. Conservatives cited neighboring North Carolina, where free blacks had the vote. Reformers replied that their plan did not give such people that right. Conservatives, they argued, ought to imagine how galling it was for those in the lower part of Virginia not to have the right to vote when free blacks did in the state below them.

In the end, the convention eased property requirements a bit, enough to add several thousand to the polls. Under the reform one could qualify to vote with an estate worth $25 or a long-term lease of $20 annual value. Those with insufficient property would have to wait over 20 years for the state to abandon property restrictions. Some who spoke at the convention thought as many as half the adult white males did not have the right to vote. Delegates assumed that fewer whites east of the Blue Ridge were disqualified. Others thought the number and percentage a lot less.

A recent study found over 50% not living on land they owned in the west in 1860. Another study, however, gives fairly high turnouts of the adult white male population for all parts of Virginia in the presidential election in 1840, suggesting that around 70% of the adult, white male population was entitled to vote in presidential elections with roughly 80% of those eligible actually voting. Moreover, when restrictions on voting were removed in 1851, the increase in participation only rose from 5% to 25%, depending on location. It should also not be assumed that most of the previously ineligible voters resided in the West, as the East showed as much of an overall increase after the reform and several memorials favoring expanding the right to vote came from eastern areas.

The western argument for more representation met bitter resistance in the convention. Easterners contended that the Trans-Allegheny paid little in taxes, as land there was less valuable and only a few had slaves. Westerners responded that the number of slaves was growing, especially in the Valley, and land values were rising all over the west. Some Easterners foresaw the possibility that once the west obtained power, they would vote to end slavery and should that happen, Virginia would separate in two, closely followed by the division of the entire nation. One delegate thought that the west really would not demand emancipation of slaves, for such an act would unsheathe a sword that would "be red with the best blood of this country, before it finds the scabbard," but he figured the westerners might tax slavery to death.

The convention bogged down in its efforts to find some combination of numbers and taxation to figure out representation. Some conservatives hoped for, but never got, the federal ratio of five slaves being equivalent to three free people to determine membership in both houses. To settle the matter, William Gordon of Albemarle County concocted an arbitrary reapportionment in both houses, wherein he counted all the whites and an arbitrary portion of the slaves. Under his scheme some parts of the western Piedmont, where Gordon lived, and a few of the more populated districts of the Valley picked up delegates. Thus the Tidewater got 26 delegates, the Piedmont 42, the Valley 25, and the Trans-Allegheny 31. In the Senate, the West would have but 13 of 32 representatives. The Tidewater lost a large percent of its share of delegates and senators. All three of the other sections gained, with the Valley and the western Piedmont gaining the most.

Whereas the original constitution gave each county two delegates, sectional divisions now became fixed. Westerners would no longer be able to follow break up their counties to obtain greater delegate strength. The new constitution required a two-thirds vote in both houses of the legislature to change the distribution. Hereafter a county could be divided, but the ratio from each section in the Assembly remained the same. Thus as of 1840, when white Virginians west of the Blue Ridge slightly outnumbered those east of it, 19 senators came from the east as compared to 13 from the west and 78 delegates came from the East as compared to 56 from the West. By 1850 when some 90,000 more whites lived in the West than in the East, the distribution of seats remained essentially the same.

The convention approved of a three-year nonrenewable term for governor. It rejected proposals to have the electorate make the choice, even though the conservative Abel Upshur agreed to the idea. The new constitution also retained the Council of State, with a smaller membership, and the system of local government. The governor continued to approve recommended county justices, but the legislature took over selections to the higher courts.

Having deliberated through much of 1829 and 1830, the delegates voted 55 to 40 to submit the matter to the qualified voters. Some 26,055 voted for, 15,563 against it. This time, as compared to 1828, the West overwhelmingly cast negative votes; the East voted solidly for the new constitution. In most cases, the eastern counties that did not want the convention now approved the new constitution by wide margins. The Valley showed almost an even division. The Southwest and Trans-Allegheny were obviously displeased. Grayson

County rejected the changes by 649 to 70, Greenbrier 464 to 34, Lewis by 546 to 10, Randolph 565 to 4, and Harrison 1112 to 8.

In the years ahead, Westerners, especially in the northern areas, expressed interest in a division of the state. The issues of slavery and sectionalism troubled relations. Secessionist feeling on the part of westerners toward the rest of the state, however, never reached a critical stage. Parts of the Valley and the Southwest remained less disposed to such a radical course.

Virginia got off to an excellent start to the 1850s as it reformed its constitution. With Westerners still objecting to the old system, elected delegates without a single "giant," assembled in Richmond in 1850. After some wrangling, they arbitrarily assigned the West 83 delegates to 69 for the East, but gave 30 of the 50 senators to the East. The convention also called for reapportionment in 1865, when the number of whites west of the mountains would far exceed those east of them (1850 data counted over 90,000 more white Westerners) on whether to accept the "white basis" for purposes of representation for both chambers. Slaveholders, however, would be protected from excessive taxes by not permitting any taxes on slaves under the age of 12 and fixing a maximum value on any slave above that age at $300.

As Virginia caught up with the wave of democracy then enveloping the nation, the convention eliminated property qualifications to vote. It passed a head tax on all adult white males, one-half of the income to be directed to public schools. All adult white males now had the right to elect members of the assembly as well as the governor (who now had a four-year single term), a lieutenant governor, members of the Board of Public Works, and judges of appeals, circuit, and district courts for various terms. The new constitution also reformed local governments by mandating the election of local justices of peace, clerks of county courts, surveyors, commonwealth attorneys, sheriffs, commissioners of revenue, and even constables. Many cities had already broad electorates and were voting directly on mayors and other municipal posts. The appendix-like Council of State ceased to exist, and voters, finding few reasons to reject the document, approved it by a margin of roughly seven to one.

Easterner Henry Wise played the most influential role during the proceedings, giving speeches that ranged up to four hours in length. He made sure the convention took a strong stand for slavery as it simultaneously diminished the weight of the number of slaves in distributing legislative seats. He understood the importance of mollifying western Virginians, both for his future political career and the troubles that likely loomed as a result of rising interest in the issue of slavery.

One reason Easterners resisted attempts by Westerners to have a greater say in state government was because they feared people west of the Blue Ridge wanted to tax them for public works in the West. But the East took more than its share of state funds for internal improvements.

Although roads remained impassable at times, the rapidity, certainty, and cost of moving people and goods all advanced during the 19th century. Turnpikes, plank roads, steamboats, canals, and railroads all played roles. Travelers thought Virginia's roads the worst in the nation during the Revolutionary era. They were not the best in 1860, but the state, following a national trend, experienced a drastic change, mostly due to the introduction of steamboats and trains. Roads improved, but even after the Civil War, many were often little more than a series of ruts, sometimes several wagon widths wide, meandering through the landscape.

By the 1820s more or less regular steamboat service tied Norfolk to Richmond, the first steamboats putting in an appearance shortly after the War of 1812. In the 1830s and 1840s rival lines, often resorting to price wars, fought for control of the James River traffic. Sometimes competition became so ruthless that steamboats ran into each other in efforts to reach passengers first. In the 1830s the forerunner of the Baltimore Steam Packet Company ran at least three times a week between Norfolk and Baltimore. The Potomac and Rappahannock ports soon had such service, as did Cherrystone and other places on the Eastern Shore. In the early 1850s Norfolk developed daily connections to northern ports. Virginia's Ohio River ports introduced steam traffic at the same time and came to rely on it even more than coastal residents. Unlike the coastal communities, they also developed a penchant to manufacture steamboats.

Coming south on the stage through Fredericksburg and into Richmond, a traveler contrasted the tedious movement on land with that of the steamboat along the Potomac and James rivers in 1827. The latter proved quicker, safer, and less costly. Steamboats could be dangerous because of defective boilers, but horse coaches encountered bandits as well as other obstructions. Another traveler contrasted the rather pleasant, though crowded, conditions on a steamboat coming from Washington D.C., to Aquia Creek on the Potomac River in the early 1840s. The second part of the trip from the steamboat depot to Fredericksburg proved exciting as the black drivers, dressed in strange costumes, compelled the horses to carry the overloaded stage up hills and through dangerous waterways. At Fredericksburg, passengers could again enjoy their travels as they went by train to Richmond. A little later the railroad went all the way to the port on Aquia Creek, thus necessitating only one transfer from rail to steamboat to reach D.C.

Virginia put much of its effort in transportation into building canals. The James River and Kanawha, which tried to link the Ohio River to Richmond, fell short of its goal. Reorganized several times, it became the state's favorite project in the mid-1830s. Private and public investors poured money into the enterprise. Political pressures kept the state contribution to a few million, and Virginia did not have enough wealthy private investors to make up the difference. State and private investors also diluted their resources as a wide variety of local turnpikes and canals shared investments. Even had the canal been completed, railroads would have reduced the need for it, and the impact of the flow of commerce over it would not have produced a great urban port, as Virginians envisioned.

Railroads served much of Eastern Virginia by 1860. In the 1830s chartered companies built three separate lines. One linked the Roanoke River in North Carolina with Petersburg. Another line went from Petersburg to Richmond. A third connected Richmond with a spot near the Potomac River about halfway between Fredericksburg and Washington D.C. Although these companies sometimes collaborated in creating through tickets for passengers when it suited their purposes, they failed to provide single and uniform tracks. Thus passengers and freight had to load and unload at least three times as they went from the Roanoke to the Potomac. Two of the lines cooperated in competing against a rival rail line built by Portsmouth and Norfolk interests. After the Petersburg people destroyed the rival line by tearing up its tracks, the remaining corporations then fought each other in ruinous warfare. Each side employed steamboats on the James as part of the struggle.

In the 1850s the situation improved. In that decade Virginia put more money into railroads than any state in the union. The coast, with the help of capital from Boston, was able to reactivate the old Portsmouth and Roanoke as the Seaboard & Roanoke Rail Road. Late in that decade V.M.I. graduate William Mahone superintended construction of a road between Norfolk and Petersburg, an engineering marvel of the time, as it required something of a plank road as a base to overcome the swampy conditions near Suffolk. Richmond got access to the York River at West Point (Eltham). The Piedmont had a half dozen major projects built in the 1840s and 1850s. The South Side Rail Road joined Petersburg and Lynchburg. Southwest Virginia had the tracks of the Virginia and Tennessee. Completed in the mid-1850s, they linked Lynchburg with Bristol on the border with the Volunteer State. The political significance of the completion of this line is hard to overestimate. Northwest Virginia had the Baltimore and Ohio and a spur line that tied it to Wheeling. The Valley had several lines (the Virginia Central went through it from east to west), but none ran its length.

The state put over $20,000,000 into building these roads. Unfortunately, urban rivalries and local interests created a crazy-quilt arrangement. The government divided the state into sections based around key communities. The residents of different cities all received some help from the state. No single great enterprise emerged from the variety of ventures. The closest thing to a rational situation involved the three lines that ran across the bottom of the state. On the eve of the Civil War, western freight started to flow in some volume through Lynchburg and Petersburg and on to Norfolk. These lines, however, remained separated from one another until the Civil War. Virginia had no through railroad for the entire period. Interests in the towns tried to prevent lines from coming together, as passengers and freight would merely pass through without stopping. Lines had different gauges (the width separating the tracks), which made through traffic impossible.

In the 1820s and 1830s, wealthy slaveholders comprised about 80% of the private capital for one of the Albemarle projects. In the 1850s those investing in the Virginia Central Rail Road included far more small farmers, professionals, and skilled workers. The earlier improvements helped produce more members of the middle class, but Albemarle County, like most of Virginia, still trailed much of the North and Midwest in creating middle-class investors.

In addition to changing its constitution and more enthusiastically embracing state aid for internal improvements, Virginia also progressed, if ever so slightly or slowly, on other fronts. Reforms in agriculture and society took place, sometimes against a strong conservative tide. The state also gradually shifted toward a more urban and industrial society, although farming and rural life remained dominant until long after the Civil War.

# Chapter 10

## The Virginia Way

John Randolph of Roanoke thought young Virginia males of the early 19th century were, among other things, petulant, arrogant, supine, listless, indifferent, loud, boisterous, overbearing, dictatorial, awkward, and contemptible. They sometimes knew a bit of Latin but often spoke profanely. Other critics complained that many young men pretended to be orators like Patrick Henry, but their bombastic style conveyed little thought. Although most eastern Virginia planters questioned this assessment about the young men of the Old Dominion, the mere existence of such a view suggests an entrenched notion that people in the past were better than they would be in the future.

Some Virginians saw two disparate cultures east and west of the Blue Ridge. Westerners coming east commented unfavorably not only about the presence of so many slaves and poor free blacks, but also about the torpid nature of white Easterners. Foreigners and Northerner Americans thought Southerners were flighty, excessively passionate, and shallow in intellectual pursuits. Southerners believed Northerners were sly, smart, standoffish, stingy, and greedy. Northerners, it was said, liked to make money, Southerners to spend it. Southern men rode horses and fired guns better than Northerners. Northerners refused to stop work to have an amiable chat with a passerby. Only a germ of truth can be found in all this, yet even Jefferson thought planters of eastern Virginia were less volatile than South Carolinians but more impetuous than Northerners.

Reforms affected different parts of the South and of Virginia to varying degrees. In the 19th century, eastern Virginia planters resisted reform. One conservative Southside politician thought that voting rights, wheat weevils, almost everything bad came from the west and the north. Residents of the Old Dominion laughed at the communes in the North. The few that appeared in Virginia soon failed or remained confined to parts of the Northwest. Virginians made fun of the women's rights reformers. They defended duels, even though the practice violated their own laws.

Throughout the colonial era and beyond, Virginia farmers were considered "the slovenliest husbandmen imaginable," failing to plow their fields, hoe their corn, or weed their wheat. They let animals roam and rarely fed them, thus having small animals that produced little manure. They did not even wash their sheep before shearing. Slovenly farm practices spilled over into the appearance of the farm buildings. Well into the 19th century, many slaveholders lived in rude shelters.

In a tobacco economy with plenty of cheap land, owners rotated their main crop for several years and left vast areas unused, hoping the soil would replenish itself. A visitor to Albemarle County just after the Revolution noted several plantations of over 5,000 acres where the slave workforce could not possibly cultivate it, but the owners had no thoughts of selling off the excess land. Thus renters prevailed in some districts simply because owners insisted on controlling the land. The neater farming practices of Pennsylvania simply did not exist in the Piedmont, except where Germans settled.

As described by a British officer roaming about the Piedmont in 1779, a typical plantation had a dwelling house, usually made of wood, near the center of the estate with kitchens and numerous outbuildings, a "small village." The estates usually contained peach and apple orchards. The better homes had shingles for roofs, painted lathes for siding, and brick chimneys. A few had glazed windows; most had only wooden shutters. Wood huts for the slaves and larger houses to store tobacco were scattered over the plantation. Jefferson seems to have been an exception in clustering his slaves in residential areas and assigning parts of his plantation to specific slaves.

In clearing their fields, Virginia farmers, girdled large trees and burned the brush, thus creating a number of dead trees spread across fields. A German baroness, almost hit by a decayed and falling tree, observed that the slaves often made fires under trees, probably to heat their hominy cakes. Left unattended, these fires burned over large areas. Except to create a lot of smoke, it mattered little, for the practice simply opened up more land. Summer storms, she noted, blew down hundreds of weakened trees. Better farmers sometimes ran fences, built in a zigzag fashion and composed of 12-foot split rails. New Englanders called them "Virginia fences," for they looked like the work of a drunk. In surveying land Virginians used "metes" and "bounds" whereby the owner marked off his supposed land by notching a convenient tree and walking off the property, avoiding the less valuable acreage. Using these rough estimates, a surveyor would then determine the dimensions of the estate. This practice led to oddly shaped plantations throughout the entire region, including western Ohio, where a large number of Virginians migrated. Foreigners would occasionally run across a Jefferson or some other reform-conscious farmer, but this breed proved rare, and even Jefferson's estate ran into serious financial problems, mostly because, like other members of the gentry, he was not frugal. Jefferson promoted machines to make farming easier—threshers, drills, and plows, but none of these ideas or inventions helped most eastern Virginians develop efficient farms.

Many Westerners practiced a saner approach to agriculture. Owners often worked directly with their small number of slaves on small farms. They used sickles rather than scythes, a practice that increased crop yield, although it required more work. Their limestone-rich fields also gave them more resilient soil. The Germans, travelers noticed, tended to rely on slaves less and to fence in their cattle more, leading to bigger cattle and more manure. Westerners also made more of their own clothes.

But even parts of the Valley presented stretches of poorly managed farmland with homes little more than hovels. Some houses did not need windows for all four sides had natural ventilation in the walls. Pigs and cattle ran free, rarely fed by farmers. Oddly, the area above Winchester, where people from the lowlands had brought in some slaves, presented the best appearance. One also suspects that proximity to Pennsylvania had something to do with the sustained prosperity of the Shenandoah Valley, along with its natural physical advantages

Although western Virginia seemed more reform minded in some matters, the Scots-Irish, who also settled in the Valley and occupied parts of the western Piedmont, usually in enclaves, exhibited habits similar to those prevalent among eastern planters. Some scholars think a Celtic style of farming came across the Atlantic with the Scots-Irish to influence herding practices and farming methods of the backcountry. If so, some of the orderliness of German culture rubbed off, because on the whole the northern Valley of Virginia exhibited an exceedingly productive society throughout the 19th century and beyond.

The Valley produced wheat as well as Cyrus McCormick, one of the few prominent inventors in the state's history. Eastern Virginia's agricultural economy was at low ebb in the mid-1830s, when McCormick tried to convince grain growers of the virtues of his $100 machine, so he had few sales east of the Blue Ridge. The Valley itself, though it grew a lot of grain per capita, was comparatively small and had a surplus of farm labor. In trying to reach the expanding Illinois market, McCormick sent a machine across the Blue Ridge to the James River, where it was shipped to Richmond and thence by water to New Orleans, then up the Mississippi and Ohio rivers to reach its destination. Faced with such a roundabout route, he located his new factory near Chicago. During the Civil War his firm produced thousands of machines. Each one released Northerners to help fight his home state.

Before the Civil War, Appalachia participated in the market economy, as Drovers herded thousands of cattle east across the mountains every year and teamsters drove wagonloads of wheat through the gaps in the mountains. Ranchers in the Southwest and in the Valley often bought cattle to fatten for market. Overall, the area produced surpluses of agricultural products and even some industrial goods that fed national and some international markets. Salt came out of the Kanawha Valley produced from coal-fired facilities. In the 1850s the Blue Ridge area in the Southwest produced small amounts of copper, lead, and iron. On the Ohio River around Wheeling, residents enjoyed the kind of growth and income experienced in Pennsylvania. The northern portions of the Valley of Virginia did quite well, but small forges and furnaces added to the agricultural resources up and down the Valley.

On the surface, this predominantly rural culture looked like Jefferson's embodiment of the republican idea where yeomen farmers served as the backbone of society. In this scenario a family owned a farm of 100 acres and produced nearly all its own needs. Recent studies, however, reveal that even as late as 1860, possibly as much as 50% of the area's total population rented for long terms or served as agricultural laborers. How many belonged to each of these groups varied considerably. Throughout the region, a large number labored for others, using a variety of arrangements. Such a family often received $15 a month and the use of a cottage and an acre or so. They did chores on the estate throughout the year and during harvests, they became part of bands of laborers that went from farm to farm to bring in the crops. One Southwestern Virginian paid his white workmen $120 a year. Neither they nor his slaves were worth the money tied up in them, he complained. Some rural folk doubtless made up for deficiencies in their diet through their knowledge of the woodlands.

Even Western Virginia, with such a large percentage controlling such a small amount of property, fell considerably shy of the Jeffersonian ideal. Some 10% of the richest landholders controlled 40% of the property. The bottom 10% of those who owned land had but 2% of the rural landscape. Although slavery played a minor role in what later became West Virginia, a least half of the propertied white households in the Valley and in Southwest Virginia had one slave and usually more, despite the fact that the overall proportion of slavery ran below 15% of the total population. The proportion of slaves in the Southwest rose during the prosperous 1850s.

In contrast, parts of Southeastern Virginia seemed depressed in the extreme. A traveler in 1827 saw a "miserable country," with barrens and swamps. At one point Nansemond County farmers grew corn at the rate of eight bushels to the acre. At the time residents grew a little cotton, but they soon gave up on that crop. Slaves wandered about with "hardly a rag to cover them." The whites, she thought were "almost as wretched in appearance as the blacks, and far more degraded." The poor in Ireland could be no worse, she opined. The driver warned the passengers to keep an eye on their bags at the rear of the stage, for robbers often cut the ropes and ran off with the loot. While this problem existed elsewhere, a rough and poor white population resided in much of lower Virginia. Although they improved considerably by 1860, they could not be depended on to sustain large markets.

As the 19th century advanced, eastern Virginia farmers gradually improved their methods. Early agricultural reformers like Jefferson and John Taylor, who urged growers to replenish soil naturally with manure and offal (corn stalks), failed to convince many to change their ways, but the proposals of Edmund Ruffin in his *Farmers' Register* elicited a more positive response in the 1830s.

Envisioning a Virginia of efficient farms spread across the countryside, this radical politician called for stricter fencing laws, a practice that would promote improvement in the quality and size of cattle and pigs while at the same time make manure available. Ruffin also hoped big planters, because they were not as wealthy as they had once been, might give up being so hospitable. Following the ideas of an English chemist, Ruffin urged Easterners to use natural deposits of lime-rich marl (decayed marine life), sometimes found in pockets several feet deep near the rivers and shorelines. Dozens of articles reported on various experiments using marl and other fertilizers along with numerous kinds of crop rotations. John Hartwell Cocke made Bremo on the James River a model for others to emulate. The application of guano in the 1850s also helped revitalize farms, but the comparatively prosperous 1850s owed its prosperity mostly to the higher price for tobacco and wheat.

Virginians also diversified what they grew and sold commercially in the years before the Civil War. The emergence of truck farming in the vicinity of Norfolk and Portsmouth totally changed the appearance of the outskirts of those two towns. Introduced by New Jersey farmers, simple techniques allowed the area to produce a wide variety of crops for northern markets. By the 1850s daily steamboat service permitted sales of a variety of fruits and vegetables in the spring and summer. A northern visitor in the mid-1850s thought the small truck farms interspersed among the traditional Virginia estates presented a productive scene despite the almost total lack of agricultural machinery. In skiffs and rowboats, truckers met the steamers in the middle of the river to load their crops.

Albemarle's farmers made progress in the 1850s. An agricultural society with about 500 members brought farmers together to discuss better ways to use their resources. A local agricultural journal raved about individual successes and forecasted wonderful futures, as Albemarle could grow crops for the Richmond market. Soil erosion became less noticeable, and less silt drained into the rivers. The small farmers of the 1850s greatly increased their output of tobacco throughout eastern Virginia as leaf prices rose. Wealthy planters grew more wheat as small growers turned to the more lucrative leaf. Corn, wool, and home manufacturing also dropped among all farmers. Farmers bought more dry goods and tools despite the fact that tobacco needed few sophisticated implements. The cash value of small and medium farms doubled as wealthier farmers enjoyed a more modest growth.

Despite the successes of small farmers due to the revival of tobacco, Albemarle retained a number of plantations that ranged above 500 acres, about double the size of farms in a comparable Pennsylvania county. The density of population reflects this difference. In 1830 Albemarle had 32 people per square mile (16 free per square mile). A typical Pennsylvania county had 53 people per square mile. Thirty years later, Albemarle attained 38 overall (18 free) while Cumberland reached 73 persons per square mile (all free). The value of acreage in Pennsylvania doubled that in Virginia. Their farmers tripled the per capita investments in farm implements. With its large number of middle-class farmers, the northern county remained far ahead of the Virginia representative.

Efforts to reform farming in the Southside suffered the natural tendency toward soil exhaustion, regardless of methods used. Production of tobacco dropped, and nothing could be done to raise yields except to switch to bright leaf tobacco, which prospered on thinner soils. As a result, Pittsylvania County enjoyed a revival, and nearby Henry County began to grow large amounts of tobacco for the first time. This boom obscured the fact that much of the land south of the James could not be revived through any knowledge available at the time. The new areas of cultivation would need natural rest. Hay, timothy, certain clovers, and other cover crops did not do well in the climate. Most crop rotation efforts proved fruitless in lower Virginia, which despite progress in the 1850s, remained behind Albemarle County in overall development.

Overall Virginia had a deficiency in investments in agricultural equipment, but not necessarily because of slavery. The Old Dominion even trailed Georgia in that regard. The Northern Piedmont and Northern Valley, with few slaves and little tobacco, did have a comparably heavier investment in machines. But the Southwest, with comparably fewer slaves, had less investment. The tobacco belt ran close to the state average in possessing machines despite the fact that tobacco required little in the way of machines, because those who used slave labor to grow tobacco were able to raise cash to buy tools from selling their crops as well as their surplus slaves.

In 1779 a British officer observed that the typical "abominably lazy" planter of eastern Virginia rose around 8 a.m., drank a "julep," which consisted of a large glass of rum sweetened with sugar, rode about the grounds until 10 a.m., when he consumed breakfast along with some hard cider (women drank tea or coffee), and then "sauntered about" and played with the little Negroes or "scrap [ed] on a fiddle." A noon he had another toddy or two to prepare for dinner at 2 p.m., after which he rested until 5 p.m., when he had another toddy. Thus he went through the day "neither drunk nor sober." On court days he repaired to the village and conducted business or watched a cockfight "at which he got so egregiously drunk that his wife sent a couple of Negroes to conduct him safe home."

Coming south toward Richmond from Aquia Creek on the Potomac in 1827, an Englishman noticed that the stage stopped ten times. At each tavern two Virginia farmers, pleasant at the start of the trip, had their toddies. "Drinking is carried to a greater excess in the South than it is in the North" was the way one English woman explained the situation.

Early in the century, an Episcopal minister tried to jumpstart a moral crusade. Mason Locke Weems, a peripatetic parson and biographer of George Washington, concocted the myth about the cherry tree to convince people not to lie. He also urged bachelors to take up the married life as he spent much of his time on the road peddling books. And he battled gambling and drinking in two publications *God's Revenge Against Gambling* and *The Drunkard's Looking Glass*. His crusade, however, had little impact.

In one of those rare instances where an older generation praises the younger, a delegate at the Constitutional Convention in 1829 (obviously not Randolph) noted "the temperance and sobriety of the rising generation" compared to their elders. "Morality and virtue," along with "industry and energy" seemed on the rise within the past 10 years as schools multiplied and religion diffused its positive impact on the people. In 1819 a local tavern keeper reported that Strasburg, with preachers playing no role, had recently reformed. Previously known for the "vicious habits of its inhabitants," the local grand jury forced an end to drunkenness, swearing, and quarreling.

The first temperance organization dates from 1826, when Charlotte County clergy decided to battle demon rum. Within three years the state had over fifty similar groups and by 1836 some 250 organizations with more than 50,000 members. Chapters of the American Temperance Society, with a goal of freeing the world of drunks, could be found in Virginia and in many other states. A more radical Baltimore group, the Washingtonians, called for members to swear off all alcohol. In Petersburg some 1,000 converts pledged not to consume any spirits. The Sons of Temperance appeared in 1843 in Norfolk and Charlottesville among other places. By 1852 it had 11 chapters in Richmond alone. Sisters of Temperance and Martha Washingtonians called for women to cease drinking. Blacks also joined these crusades, which enjoyed their greatest success in urban areas.

Yet Virginia still had many drinkers and those who condoned excessive drinking. In the mid-1840s a Congressman named George Dromgoole of Brunswick County often appeared in an inebriated state in the halls of the capitol. In winning a stiff contest for reelection, the Democrat, fortified by "a quart of toddy, three fourths whiskey and one fourth water," campaigned by saying that his Whig opponent sober was less reliable than a drunk Dromgoole. Democrats knew about John Hartwell Cocke, a Whig who succeeded in persuading several prominent Virginians to fight demon rum. A Democrat convention condemned this crusade and its temperance societies. Thomas Ritchie, the leading Democrat, opposed anything that smacked of prohibition. Many Democrat leaders thought temperance and prohibition were Northern inventions designed to destroy Virginia's way of life. The General Assembly banned retail sales of hard liquor in the early 1840s, when the Whigs had temporary control, then reversed itself when the Democrats regained the upper hand.

Despite these setbacks, the cause of temperance gained ground. A traveler in 1839 along the Wilderness Road noticed that none of the passengers on the stagecoach purchased drams at taverns. Freemason lodges began to forbid drinking during ceremonies. Then they prohibited alcohol at any functions. In the 1870s, they ousted members who appeared drunk in public. By the 1830s Baptists and Methodists condemned alcohol in any setting, including for communion. Petitions that called for banning the sale of such beverages except for medical or sacramental purposes continued to come from various counties throughout the 1850s. In 1855 the Court of Hustings in Danville banned the sale of alcohol. Manufacturers and merchants supported this move, for they hoped to have more sober workers and customers. Residents of Lexington restricted the number of saloons, had several people jailed for selling liquor without a license, and regulated bowling alleys (presumably within or near saloons), but rural interests prevented the town from eliminating alcohol. In the late 1850s the temperance crusade lost membership, but anecdotal evidence suggests that the typical Virginian drank less than formerly.

Laws expressly forbade dueling, but they were rarely enforced. The constitutional convention of 1830 even discussed banning duelists from holding public office, but those determined to shoot each other found isolated locations to avoid prosecution. The Dismal Swamp Canal at the boundary between North Carolina and Virginia proved a favorite spot. In Brunswick County, Congressman Dromgoole once insulted the owner of the local hotel, a good friend, who pushed the drunk out of his chair. When others told him what had taken place and after rival Whigs spread the word about his alleged cowardice, the Democrat sought satisfaction. The friend apologized orally, but he would not provide a written apology. In the ensuing duel, the military-trained Dromgoole killed the former friend, who had almost no knowledge of pistols. Even after these actions, this known drunk and duelist retained his seat in Congress. Henry Wise, a congressman and later governor of Virginia, had so many potential duels that one man refused to accept his challenge because he thought the man had too many unresolved previous challenges. Wise carried a concealed gun in the capitol in the belief that someone planned to kill him, but complied when a committee chair asked him to give it up before attending a meeting. Foreigners complained that Virginians often walked around with pistols or dirks.

One of Virginia's most notorious gamblers of the early 19th century claimed he was arrested only once in his lengthy gambling career, and on that occasion only when he upset some ladies when he would not let them use his hall for a dance. Bailey, who spent almost his entire adult life earning a living by playing faro, seemed quite unrepentant. A Frenchmen in the 1780s thought that Winchester, with few small churches, was experiencing a big increase in gaming tables all "assiduously frequented...[as] a sort of worship." Gambling also often led Virginia males open to the "charge of infidelity."

Public opinion ran against professional gambling during this era, but Petersburg and Richmond remained centers for horse racing, even as that sport declined elsewhere. Early in the 1850s the state reportedly exempted horse racing from betting rules. Although this particular act apparently failed to be published, it changed little, as laws against gambling had rarely been enforced at these sites anyway. In 1779 and again in 1792 the legislature outlawed gambling dens. When gamblers used the occasion of horse racing near Norfolk in 1811 to set up faro games near the track, a local editor called for local authorities to crack down, but in the face of an inability of local law enforcement, the local jockey club ended the races. In 1819 an updated version of these laws made keeping a gaming table an offense for which one could do a year of hard labor and be fined up to $500. A committee in 1833, talking about "black-legs" running faro tables in Richmond and the resorts "to the great injury of the unsuspecting and unwary," recommended stiffer penalties for those running the tables. Politicians considered amateur gambling less of a menace. The winner of bets on horse races, cockfights, or similar activities had to return the gains to the loser or pay a fine. Private games did not come under the law if losses did not exceed $20, except for whites who gambled with blacks. Virginia's legislature acted against lotteries in 1852, but they were still in business at the time of the Civil War, if the number of advertisements in newspapers serves as an indicator.

Like many Southern states, Virginia trailed much of the nation in developing a system of public education for elementary students. This failure had two primary causes. First, the white population was spread too thin, thus making it difficult for children to attend school. Secondly, Virginia inherited a tradition that only a few should benefit from a first-rate education. But the rise of republican government encouraged citizens to read to keep abreast of political affairs so they could cast an enlightened vote. In 1796 Virginia's legislature appeared to accept part of Jefferson's 1779 proposal, giving all free males and females three years of tuition-free education in local schools to pass on "the wisdom of the ages," enhance republican government, and promote equality, liberty, justice, and order. But the state left the specifics to local authorities. The state did develop a Literary Fund, which after 1810 distributed diverse funds to the counties to educate the poor. Charles Mercer, a National Republican from Loudoun County, arranged for the Literary Fund to receive $400,000, the repayment of a loan to the federal government. With other incomes the fund would have over $1,000,000. Jefferson, however, convinced the state to divert much of this money to Central College (the University of Virginia), chartered in 1819. Thus depleted, the Literary Fund failed to underwrite a full system of public education. Under the existing program residents sent their children to neighborhood schools for 90-day terms each year. They subscribed construction funds and teachers' salaries. The state supplemented the teachers' pay based on the number of indigent children taught. The county courts appointed commissioners to supervise the expenditure of about $2 per indigent child per year. Only about half of those qualified took advantage of the program, as many people lived in remote areas that had no schools. In some cases poor parents felt embarrassed to be the object of charity or they needed their children to work. In 1816, with the help of Thomas Ritchie, Richmond started a Lancastrian School, as part of a national movement. Other cities of the commonwealth did the same. These schools aimed to teach a large number of people by using older students to drill the younger ones in the basics. For cost effectiveness nothing could beat this system. Unfortunately, it failed to educate children to a reasonable level of understanding.

In 1829 the legislature created a district system of free schools, but it provided no additional money and did not require the county governments to supply any. In 1841 the Whigs, with temporary control of the House of Delegates, voted to take the money distributed to Virginia from the national tariff and land sales to create a state system of public education, but senate Democrats killed the idea. Reformers in 1846 obtained minor changes as the legislature cut the size of the educational districts in the counties in the hopes of making more schools available. County commissioners picked a superintendent to oversee the system. Counties and cities could create tax-supported schools and receive a portion of the $2 head tax called for in the 1851

Constitution, but only if two-thirds of the voters approved. Only a handful of counties and a few cities responded. Thus in 1860 the situation remained much as it had been. One typical county took in $594 from the state and $6,510 from private sources, which allowed its neighborhood schools to continue. The Norfolk council divided the city into four districts and provided schools for the young. A board of education picked one of its own to superintend the system, but within a few years teachers and janitors complained about the lack of pay, several thousand dollars could not be accounted for, and even more disturbing, about 40% of the children failed to attend classes.

Even some Democrats occasionally thought public education might be worthwhile, but that party in the state legislature usually balked at such measures. When Henry Wise campaigned for full funding of public schools in 1855, fellow Democrats accused him of "agrarianism," a form of land distribution equated with communism and usually associated with northern states. Wise won the election, but he never attained his goal while in office.

Private education made up some of the deficiency. Every county and city, at least in eastern Virginia, had a respectable academy or two for the older children of the elite. They also had a wide array of church schools and other private establishments for both sexes and some children of the middle class. Children continued to learn in the home, often from older brothers and sisters. Tutors taught the elite at plantation schools. Schools and teachers were more available than before, although well-trained teachers remained at a premium. Richmond had a private school to educate them, but Virginia made no progress at all in establishing normal schools (colleges for teachers).

Many Northern states turned to tax-supported compulsory elementary education and created public normal schools to train young ladies to be teachers. Virginia's failure to follow this model meant that the state ended up with among the highest illiteracy rates in the land. Over 77,000 adult whites (about 15% of that population) could not read at the most rudimentary levels in 1850, and the inability to write ran much higher, especially in the area west of the Blue Ridge, which had about half the schools proportionate to their white population compared to eastern Virginia. Several eastern counties, with rates of slavery around 60%, had the lowest rates of illiteracy among whites.

Virginia did use public funds for higher education. The state gave the University of Virginia $15,000 in 1850. It also subsidized Virginia Military Institute, founded in 1847 with five times as much. Only these two schools received direct state subsidies. As a whole Virginia had twelve colleges with 1,343 students. About 500 students attended public institutions, over 300 at the University of Virginia. Founded by Jefferson as a "nursery of republican patriots," the University presumably would attract only the best scholars and those unafraid "to follow truth wherever it may lead." Jefferson, bent on establishing a university from the ground up, staffed it primarily with European scholars. The students who attended schools of higher education reflected the plantation order at the beginning of the 19th century. As sons of planters, they had less than serious attitudes about learning. Fathers frequently forked over hundreds of dollars to keep their youngsters properly attired. Students challenged each other and sometimes faculty to duels with alarming frequency. They amassed huge debts in drinking and gambling. Edgar Allan Poe's stepfather paid off his stepson's legitimate bills at the University of Virginia in 1826, but he refused to cover the lad's $2,500 gambling debt. One observer claimed that about a third of the youngsters rarely studied, often drank, and generally behaved badly. In 1826 the students rioted. One even killed a faculty member. A much-despised instructor in foreign languages lost his job after beating his wife in public. Fortunately, the caliber of students and faculty improved over time. Of the students at the University of Virginia in the mid-1850s, only a handful came from west of the Blue Ridge. Thus Westerners missed out on learning from William McGuffey, a moral philosopher and moderate abolitionist. After 1857 George F. Holmes told them about the virtues of slavery. McGuffey gained great fame for blue-back readers, and Holmes, who also produced spellers and readers, taught history and literature, later developed a specialty in the science of society (sociology) as a follower of the philosophy known as "positivism." The staunchest defender of slavery at the university, Albert T. Bledsoe, a graduate of West Point, taught mathematics. Strongly religious, he detested Jeffersonian egalitarianism, worried about industrialization, and opposed abolitionism. Imparting any of these ideas to his students may have been a problem, for they often found him so deep in thought (even during his lectures) that they had to make sounds to revive him from his stupor. Less sanguine about the benefits of slavery, George Tucker taught political economy for about 20 years and published at least two major volumes, including an economic text and some fascinating novels. The state school in Lexington played a major role in preparing students to be engineers and military officers. Claudius Crozet, a French engineer who also worked for the Board of Public Works, served on VMI's Board of Visitors. The school enjoyed a better luck in students than the University in Charlottesville, as some poor but aspiring young men achieved considerable success there. One of its instructors, Thomas Jackson, had a less than inspiring record as a teacher but went on to attain great fame on the field of battle.

Among the other schools, the College of William and Mary operated on an endowment of $7,000 for six faculty and 35 students. Emory and Henry became a fine private labor school, where students took courses in the morning, worked in the afternoons, and studied at night. A Baptist college in Richmond tried the same experiment but eventually gave up the practice. Richmond College, however, survived and eventually enjoyed marked success.

In prison and asylum reform, Virginia maintained its programs. At the constitutional convention of 1830, one of the delegates argued that Virginia was relatively free of crime, as it had about one-fourth the proportion incarcerated as some northern states. Because the Old Dominion had a reputation for violence, this finding suggests that many crimes went unpunished or, as in the case of slaves, were dealt with by local authorities. In the 1850s, the director of Virginia's state penitentiary employed the Auburn System, modeled on the methods used in New York, where prisoners were not allowed to communicate either orally or by signals and had to work. In the 1850s inmates consisted mostly of free blacks and outsiders, a number of these having run afoul of Virginia's laws against helping slaves escape. The state added a convict-lease system late in the late1850s. Every year the state executed about a half dozen murderers, about the same rate as in the colony. Violent crimes certainly took place through all of Virginia history, but punishment varied. A shootout in a Franklin County in 1860 produced several victims but no guilty verdict. Unlike some states, only on rare occasions did Virginia invite the general public to watch one of its executions at a "carnival of death."

Virginia kept the Eastern States Asylum at Williamsburg and added the Western State Asylum in 1828 at Staunton. The Williamsburg facility actively tried to address the mental problems of the patients. In the 1820s the facility housed several hundred inmates, including about 100 free blacks. In 1850 the Western Lunatic Asylum had 379 inmates; its eastern equivalent served 257.

If America had to depend on Virginia to lead the cause of the rights of women, then very little would have happened in this reform. Whereas states in the North passed legislation to allow married women to own property and women's groups agitated for the right to vote and equal pay, these ideas had little impact in the Old Dominion. For years Democrats blocked Whig efforts at changing property rights, and so Virginia did not give women control over property until 1877. Yet property a woman inherited could be protected through a trust, should a husband be a known gambler or drinker. The court allowed separation, but rarely permitted divorce, even from abusive husbands, except where the husband substituted a black mistress for his wife. Women, it was believed, would be soiled by the corruption of political activities. They belonged in the home or possibly in the churches, where their influence on matters of morality could best be felt and where they could have a male protector. Free black or slave females did not come under any cloak of protection. Nor, in fact, did a number of white females. Lucy Barbour, the mother of two prominent politicians, became active enough to write letters in newspapers on behalf of Whigs, that Democrats objected to her intrusion into the political arena. In an autobiography a woman recalled accompanying her Whig father on political outings, where he explained the issues to her. Some men did admit that their wives decided how they should vote.

The economic situation for women changed during this era. Hundreds of white women found work in the textile mills of Petersburg and Alexandria. Free black women constituted much of the workforce of Petersburg, but not in the clothing mills. They did everything from tobacco stemming to midwifery. Some even owned their own small shops and other enterprises. As opportunities opened up in the cities, widows and other single women continued to run farms. Even on the more prosperous farms women often did the milking and garden chores to go along with numerous household duties, including sewing. The introduction of sewing machines in factories made clothes available at cheap prices in the retail markets just before the Civil War. Some women retired spinning wheels and looms, as cheaper cloth became generally available.

Impressions about Virginia around 1850 suggest the appearance of a substantial female if, indeed, she had ever been missing. Mothers took active roles in the education of the youngsters. Some were determined to make their sons into productive citizens, even though it meant acting more like Yankees. Women taught in the schools, and in some counties women were appointed as school commissioners. They also dominated many churches. One man claimed he and the minister were the only male members of his church. Women ran most Sunday schools, distributed religious tracts, arranged many religious activities, and even led prayer sessions. Ideas associated with Queen Victoria in Great Britain (what later became known as "middle-class morality") influenced most Americans and Virginians. In certain lines of work, at home, at church, and to a degree at school, women directed and often dominated matters.

Virginians were much more religious at the end of this era than at the beginning. Few Virginians attended church in the 1780s, despite the efforts of evangelicals. The Second Great Awakening, launched from Kentucky just after the turn of the century, converted an undetermined number of Virginians to become active Christians. Methodists had camp meetings on Tangier Island, in the neighborhood of New Bern in the Southwest, and in other locales. In 1831 Presbyterians and others made a concerted effort to convert Virginians not only to their kind of Christianity but also to a different style of living. Anne Royall, a notorious social critic who toured the state that year, claimed the "Long Coats" captured several towns in the west as well as Charlottesville and the University of Virginia, and Prince Edward Court House. The situation became so bad in Lynchburg that when these religious raiders banned dancing and drinking, one man left for Texas. Presbyterians took almost permanent control in Lexington, where men could approach young women only at church. Whereas in colonial times, women loved to dance, a passerby near Lexington in the 1830s discovered several men at a dance where there were no women.

Although such changes remained localized and impermanent, churches tended to find greater numerical strength with passing decades. A survey of Virginia in the mid-1830s found hundreds of churches, though not all of them impressive. By 1850 most counties in Virginia had about as many pew spaces in their churches as they had adults in their overall population. A Baptist church for blacks in Richmond had room for a congregation of 1,500. Baptisms in the James River brought out throngs. Contrast this description with that of the traveler in the 1780s that claimed the Richmond church had only enough space to accommodate a fraction of the town's 2,000 residents.

Tastes in literature followed British trends. Virginia women of the elite and increasingly of the middle class liked the works of British writers, including Sir Walter Scott. Stories set among England's gentry or in medieval times had romantic appeal. The wife of the man who supervised construction of the Norfolk and Petersburg Rail Road became so enamored with British novels that she had her husband name the little depots for references in these stories (Windsor, Wakefield, Waverly, etc.). Virginians read some northern writers, but Stowe's *Uncle Tom's Cabin* met a firestorm of criticism. That Stowe also set one of her stories, *Dred: A Slave of the Dismal Swamp*, in Virginia and based her main character on Nat Turner in a sympathetic fashion also did not sit well with Virginians. A few Virginia women, however, thought the writer's portrayal of slavery accurate.

By far the most influential literary person from Virginia in this era was Edgar Allen Poe. Left as an orphan when his actress mother died in Richmond in 1811, the 3-year-old Poe was taken in by a merchant named Allan. A vigorous lad able to swim the James River against the current and engage in pugilism, he attended the new University of Virginia for a year but left largely because of financial improprieties. A successful hitch in the army while stationed at Fort Monroe led to an appointment at West Point. After a brief time there, he launched a brilliant career as a poet and writer. Critics consider his mysteries and detective stories path breaking. He also returned to Richmond for a time to help edit a southern literary magazine. Estrangement from his stepfather, peculiar relationships with the opposite sex (he married his 14-year-old cousin), and a sustained drinking problem marred his life, which ended in Baltimore under mysterious circumstances. Early in the 19th century William Wirt's *Letters of a British Spy* attracted notice. Nathaniel

Beverley Tucker wrote George Balcombe, about his experiences in Missouri as an advocate of slavery, and *The Partisan Leader*, where he forecasted Virginia's participation in a future civil war. William Caruthers of Lexington produced *The Kentuckian in New York* and *The Knights of the Golden Horseshoe*. John Pendleton Kennedy, a frequent summer visitor, authored *Swallow Barn*, which described plantation life, and other novels and historical romances. He often provided Virginia settings for his works. His political ideas contrasted rather sharply with those of Nathaniel Tucker as Kennedy, a strong Whig and champion of moving slaves to Africa, strove to keep the nation together. Civil War soldier John Esten Cooke, in *Ellie*, wrote about a poor girl from Richmond, among other themes in a productive, if somewhat hurried, career in romantic literature. George Tucker produced *The Valley of the Shenandoah or Memoirs of the Graysons*, *Voyage to the Moon*, and *A Century Hence*, a manuscript not published until 1977. Although none of these works rose to the stature of great writing, they and other writings, hinted at the existence of creative juices in the Old Dominion.

Virginia had some talented artists. Edward Peticolas, a baby when his family fled from the ravages of the Santo Domingo rebellion to Richmond, specialized in portraiture. John Gadsby Chapman of Alexandria became an illustrator, but had to leave Virginia to attain fame as a painter. William Hubbard, an Englishman, did portraits of many famous Virginians and others. Alexander Galt, born in Norfolk, studied sculpturing in Italy, and produced the statue of Jefferson at the University of Virginia. A number of other artists attained fame after the Civil War.

The emergence of the health springs of Virginia changed rural Virginia. By the 1830s one could ride a stagecoach to New Bern along the Wilderness Road, board a stage going west, and tour one or several springs, before coming back on the main highway at Fincastle. By the 1850s this trip offered the three springs named for different colors plus Sweet Springs. In Virginia's northern extremity, one could stay at Berkeley Springs, or to the south at Warm or Hot Springs. The eastern slope of the Appalachians and the Valley had several springs, usually just a few miles from the old Valley Road. East of the Blue Ridge, Fauquier County had the impressive White Sulphur Springs. Almost all the mineral springs expanded in the 1850s. In that decade railroads made the overall trip to the various sites much quicker. The spas, which had been little more than a series of shacks at the beginning of the century, had hotels. One had a row of cottages in the Greek style matched by another set in Gothic Revival, befitting the medieval interests of the culture of the 1850s. The layout of several of these resorts resembled Jefferson's plan for the University of Virginia. The effort to develop these spas reflected a desire to bring order to the wilderness and at the same time to blend with nature. The owners, of course, wanted to make money, and in a part of Virginia where traditional plantations could not really function, the resorts, which in some cases catered to almost 2,000 visitors at a time, gave a significant commercial boost. In time emphasis shifted from the health-giving properties of the hot sulfur water to the cultural activities of Virginia's summer elite. So many urban Virginians went to the spas in the summer that normal social activities of the elite virtually ceased in the towns and cities. In summers such as in 1832, when cholera stalked the land, or in 1855, when yellow fever raged, moving to the various springs saved lives. Spas also provided a pleasant place for the elite to display their romantic love for nature and an imagined medieval lifestyle based on the works of Sir Walter Scott. At the end of the summer, each spring had an elaborate jousting tournament as Southern blades showed their skills riding horses and wielding lances. Young men and women carried on courtships as costume balls, musical performances, and dances provided entertainment. Slaves served their masters, but they also developed their own forms of entertainment, and black musicians played an important role in spa culture. Although servants still had to perform menial tasks, they were treated less like plantation slaves, probably because owners wanted to present a positive image of the institution of slavery, which looked like medieval serfdom in a resort setting. Some critics, however, thought that the resorts went too far in letting servants ride on coaches and promenade on picturesque paths. The spas doubtless made people more aware of nature and did limited long-term damage to what was being admired. If landscape architects of the time were correct in believing that pleasant surrounding made for better behaving people, they could have cited resort life as proof for their assertion, but beautiful surroundings did not guarantee the best in people, witness the presence of professional gamblers, who hoped to take advantage of the unwary. In addition to the spas in the mountains, antebellum Virginia featured a few resorts on the coast, such as the Hygeia right next to Fort Monroe, near Hampton. Commercials in newspapers of the time urged folks to take advantage of sea bathing as well as local fish and oysters.

The changes associated with this era, limited though they were, had an impact on the environment. The rail lines and steamboats doubtless changed the landscape, as they required a good bit of timber for fuel. Steam engine smoke changed the quality of air, but because these enterprises were comparatively small, at least in comparison to what followed, they did not intrude deeply into the environment. In time, the trains and their small depots fit the bucolic image romantics could admire. Although farming practices improved during this time, soil erosion and ancient techniques continued to cost farmers and injure the environment.

In the years before the Civil War, the Old Dominion experienced some urban growth. By 1860 around 9% of the population lived in 14 communities that each had 2,500 or more residents. The nation as a whole had over double that proportion. Despite this tendency to trail in the rate of urbanization, Virginia's cities, with one or two exceptions, gained population during this era. The state in 1860 also contained between 20 and 30 towns of over 1,000 but with less than 2,500 residents. A similar number had between 500 and 1,000 in population. Every one of the 150 counties had a courthouse, the vast majority located in villages. Dozens of little railroad depots with at most a store or two materialized in the decades just before the Civil War. All of these communities played cultural and commercial roles disproportionate to their numbers, but they only slightly modified the rural nature of the state.

Richmond, the state capital, had the most people with almost 38,000 in 1860. The thriving little industrial community of Manchester, just across the James River, had nearly 2,800 residents in 1860. Some of its residents worked in Richmond's foundries. Richmond's outskirts contained another 5,000 to 10,000. Commercial reasons explain its growth, its status as the capital helping only slightly. It started out as a trading post and became a cluster of tobacco inspection stations. Rebounding from the destruction of the Revolution, it soon developed large mills to grind wheat into flour. The fact that Richmond acquired operations that required large outlays of capital suggests the presence of a successful and enterprising mercantile class. Scotsmen played a significant role in the early years, New England businessmen after the War of 1812. Despite these advances, a woman in 1827 found the capital "a vilely dirty place," despite its attractive location. On a tour of the city she visited the penitentiary, "the most disagreeable sight of the kind that I have seen," the arsenal "in decay," and the room for the House of Delegates "thick with dirt," and "flooded with their horrible spitting." The developing iron foundries and nearby coal mines did little to improve the atmosphere. Comments on character and cleanliness aside, Richmond moved ahead. Flour mills needed only a few workers for everyday operations, but chewing tobacco plants required over 400 workers, including some female laborers in 1860). The Tredegar Iron Works attained an international reputation and had about eight hundred workmen by 1860. As a transfer point for cargo on the James, Richmond's future seemed secure especially after the city deepened the river next to its docks. As the largest city in Virginia, the capital was the first city to build a water reservoir, bring gas lighting to the streets and a small number of private residences, and pay firemen. Yet even the biggest city in the state exhibited economic deficiencies. Richmond, the largest city in Virginia, had little control over insurance and the movement of money, especially during the Panic of 1857. It showed only a little interest in the mountains of resources to its west. It built few steamboats (two small companies kept 88 workers busy in 1860). A northern company provided the engines for one of the first steamboats to ply the James River Canal. The city did some things rather well, but it lacked a broad-based industrial and commercial economy. City fathers invested in the Virginia and Tennessee Rail Road in hopes of pulling more traffic over the Richmond and Danville. Its middle class was growing and compared favorably in wealth to northern communities, especially when one counts the value of its slaves. Urban businessmen complained about iniquities in the Virginia tax code. In the late 1850s Virginia taxed land, slaves, capital, and personal property at 40 cents for each $100 in value each year. Retailers paid a fee for a license and $2.56 on each $100 in sales. In 1859 retailers had even more to complain about when the state, in the wake of John Brown's raid, added a 1% tax on goods not imported or manufactured in Virginia. Aimed at interstate trade, it troubled Virginians as well as Yankee peddlers, who frequented the byways of the state.

Norfolk and Portsmouth area contained about 22,000 residents on the eve of the Civil War, with about two-thirds of that total residing in Norfolk. Both communities would have been quite a bit larger save for a yellow fever epidemic that killed about 3,000 people in 1855. Sustained prosperity proved difficult because of Panic of 1819 and British restrictions on commerce with its West Indies. The Dismal Swamp Canal brought in a steady flow of North Carolina products, but shingles, staves, and corn were so low in value that merchants could make little money off them. In 1815 Bedford County men rowed a barrel of flour all the way down the Roanoke River, across Albemarle Sound, and up the Dismal Swamp Canal, leading locals to create the Roanoke Docks. At the beginning of the century Norfolk had a sizeable sail and rope-making concern with 54 slaves, but Virginia's backcountry failed to supply quality hemp, and only two small ropewalks remained in 1850. Norfolk had but one tiny textile mill and a tobacco processing company before the Civil War. In the 1820s and 1830s local steamboat builders could construct a sizeable craft, but they sent their hulls to Baltimore to have boilers installed. In 1860 local privately owned iron works hired but 36 men. When some entrepreneurs tried to build a square-rigger in the 1850s, they found tall pines nearby, but they sent to Maine for workmen skilled in building big ships. Meanwhile, the nearby federal shipyard next to Portsmouth built both steamboats and larger vessels. In the 1850s it hired dozens of German machinists, recent immigrants to the area. At the end of the 1850s the Elizabeth River ports secured the Norfolk and Petersburg Rail Road and the Albemarle and Chesapeake Canal, which linked the Elizabeth River with the sounds of North Carolina. While the reconstruction of the Dismal Swamp project in the late 1820s required heavy use of slave labor using hand tools over many years, workmen using steam shovels quickly built the Albemarle Canal in the 1850s. Almost all the goods passing through Norfolk either came from or went to New York, Baltimore, or Philadelphia. Although Southerners thought some sort of conspiracy kept their economy in bondage, the lack of direct trade had to do with what the small port could offer customers. New York, for instance, introduced scheduled departures for many ships shortly after the War of 1812. After Herculean efforts, local merchants arranged for one cargo to be shipped directly to France. After the Civil War, a similar project ended with a ship sinking at sea. On the positive side, a visitor who had seen the port in 1809 found many substantial brick buildings serving as residences and businesses thirty years later. The city added gas lighting in the 1850s and also had several humane societies such as the Norfolk Association for the Improvement of the Poor, the Dorcas Society (a religious nonsectarian organization devoted to helping women), the Humane Society, and the Howard Association, which raised money in the wake of a yellow fever epidemic. Norfolk's Board of Health failed to detect the arrival of the fever, when a captain hid a sick seaman to avoid quarantine. All cities had almshouses that put poor people to work if they were able as well as charitable societies the same as or similar to the ones in Norfolk.

Suffolk occasionally showed signs of life as a lumber town, but its thriving oyster business dwindled, the apparent victim of "foreigners" (Marylanders) with dredges. State legislation in 1804 banned the intentional use of oyster shells to obtain lime for construction purposes, showing that Virginians were aware that the supply of oysters was limited. In 1850 Suffolk authorities carried out a "war" against outside oystermen, sending out an artillery company on a steamboat to support the sheriff in arresting 75 men and capturing twelve vessels at the mouth of the Nansemond River. The local newspaper joked about the "greatest naval victory on record." The production of naval stores (i.e., tar and turpentine), at once time so flourishing that leaking barrels of tar provided Suffolk with what one observer called "an apology for pavement" virtually ceased by the 1830s.

Alexandria, on the Potomac River, founded in 1749, progressed slowly. Travelers found the river port well planned, built on the Philadelphia model, its streets being constructed at right angles It could always depend on shad and herring frequenting the Potomac River each spring, but the fishing industry was not sufficient to support a large town. It prospered by housing workers when the federal government built public buildings across the river. Early in the 19th century it became part of the District of Columbia. Its residents expected to profit from the move, but the town languished. In the 1790s wagonloads of wheat came from northern Virginia, including the Valley, but commercial interests took a hit during the quasi-war with France and during the War of 1812, the British burned many of its warehouses. Legend suggests that the backcountry farmers turned to Baltimore when Alexandria's merchants would not cover the losses. The more likely cause of this decline had to do with the failure to develop large mills because of a shortage of capital and sources of power. Visitors to Alexandria in the 1830s found many impressive looking but run down and sometimes abandoned brick buildings. Anne Royall thought the residents lacked "bold assurance." Along with the rest of eastern Virginia, Alexandria recovered in the late 1840s around the time the city rejoined Virginia (1847). On the eve of the railroad era, three turnpikes served the city. One, the Little River, entered the city from the south, providing a link with Fairfax Court House. Another pike tied the port to Leesburg, and a third proceeded west to the Long Bridge, which spanned the Potomac. Soon investors constructed the Orange and

Alexandria and later the Loudoun and Hampshire railroads. In 1852 residents were confident enough to ratify a $100,000 municipal investment in the Manassas Rail Road, an extension of the Orange and Alexandria Rail Road, by a vote of 501 to 7. As the terminus of the O & A, the city even had a locomotive and railroad car making plant, albeit a small one. One steam flour company, established in 1854, put out 800 barrels of flour per day, the second largest output of all the mills in Virginia. A coal company handled the cargoes coming over the Hampshire railroad line. By the time of the Civil War, a short line connected Alexandria to the southern side of the Long Bridge. One of the more unusual manmade physical structures of the time, an aqueduct carried barges from the end of the Chesapeake and Ohio canal at Georgetown across the river, where a canal bore the traffic to Alexandria. Investors could put their money into canals, railroads, iron works, coal companies, a cotton factory that hired over 100 white women, waterworks, and the Bank of the Old Dominion. Conditions became so salubrious in the old port that residents revived the long-dormant theater in 1859. Despite it all, Alexandria had less than 15,000 people in 1860.

In 1826 Anne Royall found Fredericksburg "far from flourishing," seeming to suffer from the same defects as Alexandria with a more untidy appearance and limited commerce. But in the mid-1830s improvements to the upper Rappahannock River helped the town by providing a waterway 50 miles west of the city. Ships of 140 tons annually carried off exports including about 500,000 bushels of corn, 150,000 bushels of wheat, but only 400 hogsheads of tobacco, along with $75,000 in gold dug out of nearby mines. At the time it had just over 3,300 residents. By 1860 it contained about 5,000.

Petersburg, "the Cockade City" stood on the south side of the Appomattox River, a few miles from the James. A canal company, chartered in 1788, improved the flow of commerce on the Lower Appomattox, while another company, organized seven years later, worked on the Upper Appomattox. Although both companies improved the situation, Petersburg never acquired a canal that could bear even medium-sized ships, but the flow of water did allow industrial development. After a major fire shortly after the War of 1812, residents rebuilt the town, primarily with brick. The city added amenities like gas lighting in the 1850s. As early as the 1820s the area possessed several textile mills. Their owners brought cotton from the lower part of Virginia and North Carolina. People called the city, "the Lowell of the South," but it failed to develop a large machine tool industry as a spinoff from its textiles. The textile industry remained but, possibly because of the loss of the protective tariff, did not expand. In 1860 the city contained seven cotton mills that kept about 600 women and 500 men at work. Five of these mills operated on the north side of the river, which technically placed them in Chesterfield County. A resident of the town invented a machine that replaced the hand-operated chewing tobacco press. Proportionate to its population, it had a big industrial base, and it more than doubled in population between 1830 and 1860, reaching over 18,000 at the later date.

Lynchburg, the Gateway to the West, handled the tobacco crop and contained several tobacco manufacturing firms. It benefited some from the canal along the James River. Its flour milling remained a secondary line of work. A large foundry produced iron in the 1850s. At times the city seemed prosperous, though its official population dropped in the 1850s. At its peak it contained close to 9,000 residents. The city served as the western terminus of the South Side Rail Road and the eastern terminus of the Virginia and Tennessee. Its waterworks were considered ahead of their time.

Danville, a southwestern Piedmont community destined to become a large industrial city, had about 3,000 folks in 1860, but was growing rapidly. The great increase in tobacco production in Pittsylvania County helped its commercial situation, even though it lost its status as an inspection station in 1836. Pittsylvania farmers brought much of their leaf into town for auction sales to the manufacturers of plug or chewing tobacco.

Wheeling, in the far northwestern part of the state, experienced growth during this era. As an industrial town, it had gas works, woolen mills based on nearby sheep ranches, a glass factory, and two foundries producing more nails and spikes than any other such place in the nation. It and several smaller communities on the Ohio River specialized in making steamboats. Wheeling far outpaced any city in eastern Virginia in this category with 188 workmen in 1860. The mix of businesses allowed it to grow to over 14,000 residents by 1860, the only city of any size in the Northwest.

The Valley in 1860 had some neat communities and a large share of the state's medium-sized towns. Martinsburg (3364), Harpers Ferry (1339), Winchester (4392), Woodstock, Strasburg (1583), Front Royal, New Market, Harrisonburg (1023), Waynesboro, Staunton (3875), and Lexington (2135) gave the Valley some lively towns. Most of these towns had existed before the beginning of the new century and had been helped in their development by commercial wheat farming and flour milling. Located along a relatively narrow strip of land, they contained numerous tradesmen and artisans The Valley also had a string of stage stops and several mill villages located near forges and furnaces.

Winchester commenced its communal existence in the late 1740s, when a resident received a charter for a town of some 80 half-acre lots, each connected to five acres outside the town. After the Revolution, Winchester and its rural neighborhood, as well as other communities in the Shenandoah Valley benefited from increased prices for wheat in Atlantic markets. Several merchants made Winchester a transshipping point for flour and limited amounts of tobacco and hemp carried mostly by wagon from the Valley to Alexandria and other ports. Winchester storekeepers acquired most of their stock and credit from Philadelphia, although some came from Alexandria. Farmers expanded their arable lands and increased production of a wide variety of necessities and surplus crops. An area endowed with a rapidly descending stream right next to Winchester and a fairly well populated adjacent countryside, the town prospered. It had a public square, about 30 stores, plus an assortment of wagon makers, smiths, weavers, and other skilled people. The traveling public could access about a dozen inns or ordinaries. Winchester grew with comparatively few problems until the Civil War.

A traveler in 1839 found the crowd at the old colonial courthouse at Fincastle numerous but only because the court was in session. The Southwest had Salem in Roanoke County, an attractive community. Snowville, founded in the 1830s on the Little River in what became Pulaski County, was located several miles from the Wilderness Road, but it contained over 100 residents. With a single building devoted to a wide variety of manufacturing endeavors, the community strongly resembled the industrial villages of eastern Connecticut, partially explained by the its physical surroundings but also because many of its residents came from New England. Wytheville had over 1,000 residents and possibilities. Abingdon in Washington County looked bigger but was overlooked by the published census. Bristol, on the Tennessee border, got its start in the 1850s with the coming of the Virginia and Tennessee Railroad.

Every county had a courthouse community, which possessed public structures and at least a few permanent residents. But throughout the early 19th century several counties developed numerous, and in some cases populous villages in contrast to colonial times, when such places could rarely be found. These communities were usually located along the various turnpikes or better country roads. Villages had a far greater importance than their small populations might indicate. They were convenient locations for post offices (sometimes in homes) stores, taverns, and churches as well as social organizations such as Freemasons and even occasional chapters of the colonization society. Such communities also usually contained blacksmiths, coopers, and other artisans, many of whom were free blacks. Their presence explains in part why several counties, although almost wholly rural by standards of the time had a large number of their working people doing something besides farming

Northern Virginia had more of these its share of these communities. Loudoun County had almost a dozen large villages. All of these could be found near or on one or more of the turnpikes that crisscrossed the county. Neighboring Fairfax had its courthouse community situated on a turnpike, plus at least three other villages, included Falls Church, on the Leesburg Pike. Other villages included railroad depots for the Orange and Alexandria and a smaller line traversing the county. In the southern part of the county, Centreville took advantage of whatever traffic passed on the turnpike to Warrenton.

Industrialization closely follows urbanization and vice versa. Much of the state's manufacturing capacity and capital concentrated in cities like Wheeling, Richmond, Petersburg, Lynchburg, Alexandria, and to a lesser extent in places like Fredericksburg, Norfolk, and Portsmouth. In addition, industrial villages were scattered over parts of the Piedmont and western Virginia. The iron industry flourished in some places and times and not in others. In the years following the Revolution, blast furnaces did rather well, as iron producers used charcoal and local deposits of iron ore. By the Civil War, however, many of these establishments closed, unable to compete against coal and coke-fired foundries and cheaper transportation costs. The works in Franklin County, operating since before the Revolution, closed down on the eve of the Civil War, as its main market at Danville sold ironware at cheaper prices. Winchester lost a number of skilled artisans when the railroad reduced costs to allow outside competitors to sell cheaper at local stores.

Since the Revolution, Virginia had been progressing toward a more diversified economy. By 1860 the state, although it remained largely rural, had more free people employed outside farming than in it. It had over 4,000 blacksmiths, some 1,600 wheelwrights, over 9,000 carpenters and a wide array of other occupations, including 2,200 apprentices. It had just over 1,000 grocers and almost 5,000 merchants. Curiously, Virginia, with its long bay and coastline, had but 1,600 mariners, and it had only 1,200 weavers and only 226 free ironworkers, evidence of weak manufacturing base. Because the overwhelming majority of almost 500,000 slaves lived on farms, Virginia agriculture retained its dominance.

# PART THREE: ERA OF THE CIVIL WAR

Around 1850 Virginia entered what proved to be two decades of rapid and drastic changes. Virginians had a long track record on the rights of the states, and as matters stood around 1850, the majority view in Virginia in defense of the states against the power of the central government prevailed. The one wild card in the political deck that strained and finally ruined relations with the North was the issue of slavery. The strengthening of that institution in the state, a related decline of the rights of free blacks, and the issue of slavery in national political scene are discussed in Chapter 11. The election of the Republican Abraham Lincoln in 1860 convinced several states of the Deep South to secede from the union. During the ensuing crisis, Virginia seceded and joined the Confederacy and then fought in a protracted civil war, covered in Chapter 12.

As home to the most important front in the fighting, Virginia became the scene for much death and destruction. The loss of the northwestern part of the state accompanied the war. The financial cost of the war took the form of the demise of most banks in Virginia, a high level of inflation, and no progress on paying the pre-war state debt. The war ushered in an era of corruption known as "the Gilded Age," and a longer era of business dominance over the federal government.

On the positive side, President Lincoln found an ingenious way to bring the institution of slavery to an end, although the status of the newly freed blacks remained in question. As part of a lingering legacy on the positive side, hallowed battle sites later greatly encouraged tourism in Virginia.

Changes did not end with the war, as will be seen in Chapter 13. The reconstruction that followed produced a new constitution for Virginia, which brought universal voting rights for all adult black males, along with a system of segregated public schools. After a brief decline in black participation in politics, a biracial movement to readjust the state debt and save the schools caused great political turmoil. By the mid-1890s blacks were pretty much removed from the political process in most of the state, causing some Virginians to think the era before the Civil War had been restored.

# Chapter 11

## Slavery and the Coming of War

In the 1790s the movement against slavery slowed and steps to control free blacks began to increase. As of 1793 free blacks could no longer enter Virginia. In the middle of the decade, St. George Tucker, a prominent judge, developed a complicated plan to end slavery, wherein at a specified age those born into slavery would be granted freedom as if they were indentured servants, but they then had to leave the state or sign annual work contracts. The legislature did not even consider the proposal. A massive slave uprising in Haiti sent hundreds of French refugees, along with many of their slaves, into Virginia. A French visitor to the Norfolk area in the mid-1790s observed that Haitian blacks were prone to believe in sorcery and practiced voodoo. Whites feared both sorcery and the dangers from blacks that had seen a slave insurrection. Nothing could be done about slavery in such an atmosphere.

During the first part of the 19th century most educated Virginians believed slavery was a necessary evil that had been forced on the slaveholders. The decline of the tobacco industry in the Tidewater meant that planters need not rely on slave labor as much as before. By 1800 both the Piedmont and Tidewater north of the James River, exhibited the same traits, with many planters having surplus slaves. The religiously-minded Robert Carter of Nomini Hall on the Northern Neck freed hundreds. George Washington, far less susceptible to religious emotionalism, provided freedom for some of his slaves in his will, and his widow manumitted many slaves before she died. But although some prominent people freed their slaves, most planters preferred to sell their chattel or moved with their slaves to areas where they could be more useful. Many hired out their slaves in the rising towns or among fellow planters who could still make money in commercial agriculture.

In 1800 the Gabriel Conspiracy sent a shock through Virginia and the South. A slave in the Prosser family, which had a plantation just north of Richmond, plotted with others to set fires in downtown Richmond, capture the state arsenal and secure its weapons, and kidnap Governor Monroe. Gabriel, a blacksmith more or less on his own in Richmond, advised his coconspirators not to kill Quakers, Baptists, and French people. Gabriel had white friends among the mechanics of Richmond and also did not like certain Federalist merchants or their political ideas. His old master had recently died, and a younger man now owned him. In a fight with the overseer of the neighboring plantation, he bit off part his adversary's ear. Facing death, he pled benefit of clergy and by reading and explaining scripture escaped death.

A sudden thunderstorm and a slave telling his master about the potential rebellion prevented the conspiracy from being carried out. Warned in advance, Monroe called out the militia. The authorities arrested the conspirators, plus a few that likely had nothing to do with the plan. Gabriel jumped into the James River, where a cooperative ship captain carried him to Norfolk. Authorities there apprehended the captain and Gabriel, when another slave informed on them. The captain posted bond and disappeared. Gabriel returned to Richmond, where he was tried and executed. One of the leaders, facing the gallows, supposedly said that, like George Washington, he would give his life for his people. When about a score of slaves had been executed, several slaves implicated in the plot were sold out of state.

In the aftermath of this affair, white Virginians learned about the extent of the conspiracy. Two years later Norfolk authorities executed a slave thought to have been part of the same or another plot, despite evidence that the witness against the alleged conspirator committed the crime, not the accused, but an appeal to Governor Monroe failed to save the victim. The execution of an innocent black mattered little compared to the need to maintain order.

In the aftermath of the conspiracy, the legislature beefed up slave patrols, arranged for better protection for the arsenal, and, believing blacks that navigated waterways acted as messengers for conspirators, made it impossible for blacks, either slave or free, to pilot boats in the commonwealth. Free blacks under a law passed in 1805 could not possess or carry either arms or ammunition without a license.

The legislature also placed restrictions on educating slaves. Jefferson thought it permissible to teach slaves to read but not to write, but under the law, they were not to be taught at all. In a belated reaction to the Gabriel plot in 1805, the Assembly sharply reduced the chances for manumission by requiring all newly freed slaves to leave the state within a year. A handful with especially meritorious credentials were exempted, but those who remained in the state after being manumitted could be sold, the proceeds going to the local overseer of the poor. These officers also received income from the sale of slaves imported into Virginia.

Yet despite the tendency for the state to take away rights of free blacks, occasional lack of enforcement of applicable laws left some mulattoes with a peculiar status in society. In 1816 Robert Wright, a Campbell County slave and property holding mulatto planter (the son of a white father and an African mother) petitioned the state legislature for a divorce after his white wife deserted him for the second time. Because interracial marriages were illegal, the authorities turned down the request. Curiously, though, not only did Wright's white neighbors fully support him in his quest, but they had also previously prevented white relatives from taking his inherited property. The state's failure to grant a divorce thus prevented Wright from remarrying and left his infant son in legal limbo.

The charge that Baptists and Methodists might be involved in the Gabriel incident also discouraged members of those denominations from associating with blacks. Over a decade before, a leading Methodist figured out that efforts to end slavery discouraged recruiting converts. Another noted in 1780 that his congregation did not want to hear about the topic. Itinerant ministers were shot at, bullied, cursed, and otherwise molested as they tried to recruit blacks In 1785 Virginia Methodists suspended their rule that required members to free their slaves within two years of joining the organization. In 1804 the Methodists dropped the restrictions on buying and selling slaves. Although Methodists abandoned abolitionism, some Baptists held on longer. They had integrated churches, even black ministers with mixed congregations after 1800. As a possible result of this trend, blacks retained their preference for the Baptist religion. Quakers stuck to their moral guns. In 1784 Quakers in Virginia no longer could hold slaves. They opposed slavery, but in 1798 neither they nor any other abolitionists were allowed to sit on any jury in the state that considered the status of slaves. Virginia had far too few Quakers to make an impact on the issue.

Over the next two decades, the number of slaves and free blacks continued to increase, but in absolute numbers slaves vastly outnumbered free blacks. In 1790 Virginia had about 12,000 free blacks and 292,000 slaves; by 1810 the state had three times the number of free blacks but 100,000 more slaves. Despite the more rapid growth of slaves, the number of free blacks, especially in the few towns in Virginia, seemed especially troublesome to whites. The invention of the cotton gin in 1793 and the legal end to the international slave trade in 1808 on a national level affected the marketability of Virginia slaves that could now be sold in ever greater numbers to other parts of the South. Despite the loss of several thousand slaves during the War of 1812, the numbers of slaves continued to grow but at a reduced rate, largely because so many went into the newer and more productive slave states. The proportion of slaves of the total population was about 40% until 1820, when the percentage began a slow descent.

In December 1800 the general assembly, in a secret session, asked Governor Monroe to write to president-elect Thomas Jefferson to help find a new place of residence for free blacks. Jefferson mentioned the West Indies, with Santo Domingo the best bet. A last resort might be the west coast of Africa. Around this time the British opened Sierra Leone with a population consisting at least in part of some black Virginia loyalists that went to Canada after the Revolution. Various proposals had free Virginia blacks headed to Haiti or the unsettled parts of the American west.

In 1816 leading Virginians joined the American Colonization Society, which hoped to send free blacks to Africa. Virginia-born Henry Clay, who had tried to stop slavery from getting a foothold in Kentucky, President James Monroe, and Bushrod Washington, the nephew of George and a prominent judge, belonged to the society. Charles Mercer, a nationalist Congressman from northern Virginia, saw the need to erase the one major blot on the state. The federal government and the society sponsored a shipload of former slaves and free blacks out of Norfolk to Africa in 1821. The state kicked in $20,000 in 1826. Lot Carey, one of the early settlers, became a leader in Liberia, and Joseph Roberts, reared in Petersburg and Norfolk, became president of the new republic. That new nation helped stem the flow of slaves out of Africa, but the newcomers also became oppressors over the local tribes. Despite herculean efforts, the movement of free blacks to Africa attracted only around 1.000 Virginia blacks. In 1830 more slaves and free blacks were in Virginia than had been there ten years earlier. The same held true for each decennial census that followed.

In 1787 Thomas Jefferson persuaded Congress under the Articles of Confederation to prevent slavery from moving into the Northwest Territory. Thus in the early years of the republic the area west of the Ohio was off limits to slaveholders. As Virginians migrated into that area, they sold their slaves or in a few instances freed them. Edward Coles, a neighbor of Jefferson in Albemarle County, told his slaves, as they sat on a barge in the Ohio River, that they were free. They joyfully agreed to help establish his estate, and he, in turn, arranged for their transition to freedom. Later as governor of Illinois, he prevented that state from opening up to slavery. The few thousand Virginia blacks that made it across the Ohio River found racism there about as strong as in the Old Dominion. Residents of the Old Northwest did not want free blacks in their area. When John Randolph of Roanoke freed slaves in his will, probated in 1831, he also provided money for their resettlement in Ohio, a process resisted by residents of the Buckeye State.

In the years following the War of 1812, many Virginians moved to Missouri. Most of them gave up their slaves, but a number brought their property with them. Nathaniel Beverley Tucker, one of the leaders in this enterprise, soon returned to his home state to become a strong spokesman for the retention of the slave system. Enough slaveholders entered Missouri so that in 1819 Missouri petitioned the federal government for statehood as a slave state. Northerners accepted the idea only after the Maine district in Massachusetts was given status as a free state. More importantly, the area in the Louisiana Territory above the 36th parallel could not contain slaves. The Northwest Ordinance, drawn up by Jefferson, would now be extended into the bulk of the nation's territories. Jefferson himself, though pleased that Congress produced the Compromise of 1820, regarded the raising of the issue itself as a "fire bell in the night." Afterwards the author of the Northwest Ordinance argued that allowing slaves into the western territories might be a way to dilute the institution. Some sarcastic Southerners urged that slaves be spread evenly across the entire nation.

Jefferson had serious doubts about the innate abilities of people of African descent and the possibility of progress for blacks in American society. Scholars of the time, like Jefferson, wondered about a link between apes and humans in Africa. Doubting the biblical stories of creation, they had ideas, forerunners to evolution, about man belonging to a "chain of being." They believed blacks were a lower order of animal and could not function in American culture as free people. Medical literature of the time found physical differences of the races. Jefferson saw Virginia inhabited by two distinct nationalities that simply could not mix. On the humanitarian side, Jefferson worried that mean-spirited whites would persecute blacks. Jefferson, therefore, opposed slavery but, like most Southern whites, thought free blacks had to be removed. Such an undertaking simply overwhelmed his generation, and thus he and numerous others gave up on the idea of actively pursuing the abolition of slavery. As Jefferson saw the problem in 1820, his generation had a "wolf by the ears."

There the matter stood when news of the Turner Rebellion reached terrified whites in the summer of 1831, when a black preacher in Southampton County organized and carried out the execution of 55 whites, including many women and children. Nat Turner thought he was carrying out the will of God, having seen numerous omens. Gathering what weapons they could and consuming a "last supper," the rebels moved toward Jerusalem, the capital of the county. Turner himself apparently killed only one person as he persuaded others to follow his orders. Only a few people participated in the plot, and it covered only a small part of the surrounding area, but whites fled from Southampton in droves. They so flooded the nearby town of Hicksford (Emporia), that Brunswick County militia had trouble helping suppress the uprising. When the rebels met resistance and then encountered slaves that defended their masters, the rebellion fell apart. Turner hid for several weeks until a passerby apprehended him. By the time he was brought to trial, mobs had killed or harassed hundreds of blacks with no role in the rebellion. Turner followed his fellow rebels to the gallows. The only mass killing of whites ever carried out by slaves in the Old Dominion, this rebellion shocked white Virginians. The wounds inflicted on the victims reminded people of Indian brutalities. Although they had long feared the possibility of such an occurrence, they simply could not believe that slaves on their own would or could plan and carry out such an atrocity. Governor John Floyd blamed northern abolitionists and evangelicals. The radical William Lloyd Garrison, who started publishing a new abolitionist journal earlier in the year, advocated immediate legal steps against slavery. A year earlier a free black in Boston urged slaves to take direct action against slavery. A copy of this incendiary literature apparently surfaced in Richmond and possibly influenced the legislature to prohibit teaching free blacks to read. No one ever traced any of this literature into Southampton County, but all over Virginia and North Carolina mobs broke into homes of free blacks looking for such literature. Turner himself, though he could read, knew nothing about these abolitionist writings. Floyd, knowing that Turner was a preacher, also thought the evangelical disturbances of that same year helped promote unrest. It might well be that talk during the constitutional convention in 1829 and 1830 about western Virginia being interested in ending slavery may well have encouraged Nat and his followers.

In the wake of the rebellion, the search for scapegoats, and the ensuing panic, the Virginia legislature ordered that neither slaves nor free blacks could have guns, conduct church services without white supervision, or own slaves unless they were close relatives. The House of Delegates later passed a bill that would ban free blacks from any mechanical or trade other than barbering, but the Senate would not go along with this blatant effort by skilled white workers to reduce competition.

The legislature, at Floyd's behest, then discussed slavery. Over objections of delegates from the Southside, Thomas Jefferson Randolph submitted a plan for the gradual end to the institution. Not unlike a proposal made much earlier by his famous grandfather, Randolph called for all children born after 4 July 1840 to receive their freedom at maturity, whereupon they had to leave the state. The proposal contained a loophole for slave owners in that they could still sell children, but the plan would eventually have ended slavery in the state. A conservative counter proposal called for the state to purchase and remove six thousand slaves each year. A Southside representative who helped put down the Turner Rebellion saw slavery as a mildew stagnating about a third of the state. A small tax plus money from the federal government from land sales might do the job, he hoped.

After Easterners failed to postpone the matter, the house debated the proposal. James McDowell, expressing the western view best, parried every negative argument raised. Scriptures may not have explicitly forbidden slavery, but slavery in ancient history differed considerably from contemporary times. McDowell thought the idea that Virginians had inherited the problem provided no excuse for doing nothing. To the contention that the state could do nothing about private property, McDowell argued that public safety trumped property rights. Some conservatives thought Turner and his cohorts were little more than a drunken mob that twenty members of the militia could have brought to heel, but McDowell believed the threat posed more of a problem than the recent British attack. Written testimony and common sense suggested slaves understood the concept of freedom. A favored few might forgo freedom, but most innately desired to be free. Although repressed, their idea of liberty was essentially the same as their masters and had been granted by God, who did not mean for it to be extinguished by man. Although sounding like a northern abolitionist or at least a member of the Scottish Common Sense School, he argued against allowing the issue to bring Virginia to a point where it would take the unconstitutional step of seceding from the union and joining a confederacy of slaveholding states. Such a step would lead to anarchy and then dictatorship, the prescient McDowell predicted. Despite McDowell, the House defeated the proposal 73 to 58, with almost all delegates from west of the Blue Ridge voting for, and Easterners against, it. All delegates from the Trans-Allegheny and about 90% from the Valley condemned slavery, as the House passed that measure by seven votes.

Many delegates, agreeing that whites of low character took advantage of the prejudice existing against the colored people to mistreat them, wanted to remove free blacks from their midst. One delegate with a more positive view thought slavery part of God's master plan wherein Africa sent savage slaves and received citizens and Christians in return. Overcoming a combination of liberals and conservatives that doubted the wisdom of subsidizing efforts to send free blacks to Liberia, the legislature initially agreed to fund some $90,000 in the project. During the same debate, the delegates turned down a proposal to force all free blacks out of the state. When the situation calmed down and the legislators found out that few free blacks would leave voluntarily, the Senate rejected the idea of paying for colonization. Some years later the Assembly changed its mind again and provided an annual appropriation of $30,000.

As mentioned earlier, just before Turner's Rebellion, the legislature banned anyone from teaching free blacks to read. In Norfolk in 1853 Margaret Douglass and her daughter went to jail for a month for operating a school for blacks, the judge giving a lengthy rationale in support of the law. Authorities usually took no action against slave owners who taught their own servants. The wives of court officials even ran schools, and one Baptist church had six black Sunday school teachers. In Hampton, Mary Peake, the daughter of a free black woman and an Englishman, ran classes for up to 500 hundred black students. Overall, however, the law deterred advances in education for slaves and free blacks. A Portsmouth slave that learned to read and write without instruction upset his overseer who worried that the authorities might find fault with him.

Using some of the points raised by conservatives during the legislative debate over slavery, Thomas R. Dew, a professor and future president at the College of William and Mary, opposed deporting slaves to Africa, basing his argument on seemingly immutable laws. Virginia, he argued, needed its slaves to rebuild its agricultural economy. Older slaves would be unhappy had the Randolph proposal carried, he contended. Dew doubted that any method could be devised to pay for slaves whose $100,000,000 in value was about one-half the total worth of all property. Freeing slaves would force the value of that property to fall even further. Raising taxes to pay for freeing and moving blacks would encourage whites to flee the state and discourage others from taking up residence in it. If somehow all the slaves could be bought and removed, Virginia would be nothing more than a desert. Dew knew the typical planter of lower Virginia could not afford the philanthropy of not taking payment for slaves. Europeans, he argued, had not given up serfdom until it was in their interest. Counteracting McDowell's views, Dew made selective use of the ideas of Adam Smith, given the latter's opposition to slavery, that philanthropy was not necessarily a virtue. Eventually as Virginia industrialized, it might have less need for contented slaves, but for the time being the institution was not only necessary but good for the state and the slaves. Published in 1832, his volume remained popular in the South for years. It was neither the first nor the last defense of slavery.

A favorite proslavery position was to compare slaves in Virginia to workers elsewhere. A visiting Englishman responded to a Richmond resident's claim that English workers were far worse off than slaves in Virginia, pointing out that traders sold slaves (men, women and children) as if they were cattle. He wept with the slaves when they he heard their pitiful cries as he watched a slave auction in Richmond. In material things the poor in his homeland might live similar lives, but all people in England had essential rights. In Richmond a young boy threw some lime on a slave. In brushing away the lime from his face, the slave inadvertently dusted the assailant's eyes. The boy's brother demanded that the slave owner whip his slave, and the owner obliged. In England, a poor person had the right to resist, but Virginia law failed to protect the slave.

George Fitzhugh of Prince William County argued in the 1850s in *Sociology for the South or The Failure of a Free Society* and *Cannibals All or Slaves Without Masters* that Southern slaves lived better than northern workers. The masters, he thought, took care of their elderly slaves while factory owners left their aged workers to fend for themselves. That northern workers could change their place of employment was irrelevant. Most Virginians found little Fitzhugh's novel notions to admire, nor were they interested in resuming the importation of slaves from Africa, another of Fitzhugh's ideas. By the time Fitzhugh published his views, eastern Virginians wanted the constant agitation about the issue to cease. They wanted to go about the business of exploiting slave labor, buying and selling people, apprehending runaways, and taking their slaves wherever they went without restrictions and without being constantly reminded of their moral failings.

Dew's book signified the end of any real opposition to slavery in eastern Virginia. Opposition to slavery did not prevent McDowell from becoming governor in the early 1840s, but he said nothing more to deter slavery. A young man from Lynchburg, Jesse Harrison, wrote a rebuttal to Dew, but then left for Texas. John Pleasants, the editor of a Richmond newspaper, who tried to prevent state censure of abolitionist literature, died in what passed for a duel. John Hartwell Cocke fought for abolition and numerous other reforms, but he was out of step with his times. Only one major eastern Virginia politico, John Minor Botts, opposed slavery in the late 1840s and 1850s.

Even in parts of western Virginia antislavery voices began to fall silent. Henry Ruffner proposed a plan in 1847 to end slavery west of the Blue Ridge, but the legislature would not act on this idea. In time any western Virginian who cared to run for statewide office had to renounce any previous endorsement of even the slightest antislavery sentiment, if he wanted to be elected. Firmness on behalf of slavery became a litmus test.

The institution troubled religious leaders, but few eastern Virginia clerics openly attacked slave holding. Concerned about the destruction of families, they agreed that when a spouse was taken away, the remaining one could remarry as if the other were dead. Many ministers agreed with Dew that scriptures sanctioned slavery, as the institution had existed in ancient times and various verses suggested obedience to a master. Robert Dabney, a member of the faculty at a seminary, also argued that domestic slavery was an integral part of the civil government.

On a national level, several major Protestant denominations broke up over the issue. The Presbyterians split over theological questions in 1838 and did not divide over sectional and slave issues until 1861, but in the mid-1840s the Methodists broke in two over the question of whether a bishop could own slaves. The antislavery side remained active in northern Virginia above the Rappahannock and in the Valley and the Northwest. In responding to a national decision to prevent laymen from having slaves in 1855, proslavery Methodists wanted to rid the entire Valley and the Northwest of the "foul leprosy of anti-slavery Methodism." Even after the Civil War northern-style Methodism faced hostile receptions in Virginia. The Baptists, already rent with factions, ended up with northern and southern divisions.

As Dew was writing, the number of slaves sold out of the state was growing toward a peak in 1836 of about 40,000. Nearly all sales broke up families. Some owners expressed great remorse about selling their slaves but did it anyway. Dew pointed out that most slaves loved their masters and would follow them, even if it meant leaving their wives and children. Ensconced in academe the president of the College of William and Mary, Dew concerned himself not at all with moral questions but worried that the state might be depleting a necessary workforce. Just as he thought government should play no role in acquiring and moving slaves to Africa, he argued that no restraints should be put on the sale of slaves into the Deep South. The latter depleted the workforce, but the sale price offset the loss of population. As it turned out, sales peaked in 1836 and fell back in the years that followed as a depression discouraged land development in the Southwest. From 1790 to 1860 over 500,000 slaves born in Virginia ended up in other slave states. Thousands went out during the boom following the War of 1812. About 120,000 left in the 1830s and 80,000 in each ensuing decade.

A former slave described the movement of slaves through Norfolk harbor in the wake of the Turner Rebellion. He saw :two vessels came from Eastern Shore of Virginia loaded with cattle and colored people." As the cattle were lowing for their calves, "men and women were crying for their husbands, wives, or children" despite the presence of men with whips who tried to compel them to remain silent. When in 1839 in Hampton Roads slaves took over and steered a ship into British Bermuda, where they were freed, slave traders shifted to inland routes. Thousands crossed the New River in cofles (a group chained together). In approaching the river just after dawn, a British traveler, coming upon a huge encampment, saw an unusual spectacle. Well-dressed slave drivers, who wore broad brimmed white hats with black crepe, stood smoking cigars in front of about 300 slaves that had camped in chains that night. Led by a white rider, some 200 male slaves, in a double row, manacled and chained to each other, forded the river on foot while wagons and single horse carriages carried whites and rafts conveyed black women and children. The observer lamented their fate on leaving familiar homes to work in the unhealthy Louisiana's sugar industry where he understood the life span to be but seven years. The drivers encouraged all to sing "Old Virginia" to the banjo as they marched. The traveler, who thought Jefferson's ideas about equality and religion had led Virginia and America astray, was especially annoyed that men that talked about liberty could treat human beings in such a fashion. Virginians supposedly despised slave traders and complained about the auction houses in every major town, but one of the most famous traders served as mayor of Petersburg and as a congressman. Folks in Norfolk and Portsmouth hated him not because of his involvement in the slave trade but rather for his destroying their railroad to the Roanoke River.

The story of Moses Grandy belies the myth that Virginians treated their slaves well. A slave and boat captain fetching shingles out of the Dismal Swamp, he returned from work one day to find his wife, who was owned by another slaveholder, sold and being moved to the Deep South. The driver allowed him to talk to her from a distance but not touch her even though he would never see her again. Grandy purchased his freedom three times. After one sale he delivered a cargo at Norfolk, having paid his owner for his freedom, but a merchant introduced him to a stranger, praising him as the best boatman in the area. The man went to his former owner and bought him, even though he was free. As a slave, he saw the use of whips and paddles, and the application of brine to make wounds smart. On a plantation, where Grandy worked after one of his owners was forced into bankruptcy, overseers whipped new mothers so bad that breast milk and blood mingled. Should the black driver not strike firmly enough, he received a whipping. Slaves slaked their thirst by drinking swamp water and received gruel to eat. The treatment was even worse for those digging canals in the swamp. Grandy thought that treatment improved the closer one came to states that had no legal slavery and also pointed out that no slave wanted to work on a plantation with his wife because he could do nothing about the brutality she faced. Grandy eventually did secure his freedom and left the state. He also bought freedom for his second wife and at least one of his children. The former slave contended that no free black wanted to go to Liberia, but the slaves would go there for freedom, if given the chance.

Not all masters were brutes. A black man who later became a delegate to the assembly after the Civil War remembered his owner fondly, for she even allowed him to go to Europe. Had she freed him, he would not have been able to return to the state and try to find his wife taken by a slave dealer. At least one white woman went into the holding pens at auction houses in Richmond to save slaves.

It is also likely that treatment improved over time. The temperance movement reduced the chances of planters striking slaves in drunken rages. The authorities occasionally even tried people for killing their slaves. Evidence gathered by abolitionists of mistreatment of slaves convinced some slave owners to mend their ways. Most importantly, the increased market value of slaves made many owners desist from excessive whipping. The worth of a prime slave rose from about $400 in the 1830s to nearly $2,000 in the late 1850s during a time with virtually no inflation. But the agricultural revival of that time likely meant that slaves worked harder.

Compared to the Deep South, Virginia had few truly big plantations, but slaves were so distributed throughout the state and within counties that most slaves resided on farms with an average of between 20 and 30 slaves. Such is the case despite the fact that the majority of slaveholders, even in eastern Virginia, had few slaves. About 10% of the slaves lived in parts of Virginia that had few slaves. Thus they were in a situation with few other slaves and where masters worked in the fields, which was not necessarily something helpful to slaves. Slaves living near large numbers of slaves developed a greater sense of community and engaged in more cultural activities. The concentration of slaves in one or several large farms also allowed more opportunities for family life. All sorts of family, neighborhood, and religious gatherings were possible when dozens of slaves lived near each other. Church services took place often without white supervision, despite the legal proscriptions.

Slaveholders faced an ongoing problem with runaways. Even slaves treated rather well simply left for the North, often receiving help from friends. Henry Box (he officially changed his middle name) Brown carried out the most famous of these flights, when friends sealed him in a box in Richmond. Handlers turned the box over several times as it made its way on the railroad to Aquia Creek, along the Potomac River by steamboat, and by rail from Washington D.C., to Philadelphia, where conspirators released a bit dizzy and fatigued Brown. One escaped woman hid out in Norfolk for nearly two years before heading north. Another Norfolk slave made his way to Boston, where the authorities arrested him, but fellow blacks rescued him. He ended up in Canada, as did many fugitives. Although these stories gave heart to the abolitionist movement and slaveholders vehemently complained, only about 200 Virginia slaves, at most, successfully escaped slavery annually. About forty times as many were being forcibly removed to the Deep South at the same time.

The impact of urbanization and industrialization on diminishing slavery can be overstated, as white Virginians found slaves could be employed in a wide variety of nonagricultural activities. Those in the coal pits of Chesterfield County numbered in the hundreds. One observer in the 1830s thought the black miners preferred that kind of work, dirty and dangerous as it was, to plantation labor. Such a remark is not a positive endorsement of the supposed easy life slaves experienced on Virginia farms. Several thousand slave men, women, and children worked in the tobacco factories of Richmond, Petersburg, Lynchburg, and Danville. The foundries of Richmond hired many slaves. By 1850 some 85 plants in Richmond, Petersburg, and Lynchburg used about 6,000 slaves. Although the textile industry had few slaves, the number of slaves employed in something besides agriculture approached 30,000. Slaves could be found working in tiny forges in the Valley of Virginia, processing tobacco in little mills in Patrick County, fetching shingles in the Dismal Swamp, cutting for lumber companies, fishing and gathering oysters in York County, and repairing or building boats near the coast.

Despite of the adaptability of such labor, the percentage of slaves fell faster in those areas where alternatives to agriculture existed. Throughout the 19th century urban areas had smaller proportions of slaves compared to the surrounding countryside. The decline of slavery in the cities and towns usually exceeded that in the nearby counties. In the 1850s a marked decline took place in growing cities. In the 1850s Norfolk dropped from 30% slave to 22% and Portsmouth from 22% to 10%. The percent of free blacks grew in these places early in the century, then leveled off, and finally began to drop.

Urban slaves proved harder to control than those in the countryside. Owners and managers of industrial enterprises were chiefly interested in production and less in social control and usually found quarters for their workers away from the plants in designated enclosures. They rarely effectively supervised off work hours, even though local laws mandated restraints. From the point of view of those trying to reduce slavery in the state, this trend looked good. But in 1860 less than 9% resided in urban areas. A major trend among the towns became a minor movement for the state as a whole.

Problems usually attended what appeared to be progress. Certainly Petersburg's textile mills did not provide a healthy environment for their many female employees. Because lighting in cities often came from gas derived from coal, noxious and toxic odors filled the air near these plants. Early gas plants often burned up, leaving short-term financial losses and long-term damage to the environment. Living in cities without public sewage systems had its hazards. Death rates in urban areas exceeded those in the countryside, largely due to the prevalence of communicable diseases. So it may have been just as well that urban growth was restrained in Virginia.

Those who did not think slavery was a healthy institution took comfort from the fact that after 1820 the proportion of slaves out of the overall population fell for the entire state. Starting in that year, when 40% of the population was in slavery, the percentage dropped in each succeeding decade until it reached just over 31% in 1860. On a superficial level, it looked like the institution would disappear in another half-century or so, but the absolute number of slaves was still increasing, though at a low rate of between 3% and 4% each decade. The institution was losing ground mostly in urban areas and in the northwestern part of the state, but in absolute numbers it was still growing.

Many counties in the Southside and in parts of the Tidewater and in northern Virginia held tightly to slavery. The theory that eastern Virginia needed its slaves for agricultural revival proved accurate. The sale of surplus slaves allowed the purchase of fertilizers, and machinery brought back many depleted farms. The slaves remaining in Virginia once again became productive workers, thus giving Virginians no economic incentive to end the institution. As one Richmond newspaper put it, the slave "is here and here forever, is our property and ours forever, is never to be emancipated and is to be kept hard at work." It would take events of seismic proportions to rid Virginia of slavery.

As Virginia passed the middle of the 19th century, the state presented a picture of a balanced economy, a reasonably sober and industrious people, and a calm demeanor. In the mid-1840s the long depression began to lift, slowing down the exodus from the state. With the Constitution of 1851, western complaints moderated. In the 1850s the state seemed on the verge of a new golden age, but one without the grandees of colonial times. The rural elite still ruled, but the state had a growing middle class. Only the institution of slavery marred the scene.

In the late 1840s the slavery issue took center stage in national politics. During the Mexican War, amendments to war appropriations bills proposed by a Pennsylvania Democrat that would exclude slavery from any territories acquired as a result of the war passed the House of Representatives on several occasions, but each time the Senate blocked passage. The Calhoun and Ritchie wings of the Democratic Party divided only over the degree of hostility to this provision.

In 1849, the Whig Zachary Taylor assumed the presidency, narrowly losing the electoral vote in Virginia. Later that year, as Congress debated the issue of bringing California into the union as a free state, Southern secessionists called for a meeting in Nashville to discuss leaving the union. The Virginia legislature authorized elections to send delegates to the convention. As disaster loomed, Congress came up with the Compromise of 1850, whereby Congress voted separately on California statehood, the fate of slavery in the other territories acquired from Mexico, ending the slave trade in the District of Columbia, a tougher fugitive slave law, and the Texas boundary and debt question. Virginia Congressmen followed the rest of the South in opposing the admission of California and ending the slave trade in DC, and they also voted for a strong federal fugitive slave act. Senator James M. Mason from Virginia delivered Calhoun's final address denouncing the North for its antislavery views. The Compromise of 1850 undercut the meeting in Nashville. Delegates at meetings in Hampton and Charlottesville elected Nathaniel Tucker and William Gordon as delegates, respectively. Robert Mercer Taliaferro Hunter, a sitting U.S. senator, also went to Nashville, ready to vote for secession. Of 15 districts, 7 picked 14 representatives. With news of the compromise, the need for meeting in Nashville to consider separating from the union evaporated. Only six Virginia delegates showed up in Tennessee, and one of them opposed any talk of secession. The failure of the convention disappointed ardent secessionist Nathaniel Tucker, who considering the union a curse, contended that, "if we will not have slaves, we must be slaves."

Some of the congressmen from the western part of the state supported California as a free state, and one Whig delegate from the northern Valley favored ending the slave trade in Washington D.C. James McDowell, the Democrat from Rockbridge County, unlike other Virginia delegates, voted to admit the western state, but he opposed ending slavery in the nation's capital, a considerable modification of his former strong opposition to slavery. McDowell, not wishing to stir up the "fire-eaters," urged abolitionists in the North to desist so that the union might be saved. Even the congressman from the Wheeling area, where comparatively few slaves resided, voted with the majority of the Virginia delegation. Support for a new fugitive slave law prevailed throughout Virginia.

One congressman from eastern Virginia took the northern side on such issues. Occasionally, when the Democrats split in the district embracing the city of Richmond and Henrico County, John Minor Botts could win election. In 1851 this maverick Whig not only ran on a record in favor of the Wilmot Proviso and California statehood, but he also opposed as unconstitutional the notion that a state could secede from the union. He argued that any president who would allow a state or states to leave the union would be guilty of a felony. A united Democratic Party defeated him, but Botts carried the Whig stronghold of Richmond, although by a narrower margin than usual. At the height of the controversy over California, the voters of the city of Richmond claimed the right of secession, 214 to 105. Despite these differences, Richmond voters, more often than not, supported Botts in his occasionally successful campaigns.

Over the next decade the slavery issue failed to go away. *Uncle Tom's Cabin*, published in 1852, fired up the abolitionists. The formation of the Kansas Territory, with the potential to have slaves in an area already exempt from slavery, induced Northerners to create a new Republican Party in 1854. The Whig Party ceased to exist as a national party as Kansas experienced a civil war. Democrats joined with people of like mind among the remaining southern Whigs in supporting any legislation that might contribute to making Kansas a slave state

Democrats dominated the political scene in the Old Dominion. Senators John M. Mason and R.M.T. Hunter favored any measure to further Southern interests. Mason, who lived near Winchester, had favored the western position on representation at the Constitutional Convention in 1830. After flirting with the Whigs, he rejoined the Democrats as a strong advocate of states' rights and supporter of John C. Calhoun. The Assembly sent him to Washington to fill out an unexpired term in 1847and elected him in 1850 and again in 1856. Starting out as an independent, Hunter became a states-rights Whig, even serving as a Whig leader in the House of Representatives. A consistent supporter of Calhoun's efforts at the presidency, he took a U.S. Senate seat in 1847 as a Democrat and, like Mason, was twice reelected.

These senators and their allies also warmly endorsed the Supreme Court (1857) decision that made restricting slavery in the territories unconstitutional. Dred Scott, a Virginia-born slave, based his claim to freedom on residency in areas where Congress outlawed slavery. Chief Justice Roger Taney, the Jackson Democrat, who removed government deposits from the national bank and as a reward replaced the deceased John Marshall on the court, thought that no black, free or slave, could bring a case before his court. Because the case needed closure, Taney and the majority decided that Congress had erred in the Northwest Ordinance and the Missouri Compromise. The right to property in slaves was inviolate. Peter Daniel, a Virginian on the court who concurred with the majority decision, believed freed slaves had no rights as citizens, this despite his prior reputation, while a judge in Virginia, to defend the rights of accused free African Americans. A member of the Virginia family that had previously owned Scott purchased his freedom.

Fugitive slaves remained a hot button issue in the decade. The case of Anthony Burns, a slave who escaped from Alexandria, added to hostile feelings. Apprehended by federal marshals in Boston in 1854, he was returned to Virginia but only after a federal officer died during a riot. Federal law counteracted the laws of several northern states, but Massachusetts made it clear that it would interpose itself between escaped slaves, plus those who would help them, and the new federal law. Virginians opposed the idea of the rights of the states in this instance. Some sympathizers purchased Burns's freedom at an inflated price. A Virginia court imposed a virtual life sentence on a steamboat captain for his part in a conspiracy to save a slave from the auction block. Like many others, the captain went to the state penitentiary. During the Civil War, the governor commuted his sentence, allowing him to be exchanged as a prisoner of war. Even though the numbers involved in these episodes remained quite small, they received a great deal of publicity and kept the public in turmoil.

Whigs tried to stay in business by attaching themselves to Know-Nothingism, a movement that tried to distract people from slavery by pointing out the dangers and deficiencies of the large number of German and Irish immigrants. The American Party ran against both the Democrats and Republicans in the presidential race in 1856 and received nearly 25% of the national popular vote. Those affiliated with this party carried Norfolk and Lynchburg, where enclaves of Irish and German immigrants resided, but they lost the election for governor in 1855 to Democrat Henry Wise. In 1850 only about 22,000 of about 1.4 million then living in Virginia had been born outside the United States. Of these about half were Irish and a quarter of them were German. The Irish and Germans tended to be concentrated in Wheeling, Richmond, Norfolk, Portsmouth, and to lesser degrees Petersburg and Lynchburg. Richmond, for example, had 2,244 Irish and 1,623 Germans out of its 36,000 residents in 1860. Norfolk ruffians tried to kidnap a priest and a Catholic church burned under mysterious circumstances. Although some residents of the cities took seriously the anti-foreign, especially anti-Catholic, rhetoric, most of the support from these candidates came from old Whigs who simply could not bring themselves to vote Democrat.

The Democrat Wise, who rivaled Hunter in trying to be the most radical in defending slavery, won the governor's race rather convincingly. A consistent hawk on the question of slavery, the controversial Wise once said he "would arm and equip 50,000 men the next morning, ready for revolution" should the Republican candidate for president in 1856 win.

Into this volatile mix came John Brown, a veteran of the war in Kansas. In October 1859 Brown and his band captured the federal armory at Harpers Ferry, Virginia. He hoped to incite blacks in the South to rise in rebellion. Several died in capturing the armory and in the ensuing skirmish with state militia. U.S. Marines, under Robert E. Lee and J.E.B. Stuart, broke through the armory door and captured Brown. At his trial the old man expressed a willingness to "forfeit my life for the furtherance of the ends of justice." The religious Brown told Wise that he and his fellow slaveholders had far more to atone for than he did. Having been found guilty of murder, treason and inciting rebellion, he was hanged on 2 December 1859. A large body, including students from VMI, stood guard. In the wake of the incident, Wise urged students in northern colleges to attend the new medical college in Richmond. In the aftermath of the hanging Virginians learned that Northern money backed Brown. His status as a martyr upset residents of the Old Dominion and the South. When the governors of Iowa and Ohio refused to extradite some of Brown's band for trial in Virginia, the newly elected moderate governor John Letcher called for boycotts against northern goods, as more extreme Southerners agitated for secession.

In 1859 John Letcher from Lexington received the nomination of the Democratic Party. In 1847 Letcher had endorsed the Ruffner pamphlet, which called for an end to slavery in western Virginia. Later elected as a congressman, Letcher soft-pedaled his earlier view, but Wise and other southern-minded Democrats still considered Letcher unsafe on slavery. During the campaign in 1859, he addressed audiences only in the West, and the party machinery ground out victory for him.

The next year the national party structure fell to pieces. Meeting in Charleston, Democrats failed to compromise on a federal slave code for the territories. They reassembled in Baltimore, where 23 of 30 Virginia delegates walked out, along with most Southerners, over allowing delegates loyal to Stephen Douglas of Illinois to gain the upper hand at the convention. About four-fifths of the Virginia delegation then met at another convention in Baltimore and nominated the incumbent vice president John Breckinridge for president. They announced a pro-slavery platform. Old Whigs tended to favor the new Constitutional Union party, its platform to save the union, and its candidate, John Bell. The Republican Party nominee Abraham Lincoln carried enough northern states to win a plurality of the popular vote and a majority of the Electoral College. Less than 2,000 Virginians voted for the "Black Republican," almost all of these in the extreme northern parts of the state. Virginia cast some 53,506 for Bell and 52,362 for Breckinridge. Only a little over 11,000 supported the regular Democrat. Western Virginians, who usually opposed secession, may have voted narrowly for Breckinridge because they saw him as the true Democrat amid much talk about fusion tickets. A plurality of Virginians voted for the old Whig, John Bell, who stressed preserving the union.

With the Lincoln election in 1860, South Carolina and other Southern states began to call conventions that would eventually carry them out of the union and into their own confederacy. The nationalist Botts approved the departure of South Carolina, a disturber of the "peace for the past 30 years." Secessionist opinion gained strength as the Deep South sent emissaries that called for Virginia to join them. John B. Floyd, a former governor and son of a governor, returned from Washington to a cheering crowd of Richmond radicals, after being removed as secretary of war for malfeasance.

Governor Letcher finally agreed to convene a convention to consider secession and announced his own agenda for the national government to avert disunion. Letcher wanted the North to end all state laws opposed to the fugitive slave law, protect slavery in the District of Columbia, and give holders of slaves the right to move their property into western lands. He also called for the federal government to pass laws against those who tried to end slavery, allow no opposition to slavery in the slave states, and affirm the right of secession. In dealing with the immediate future, the governor urged a convention of delegates of all the states to work out compromises. Despite these tough demands, radicals chastised Letcher for being too lenient on the North. The House of Delegates voted 108 to 0 and the Senate 37 to 0 to join with the South should efforts at compromise fail. John Tyler represented the state at a conference of representatives from the states of the Upper South. In February Virginia voters sent delegates to the state convention. Despite of the dominance of secessionists over the public mind, those who first assembled in Richmond overwhelmingly opposed secession. Only one-fifth openly advocated severing connections with the union. A large group of moderates dominated the vote. Hard-core unionists controlled at least one-third of the representatives. A few unionists came from the southwestern Piedmont and from the Norfolk area. Most of the unionists came from a few counties in the most northern parts of eastern Virginia, the Valley of Virginia, and the extreme western part of the state.

Radicals argued that should the state secede, it could join the Southern Confederacy and thereby become the industrial part of a new country. Representatives from the Confederacy promised a 10% tariff to protect Virginia's industries in the new nation. At the time this issue arose, the United States, sans its

Southern anti-tariff representation in Congress, prepared to raise the national tariff. Should Virginia remain in the union, she would find herself at a commercial disadvantage.

As the crisis worsened, the Virginia convention held on to its unionist views. Lame-duck President James Buchanan insisted on holding onto the federal forts in the Southern states but made no effort to suppress the rebellion. Negotiations to reach a compromise failed as president-elect Lincoln refused to accept proposals to amend the constitution to protect slaveholders in the territories or allow slavery all the way to the Pacific Ocean below the 36th parallel, but he would take no action against slavery where it existed nor would he reinforce the garrison at Fort Sumter.

As Lincoln took office, the convention still refused to recommend secession, but when South Carolinians attacked Fort Sumter and Lincoln called for 75,000 volunteers (Virginia would be expected to furnish 8,000) to put down the rebellion, the Virginia convention voted 88 to 55 to recommend withdrawal from the union. In the aftermath of the successful attack on the fort, Confederate flags flew over Richmond and Lynchburg and hundreds of guns saluted the victory. A throng at the capital hissed Governor Letcher when he delayed endorsing secession. With Lincoln's call for Virginia's help in putting down the rebellion, the remaining moderates yielded to the demand to sever connections with the union. The Tidewater voted 23 to 6, the Piedmont 32 to 4, and the Southwest 18 to 3 for secession. Valley delegates cast 17 votes against and 10 for secession. The Northwest went against separation 25 to 5. Delegates from the Northwest left the enthusiastic crowds in Richmond and made their way home to prepare for the separation of their area from Virginia.

In late May the voters of Virginia confirmed secession by a margin of six to one at a time when voice voting prevailed. Only the Northwest dissented, although pockets of unionism remained in the northern Valley, in Loudoun County where one of three voted against secession, and among unionists near the coast. One secessionist officer in Portsmouth prevented his men from going to the polls when he found out they planned to vote against separation. In the mountains secessionists physically threatened their opponents. Many who voted to carry Virginia out of the union no longer argued its constitutionality; they simply believed Virginians had the right to rebel as their revolutionary forefathers had. Many still had serious doubts that not guaranteeing slaveholders certain rights outside the state of Virginia constituted a legitimate reason to leave the union. Most could not accept the idea that they might have to assist in suppress other Southerners. The legislature quickly placed Virginia in the Confederacy.

During this process communications between Lincoln and representatives to the Virginia convention broke down. The president might have agreed not to send relief to Fort Sumter had the Virginia convention decided to adjourn without action. Participants give different accounts of the events and opinions. Lincoln later allowed Kentucky to opt out of the effort to put down the rebellion. We will never know the reaction had he offered such a deal to Virginia. It would certainly have strengthened the hand of the unionists in the convention. But by that point much of the public wanted secession and war if necessary. The moderates caved in to the demands of the radicals in the wake of the Sumter crisis. War was now at hand.

# Chapter 12

# The War of the Rebellion

Amid great excitement the nation prepared for war. Assuming that the fighting would last but for a few months, Northerners responded with enthusiasm when Lincoln called for troops after the fall of Fort Sumter, as Virginians prepared to repel the invaders. The Confederacy moved its capitol to Richmond, where President Jefferson Davis took up residence. The city on the James now served a double political role as the capital for a new nation and an old state.

Some Virginians thought the North, being a land of tradesmen, textile workers, and tailors, could not stand up to the South with its stronger rural traditions. They believed that, as a virtuous people, God would be on their side in what looked like an unequal contest, but defending their state gave them a major advantage, both psychologically and physically, over perceived aggressors. Even without seeing the results of the 1860 census, Americans knew the North had huge advantages in raw numbers. The Confederacy consisted of but eleven states, half the Northern number. Northerners outnumbered Southerners 2.5 to 1. Moreover, the South had over 3,500,000 slaves among its 9,000,000 people. In railroad mileage, merchant ships, naval vessels, textiles, iron, coal, firearms, and other industrial lagged way behind the North. But the situation for the South was not as perilous as it seemed. Many Southern sympathizers lived in Kentucky, Missouri, and Maryland and even in the southern parts of the Midwest. Though it trailed the North in per capita wheat production, the South produced more corn and livestock per person. At the end of the war the South still had food, but its transportation system could not deliver it to critical areas. With the Deep South a world-leading producer of commercial cotton, the South could use cotton for clothing and diplomatic leverage. Most importantly, the North had to conquer a vast territory and a people who had recently developed a strong military tradition. The South, it turned out, would only lose the will to fight when it had been totally defeated on the battlefield. In order to attain this objective, the North fought a war for four years without losing confidence in its objective to save the union.

Virginia's situation shows the difficulty in assessing strengths and weaknesses. Even though the Old Dominion trailed the Northeast and much of the Midwest in industrial capacity, it had far more than other Southern states. The ability to make cannons and cloth kept Virginia and the Confederacy in the fight. At the outset of the war Virginia had almost 200,000 white men of fighting age, but some 40,000 came from what became West Virginia and over three-fourths of them fought for the North. In the northern parts of the Valley and Loudoun County hundreds of Virginians sided with the North. The nearly 500,000 slaves in Virginia would also prove a problem, for although most remained loyal to their masters and some aided the Confederacy through industrial work and other services, thousands more ultimately helped form black regiments that brought defeat.

Many skirmishes and a few major battles took place near railroad depots such as Manassas, Fair Oaks, Savage Station, and Brandy Station. Late in the war a small Union force marched across the mountains, brushed aside local resistance, and destroyed the bridge across the New River at Central Depot on the tracks of the Virginia and Tennessee. The showdown of the war occurred at Petersburg, a major railroad center. The Yankees used the short Appomattox Railroad and an extension to bring supplies from City Point on the James River to help in the siege of Petersburg. The Confederates utilized the tracks of at least three major roads during that partial siege. Inability to supply Lee's army by rail as he retreated from Petersburg finally brought the war in Virginia to an end. Evidence also suggests that Union sympathizers that held management jobs with Virginia railroads diverted or delayed the movement of materials and men.

Just after the convention called for secession but before the public voted, Virginia militia captured the federal arsenal at Harper's Ferry and moved its machinery to Richmond. At about the same time Federals failed to blow up the navy yard at Portsmouth as they evacuated the yard in the face of incoming militia. With little damage from the fire, the Confederates were later able to restore the buildings and convert one of the ships in the dry dock to an ironclad.

Soon after Virginians voted for secession, a northern army under General George B. McClellan advanced into the northwestern part of the state, where sentiment for the union was strong. Facing more resistance in the Kanawha Valley, the advance finally stalled in the Greenbrier area, but the union now had control over most of the area. Two Confederate generals, John B. Floyd and Henry Wise, both former governors, failed to cooperate with each other, but the loss of the region had more to do with other disadvantages under which the Confederates labored. Even Robert E. Lee could not change the outcome in the west. A graduate of West Point and veteran officer Lee considered secession a revolutionary step. He also did not consider himself a defender of slavery, though his family owned a few slaves. As his state faced invasion he turned down Winfield Scott's invitation to take charge of the federal army and accepted overall command of the Confederate forces.

In early July 1861 the Federals failed to stop Confederates at Harpers Ferry from moving east to assist anther rebel army at the junction of two railroads. When the Federals pressed hard, the Confederate left gave way, but a brigade under the command of General Thomas J. Jackson (nicknamed "Stonewall" for actions that day) and other rebel units drove back attack after attack. With the arrival of troops from the Valley, the Confederates counterattacked and drove the Federals from the field. Defeat quickly became a rout as inexperienced soldiers hastened away from the action. Crowds of civilian onlookers fleeing toward the Potomac River further complicated the union retreat. With over 2,000 casualties it was the costliest battle in American history to that point.

Although many Virginians assumed the North would give up, Northern opinion called for greater effort. The Virginia-born Winfield Scott had already drawn up his Anaconda Plan. Though considered something of a joke at the time, it came quite close to reality over the next several years. A large federal navy did gradually encircle the entire south and cut off foreign commerce. Naval and army units gained control of the Mississippi River and carved up the Confederacy piecemeal. The plan also called for the capture of Richmond, but Scott knew the difficulties that assignment entailed. Two years into the fighting the union controlled the Mississippi and had much of the coastline blockaded. Even though it had captured the Norfolk area and occupied parts of northern Virginia, the campaign to capture Richmond fell far short of realization.

Now in command of the new Army of the Potomac, General McClellan took the better part of a year to organize and equip about 190,000 men. The young Napoleon may have matched his namesake in organizational ability, but he disliked and did less well in tactics. Ordered by President Lincoln's to act, McClellan, as part of what came to be called the "Peninsula Campaign," moved his troops down the Potomac to Fort Monroe, from where he launched a campaign to capture Richmond. Federal gunboats on the James and the York would provide support as he moved up the Peninsula. A nervous Lincoln, who did not really like the idea, agreed to it as long as thousands of troops remained to protect Washington D.C.

As McClellan made his move, the Confederates threw a wrench into the proceedings by launching an ironclad they had been working on at the navy yard in Portsmouth. Slave seamstress Mary Louveste and other spies gave the union Secretary of the Navy details of the old federal ship *USS Merrimac*. Only partially damaged by the earlier explosion, the Confederates made it into an ironclad. Renamed the *CSS Virginia*, she sailed cumbersomely into Hampton Roads on 8 March 1862 and took on the federal warships. One she rammed into submission; the other she raked with cannon fire; a third one she saved for the next day. With a damaged ram and wounded chief officer, the Confederate vessel withdrew. The next day as she returned to dispose of the remaining federal fleet, the crew of the Confederate ship came upon a small and curiously shaped vessel. Knowing what the Confederates had been up to, the U.S. Navy contracted for the construction of an ironclad from the keel up. With its parts made in different places, the *USS Monitor*, once assembled, came down the Atlantic Coast. So low in the water it barely made the ocean voyage to Hampton Roads, the "Cheese Box on the Raft" now took on the craft that looked like a turtle. For several hours they clanked cannon balls off each other to little effect. With its greater ability to maneuver and a revolving turret, the

Monitor evaded ramming attempts. The stalemate ended with the Yankee ship in shallow water, as the Confederate ship returned to the navy yard. Naval warfare would never be the same.

With the Confederate move checkmated, the union moved on Norfolk and Portsmouth. Lincoln visited Fort Monroe as the Yankees sent a small army across Hampton Roads. Union forces had already driven the Confederates under General Henry Wise out of Roanoke Island and much of Albemarle Sound, thus exposing the southern flank. The main force landed at Willoughby Spit and marched overland to Norfolk and the important shipyard, the home of the infamous ironclad. The Confederates abandoned their elaborate earthen works and retreated up the James to help defend Richmond. They sank their ironclad because it was too big to ascend far up the James and not sufficiently seaworthy for ocean travel.

After a month of preparation at Fort Monroe the Federals finally moved up the Peninsula toward Yorktown, where General John Magruder had his limited number of troops pretend they were a huge force. The Union had a detective service, an elaborate system of spies, and balloonists. Although one spy reported Magruder's ruse, reports consistently overestimated the size of the defending army and the pessimistic McClellan believed the enemy had even more men than reported. After an elaborate buildup, McClellan's men took Yorktown, finding no Confederates there to defend it. Hastening the pace, Federals moved on to Williamsburg, where they finally fought a battle, as the Confederates retreated toward Richmond and Confederate General Joseph Johnston stalled for time.

Meanwhile, Lee ordered a small force to keep an eye on a Union Army under General Irwin McDowell (the loser of Manassas) at Fredericksburg and sent a larger force under Jackson to raise havoc in the Valley of Virginia and thereby take pressure off Richmond. The plan worked to perfection. The Union had a large army under Nathaniel Banks, another politician turned general, in the lower Valley. McClellan hoped McDowell could attack Richmond, leaving Banks to defend Washington. Although his forces were defeated at in one battle, Jackson forced Banks to reconsider moving east. Splitting his small army, Jackson took on a force under General John C. Fremont, once known as the "Pathfinder of the West" and the Republican presidential candidate in 1856. Fremont's military training did little against Jackson's tactics. Jackson moved deceptively toward Front Royal, where, with the help of young Belle Boyd (her report prevented the Federals from destroying an important bridge), his men took the town. With Hunter still coming from the west and McDowell moving from the east to help Banks, Jackson slipped away and watched as union armies moved south on both sides of Massanutten Mountain. One part of his army struck Freemont in early June at Cross Keys. The next day his main army raked another Federal army at Port Republic. As their adversaries retreated, Jackson and his men headed east to help defend Richmond. No Federals followed.

As Jackson wore out his opponents in the Valley, McClellan drove within sight of Richmond. The swampy Chickahominy River divided his large army nearly in half. At Seven Pines, near the rail depot at Fair Oaks on the tracks of the Richmond and York River Railroad, the Confederates struck the weaker half of McClellan's army. In the resulting bloody standoff, Johnston incurred a serious wound, and Lee, assuming battlefield command, launched a series of blistering attacks. Cavalry officer James Ewell Brown "Jeb" Stuart rode around the federal army and told Lee the location of the union right flank. Starting northeast of Richmond near Mechanicsville, Lee attacked again and again. The northernmost Union regiments held when Jackson's men did not arrive in time. The next day at Gaines Mill, Jackson weighed in toward the end of the day for a Confederate victory, but one achieved with huge losses. The Confederates then struck at Savage Station and another rail depot, with both sides taking heavy losses. At Malvern Hill on July 1, Confederates, running uphill, faced massive cannon fire from the top and from union gunboats, and fell back in apparent defeat, but it was McClellan that moved his army away from the fighting—to Harrison's Landing, on the James River. The Seven Days ended McClellan's efforts to capture Richmond. His failure to counterattack, even though he had really lost only one of the battles and despite the fact that Lee had lost more men, indicated that the union general would never attain his objective. Although a series of losses, Seven Days proved to be a strategic victory. A shaken McClellan abandoned any hope of taking Richmond with his Army of the Potomac and withdrew down the Peninsula.

McClellan was finished, but Lee was not. Lincoln had belatedly organized the three armies that had faced Jackson into the Army of Virginia. Seventy thousand strong, it moved toward Richmond under the command of cocky General John Pope. On August 9, 1862, south of Culpeper at Cedar Mountain, Jackson and later General A.P. Hill stunned Pope after initial Union advances. With Lee's army moving north of Richmond, Jackson then moved to the rear federal forces strung out along the Rappahannock River. Using forced marches as they had in the Valley Campaign, Jackson's men reached the tracks of the Orange and Alexandria and then moved to Manassas Junction, where they feasted on or destroyed a mountain of Union supplies. Major fighting broke out as Pope's army made contact with the Confederates. Then half of Lee's army, under General James Longstreet, hit Pope's flank. Thoroughly defeated Union soldiers withdrew toward Washington, having been beaten for the second time at a place they called Bull Run and the Confederates called Manassas.

Having freed much of the Old Dominion of the invaders, Lee took the war into Maryland in hopes of persuading Northerners to pull out of the war and convince the world that the Confederacy could win. With his army split into three parts, Lee moved at will through the entire area. Jackson captured the federal garrison at Harper's Ferry. Leaving A.P. Hill in charge, he then united with Lee. In the meantime at Frederick, Maryland, where Lee's army had been camped, a Union officer found the Confederate battle plans wrapped around some cigars. McClellan, who had been placed back in command of the Federals, knowing Lee's intentions but still believing his forces outnumbered, moved cautiously. The two forces met near Sharpsburg in the bloodiest day of fighting of the war, with Lee losing nearly a third of his army. The arrival of Hill from the Valley saved the day. McClellan never did use his reserves and refused to attack the next day, as the Southerners withdraw. The main Confederate Army camped around Winchester and the Yankees reoccupied Harpers Ferry.

Tired of the lack of action, Lincoln put General Ambrose Burnside in charge of the Army of the Potomac. Despite his victory at Roanoke Island, Burnside knew he was not qualified for such a command. In December the hairy-faced but balding Burnside sent some 130,000 troops east in the hopes of crossing the Rappahannock and forcing Lee to chase him for control of Richmond. A delay in fording the Rappahannock near Fredericksburg enabled Lee to take control of the heights south of the city. Union men finally forded the river with heavy casualties to occupy Fredericksburg. Burnside then insisted on a full assault on high land south of the city. His men marched forward as if committing suicide. Thousands died, and Lincoln removed Burnside from command.

In the spring of 1863, "Fighting Joe Hooker" took on Lee. Longstreet's corps headed to southeast Virginia to locate additional supplies. While in the southeast, Longstreet tried unsuccessfully to drive untested Yankees from Suffolk. Meantime Hooker met Lee at Chancellorsville. On the offense Hooker sent cavalry toward Richmond and held several corps in reserve at Fredericksburg. His main force tried to reach Lee's rear by passing through the Wilderness. Lee knew the location of the union right flank through Stuart's exertions, while his opponent, lacking cavalry, had no idea where Lee was. With a limited number of men watching the Federals at Fredericksburg, Jackson moved his columns to the left. In a surprise attack the Confederates folded enemy lines. As Lee blocked the army in blue coming from Fredericksburg, Hooker withdrew in disgrace, having failed to use reserves. But this brilliant Confederate victory cost Lee lost over 12,000 men. Hooker lost more, but several more victories like that might mean the end of the Confederacy. Among the casualties was the heroic Jackson, who in reconnoitering after the fight, was wounded by friendly fire wounded him and died a few weeks later.

In one last bold step to save Virginia and the Confederacy, Lee invaded Pennsylvania, threatening Washington D.C. and the Northern heartland. Whether a great victory for the Confederates would materially change Northern opinion will never be known, for the outnumbered Lee lost at Gettysburg. When detachments that had been wandering about unaware of the location of the enemy began to fight around Gettysburg on 1 July 1863, Union forces held the high ground around the town occupied by the rebels. On the second day in hand-to-hand fighting, the Confederates failed to take Little Round Top, from where their cannon could have raked the enemy. On the third day, Lee sent General George Pickett's division of Virginians and others directly into the teeth of the Union regiments on Cemetery Ridge (aptly named). With

Federals yelling "Fredericksburg, Fredericksburg, Fredericksburg," a few rebels, reached the Union lines, but northern reserves quickly enveloped them. With casualties approaching 30,000, Lee and his men staggered back into Virginia, once again not pursued by the victorious Federals. At the same time, Yankees under General Ulysses S. Grant captured Vicksburg, after a prolonged siege, to gain full control of the Mississippi River. In the fall, amid the tough terrain around Chattanooga, the union, with the help of the Virginia-born George Thomas, broke the back of rebel resistance in eastern Tennessee.

In many ways the actions in the summer and fall of 1863 decided the outcome of the war, but few of the participants realized it at the time. In Virginia, after some Union victories near railroad depots, the two sides halted the fighting for the winter with Lee south and General George Meade north of the Rapidan. For the North, the situation looked a lot better than it had the previous winter.

After Antietam, in September 1862, Lincoln issued a preliminary proclamation for emancipating the slaves. Congress had already ended slavery in the territories and in the District of Columbia. Some Union commanders started freeing slaves under their jurisdiction. Lincoln halted this practice, but Congress made it policy. The abolitionist wing of the Republican Party put sustained pressure on the president to take a bigger step against slavery. In the wake of the victory in western Maryland, Lincoln responded with a war measure. To the disaffected Southerners he offered peace within the union if they would stop fighting. If they continued the rebellion, then on 1 January 1863 all the slaves in the rebel-held areas would be free. Slaves in union areas remained in bondage. Thus the Emancipation Proclamation did not free any slaves in Alexandria or the Norfolk area, which the Federals occupied, nor did it free any slaves in Maryland or in other border states. The act helped keep Great Britain and France from seriously considering recognition of the Confederacy. Just as importantly, emancipation infused new enthusiasm into the Union cause, but it lost support particularly among the Irish in the northern cities. A related use of conscription to beef up northern numbers also met resistance. By not ending slavery where he could, Lincoln retained the backing of unionists in places like Missouri, Kentucky, and Maryland. The Union also now tapped into the huge reservoir of free blacks in the North and slaves in the South. Thousands of these could now join the Federal Army. As the North began to carve up the South, newly freed blacks signed up for service for a nation that intended to end the institution of slavery. Lee urged the South to respond to this war measure by freeing some slaves to help the Confederates, but because most Southern politicians were fighting the war to protect slavery, they dismissed such a proposal. Not until the very end of the war did they agree to the idea.

With both sides determined to fight the war to a bitter end, Virginians endured two more winters of privation. Confederate currency had already reached the point where it took $30 to buy a barrel of flour. In Richmond the previous April several hundred women carried out a bread riot. The capital, overflowing with destitute people along with some deserters, experienced a break down. Soldiers and civilians alike had difficulty finding shoes. Some soldiers knew that it was "a rich man's war and a poor man's fight" as conscription, put into effect the previous year, exempted large slaveholders from service.

Major parts of the Richmond area took on the appearance of a hospital or a prison. At Chimbarazo, the Confederates built hundreds of wooden barracks to house the wounded. Phoebe Pember superintended this remarkable facility. After the war the city turned the site into a large park. Sally Tompkins ran a small private hospital, achieving exceedingly high rates of survival among her patients. Davis commissioned her a captain and retained her as the director when the hospital went public. Richmond had several other medical facilities. They could also be found, sometimes as temporary shelters, near battle sites. Lynchburg had some of the best hospitals in the Confederacy.

Richmond also held thousands of prisoners. Confederate authorities sent many on to camps farther south, but as the war number captured reached high levels, the provost marshal converted tobacco warehouses, Negro jails, and any large building he could lay his hands on. Libby Prison, Belle Isle, in the middle of the James River, held some 8,000 prisoners at its peak; Castle Godwin and Castle Thunder were names long recalled by their inmates. Conditions eased somewhat when both sides permitted exchanges of prisoners, but in 1863 the North decided this policy lengthened the war. Despite the shortages and mistreatment, prisoners were better off in Richmond than they would later be in camps to the south.

The war increasingly imposed hardships on a divided people. In areas supposedly under Union control in northern Virginia, "Gray Ghost" John Singleton Mosby and his Partisan Rangers, a band of several hundred unofficial Confederates, harassed the Federals and Union sympathizers. Mosby's men captured officers, robbed trains, and even meted out law and order, sometimes killing those who failed to cooperate in their schemes. Pro-Southerners helped them, but parts of Loudoun County had strong pro-Unionists while many others tried to avoid helping either side. Unionists sometimes banded together to carry out raids on those who harassed them.

In the early stages of the war, Union officers tried to entice residents of occupied areas to cooperate by restraining their troops. When Union forces occupied the Eastern Shore in November 1861, the commanding federal officer pledged to leave persons and property alone, including slaves. But such olive branches produced negligible results. And by the second year of the war, as they tired of insults and injury from noncombatants, especially women, federal troops acted more sternly. In both Union-occupied Alexandria and Norfolk, commanders silenced secessionist critics such as ministers for their inflammatory sermons by arresting and them. In time, with continued resistance on the part of residents in occupied areas such as northern Virginia, Union officers retaliated against attacks on railroads by subjecting adjacent areas to pillaging and destruction. By the end of the war, federals were burning sections of the state such as the Valley of Virginia to prevent food from reaching Lee's forces bottled up in Petersburg and Richmond.

In the mountains of Virginia and West Virginia war sometimes turned into family feuds. At the outset of the war most residents of the Southwest sided with the state, and only a few unionists and German Baptists, who opposed war on general principles, undermined the war effort. Although the Confederacy allowed members of that order to opt out of military service for a price, they still faced harassment, even murder, from ardent secessionists. As the struggle continued, the situation compelled many mountaineers to desert. Most deserters returned home to help their feed their families, flour being in short supply as farmers turned grain into alcohol. Neither the Confederacy nor the state had the ability to feed the destitute in the cities, let alone the mountains. The desertion rate stepped up in 1863 and became unmanageable in 1864. The Confederacy simply did not have the manpower to chase down deserters. Home Guards, consisting of old men and boys, tried, but in the end all they and others who pursued fugitives accomplished was to create ill will. The area below Portsmouth, on both sides of the North Carolina border, became a no-man's land. The swampy area had long been known for its outlaws and general lack of order. The war did nothing to detract from its image, as guerillas harassed one another and innocent civilians.

In the spring of 1864 the military campaign resumed. Fresh from victories in the west, Ulysses Grant brought a determination seldom seen among Union officers. As Grant contended with Lee along the Rapidan River, General William T. Sherman and his men advanced into northern Georgia. At the same time, a small army under General Benjamin Butler kept pressure on Richmond from the east. A reasonably capable administrator, this one-time Massachusetts politician left much to be desired on the battlefield. Southerners considered him little more than a thief and a petty dictator. The defenders of Richmond had little to fear from him as they still controlled the fort at Drewry's Bluff, preventing the Union from using gunboats for a direct assault on the city. Butler spent a long time and effort trying to take out a bend in the James River at Dutch Gap. The resulting explosion sent tons of silt into the air only to land about where it started.

As Grant moved south with his main army, he sent smaller forces to the Valley of Virginia and 13,000 cavalrymen under General Philip Sheridan to raid Richmond. The army in the Valley reached New Market, where the Confederates, with the help of students from VMI, drove them back. On another occasion, Sheridan's men met the Confederate cavalry north of Richmond at Yellow Tavern, where Jeb Stuart died. The main Union Army went after Lee. On 5 and 6 May 1864 at the Wilderness, on some of the same ground fought over a year earlier (those fighting ran across numerous skeletons), Grant incurred about 18,000 casualties to the gunfire and the resulting fires that engulfed the place. Determined to sustain the fight, Grant moved on to Spotsylvania Court House. After dueling for several days, Grant attacked the center of Lee's entrenched forces. In one day, during which they fought over a "bloody angle," both sides lost 7,000 men. Once again, Grant moved to the southeast. Passing up a chance for a major battle at North Anna, he moved over to Cold Harbor, near the scene of the fighting in 1862 northeast of Richmond. Lee arrived first and again entrenched his men. On 3 June, Grant's forces, attacking several times in the face of almost certain slaughter, suffered thousands of casualties in a matter of minutes.

Ignoring the outcry from Northerners and Southerners alike, Grant moved his army across the James River over a pontoon bridge and sent advance units toward Petersburg. A delay by union officers gave Lee time to rush much of his army to the Appomattox River and save Petersburg. Both sides then settled down for a semi-siege. The Confederates ended up with a string of forts and trenches that stretched from east of Richmond to south of Petersburg. In essence Grant could not get in, but Lee could not leave. There they faced each other for the next several months, during which time Pennsylvania miners tunneled under the earthworks and ignited gunpowder. Thousands of Union men, including several black regiments, pushed through the gaping hole in the defenses caused by the explosion. The sunken area then became a slaughter pen as one of Lee's aides, General William Mahone (the "Hero of the Crater"), rallied the Confederates, who kept the high ground. Mahone also stopped his men from killing blacks who had surrendered.

At this point, General Jubal Early led 13,000 men on a raid toward Washington D.C. Grant diverted some of his massive army to defend the capital, and Early withdrew. After a sharp encounter at Sheridan drove the rebels clear out of the Valley and stripped it of its supplies. Another Union force had earlier burned the public buildings at Lexington and even threatened Lynchburg until Early forced it to retreat.

On the southern front, as Grant sidled around Richmond, Sherman's army moved toward Atlanta, as outnumbered Confederates slowly withdrew. The tactics of a new and more offensive-minded commander failed, and Sherman's men captured the city. Facing limited opposition, they marched to the sea at Savannah, inflicting destruction as they went. In the wake of the victory at Atlanta, the North voted for Abraham Lincoln over George B. McClellan, the Democrat candidate, for president who had hinted at a negotiated peace with the rebels. With the Lincoln reelection, the North made it clear that the only way to end the war was for the Southerners to put down their arms.

As they faced another hard winter, the Virginians proudly rejected the idea of surrender. Suffering from diseases of the heart and stomach, Lee agreed to keep his command. Lincoln met with Confederate envoys in Hampton Roads early the next year. Gaining no concessions from the president and unwilling to give up either secession or the Confederacy, the people in Richmond held a huge rally at the massive African Baptist Church and vowed to fight on. The winter of suffering proved fruitless. As spring approached, the Union Army stretched their lines against ever thinning rebel ranks. Federals took the old rail line coming from the Roanoke River, thus reducing supplies. Grant hammered at one point, then another, and finally Sheridan broke through at Five Forks on the Confederate right flank. Lee sent word to Jefferson Davis, then attending church, to prepare to leave Richmond. As the Confederates hastily departed from the capital, fires broke out in the lower part of the city started by Confederate efforts to destroy military supplies. Hundreds of homes and businesses burned. The fire even started to burn the bridge the Confederates used to cross the James. At their departure, mobs of deserters and civilians ran through the streets. As a rebel officer prepared to cross the bridge, he noticed "bold, dirty looking women" and "scoundrelly-looking men," who now sneaked from their hiding places and pillaged the burning city. An especially nasty woman watched the retreating Confederates and scornfully commented in her Irish brogue, "Yes, after fighting them for four years, y're running like dawgs." The officer contrasted that behavior with the sad and tearful demeanor of the many Virginia women that had never failed the soldiers. He was grateful for their sake that incoming Federals restored order.

As Lee and his men made their way near the tracks of the Southside Railroad toward its junction with the Richmond and Danville in hopes of reaching Danville, the newly designated capital of the Confederacy, Federals harassed them at every step. At Sayler's Creek, Lee lost much of what remained of his tattered army. With his beleaguered men virtually surrounded and the failure to find supplies at the rail depot at Appomattox, Lee accepted Grant's invitation to meet him at Appomattox Court House, where they agreed to the terms of the surrender of the Army of Northern Virginia at the home of a man that had left an earlier home near Manassas to avoid the war. The national nightmare was apparently over.

# Chapter 13

# The Restoration of Virginia

In the days following the fall of Richmond, Abraham Lincoln walked the streets of the stricken city, welcomed by crowds of blacks. After sitting at Jefferson Davis's desk, he left for Washington, from which city news of his assassination soon stunned the nation. Blacks cried in lamentation. A few whites cheered, but most realized that the killing would stir up resentment in the North. Moreover, Lincoln had been a voice of moderation. Now that voice was gone.

Virginians now knew that around 15,000 Virginians (North Carolina sustained around 40,000 deaths) lay in premature graves, and thousands of others lacked limbs or suffered from long-term debilitating diseases. Both side absorbed huge losses in men and materials. The Northern death rate exceeded the Southern because of the differential in disease-related deaths and the battlefield losses toward the end of the war, when General Grant stepped up the pace in the fighting. The long-term effect of malnutrition could not be measured nor could the movement of sexually transmitted illnesses. Alcoholic consumption increased even as the Confederacy tried to restrict use of spirits. Pellagra and other ailments persisted in the Southern army, but Northerners were especially susceptible to the miasmas that arose in the swampy areas of the South. Diseases also spread among the civilian populations, on both sides of the conflict, especially among children. Many men at the front learned about the deaths of one or more of their children as diphtheria, typhoid, and scarlet fever ravaged the land. As diseases of the mind and body ruined the lives of many, various fevers spread among weakened livestock and raised havoc for years to come. Even plants proved especially vulnerable to pests. In short, the Civil War was an ecological catastrophe of the first order.

Virginians, of course, did their best to get by in unusually troubled times. Lacking anything that remotely resembled currency and with low returns on what they produced and high prices for what was imported, they bartered or did without. In areas where wild game remained plentiful, farmers hunted for deer, opossums, quail, pheasants, and wild turkeys. Eventually farmers restocked their supply of pigs and began to grow grain, and a degree of normality resumed.

War always brings change, and the territories over which wars take place usually endure the most negative physical consequences. The entire lower and much of the middle part of the Valley of Virginia lay in ruin with its crops, many farm structures, and public buildings destroyed. The northern Piedmont also sustained serious damage. Major parts of the cities of Richmond and Petersburg were devastated, the first by the fire started by the Confederates themselves, the second by the siege. Confederates, including some residents themselves, burned Hampton as they withdrew up the Peninsula early in the war in the belief that Ben Butler planned to use the structures to house contraband blacks that had escaped to Fort Monroe. The residents of Fredericksburg were still trying to overcome their city's sacking at the hands of federal troops in December 1862. Wherever large armies occupied the countryside for any time, the land would take years to overcome their presence. A community like City Point, which Grant used as a staging area to attack Petersburg, would soon be virtually abandoned with the end of the fighting, but it would take time for the effects of having mass movements of troops and materials to wear off. Plantation houses along the James, often used as headquarters or as hospitals, required time and money to be restored to their former state. Only the Southside, where secessionism was strongest, and the Southwest escaped serious physical damage. But throughout the entire state, where railroads still operated, worn out tracks carried dilapidated equipment, if they ran at all.

Only cemeteries seemed to be doing much business. One of the biggest tasks following the war was the relocation of bodies in makeshift graves to more formal resting places. The Union confiscated Arlington, the Lee estate near the District of Columbia as a cemetery for Union dead. Many years later, the federal government created numerous parks as memorials to those who died in the fighting.

Along with physical change, most of the Southern banking system disappeared. Confederate bonds and currency and money printed by the banks of Virginia had no value at all except as keepsakes. The House of Delegates calculated that residents lost some $237,000,000 in real estate and personal property. The state lost some $26,000,000 (and owed close to $40,000,000 in debts still climbing with interest) in its public works and another $4,000,000 in bank stock. Estimated losses in the value of slaves ran in the hundreds of millions, but the resource still existed as a freed people.

The Old Dominion experienced a revolution during the Civil War. Most Virginians went into the war in the belief that they were following the heritage of the American revolt against Great Britain. Even before Virginia left the Union, the federal government began to embark on a program that put in place the Whig ideas (originally Federalist) about the economic role of the federal government. The South came out of the war not only having failed to attain Southern independence, but also facing a Republican-style federal government with national banks, protective tariffs, and federally funded transcontinental railroads. Now in the aftermath of war, Virginians faced still more revolutionary change. Lincoln's proclamation meant the end to the "peculiar institution" in much of Virginia as Northern troops conquered more areas. In Virginia many people celebrate Emancipation Day on 9 April, the date when Lee surrendered, but federal officers declared an official end to slavery throughout the state a few days later, and the nation ended the institution with the 13th Amendment late in 1865. An occasional farmer neglected to inform his workers of their freedom in remote locations, but sooner or later slavery ended throughout the state.

White Virginians probably thought the blacks were worth more as slaves, but they were most concerned about what blacks might do as free people. Without the control of masters, freedmen allegedly roamed about with few restraints unproductive for themselves and society. In reality, most former slaves, after celebrating their freedom for a few days, went back to work in the neighborhood where they had formerly been enslaved, hiring out to one of the nearby white farmers or to their old masters. A great many worked on someone else's land, and received a share of the commercial crop. The Freedmen's Bureau oversaw contracts between the former slaves and the property owners. Several thousand freedmen left their rural homes to live in one of the growing cities like Richmond or Norfolk, where more opportunities for competitive work prevailed.

As a result of the war, Virginia lost the entire northwestern part of the state, plus some of the counties in the lower Valley. About 375,000 people became residents of the new state of West Virginia. Soon after secession, delegates from several counties, often elected in an irregular fashion, met in a series of conventions at Wheeling. Out of those meetings came a restored government, a governor, and eventually a constitution, which took effect in 1863, approved by voters and by the Lincoln administration.

Two nagging questions remain about the entire process. To what extent did the formation of a new state reflect the wishes of the people? And how does a section secede from a state without the permission of the state? Most historians now agree that the majority of citizens of what became West Virginia favored statehood. Some sources ascribe heavy ratios in favor of the step with at least 60% to 70% advocating the move. Although some of the wealthy, as far north as Wheeling, sometimes secretly aided the Confederacy, considerably more West Virginians served in the Union army than for the Confederacy. Yet the southern and extreme eastern parts of what became West Virginia had deep reservations or were decidedly against being separated from Virginia. In sum, West Virginians carved out a bit too much acreage when they formed their state if the desires of residents had meaning. As to the second question, Congress accepted West Virginia and Lincoln proclaimed it as the 35th state. Because the restored government, operating at Wheeling with links to other occupied territories, validated statehood, Congress and Lincoln could allow West Virginia to enter the union. Oddly enough, West Virginia seceded from Virginia because the southern states could not secede from the nation. Congress approved West Virginia statehood when its citizens amended the proposed new constitution to end slavery. After West Virginia became a state, Lincoln moved the restored government to Alexandria, the capital of occupied Virginia, a territory that included the Norfolk area. Because in Lincoln's mind Virginia never separated from the union, the government in Alexandria represented the state in its relations with the federal government. Francis Pierpont, one of the leaders in the movement for West Virginia statehood, moved from Wheeling to Alexandria as governor of Virginia. Two residents of Alexandria now

120

represented Virginia in the U.S. Senate. Pierpont feuded with General Butler over the Hampton Roads area. Butler, the commander at Fort Monroe, convinced the unionists in the area to vote for martial law, thus making the civilian government irrelevant. After the war Virginia sought reunification with their western brethren, but few people in West Virginia expressed any interest. The majority of Virginians concluded that the westerners deserved their fate in much the same fashion as the British viewed Americans after the Revolution. Virginians felt sorry for the people in the lower Valley, whom they thought had been coerced. Current boundaries were finally fixed in 1871. The Virginians also let it be known that West Virginia would have to share the payments on the debt Virginia had amassed before the war. That matter would not be resolved until deep in the 20th century.

Soon after federal troops entered Richmond, Pierpont moved into the governor's mansion. Dominated by old Whigs the General Assembly elected in the fall of 1865 approved the 13th amendment and made marriages legal for former slaves, but blacks still could not marry whites. It also rescinded an act of the Alexandria government allowing West Virginia statehood and another piece of legislation that exempted those that had served the Confederacy from voting. The Vagrancy Act aimed to put destitute newly freed men and women to work. This act, and others like it in other Southern states, fired up Northern opinion because it seemed Virginians were undoing emancipation. In some cases apprenticeships were used to keep young blacks in bondage. The mayor of Richmond routinely assigned the apparently destitute jobs or a jail time until Radical Republicans removed him.

The death of Lincoln set in motion events that would ultimately lead to a much more pervasive policy of reconstruction. Lincoln had earlier suggested that male freedmen that knew how to read or served in the Union military might be accorded the right to vote. With his death, radicals within his party began to push for citizenship for all blacks, including the right to vote for adult, black males. As early as February 1865 Norfolk freedmen sought to obtain that right. Mass meetings in Alexandria called for the same. Lincoln's assassination brought into office Andrew Johnson, who had run as a war Democrat on a Union ticket with Lincoln. A sometime Tennessee tailor, Johnson, expressing disdain for the elite of the South, initially did not even want to accept Grant's and Sherman's generous peace terms agreed to in two surrender ceremonies. He even considered proceeding with treason indictments against Lee and other Southern military and political leaders.

Not long after assuming the presidency, however, Johnson in a blanket amnesty allowed the less wealthy to have their property returned as long as they took an oath of future loyalty to the Union. He also pardoned wealthy or prominent ex-Confederates that did not qualify under this program. A few ex-Confederates that owned estates thought long and hard about taking such an oath, but the great majority agreed to the requirement. One man allegedly fell down in his haste to reach the court. Any idea of compensating slaves for their years of toil by giving them "forty acres and a mule," a policy associated with General Sherman, disappeared with this act. It also meant that several estates that had been turned over to blacks under the Freedmen's Bureau and in some cases even included schools were now returned to their original owners.

Late in 1865 Congress decided not to accept the Southern delegates sent to Congress under Johnson's liberal program of restoration. Congress also organized a Joint Committee on Reconstruction, which conducted interviews about the treatment of freedmen and northerners. Although Robert E. Lee thought most Virginians cooperated in a peaceful manner, other witnesses cited grave violations. Black and white teachers were routinely harassed despite which they were able to put hundreds of former slaves on the road to literacy. A black man died in a racial incident in Alexandria on Christmas Day. A Fairfax County jury sentenced the murderer of a unionist to but a year in jail. Unionists in northern Virginia understood that John Mosby had advised his guerillas to be ready to move at a moment's notice. That such a situation could exist in Alexandria and Fairfax did not bode well, for these places had hundreds of Unionists, many Northern-born. Fairfax's pro-Union sheriff testified before the committee that secessionist-minded members of juries diverted justice. At the end of the war, most Confederates admitted defeat and hoped to return to home and resume normal living. Some eight months later, some hoped the United States might become involved in a foreign war, allowing them either to fight for the enemy or forcing the federal government to leave them alone.

In 1866, as Johnson and the Radical Republicans in Congress came to blows, Congress approved, over the president's veto, a Civil Rights Act, which validated citizenship and, therefore, voting rights to blacks as well as a measure to increase the role and power of the Freedmen's Bureau. The new Congress that met in March the following year passed over the president's veto a series of reconstruction acts that compelled all the former states of the Confederacy, save Tennessee, to go through a lengthy process to be readmitted to the union. Lincoln's idea of a simple restoration of the Union was no longer possible.

In April 1866, as Congress conducted its investigation of the South, some 300 blacks in Norfolk celebrated the anniversary of Appomattox as part of a campaign to obtain the right to vote. Angry whites precipitated a race riot, during which a Confederate veteran wounded a black man. With blacks in pursuit, he panicked and fired a shot into his stepmother's throat, killing her. Someone then shot him in the back. In response to this incident men dressed in Confederate gray carried out a night of terror, killing and maiming many blacks. When the veterans fired at U.S. infantrymen, Norfolk and Portsmouth went under martial law. As a result of the imbroglio, a black man went to jail for murder, but no charges were filed against any whites. Race relations continued to deteriorate as an inquiry determined that in Norfolk many blacks and white unionists feared to go out at night. The head of the Freedman's Bureau reported the appearance of the Ku Klux Klan in Virginia. Whites expressed concern about efforts to stir up former slaves. In 1869 in Princess Anne County, Willis "Specs" Hodges, a native free black from the area who had fled north well before the Civil War but who had returned to guide Union troops through the area against guerrillas late in the war, allegedly urged black squatters to resist removal. When federal troops tried to oust occupants on one plantation, a blast from a shotgun felled a federal soldier, and other soldiers quickly shot down three blacks. Clashes between blacks and union troops made it evident that Northern soldiers often sided with the ex-Confederates. At that time former governor and general, Henry Wise, had reacquired his estate after a legal battle with the Freedmen's Bureau, which had been using the estate as its headquarters. The local press advised Wise not to use force to evict squatters. Eventually he secured possession, but the place proved to be in a ruinous state.

Radical Republicans pushed ahead with their idea to give suffrage to all adult black males even though many Northern states failed to. Hundreds of blacks cast votes in the legislative elections held right after the war, but local officials refused to count them. Many Republicans felt it necessary to assure black voting, because when all former Confederate states rejoined the Union, the Democrats would likely regain control of the federal government unless newly franchised blacks could offset whites in the South. In order to ensure the constitutionality of the Civil Rights Act, the Republicans passed the 14th Amendment. A complicated measure, it called for a reduction in representation in Congress and in the Electoral College for those states that did not allow blacks the vote. Congress later turned to the 15th Amendment, which simply barred any government from denying or abridging anyone the right to vote on the basis of "race, color, or previous condition of servitude."

Congress passed the First Reconstruction Act over a Johnson veto in March 1867. Under it, Virginia became Military District #1 under the command of General John M. Scholfield, an honest and capable officer. Like other Southern states, the Old Dominion now had to create a new constitution. Once Virginia approved the 14th Amendment (the legislature overwhelmingly turned it down in 1866), it could request statehood as if it were a territory. Under this act, voters had to take an oath that they had not voluntarily aided the Confederacy. With Scholfield supervising the elections, several thousand more whites than blacks registered, but a much smaller white turnout on the day of the election meant that Republicans, both white and black, far outnumbered conservative-minded delegates at the convention. Radical Republicans, consisting of what Southerners called "carpetbaggers" (outsiders) and "scalawags" (natives who cooperated with the Yankees) took almost 50 seats with blacks counting another 25. The combination far outnumbered conservative whites.

Republicans, both white and black, played major roles at the convention. Judge John Underwood chaired the session, his name being attached to the document. A one-time resident of Virginia who had been driven off before the Civil War for opposing slavery, Underwood was no friend of most white Virginians despite having ordered the release of Jefferson Davis from Fort Monroe, when prosecutors failed to present evidence implicating him in the Lincoln assassination. Another delegate, James Hunnicutt, an unusual "carpetbagger" as one-time secessionist and racist editor of a religious magazine from South Carolina, urged blacks to commit violent acts against whites. They elected him as a delegate but failed to heed his advice. John Minor Botts, the old Whig opponent of secession, resident of a Richmond jail early in the war, and under plantation arrest for much of the war, tried to tone down the harsh rhetoric. Leading black representatives included Lewis Lindsay, a Richmond bandleader; J.W.D. Bland, from the Appomattox area; and Dr. Thomas Bayne, a Norfolk dentist who fled from slavery before the war. The white press poked fun at the part-time minister, an articulate and exciting orator. A few years later, when Bayne sided with conservatives on another matter, an editor decided that he possessed great skills in public speaking.

The document these delegates produced contained many reforms, including the written ballot, a system of public education, and protection for private debtors. An amendment on usury ratified in 1872 imposed a 6% rate in certain instances. Under the document, the state would have to retire its debt and issue no more bonds for public works. Elected supervisors would govern the counties, but voters no longer picked judges. Counties would be divided into towns, but in 1872 voters amended the constitution so that each county contained a minimum of three magisterial districts, with at least one supervisor elected from each district. Each county should have a sheriff, an attorney, a clerk, treasurer, and commissioners of the revenue. Each magisterial district would have three justices of the peace, a constable, an overseer of the poor, and three trustees of education. The governor, who would still serve one four-year term, could now veto bills and pardon criminals.

Most importantly, the proposed constitution allowed blacks to vote and disfranchised anyone that had formerly held a federal or state position and then fought for the Confederacy. To hold state or local office one took an "iron clad oath" never to have voluntarily fought against the United States. Only a few hundred whites would lose the right to vote, but the clause would certainly put a damper on the number who could hold office. Schofield had asked the convention not to put these disabling clauses in the document. Worrying about the possible disastrous consequences of the Underwood Constitution as drawn up in Richmond, Schofield convinced General Grant, who was in charge of the military occupation but would soon be elected president, to let him delay submitting the results to the voters. That delay gave time for a compromise to materialize, but it also meant that unlike many other Southern states that met the requirements of the Reconstruction Act, Virginia, still being a territory, had no vote in the presidential election that year. Some young men down an especially tall tree they found in the Dismal Swamp on which to wave a banner for the Democrat standard bearer that year, but they never had the chance to cast a vote. Meanwhile, under various acts Congress charged the secretary of war and the military with implementing reconstruction through a chain of command. When President Johnson tried to evade the system, the House of Representatives impeached him, but the Senate narrowly failed to remove him from office.

A "Committee of Nine" urged acceptance of the black vote and the rest of the Underwood Constitution, if the clauses restricting white voting and holding office were voted on separately. The newly elected Grant agreed with this compromise, and in the 6 July 1869 canvas, after a vigorous campaign, the voters approved the new constitution by a wide margin and rejected the two clauses by about 40,000 votes each. In elections held the same day for statewide office as well as Congressional seats, a moderate Republican Gilbert Walker, a New Yorker and a Norfolk businessman, defeated the radical Republican H.H. Wells, a former military officer, and interim governor by about 18,000 votes. With white civilization hanging in the balance, according to the press, Conservatives, who had earlier pulled their candidate from the contest, voted for Walker. Other elections had similar results as Conservatives also secured control of the assembly and took six of nine Congressional races. The Conservative press considered the time when it became clear that Walker had won a "day of deliverance," but the verdict of the voters had to be submitted to Congress, which somewhat reluctantly accepted the package, but only after it added some twelve reservations, including Virginia's acceptance of the 13th, 14th, and 15th amendments plus West Virginia statehood. The third clause of the 14th Amendment jeopardized some elected Congressmen that had previously taken an oath to support the federal government and later helped out the Confederacy. The agreement, however, meant that Virginia had regained statehood.

The matter of occupation, however, remained unresolved, at least in Richmond. Walker took office in late January 1870, but a general that replaced Schofield remained in the city with some occupation soldiers. In the capital, the Radical Republicans and Conservatives vied for control of the municipal government, with each side embracing violence. During a packed meeting at the state capitol building, the gallery collapsed, leading to the deaths and maiming dozens of spectators and participants. After this catastrophe, the two sides ended their dispute and federal troops withdrew from the city. The ordeal that started in 1861 was finally over.

As Virginia entered a new decade, the state contained nearly 1,225,000 people or about the same as it had ten years earlier, not counting the part that became West Virginia. Despite all the disasters, including battle deaths and diseases like scurvy and cholera, the state grew. The percentage of blacks in Virginia, as it came out of Reconstruction, increased by only 1%, suggesting some blacks left the state. During the 1860s, many blacks migrated to cities like Alexandria, which almost doubled its African American component while losing a few hundred whites. Petersburg grew from about 9,000 to over 10,000 blacks as it lost about 600 whites. Richmond surged to over 23,000 blacks compared to about 14,000 some 10 years earlier, as its white population climbed but about 4,000. Portsmouth's black population jumped to close to 40%, and Norfolk showed similar increases. Fredericksburg, one of the few large communities to suffer a population loss, had far fewer blacks and whites, losing overall about 1,000 residents.

On a lighter note, the era right after the Civil War produced something more than a series of ceremonies for deceased Confederate soldiers. Several traditionally Northern pastimes, such as sculling and baseball became commonplace. In October 1865, Norfolk lads lost to a team composed of Union troops from Illinois 44 to 30. The game appeared in Richmond at about the same time, and it soon showed up at the campus of VMI. In 1867, around the time the new constitution was being drawn up in Richmond, teams from Petersburg and Norfolk vied for what they considered a state championship. Called the "national game" since around 1857, its appearance south of the Potomac signified sectional accommodation. Richmond residents, not wanting to become too close to Northerners, resisted efforts to play the Union Club from the DC, for "we are southerners." A Northern newsman thought the national association could get along without Richmond and suggested a contest between the Virginians and African Americans. Despite the bantering, the nation, including Virginia, experienced a surge of interest in the sport. Everyone seemed to be suffering from baseball on the brain. When balls began to strike those passing by the games, the Radical Republican mayor of Richmond banned the contests within city limits.

During his four years in office, Walker, a banker, materially aided business interests, a fairly common practice in the "Gilded Age." William Mahone had raised funds to help Walker win election. As governor, Walker approved legislation that authorized the incorporation of the Atlantic, Mississippi, and Ohio Railroad (the A.M.&O. or as some wags put it, "All Mine and Otelia's," a reference to Mahone's wife). Mahone, the president of the Norfolk & Petersburg, lobbied the legislature to approve the formation of a trunk line, with limited and temporary state ownership. This long-needed line had uniform gauges and passed through cities and towns with no need to transfer cargo. Responding to the requests of the rivals of the A.M.&O., Walker then, over Mahone's objections, approved legislation that allowed the backers of the Baltimore and Ohio and other railroads to buy out the state's investment for around $1,000,000 and giving them control of most of the tracks north of Richmond. The state retained only its interest in the Richmond, Fredericksburg, and Potomac. Northern railroad money and Mahone's funds fueled the vote on the measure. When some people blamed the few black representatives for the sordid business, one of them said he simply followed the advice of reputable Conservatives. The Conservatives, a combination of old Whigs and prewar Democrats, dominated the House of Delegates, which contained but 27 blacks, only three of whom did not support the Republican Party. That party, with connections to businessmen from the North, had no reason to oppose this legislation. But this sale of railroad stock disturbed many voters.

Some residents also reacted against the Funding Act, which stated that Virginia would pay full value for two-thirds of the state debt, assuming West Virginia would pick up the other third. This debt had been incurred before the war to build internal improvements. With interest, it now stood at about $45,000,000. In effect, Virginia received about 10% of the original of $30,000,000 in bonds at 6% interest and coupons for the other $15,000,000. Knowing a bad deal when they saw it, the voters retired many of the members of the Assembly that passed the measure. The new legislature rescinded the act, but Walker, who had switched political parties, overrode their objections. Westerners particularly wanted to scale back the size of the debt so bondholders would share some of the loss. At least the accruing interest, they argued, should be eliminated. The Funding Act received marked support among the old planter class, which had concerns about honor. Walker strongly supported both the Funding Act and the related sale of state properties. He contended that Virginia's wealth amounted to three-quarters of a billion dollars, which should yield more than enough to pay the debt and develop public schools, a priority the Republicans had implanted in the Underwood Constitution.

Speaker of the House James Lawson Kemper replaced Walker as governor in 1874. A survivor of Pickett's Charge, the new governor carried out a rigorous and racist campaign to win the office, saying that his opponent was worse than a carpetbagger. But after assuming office, he refused to allow Petersburg to have a new charter that would have given the Assembly power over appointing municipal judges. Because the Conservatives had absolute control over the Assembly and blacks held sway in the "Cockade City," the change would strike a blow for white supremacy. But when Kemper vetoed the measure, Conservatives in Petersburg hung him in effigy. Even General Jubal Early became upset with his fellow Confederate veteran when Kemper said he would let blacks march in a parade to honor recently deceased General Pickett. A moderate on fiscal matters, Kemper hoped the bondholders would voluntarily take smaller payments. Because neither they nor the legislature took any step to reduce the debt, the governor felt obligated to keep funding for schools at low levels. While he supported public education in theory, the state did not have sufficient funds to cover both school costs and debt payments. To complicate matters, the economy turned south with a market crash in 1873. Anticipated revenues for the state failed to materialize. In Kemper's last year in office, the legislature created posts for a railroad commissioner and a commissioner of agriculture (both with severely limited powers) and even allowed women to own property while married. Mindful of the rising power of religious folks, the legislature also rewrote laws concerning the Sabbath in the guise of a labor law, so that it would be a violation to work at one's regular job on Sunday.

Kemper's replacement, another wounded hero of the Civil War F.W.M. Holliday, avoided expressing his views on the debt during the campaign in 1877. After he took office, the Assembly passed a bill to change the debt agreement, thus making more funds available for education. Spokesmen for the bondholders argued that public education was a communist idea. Rising politician John Daniel, known as the "Lame Lion of Lynchburg," said he would rather see all the schoolhouses burned than allow for a reduction in the debt. Noting that the previous generation did not need free schools, Governor Holliday vetoed the measure. Thus about half the schools did not operate in 1878, despite an improving economy. With the state owing some $1,500,000 to the localities for public education, teachers went without pay. By this point, when many northern states were creating public high schools, Virginia law expressly forbade state aid to such schools, because the state had a hard enough time covering existing obligations. Faced with a crisis in education, Governor Holliday finally agreed to a slight reduction in interest payments on the debt and relief from the burden of carrying West Virginia's share of the debt. The new funding program left the creditors with coupons redeemable in tax payments. Thus the actual money available to the state for expenses remained at low levels. The measure proved insufficient in heading off a major reform of the issue.

From the outset public education remained segregated. The Underwood Constitution, despite efforts by black delegates, failed to integrate the newly created schools. The federal Civil Rights Act of 1875, which required integration of public services, omitted any reference to education. William Ruffner, the first state superintendent of public instruction, strongly opposed any effort to integrate schools, noting it would kill public schooling in Virginia. During the financial crisis of the 1870s, limited funds went mostly to white schools. Northern benefactors made up some of the difference. The Peabody Education Fund, for example, pumped about $20,000 a year into black schools. Some years later the Jeanes and Slater funds, both supported by Northerners, also helped black education.

William Mahone, who failed to garner much support in his bid to be the Conservative gubernatorial candidate in 1877, organized the Readjusters at a convention in Richmond in 1879. With his railroad in receivership because of the Panic of 1873, Mahone went into politics. A Baptist preacher from Albemarle

County, "Parson" John Massey, who considered himself the founder of the Readjusters, turned his oratorical skills from preaching to politics. Assemblyman Harrison H. Riddleberger, an old Democrat from the Valley, switched sides from the Funders (Conservatives) to the Readjusters. When they failed to persuade large numbers of blacks to switch to their party, the Readjusters worked out an alliance with the Republicans. The Readjusters courted black voters with reforms that involved money for schools, including higher education for blacks. By not running candidates against each other, the alliance carried the legislature with over a 20,000-vote margin, netting them majorities in both the House and Senate.

Lacking the two-thirds vote necessary to override vetoes, the Readjusters and their Republican allies waited for the next election. Late in 1879 the legislature picked Mahone as U.S. senator. In Washington, for supporting Republican positions, Chester Arthur, who assumed the presidency on the assassination of his predecessor, gave the dapper Readjuster control over federal patronage in the state. That meant that political boss Mahone could demand a percentage of the officeholder's salary. In 1881 the alliance retained control of the Assembly and elected William Cameron, a newspaperman and mayor of Petersburg, as the new governor. The next year the Assembly drew up a bill that arbitrarily cut away much of the accrued interest on the prewar debt and left Virginia responsible for paying about $21,000,000. The state issued new bonds, called "Riddlebergers" (named for a legislator) bearing 3% interest. None of the debt was redeemable for tax payments.

That Assembly rewarded blacks by eliminating public whipping and the poll tax, measures the Conservatives employed to reduce black voting. The legislature funded the Normal and Collegiate Institute for Negroes in Petersburg and the Central Hospital in the same city for the mentally ill. Members appropriated almost $800,000 for the Literary Fund and payments directly to schools, giving black education a significant boost. Governor Cameron also appointed two black members to the Richmond School Board. This act, more than any other, sent Conservatives into a frenzy because white schoolteachers would theoretically be taking orders from black trustees. In addition, the legislature cut property taxes and raised rates on corporations. It funded the Virginia Agricultural and Mechanical College, created in 1872 at Blacksburg. An earlier legislature had directed federal funds from land sales to the new college and to Hampton Institute, a private school for blacks endowed with Northern money after the Civil War. The Readjuster-Republican Assembly and Governor Cameron also meddled in the affairs of the public colleges by appointing a new board of visitors at the University of Virginia. The university administration and students eventually accepted the reforms instituted by the new board. Curiously, Readjuster judges refused to let their own party members control the medical college in Richmond.

Duels accompanied these tense political times. The editor of the Mahone-backed Richmond paper ended up with wounds to his jaw and lower body. In one of the numerous affairs Delegate H.H. Riddleberger, "the Game Cock of the Valley" participated in the participants shot three times to no effect. In reaction to these encounters, the legislature toughened the laws on dueling. Finally, in 1885 the practice ceased when a prominent editor spurned the demands of an obviously demented duel seeker that had already served a prison sentence for manslaughter.

Despite these successes, the period of Readjuster-Republican dominance proved short-lived. As early as 1883 the alliance lost cohesiveness, and within a year or two the Readjusters disappeared. Some of them, like Mahone, became Republicans, while others rejoined the Conservatives, now known as Democrats. Massey joined the revived Democrats and narrowly lost a fight for a congressional seat against John S. Wise, son of a former governor and another wounded veteran. Mahonites cheered, "All de Funders am a-weeping/Poor Massey's in de cold, cold ground," but four important state senators bolted the alliance and blacks were disgruntled when Mahone rewarded members of their race only with low level posts. Cameron proved more accommodating as he appointed blacks to paying positions such as doorkeeper and penitentiary guard. In Danville a charter change gave blacks control of the city council, which meant black influence among justices and police, but Mahone refused to meet black demands in Petersburg to replace white schools teachers with blacks. Black citizens complained that many of the whites failed to pass competency tests for teaching and also did not understand black culture.

In October 1883, Orra Langhorne overheard a caucus meeting of the State Democratic Convention in Lynchburg. Even though the race question still divided Liberals and Conservatives in Virginia, she thought blacks had advanced despite the Democrat longstanding protest against progress. Even Democrats, she hoped, might recognize black achievements. Possibly an educational requirement might remove some of the problems that had resulted from black voting. When she heard that the Supreme Court made the Civil Rights Act unconstitutional, she overly-optimistically presumed it would not cause great harm because of black progress in the past ten years. Born and raised in Rockingham County in a wealthy pro-Union family, Langhorne closely followed race relations. Riding the rails between Lynchburg and Charlottesville, she noticed that as the cars filled up, whites took seats next to blacks. Some years earlier, Langhorne observed, the mere presence of black people in a first-class car, except as attending servants would have created a commotion, but now no one seemed to notice. She also praised the progress of those she had known as slaves in Harrisonburg. Most of them now owned property and had not become maids. A mulatto teacher reported that curious but friendly whites often came to her school to inquire about new ways of teaching. A young black man served as a policeman and reported no trouble with white people recognizing his authority. That observation may well have been true for Harrisonburg, but on the eastern side of the Blue Ridge, a stronger brand of racism prevailed, as whites resisted efforts to allow blacks to rule over them. Langhorne observed that white Southerners were having difficulty unlearning their ingrained idea that whites had to rule and blacks serve. While Northerners gave money and sometimes their lives to help blacks, they often refused to socialize with them. Southern whites wanted blacks to be near them but "keep their place." One Virginia planter said if all blacks went to Africa, he would have to go there, too. White women would not leave their children with white nurses nor feel comfortable with white maids and expressed shock when blacks left for higher paying jobs in the North. Langhorne observed that blacks did all the work in tobacco factories in Lynchburg, usually under a white boss. Negroes predominated as teamsters, taxi drivers, porters, snack sellers, and barbers, who drew their own color line for customers. Many had also recently become small grocers, hucksters, and saloonkeepers. In the skilled trades, white master mechanics refused to let them be apprentices, thus reducing chances of progress in specialized fields, but many contractors were starting to use integrated workforces.

In the fall campaign of 1883 the Democrats, after reorganizing, launched a full campaign, using the fear of a proposed state Civil Rights Act to replace the defunct federal one to help win the election. They appointed as chair John S. Barbour, an old enemy of Mahone from his railroad days. Promising not to touch the debt question or funding for schools, the Democrats campaigned against "Negro domination." The newspapers were again filled with racial invectives as the day of the election loomed. Three days before the election, a race riot in Danville, possibly contrived by the Democrats, cost four blacks and one white their lives, as several white men fired into a crowd. The public reaction allowed the Democrats to secure two-thirds control in both houses.

Under the Anderson-McCormick Act, the legislature the next year took election regulation away from judges, who for the most part were Readjusters destined to serve as much as 12 more years, and gave it to local election officials that were almost all Democrats, who naturally found in favor of their party in any disputed vote, thus sharply reducing any chances for a revival of their rivals. Party chairmen at the county level took their cues from the state chairman and appointed sheriffs, clerks of court, and treasurers. These men in turn materially aided the organization where and when they could.

Democrats also created the future Longwood College at Farmville to train white teachers and put William Ruffner in charge of it. The Readjusters had removed Ruffner as head of public education, a post he held from the start of the system in 1870. Although a constant friend of public pedagogy, Ruffner's strong stand against integration and racist comments during the congressional debate in 1875 had not endeared him to African Americans.

Readjusters disappeared, and Republicans gradually faded from the political scene. In 1882, at the height of their power, they had put Riddleberger in the U.S. Senate and thus held both seats. With the disappearance of the Readjusters, senators Riddleberger and Mahone became Republicans. In 1884 the Republicans put up a stout fight to capture the electoral vote for the Republican presidential candidate, but they lost in Virginia by but 6,000 votes. Blacks turned out in high numbers in a federal election, where Democrats had less control. Cleveland, the Democrat, won nationally and soon deprived Mahone of all federal patronage. Now in decline, the Republicans picked Congressman John Wise to run for governor in 1885 against Democrat Fitzhugh Lee, the nephew of "Marse Robert." When Lee won handily, the Democrats controlled the state legislature and the governor's office. The number of blacks in the legislature soon fell to one in each house. As soon as it could take up the matter, the Assembly replaced Mahone with John W. Daniel as U.S. senator. The Republicans rebounded in the off-year congressional election (1886) by taking 6 of 10 seats, but the 1888 election reduced that number to two. In 1888, the Democrat-dominated legislature picked John Barbour for the other Senate seat.

One Congressional seat went to John Mercer Langston, the only black to represent Virginia in Congress during the era. Langston, the son of a white planter and his former slave, hailed from Louisa County and grew up in Ohio. After attending Oberlin College, he became a lawyer, being the first black to present a case before the U.S. Supreme Court. A recruiter for the Union during the Civil War, he later served the Freedmen's Bureau. After serving as president of a college in Washington D. C, he became the U.S. Minister to Haiti. On returning to Virginia, he became the president of the Virginia Normal and Collegiate Institute. When he ran for Congress in a Southside district with a large black population, Mahone put up another Republican against him. When his opponent polled about a 700-vote margin, Langston appealed to the House of Representatives. After a considerable delay, Congress, along party lines, declared Langston the winner. In 1890, after talking about race mixing, Langston lost his bid for reelection by a wide margin. With black support deteriorating, and detested by most whites, Mahone and the Republican Party lost by a mammoth margin in Mahone's bid to be governor in 1889.

Tactics employed under state law contributed to the gradual decline in African American participation in politics. In Richmond, Jackson Ward, a center of black culture, lost political influence. Lynchburg experienced something different in 1887, when an alliance of Republicans and the Knights of Labor, a national organization of working men, won a narrow and temporary victory in the council elections. Blacks in Lynchburg, Richmond, Petersburg, and perhaps elsewhere belonged to this movement, but when the organization became associated with violent strikes, it lost support. And so the exodus of urban blacks from the political scene continued.

In 1890 Congress considered renewing federal supervision of elections to help black voters in the South. A majority of Republicans approved the measure, which passed the House, but Democrats managed to kill the bill in the Senate. The failure to pass the force bill gave Virginia and the rest of the South a green light to do as it wished regarding race. In the mid-1890s the U.S. Supreme Court allowed states to require segregation in transportation and in the late 1890s the Supreme Court paved the way for the states to maneuver around the 15th Amendment and pretty much end black voting.

In 1894 the legislature passed the Walton Act, which retained a written ballot but prevented anyone from entering a previously filled ballot or using symbols to aid in casting one. Aimed at those who could not read, it further reduced black, and to some extent white, voting. In 1888 blacks voted en masse (the greatest number of votes cast for a Republican in Virginia) for Benjamin Harrison, who lost the state of Virginia by a narrow margin. Black participation dropped off, especially after they stood in long lines in the election of 1896, only to be prevented from voting. By the end of the century, few blacks exercised the franchise even in presidential races. In Danville, where blacks outnumbered whites, only 35% of adult black males were still voting in the early 1890s. Later in the decade that percentage fell by not quite half. Virginia Republicans purged themselves of black leaders and attempted unsuccessfully, to campaign as a "lily white" party. At century's end, John Mitchell, a black Richmond editor, doubted that black rights could be any deader than they already were.

Having reduced their Republican opponents to the status of a second-rate party, the Democrats in 1892 renegotiated the debt issue. Faced with negative court decisions over the Riddleberger Act, the Assembly came up with new bonds and a new schedule whereby the state could take twice as long to pay back over $6,000,000 more than the Riddleberger agreement called for.

Agriculturists expressed a litany of complaints, some real and others imaginary. Some, thinking fertilizer companies regularly committed fraud, talked of regulation. The altered tobacco inspection system left tobacco growers under the thumb of manufacturers. Farmers complained most about railroads that charged more for sending goods within the state than across the country. They also grumbled about protective tariffs that aided industrialists and kept farm prices low. The Patrons of Husbandry (the Grange), a political action group, after helping convince the state to create an agricultural and mechanical college at Blacksburg, supported the Readjusters and Republicans. In 1885 farm organizations formed the Farmers-Assembly with Colonel Robert Beverley at the helm. White Virginians belonged to the Southern Alliance, blacks to the Colored Alliance, numbering between 20,000 and 30,000 each in Virginia. The Alliances formed several farm cooperatives to bypass middlemen. On a national level, the alliances, along with some industrial workers, formed the Populist Party in 1892. Although Populist leaders toured Virginia and James G. Field, their candidate for vice president, came from Virginia and supposedly lost his leg in the cause of the Confederacy, they received little support as a third party. Many Virginians, however, sympathized with the antagonism toward big business expressed by farm leaders. In 1893 the Populists, with the support of Republicans, ran Randolph Cocke against Democrat Charles T. O'Ferrall. Even though no blacks played any role in the Populist Party in Virginia, the Democrats saddled the Populists with the reputation of having black support. Their candidate lost the election by about 50,000 votes, as whites, following the supremacy line, voted Democrat, though few blacks cast votes.

The years following the Civil War brought great political turmoil to the Commonwealth, but when the dust settled, white Democrats had control of the state as they had before the Civil War. Although they could not return the state to the days of slavery and could recover commercial and cultural aspects of their former life only in their imaginations, they could put blacks back into more pliant roles. Wealthy eastern farmers, with a conservative mindset, held a disproportionate share of political power.

# PART FOUR: THE EMERGENCE OF MODERN VIRGINIA

Those residents who attained adulthood around the time of the Civil War and then went on to live the biblical three score years and ten witnessed great change over their lifetimes, perhaps the greatest known to any generation of Americans. Over the next half-century or so, the number of Virginians leaving the state eased somewhat, but the trend of moving to towns and cities within Virginia accelerated. Dozens of occupations besides farming materialized. Farming changed as scientists made discoveries. One invention after the other transformed homes, though many in rural Virginia were activated a bit belatedly. Electricity energized businesses and illuminated a few homes. In the 1890s, electrified streetcars remade urban transit. People talked to each other on the telephone. Folks flew in something besides balloons. Some drove cars and trucks. Powerful ideas, like those of Charles Darwin, invaded the intellectual atmosphere. Public schools became more common, and by 1910 many communities had high schools. Literacy rates grew, though a bit grudgingly. Governments expanded their roles in regulating the economy and society. An American victory over Spain near the end of the 19th century sent the United States on the road to being a world power. Modern sports commenced. Women asserted their rights and finally obtained the right to vote. Overall health improved as a Virginian figured out what caused yellow fever and public health programs took effect. The state and later the national government moved against drinking. Someone looking back from around 1915 would have difficulty taking in all that happens in Chapters 14 and 15.

In Chapter 16 Virginia and America then entered an era of booms and busts, as they experienced World War I, a postwar economic collapse, the Roaring Twenties, the Great Depression, the New Deal, and World War II. By 1945, someone who reached adulthood around 1915 could likely make a case that they had experienced at least as much change as their fathers or grandfathers had but in a shorter time.

# Chapter 14

## Changing Commonwealth

After a slow start in recovering from the effects of the "Late Unpleasantness," Virginia made considerable strides over the next three decades. As the state forged ahead, it exhibited most of the national trends such as greater urbanization and industrialization, more diversity in both the overall economy and in farming, more railroad mileage, more mines, more commercial fishing, improved literacy, and a host of other signs of material and social progress. Most of these trends commenced well before the war, but they intensified over time. They were also accompanied by negative consequences, both for people and the environment.

The trend toward urbanization in Virginia tended, as before the Civil War, to trail the nation. With just under 12% of its people considered urban in 1870, the percentage grew slowly at first and then accelerated. It stood a bit under 13% in 1880, about 17% in 1890, over 18% in 1900, and at 29% in 1920. Virginia still trailed the nation in being urban as the country at that time was divided equally between rural and urban residents, but Virginia was now becoming urban at a rate faster than the nation as a whole.

As the towns and cities acquired more size, they offered more possible lines of employment. Diversification in occupations accompanied urbanization. In 1870 about 53% of the workforce farmed, but the proportion in farming and forestry dropped to 36% about 50 years later. In 1870 some 244,000 Virginians worked on farms as owners, renters, or agricultural laborers. Another 50,000 people, almost all black females, worked as domestic servants either in the country or cities. Just over 20,000 Virginians either carried commodities or helped to sell them. About 50,000 workers manufactured or mined products. In the next decade as the number of those in farming or forestry increased slowly, those in trade and transportation jumped by 50% and then doubled over the ensuing decade. By 1900, the number in manufacturing and mining surged to about 100,000, up from less than 78,000 some 10 years earlier. Compared to national numbers, the Old Dominion still had disproportionate numbers of farm people and female servants (85,000 as late as 1920) and fewer tradesmen and textile workers, but a demographic snapshot in 1920 found over 196,000 working in manufacturing and the mechanical arts, about 16,000 in mining, almost 65,000 in transport, the same number in trade, 34,000 in professional service, over 31,000 in public service, including almost 13,000 female and 1,900 male teachers. But despite some 6,600 women typists, nearly 1,700 female telephone operators, and several hundred women in the retail trades, their overall proportion of women in the workforce did not show a marked increase after the turn of the century.

With over 300,000 occupied in agriculture in 1920, the state remained reliant on farm production, but although nearly all farmers continued to produce necessities, they also specialized more than previously. More producers concentrated on commercial fruit and vegetables. Coastal truckers significantly increased business as up country growers turned to apples and peaches. The production of hay and other crops for cattle rose through the decades, even in parts of the Southside.

As farming diversified the number of farms markedly increased, growing between 1870 and 1920 from nearly 74,000 to over 186,000, but improved acreage only rose from just over 8,000,000 to almost 9,500,000 during the same time. Farm values, sluggish in the late 19th century, rose to $625,000,000 in 1910 and then doubled during the next decade, due in part to the inflation associated with World War I. But before that war, farm prices rose in comparison to the cost of other commodities. Thus Virginia's rural population was much better off financially after the turn of the century because they received higher prices, had a better understanding of the role of pathogens in transmitting diseases, and used commercial fertilizers.

Production of traditional crops varied over the last three decades of the 19th century. Southside farmers produced about 100,000,000 pounds of tobacco in 1919 with similar amounts 1909 and 1899. Before that, the amount of production and acreage varied greatly from lows of 37,000,000 in 1869, with a much higher volume in 1879 and a considerable drop-off in 1889. Virginians continued to grow wheat and corn as they had before the Civil War, with the state's breadbasket, the Valley of Virginia, not only recovering its wheat crops, but also producing more than in the comparatively prosperous 1850s, but the price of wheat remained low due to the opening of new fields in the far West.

Nontraditional crops played bigger roles. By 1900 truckers farmed over 45,000 acres and produced around $7,000,000, with Norfolk County one of the biggest in vegetable and strawberry production in the nation. Peanut production soared in the counties southwest of Norfolk. In 1889 farmers devoted almost 59,000 acres to that product, a number that about doubled by 1919. By that point peanuts required about two-thirds the amount of space as tobacco.

Nearly every part of the farm economy faced problems. A successful truck farmer showed solid returns for a few years only to be overcome by some blight. Peanuts did well for a while, but then an unknown nematode cut yields. Wheat producers had to combat rusts or other diseases as well as lower prices. Amherst County did well with apples and peaches, but a blight sharply reduced the latter's yield. Federal and state governments created farm extension programs in the late 1880s and small signs of progress in the 1890s boded well for the next century. Founded in 1872, Virginia Tech played a major role in agricultural research. Agricultural experiment stations scattered throughout the rural areas, mostly just after 1900, also materially aided farmers.

In 1920, about a quarter of farmers were black, a proportion that had been dropping for some time, as farm tenancy ebbed and flowed. When white owners found they could not convince former slaves to work for low wages after the Civil War, sharecropping became commonplace, but renting also prevailed. Often many freedmen accepted deals that left them scratching a bare existence out of marginal lands. Tenancy dropped during the prosperous 1880s and increased in the depression-racked 1890s, and it grew some after that despite a strong economy. Farms owned by blacks were estimated to be worth about $100,000,000 in 1920, an impressive increase over the years, but white-owned farms still carried about ten times that value. Various forms of crop sharing still prevailed among those that did not own their own farms, leaving many farm owners, both white and black, in debt.

Along the coast, truck farmers supplemented their farm income by fishing and oystering. Even before the Civil War, counties such as Mathews on the western shore of Chesapeake Bay had between 150 and 200 oystermen, a somewhat smaller number of fishermen, and several dozen mariners. For the bay area, thousands, many of them African Americans, worked on the water or were employed shucking oysters in nearby cities or towns.

Before the Civil War, in response to petitions from coastal residents, the state passed acts to combat dredging to protect the oyster beds and reduce competition from outsiders, but some oystermen complained that the legislation should not be applied to deeper waters where the use of tongues proved difficult nor at the lower end of the Rappahannock River, where removing oyster "rocks" aided navigation. For a time only local oystermen along the Nansemond River could tap their beds. By 1860 the legislature produced a very lengthy and complicated system designed to reduce damage to the beds, preventing the sale and even the transplanting of oysters during from May through August, and inspecting all the ships moving oysters, both for violations of fishing laws and to apprehend potential runaway slaves. This elaborate and complicated system controlled both the planting and gathering of oysters, with special fees depending on the boat size and type of equipment.

During Reconstruction, the state imposed taxes on oysters boats, both to derive revenue in an especially financially strained time and also to regulate the industry. By the early 1870s, the state claimed ownership of all the oyster beds, but the legislature gave adjacent property owners special privileges in their use. Governor Cameron gained fame for leading an armed band aboard one of the state's "naval" ships in pursuit of oyster poachers in the mid-1880s. On another occasion the watermen of Tangiers fought a pitched battle against the state navy. A few years later Governor O'Ferrall collaborated with the governor of Maryland to reduce the depletion of oyster grounds.

In addition, the state started to protect endangered fishes by forcing dam owners to provide fish ladders or sluices on rivers. As early as 1800, residents of the Lynnhaven area in Princess Anne County failed to convince the state to restrict fishing to residents of the neighborhood because outsiders left fish to rot on the beaches. Yet, by 1860 one could not legally use nets or seines to fish in certain rivers. The state also made it illegal to shoot waterfowl at night. Hunting laws became increasingly more restrictive over time.

Rural life became more pleasant, especially after the turn of the century, with the introduction of mail delivery to rural areas, traveling libraries, tractors, hand-cranked phonographs, and a host of other implements. Kerosene replaced whale oil for lighting in the 1870s. Iron ranges for cooking and water pumps for kitchens became more common as the 20th century progressed. Curiously, observers talked more about rural isolation in the new era, as the time when farmers had limited access to the outside world and lacked many conveniences became more romantic. Through most of this era, most rural folk still did almost all work by hand: sewing and weaving, weeding, cutting grain, husking corn, hauling water, pruning plants, along with numerous other chores. Major changes began to occur after the turn of the century, but even at that time, black farmers continued to rely on the old ways, mostly because they could not afford new implements.

A description of the area north of Danville in Pittsylvania County typified rural life in the Southside, where slaves clustered in large farms before the Civil War. Orra Langhorne compared this situation with the scene in 1885 as she rode near Chatham, credited with 543 residents in 1880 and 757 in 1890 and consisting a "square or two" of houses built close together and "pleasant,...white houses with big yards and wide spreading trees" for about a half mile on either side of town. She then found herself in deep woods, with little human habitation save for an occasional log or pine-board cabin in a small clearing, which also featured patches of tobacco, scenes that reminded her of the pioneers. A mile or so from Chatham, she saw a village that had but a row of small houses. Two of these were but mud-daubed huts with great chimneys composed of sticks and clay that reminded her of the slave shelters on the old plantations. The rest were new and had weatherboards for siding.

By 1920 about half of Virginia's rural population, including both blacks and whites, did not rely on farming for their principal source of income, reflecting a longstanding trend. Many held skilled or semiskilled jobs or ran or worked in retail businesses, sometimes living in villages or small towns. During this time Virginia contained dozens of villages too small for the census to record. Census officials found 80 towns of over 1,000 but less than 2,500 people in 1890, 128 in 1900 and 159 in 1910, when about 29% of over 2,000,000 Virginians lived in all the incorporated communities of the state, while about 23% resided in places with more than 2,500 residents.

Ellen Glasgow began her extraordinarily productive career in fiction writing in the late 1890s. In her numerous works, she rejected the Calvinism of her father and accepted the ideas of Charles Darwin, the English naturalist. Professor Holmes at the University of Virginia guided her academic studies. Glasgow started her writing career with a study of a young man of illegitimate origins. Her second major work, *The Voice of the People*, dealt with late 19th-century Virginia politics. *Battleground* examined Virginia during the Civil War. *Deliverance* dealt with Virginia under Reconstruction. Her works showed considerable sympathy for the defenders of old Virginia, as she deplored rising commercialism and materialism. Her favorite characters are clearly women and a few men able to overcome adversities. Although some of her businessmen were a bit unsavory, she saw herself as a realist who strove to combat excessive sentimentality about times before the Civil War. In *Barren Ground*, Glasgow described rural life in late 19th-century Virginia. The author recognized the difficult circumstances in which rural people lived. But while isolation is a central theme in her works, many of her characters roam the rural paths and fields and also occasionally hop on a train in the morning at a nearby isolated depot and reach busy New York at night.

Although Glasgow was certainly Virginia's most well known novelist of the time, the state produced several other respected writers, especially women. Mary Johnston's *To Have and To Hold*, written as the century turned, was perhaps the best historical novel ever produced by a Virginian. Amelia Rives, Mary Terhune, and Constance Harrison also contributed fictional books as well as a wide array of articles in popular magazines of the time.

Many farmers hated railroad corporations for keeping rates high and as representatives of modern business practices. Railroads corrupted politics almost as much as the issue of race, but they also improved rural life. The process began before the Civil War, particularly in the 1850s, when Virginia acquired hundreds of miles of tracks. Once rebuilt after the war, this system substantially expanded, especially in the prosperous 1880s. At that time the Norfolk and Western emerged out of the wreckage of Mahone's railroad empire to control the tracks below the James River. In 1881 it acquired a feeder track near present-day Radford that tapped timber and coal above the New River. Branch lines linked the hollows of Russell and Wise counties. Another line headed south toward the Blue Ridge and more resources. Still another entered southwest Virginia through Cumberland Gap.

With the appearance of rail connections, mining became the mainstay in the mountains to go along with lumbering. Entrepreneurs first tapped the Pocahontas Vein (coal) in Tazewell County in the early 1880s. They developed Wise County later in that decade. The population of these places rapidly increased as black Americans and immigrants from Eastern Europe came to work. By the end of the century the number of miners in Wise County exceeded those in farming, even though the number employed in agriculture had grown, along with their incomes, in response to the need to feed the new arrivals. At that time about 10% of the residents of the county were black and a smaller percent came from overseas, but the mines had a much higher ratio of black and foreign workmen. William Lamb, the driving force in creating the coal piers in Norfolk, ended a strike in Tazewell County by discussing matters with the black workers. They found him an acceptable negotiator because of his reputation as a Republican. He could not communicate with the other miners, for none of them could speak English.

A study of the use of waterpower in 1880 revealed a wide variety of mills processing everything from cotton to paper, using river water. Major rivers like the James, especially at the fall line, offered power to many businesses, but one could also find smaller operations along sluggish and usually shallow rivers like the Nottoway and Blackwater in southern Virginia. One surveyor noted that the Dan River still had locks built for a canal nearly a half-century earlier and wondered why its power had not been tapped to a greater extent beyond supplying Danville with drinking water. Along the James, Appomattox, and the Rappahannock, companies used water backed up by dams built years earlier to supply water for canals. Sending water down sluices to create power had been a common way to obtain mechanical power for generations, but the 1880 report disclosed that Virginians had not come close to exploiting water's full potential. Certain areas along the major rivers could conceivably have produced up to 4,000 horsepower at any single time, but no single mill used more than a few hundred. Even so, this small amount of power kept dozens of workers busy producing cotton, paper, flour, iron and other items. One of the problems with using water was the variability of its volume, even with the use of reservoirs. Even with fairly consistent rainfall, mills did not continually operate, but Virginia's climate usually varies in the amount of rainfall, thus forcing the closure of mills and forges several times in any given year. Also, even minor floods (and Virginia had at least two fair-sized ones in the 1870s), swept away dams and crucial equipment if not the buildings.

Most manufacturers turned to steam made from coal for power. Only one of the cotton mills on the north side of the Appomattox opposite Petersburg used steam in 1880, but by 1909 Virginia's manufacturers were using nearly 3,400,000 tons of bituminous coal and 26,000 tons of anthracite to generate steam. Coal, along with some gas and oil plus electric power produced by the firms themselves or sold by power companies, now supplied energy needs. Waterways yielded hydroelectric power from both small and large operations, but most companies turned to coal for energy.

As a result of rail construction, town life developed where it had never been before. Indeed, the majority of Virginia's towns and cities today owe their location to the presence of the rail lines. In the late 19th century, communities of near or over 1,000 residents materialized almost overnight. Eggleston, Pembroke, Pocahontas on the New River Division, Big Stone Gap and Norton in Wise County, St. Paul, Gate City, to name a few, came into existence to accompany Bristol, which arose when the old Virginia and Tennessee put its tracks in the area in the 1850s.

Several towns in the Southwest became industrial centers based on their rail connections. Pulaski, along the tracks of the Norfolk and Western, developed the Dora Furnace and other industries, and Radford, created as a city in 1892, had pipe works and a large foundry among other enterprises. Former Confederate General Gabriel Wharton took a leading role in persuading the Norfolk and Western to tap the coalfields to the west, thus bringing even more coal through the Radford area. In 1877 George Carter, descended from the famous planters of the Northern Neck, started with a small lead and zinc company near the site of an earlier lead and iron industry. He combined some ten companies into the Virginia Iron, Coal and Coke Co., which had hundreds of coke ovens across the area. General John Imboden, another former Confederate, roamed the entire area looking for coal and iron deposits. The community of Damascus resulted, but huge iron deposits in the West took the edge off the boom in Virginia. Imboden collaborated with Rufus Ayers, a Democrat attorney general, in promoting Big Stone Gap, a major rail center. Wise County, the biggest coal-producing county for many years once it started booming in the 1890s, had the old courthouse community at Wise (Gladeville with 800 or so in 1910) as well as Big Stone Gap and Coeburn, two trading centers. The former contained just over 2,500, with almost 400 more in a suburb in 1910. The county also had Imboden and Appalachia (originally called Mineralville), located between Big Stone Gap and Norton, the second largest town in the county with almost 1,900 residents in 1910. About a dozen coal camps like Andover, Esserville, and Stonega operated as company-controlled hamlets. These places usually rose overnight and then disappeared when the mines played out. Census officials mention none of these communities, citing only Tacoma with 169 folks and Bond Town with 305 in the report on the 1910 census.

Not every area felt the impact of the introduction of rails quite as much as the mountains with their minerals and timber, but in Southside Virginia, the Norfolk, Franklin, and Danville allowed Franklin to become a paper mill town. The Camp family developed the mill and timber resources. By 1910 Southampton County had at least four major lines within its boundaries. In the 1880s the Pennsylvania Railroad built an extension down the middle of the Eastern Shore of Virginia. Cape Charles, at the southern terminus, came into being with its new homes assembled from lumber parts brought over the new rail. At least half a dozen depots grew into recognizable communities because of the rail service.

Rivals to the Norfolk and Western built a trunk line from deep in West Virginia, along the New River and all the way to Norfolk. The Virginian brought tons of coal to its piers above Norfolk by 1910. At the same time its tracks running several miles south of those of its rival (the Norfolk and Western) through the Southside, allowed the creation of at least a trio of sizeable towns.

Rail connections of the early 1880s permitted the rise of Roanoke and Newport News. Proponents of southern industrialization saw them as examples of the "New South." Newport News was largely the handiwork of Collis Huntington, one of California's infamous railroad men. Years before the Civil War, Huntington pondered the virtues of the harbor at Point Comfort. After the war he and his cohorts extended the Chesapeake and Ohio, from Richmond to the coast. They also financed the Newport News Shipbuilding and Drydock Co., which soon made battleships for the federal government. Using a land company, Huntington and his associates closely controlled what soon became a city of 20,000, with hundreds engaged in industrial work at the big shipyard. Nearby Hampton emerged from the ashes of the war to become a major fish processing center. Several Northerners invested heavily in such businesses as canning crabs and fishing for menhaden, as fish fertilizer replaced bat guano. It was connected to the railroad in Newport News by a short rail line that served both producers and tourists.

Located on the tracks of the old Virginia and Tennessee, the village of Big Lick turned almost overnight into an industrial city, when a railroad came in from the north to join the revived Norfolk and Western. Roanoke soon became known as "Magic City," as thousands of workmen, many from Pennsylvania, followed the tracks. Machine shops worked on cars and locomotives, as Roanoke became the headquarters of the expanded Norfolk and Western. By 1909, Roanoke's 3,500 employed in manufacturing, nearly 10% of its total population, added some $7,000,000 to the value of their production, roughly a 30% increase in five years in a time of limited inflation.

Small industrial and/or commercial communities also flourished along the other railroads. The Chesapeake and Ohio had Clifton Forge and Covington in the western part of Virginia. West Virginia Pulp and Paper Co. created a plant in Covington to produce high quality paper in 1899. Covington also had a sizeable machine shop established in 1892. Alleghany County also benefited for a time from the presence of the Low Moor Iron Company, named for two industrialists and located in a community of the same name not far from Clifton Forge. The Southside ended up with Blackstone and Crewe, among others along the existing road between Petersburg and Lynchburg. Dozens of the former tiny depots came to possess clusters of stores and other services.

Despite losing status as a seaport, when oceangoing ships began to draw over 16′ of water, Richmond grew in population and economic activity through its numerous rail lines and related industrial output. The tobacco industry continued to produce plugs but it also shifted to cigarettes. When a tobacco company offered a prize for anyone who produced a rolling machine, James Bonsack, from a textile village named for his family located near Roanoke, came up with a device based on the carding mechanism used in twisting fibers. The machine, patented in 1881, produced almost as much as fifty hand rollers in the same time. Richmond benefited, even though much of the tobacco suitable for cigarettes came from North Carolina and fell under the control of a monopoly. It also had enlightened businessmen despite the myth that the old capital of the Confederacy failed to respond to the new age. By 1909 Richmond contained about 127,000 residents. Its 15,000 industrial workers added some $47,000,000 value to manufactured products, a 70% increase in five years.

Norfolk and Portsmouth surged during the new age. The Norfolk and Southern Co. sent tracks into North Carolina. The area also secured another line west to Danville, the Atlantic Coast Line. Early in the 20th century a belt line linked the different lines on the Portsmouth side of the Elizabeth River, and around 1920 it was extended north of Norfolk, as investors built factories along the new route. Cotton, which started to show up just before the Civil War, increased with the century to a point where Norfolk became the third largest cotton exporter in the nation. Steam compresses reduced the size of bales so even more could be packed on the ever larger ships that entered the harbor. The value of coal exports reached about $20,000,000 compared to less than $1,000,000 a few years earlier. The Norfolk and Western opened coal piers a few miles west of downtown, in 1883. New tracks brought coal around the city rather than through it, relieving downtown of coal congestion. By the end of the century these piers made Norfolk one of the largest coal ports in the world. The establishment of coal piers by the Virginian by 1910 simply continued this trend.

Millions of board feet of lumber flowed through the area, as John Roper, a Pennsylvanian stationed in Norfolk during the Civil War, bought or rented hundreds of thousands of acres in lower Virginia and upper North Carolina. After introducing a kiln drying process for pine, Roper later invested in shipbuilding. With timber, truck farming, and peanut processing (a Norfolk firm apparently was the first to make peanut butter), and a host of industrial operations, including a knitting mill or two, its population grew from less than 20,000 in 1870 to 67,000 in 1910. At that point, its industrial workers (some 4,700 of them) were adding over $10,000,000 to the value manufactured items, with lumber products leading the way.

For a time Smithfield in Isle of Wight held the title as the leading peanut processing center, using steamers on the Pagan River for distribution purposes, but the town, lacking rail links, gave way to nearby Suffolk, where a Pennsylvania peddler originally from Greece, Amedeo Obici, formed the Planters Peanut Company. Smithfield then concentrated on hams and other pig products, for which the area had become famous, with the Smithfield Packing Co. taking center state. Over the years this firm came to control considerable market share in that industry, but the Pagan River and adjacent waterways sustained considerable ecological damage.

Alexandria showed little growth during the late 19th century, but the city did well after 1900. In the mid 1870s the waterfront possessed a tiny foundry, a fairly large grain warehouse, an old cotton mill, and a small flour mill, along with coal and lumber yards, and several small piers, including one for the ferry to the District of Columbia. Its port continued to handle cargoes, assisted greatly by the tracks of a main line that joined the Alexandria & Fredericksburg outside the city. Once a railroad bridge crossed the Potomac, the canal to Alexandria became obsolete. Shippers might still send some materials that could be shipped up the coast or overseas, but Baltimore had already taken the bulk of that business. Thus Alexandria remained a way station rather than a major terminus. Its population in 1910, at about 15,000, was about the same as in 1860.

The general appearance of Northern Virginia area remained static until around 1900. Old villages like Falls Church carried on with its depot on the Washington & Ohio line and the Leesburg & Alexandria Turnpike, but it only had around fifty buildings, including three or four stores and the same number of churches. Centreville now had Braddock's Road as well as the old road to Warrenton, but businesses remained confined to a limited area. Vienna had possibly two blocks of businesses and a handful of residential blocks, despite having a train station. Chantilly was little more than a wide spot on the Little River Turnpike. Herndon had developed nicely as a station on the tracks of the Washington & Ohio, but Fairfax Court House had maybe forty buildings, mostly residences to accompany its courthouse, jail, and school for black children. Alexandria County, carved out of the northern part of Fairfax, had the village of Rosslyn right next to the Potomac and the U.S. Military Cemetery at Arlington (the Lee estate). Just to the southeast of the cemetery was the former site of the Freedmen's Village, home to former slaves for a time after the Civil War.

By the mid-1890s, an electric railroad ran from the northern outskirts of Washington across the Potomac a mile or so above the Chain Bridge and wound its way through Fairfax County. A second traction line through Falls Church began to operate before the turn of the century, and in 1912 the old Washington and Ohio Railroad converted to electricity. The nation's capital, with over 400,000 folks in 1920, filled out its side of the Potomac, and with electric rail connections, federal workers took up residence across the river. Real estate developers now offered homes or lots for sale near Vienna and at equally romantic sounding names in other locations. By 1920 Arlington County, having been separated from Alexandria County five years earlier, had about 16,000 residents. Fairfax also grew as well, to about 21,000. Most of the population increase in these areas could be attributed to a spillover from the nation's capital, a small stream in what would eventually become a tidal wave. The District of Columbia, unlike Virginia cities, had no legal way to acquire its suburbanites.

Richmond had the first trolleys in the entire country, introduced by a railway in 1887 to link the city with a suburb and an exposition. Norfolk enjoyed the same service as of 1894 as electric cars replaced those drawn by donkeys mules. Soon tracks for trolleys stretched for miles outside each downtown. Norfolk investors built a line north of their city that served the Jamestown Exposition of 1907. Staunton and even Radford had lines in the early 20th century. The coming of the trolleys accelerated a movement toward the suburbs. As people moved from the countryside, they often took up residence on the outskirts of existing cities. There they joined folks who had moved out of the central cities. Some of these newcomers owned their own homes, as borrowing money to build residences became more common. Those who could not afford to purchase found rental units, usually located in the more built-up areas closer to downtowns. Over 70% of those living in core cities rented apartments or small homes and moved at least once a year on a prescribed day. Suburban living had numerous and obvious attractions, including home ownership, and the trolley lines made it possible for people to work in the cities and live in the suburbs. The suburbs also provided more space for each resident. As cities annexed more of their surrounding suburbs, they reduced the density of population for the city as a whole. Thus cities had fewer people per square mile over time. Almost every city had more people per square mile in 1870 than in 1920. In 1870 no city in Virginia required even an hour to walk at a leisurely pace the entire length of the settled areas. By 1920 several cities in Virginia embraced too much land to allow such a feat.

Progress came at a price. Not only did industrialization require extensive use of resources and often entail poorer water and air quality, but it also put excessive demands on workers. In a five-year span, the number of workers grew but at nowhere near the pace of the value added by their efforts. Overall, the average workmen put in between 55 and 60 hours each week. The typical Danville cotton mill operative worked 60 hours a week, a number that paled in comparison to someone employed making glass or ice, where the standard week of work consisted of 72 hours, or six 12-hour days.

In addition, each new rail line or slight modification in the route of an existing track resulted in the appearance of near ghost towns, as people moved their businesses and homes. The political power of the railroads and the increased reliance of people on their services also produced numerous problems.

In the mountain Southwest entrepreneurs either persuaded or coerced landowners to sell mineral rights for small returns. Northerners supplied much of the capital, but many local residents participated in these transforming ventures. John Fox, Jr., a resident of Big Stone Gap and a novelist who developed the theme of Appalachian uniqueness (*Trail of the Lonesome Pine*), deplored the speculators and riffraff that accompanied the booming economy, but he also favored the New South's industrial development and cooperated with respectable businessmen.

The boom of the 1880s eventually gave way to a bust in the 1890s. A bank in Lexington closed in 1895 due to embezzlement related to failed speculation in nearby Buena Vista. Advertising their community as a new "Magic City," the Buena Vista Co. played up its proximity to iron, manganese, and tin. Like Big Stone Gap, Buena Vista resembled a Western mining town with men drinking heavily and toting guns. It attracted hundreds of petty speculators (carpetbaggers) from all over the country. When the town received news of the impending establishment of a large foundry, pandemonium reigned. Claiming a far greater population than actually existed, Buena Vista secured the status of a city under state charter in 1892, at about the same time the speculative market collapsed. Something similar happened northeast of Staunton, where one-time Civil War mapmaker Jedediah Hotchkiss hoped to make Shendun (later known as Grottoes) into a major rail center and the "Norfolk of the Shenandoah Valley." After its incorporation in 1892, however, the depression reduced rail traffic. Other investors had high hopes for Glasgow, located on the James River near the confluence with the Maury River, not far from Balcony Falls to the east and Natural Bridge several miles to the west. Again rail links (the line to Roanoke and the Chesapeake and Ohio) and natural resources gave promise and developers mapped out a city extending for miles along the river, but after attaining a population of about 1,000 residents, growth stopped with the economic downturn. Farther south, Radford experienced a similar buildup in the 1880s. Newspapers gave weekly summaries of new buildings and businesses, giving the impression that thousands of productive citizens were flocking to Central Depot on the New River. The community, renamed Radford, received a city charter in 1892, only to find that in the next census its total number fell below 3,000. Along the way, one of the new foundries released something toxic into the river that killed most of the fish.

Doubtless residents of the southwestern part of the state did not all benefit from the railroads, mines, and manufacturing plants. Old folks, asked to recall life in rural western Virginia in the late 1930s, remembered the late 19th century as a time when people farmed, did carpentry work, produced pottery, or ran grain mills. People spent time hunting or gathering ginseng or chestnuts. Folks pitched in to help to raise a barn. By the 1920s, with the availability of cash, farmers paid for someone to do the work. Years before, the same farmer would give everyone a good feed. The cost would be the same, but the change diminished social life.

While Sundays remained a day of church, visiting, and rest for rural Virginians, Saturday afternoons became the time for family shopping in the nearby towns. At first in wagons and later sometimes by truck or auto they came to the nearest business district. That center of commercial activity still had skilled artisans like blacksmiths along with tobacco warehouses and granaries. In its center, usually a few yards from the train depot, one found general stores (they gave way to groceries and hardware stores), and specialty shops operated by jewelers, druggists, milliners, and photographers. A hotel or two, along with at least one café, stood not too far from the depot. Eventually these towns came to possess small hospitals.

Towns with over 3,000 people likely had a bank because the state had well over a hundred such firms in the late 19th century. After 1900, the national government allowed towns smaller than 3,000 to have national banks, and the gold strike in Alaska increased paper money nearly everywhere. Up to then, many businesses operated on a near-barter basis. As few people had cash, stores carried accounts for months. Some mining villages in the mountains remained reliant on scrip transferable only at company stores deep.

Early in the 20th century, the skylines of larger cities like Richmond, Norfolk, and Roanoke changed dramatically with the appearance of tall buildings. Although Virginia had nothing quite as grandiose as the skyscrapers in the biggest cities of the nation, the skylines did show a marked difference from what had existed in earlier times, as architects and builders took advantage of the production of skeletal steel, which became available late in the 19th century. Those who worked in these structures often had to familiarize themselves with the use of elevators.

Cities and towns served as magnets for social activities. Every sizeable community had an annual fair, a traveling circus, and a parade or two every year. Plays went back to colonial times, but the heyday of the theater took place during this time. Every city of any size had numerous locations for different kinds of theater, from the classical to vaudeville. Nickelodeons (it cost five cents to enter) showed silent films. Larger cities had at least half a dozen auditoriums of various sizes.

Middle-class urban residents and suburbanites increasingly took up membership in one or more of numerous fraternal groups that the era featured. Despite the fact that these societies met once or twice a month on a weekday evening, they still attracted large memberships. Large cities had the biggest lodges, but the small towns and villages had a disproportionate number of residents belonging to such organizations. In addition to the oldest and most respected of the fraternities, the Freemasons, there were also chapters of the Order of Seven Wise Men, which started out in New Orleans in 1853 and attracted different nationalities or ethnic associations, Odd Fellows, Red Men, Knights of Pythias (they had a considerable following among the textile workers in Petersburg), Woodmen, Macabees, later a wide array of groups honoring animals, and still later the less secretive and more service-oriented like the Lions and Ruritans (first created in Suffolk). The rapid growth of the Modern Puritans in Cavalier Virginia provides some irony and may well indicate changed attitudes.

Most of these organizations had an insurance component in an era when commercial life insurance was just becoming available. Many played major roles in charitable activities. Secrecy gave some a special aura, but multiple memberships provided a problem. A minister who belonged to 16 different secret lodges or chapters discussed some of the excesses of lodge life at a special convention to address excessive commitment to these clubs. These associations enjoyed their greatest popularity in the first half of the 20th century.

Blacks had also been creating clubs for some time before the Civil War. A secretive group of black Freemasons operated in Norfolk in 1852. Their formal organization dates from just after the Civil War, after whites refused to let them join the existing organization. During that war, two former slave women in Hampton Roads organized the United Order of Tents. After helping blacks escape from slavery, it acquired a charter as a benevolent society. The Good Templars of Richmond had a mixed racial membership. That body helped organize the United Order of True Reformers, a temperance club just for blacks that eventually evolved into a burial association. Maggie Walker became the first female bank president in the nation when she presided over the Independent Order of Luke. At this time the list of black fraternities in Norfolk included Freemasons, Seven Wise Men, Knights of Pythias, Odd Fellows, and about a half dozen similar organizations.

Sports clubs also became part of the scene, starting in the cities and colleges and spreading to rural areas. Most of the membership in these early clubs came from the mobile young men who worked in the retail trades. These gentlemen engaged in high-scoring baseball contests, observing strict rules of conduct. In the 1880s Virginia cities developed professional teams that hired young men, many from the north and west. In 1884 Richmond had a team in the American Association, considered a major league. In 1894 the Virginia State League, with six Virginia cities represented, ran a full season, with Petersburg winning the disputed championship. That league played intermittently into the 20th century and then contested for titles for every year from 1906 until 1928. The winning contender from Richmond, the Lawmakers (Colts) drew more fans in 1908 than some teams in the major leagues. By then several cities had wooden parks with stands and bleachers painted green and holding as many as 5,000. Often the team names came from the work of the area. Norfolk's came to be called the Tars, for sailors. Portsmouth professional players were known as Truckers, because the city was surrounded by truck farms or Grangers (a reference to the Grange). Newport News possessed the Shipbuilders. For a time the Shoemakers represented Lynchburg, and Petersburg reporters varied in calling their players Nuts, Goobers, and Trunk Makers. The Leafs (for tobacco production) prevailed in Danville. The folks of Roanoke called their club the Magicians, in honor of "Magic City."

Football also became a fixture. Old-style football, before officials introduced the forward pass on a limited basis in 1906, provided colleges and high schools with an extremely rough sport. Motion plays and wedges allowed backs to run before the center released the ball. The flying wedge came into play in the mid-1890s but was soon made illegal. In the mid-1890s the University of Virginia was considered the best in the South over the likes of Trinity (now Duke University) and the University of North Carolina. In the early 20th century, UVa usually won matches over the other colleges in Virginia, though VPI stunned the Cavaliers in 1905. UVa usually beat the Tar Heels, but the Cavaliers had a hard time defeating the University of the South, Georgetown University, and Carlisle, the famous Indian school in Pennsylvania. Games against this kind of competition usually took place in Richmond or Norfolk before about 10,000 enthusiastic fans. Many Virginians doubted the value of a game that injured and sometimes killed. After the death of a University of Virginia player in 1909 the state legislature considered, but finally rejected, a ban on football. John Mosby of Civil War fame urged the university to abandon the sport, countering the argument that football made good potential soldiers, noting that no Confederate soldiers ever played the game.

Oared boat racing drew the greatest attention in the 1870s. Held on the various rivers, such as the Elizabeth, the Potomac, and the James, crew attracted thousands of people, who watched amateurs and less often professionals, vie for various championships. A crew of Irish-Americans from Portsmouth and employed by the Seaboard Railroad did well at the regatta at the centennial celebration in Philadelphia in 1876. Around 1880 state individual and team championships took place on the James River above Richmond, under the auspices of the Richmond and Allegheny Railroad, which sponsored the event as a way to attract travelers.

Virginia experienced a cycle craze in the late 1860s. The fad eventually passed, but in the 1880s the ungainly "bone crusher" attracted the interest of numerous clubs and Virginia ended up with her share of chapters of the League of American Wheelmen, nearly all headquartered in urban communities. The development of the safety bicycle (it had decent brakes and two tires of the same size) made it possible for both men and women to enjoy trips in town or into the countryside.

Basketball came to Virginia in the mid-1890s as an intramural affair at Hollins College, near Roanoke. It became a competitive sport at the colleges for males in the next decade. Tennis and golf both became part of the public scene toward the end of the 19th and early years of the 20th century. Country clubs, on the outskirts of the cities, built tennis courts and golf courses. By 1920 most cities had several courses in their vicinity. Track and field events evolved in the late 19th century, first as intramural activities and then as intercollegiate events. Gymnasiums appeared on college campuses and in the cities. Athletic clubs provided a variety of services in the cities, where they sponsored indoor and outdoor track as well as basketball leagues in the winter. The Young Men's Christian Association took an active interest in promoting sports. The YMCA fielded football teams in the 1890s and then switched to basketball in the 20th century. Blacks created their own YMCAs and ran sports programs. Virginia Union and Hampton Institute had excellent teams that competed against each other and Howard University.

Urban life enjoyed all sorts of advantages but also suffered from defects. In 1880 only one-third of homes in Richmond had water closets connected to a public sewer. The rest relied on privy vaults, often improperly sealed. All cities relied on hired scavengers to move "night soil." Portsmouth had no sewer system at all. Nor did it have water other than through cisterns. Norfolk had water closets in only one-eighth of its homes, but had a system to supply the city with water through some 110 hydrants. Lynchburg and Richmond had adequate, if somewhat dated, municipal reservoirs and piping. Although nearly every city developed a way to move sewage outside the built-up areas, sewer treatment plants did not come into existence until the World War II era. Thus untreated fecal matter often seeped into waterways. And refuse dumps, once well outside city limits, often had residences built on them as suburbs grew. In addition to problems attendant to a lack of an effective sewage system, cities also had to contend with frequent fires, some of which burned down major parts of towns. Hospitals, hotels, and sometimes theaters were especially vulnerable to fires.

Cities became less perilous and more pleasant to live in over time. The number of paid police and professional fire departments helped out. In 1880 cities varied in the amount of paved streets (paving included cobblestones or shells). Only Alexandria had near half of its streets paved. In the wet season urban streets, mostly composed of dirt, became muddy, and in dry times they produced copious amounts of dust. Dead animals sometimes decayed where they fell, although in 1880 cities required owners to remove them. Owners of property that abutted the streets were expected to sweep debris from the gutters to the middle of the streets, so the city crews could heap it on carts for disposal outside the cities. By 1920 all this changed as streetcars and later automobiles began to replace animals and cities collected garbage. Hard-surface streets became commonplace, although low-income districts continued to feature dirt paths.

Because the overall death rate declined, dropping from over 16 to 13 per 1,000 between 1880 and 1900, conditions for better health likely became more prevalent, but death for the very young was common through the entire era. The average age of dying in Virginia fell below 40 in 1900, somewhat lower in 1880, but anyone that survived the first few years had an excellent chance of attaining a far more advanced age, but children's diseases like whipping cough, scarlet fever, diphtheria, and infantile cholera still prevailed. People of all ages faced the prospect of dying from apoplexy, dropsy (excessive fluids), and consumption (tuberculosis—the biggest killer of the early 20th century), but improved treatment for those who could afford it cut losses over time. In 1900 a handful still perished from smallpox, even though vaccinations had been around for nearly a century.

Patterns prevailed in the distribution of death. In 1880 black males residing in Richmond had a much greater possibility of dying than white females in the same city. Black women and their babies also had a comparatively high rate of death. However, blacks tended to survive to true old age (95 or more). Overall in Richmond, the death rate of both races and sexes ran considerably higher than the state average. Norfolk, the only other urban area in Virginia for which statistics are available, did not have as big a disparity in death between the races but did have a higher proportion die compared to the rest of the state. These numbers indicate that density of population kept the death rate higher in cities than in rural areas. Maps produced from death data show that in 1890 diarrhea-related and malaria deaths ran higher on the coast, but diphtheria and whopping cough caused more deaths in the interior of the state. Croup ran much higher in the mountains than elsewhere in Virginia. White children were more likely to die from scarlet fever than were blacks across the state, but the disease did not seem especially active in 1890. Blacks along the coast were especially vulnerable to tuberculosis. Typhoid ran higher death rates inland. Cancer carried away a few hundred, but consumption occurred more frequently. Diseases like "black lung" among miners and "brown lung" among textile workers cannot be detected at this early date.

Several cities had parks in 1880 and many added to these resources during this era. Petersburg had Poplar Lawn (10 acres), Richmond the spacious old Civil War hospital grounds at Chimborazo, Libby Hall, and the capitol, and Lynchburg ten acres at its fairgrounds run by the local agricultural society. Around 1890 Norfolk newspapers campaigned for a "pair of lungs," two small parks that might give residents some relief. Around the turn of the century, the city acquired property north of the city near a trolley line for a large open area.

Nearly every city and many smaller towns either created or expanded public libraries during the era, many obtaining funds from the Carnegie Foundation. Levels of literacy grew slowly, but readers found an ever-expanding number of magazines, newspapers, and books to peruse. Members of the United Daughters of the Confederacy canvassed the literature and removed statements that denigrated the Confederacy or the institution of slavery.

Resorts in Virginia, like the Homestead, continued to develop during this era as vacation spots for members of the state's growing elite. Nearly all these spas presented more impressive physical atmospheres than exhibited before the war. The White Sulphur Springs recovered after the war and continued on in its illustrious career. The Langhorne sisters out of Danville frequented the White. Nancy Langhorne married and became Lady Astor. She served as the first woman in the House of Commons. Sister Irene married the artist

Charles Dana Gibson. She thereby became the famed "Gibson Girl," the supposed ideal of the "New American Woman."

Virginia capped the coming of the modern age with a salute to the old. Proposed in 1900 in recognition of the 1607 settlement at Jamestown, the exposition received a charter from the state in 1902 along with funds to buy the property. The company picked a site on Hampton Roads in the northern part of Norfolk County and raised subscriptions of $1,000,000 by 1 January 1904, reaching its quota minutes before the deadline. Former governor Fitzhugh Lee led the effort until he died the next year, when former Congressman Harry St. George Tucker assumed the mantle. The federal government kicked in $250,000 and provided logistical support as well as money for a Negro Building. Several states erected houses. Although the crowds fell short of projections and many of the buildings remained unfinished at the time of the opening in April 1907, the exposition ran its course and provided the area with much excitement and publicity. Although the event failed to generate anticipated revenues and left investors with a large debt, it was truly a remarkable undertaking for an area with such a small population. The exposition at least bettered the record for timing historical observances than either the Columbian Exposition in Chicago in 1893 or the Louisiana Exposition at St. Louis of 1904, both of which ran late and also lost money.

With their Georgian or neocolonial architecture, the main buildings oozed stability, along with examples of material gain, but the directors did not lose sight of the significance of the event. The History Building featured William Couper's statue of John Smith and representations of Pocahontas several places. A poet read "The Vision of Raleigh." Accompanying literature informed the public about "Historic Yorktown," "Historic Williamsburg," and the ill-fated college at Henricus. Electric power moved an exhibit of the Battle of Hampton Roads as cycloramas highlighted it and other battles of the Civil War. An international exposition, the event brought together different cultures and reflected a new world order. The Japanese played a major role, as did the British, especially as part of an international naval rendezvous. President Roosevelt took the occasion to launch his famed Great White Fleet on its world tour.

# Chapter 15

# The Progressive Impulse

In the first two decades of the 20th century, the nation experienced change in all levels of government. Under Republican Theodore Roosevelt and Democrat Woodrow Wilson, the federal government took on the responsibility of regulating major components of the economy. It broke up large corporations and fixed railroad rates. An enlarged bureaucracy kept tabs on banks and other businesses. The national government also set guidelines for child labor and in some instances set pay. Roosevelt intervened on behalf of coal miners during a strike. Progressive thinking also showed up at state and municipal levels.

The roots of Progressivism went well back in American history, but during the depression of the 1890s, Democrats dropped conservative President Grover Cleveland and supported reformer William Jennings Bryan, who promoted the Populist idea of minting tons of silver dollars to right the ruined economy. Conservative Democrats such as Senator John W. Daniel and newspaperman Carter Glass, both of Lynchburg, hopped on the Bryan bandwagon in the 1896 election. Although they agreed about the issue of free silver and both took the traditional Democrat position against the protective tariff, Daniel, the old Confederate veteran, was less of a rebel than Glass. When a group of unemployed veterans walked toward the nation's capital to persuade Congress to hire them for public works projects, newspaperman Glass complained when Governor O'Ferrall drove them out of the state. Earlier Glass opposed President Cleveland's use of troops to put down the Pullman strike in Illinois. Glass also criticized the governor for sending state troops to help break a coal strike in western Virginia and favored a graduated income tax on the federal level. Glass believed bankers and brokers precipitated the financial crisis and that Cleveland's reliance on business interests smacked of a conspiracy. His liberalism, however, had limits, as he originally opposed a proposal in the Virginia legislature to limit child labor and the workday for women.

Even Thomas Staples Martin, the junior senator from Virginia, reluctantly supported Bryan. Although he started his career as a corporate lawyer for the railroads and a representative of business interests, Tom Martin remained a U.S. senator until his death in 1919 largely because he could be flexible. Neither he nor Daniel, who served in Washington until his death in 1910, championed progressive causes, but they did not obstruct efforts at reform. In 1896 only a few Democrats, including Governor O'Ferrall, backed a third-party candidate who favored the gold standard. The Republicans lost by a wide margin in the Old Dominion, but they carried the nation.

In the aftermath of the presidential election of 1896 a Democratic convention discussed, but finally rejected, the possibility of having a primary, where the voters, not the legislature, would pick the U.S. senator. Those who favored the idea such as Andrew Jackson Montague led the movement within the party against the Martin machine. Using railroad money and patronage, and with the cooperation of Senator Daniel, Martin kept the dissenters at bay. In 1899 the Assembly picked him for another six-year senate term, but the independents persisted. Attorney General Montague, "the Red Fox of Middlesex," bested Claude Swanson, "the Plowboy from Pittsylvania," in taking the party nomination for governor in 1901. Midway through the campaign, they both came out for primaries, employer liability laws, good roads, and good schools. At the Democratic convention the "Red Fox" secured the nomination and easily defeated his Republican rival in the general election.

As the independents and conservatives struggled for control of the Democratic Party, 100 delegates assembled at Richmond to produce a new state constitution. Despite the northern origins of the Underwood Constitution, the document generally had support among the Virginia electorate, which rejected a call for constitutional reform in 1888 by a margin of nearly 60,000 votes and again in 1897 by about 45,000 votes. In 1900 the independents pushed hard for a new constitution. Republicans, understanding that the primary objective of the reformers was to virtually wipe out the potential black vote, opposed the convention. Conservative Democrats, like Tom Martin, remained silent on the subject. Martin doubtless feared a new constitution might damage his control over city and county courts and could also produce a document that might curtail the power of railroads and other corporations. With less than a third of the qualified electorate participating, the voters approved a convention by a 17,000 margin.

The chief reason for changing the constitution was to eliminate black Virginians from the polls. Because the Republican Party had virtually abandoned black voters, the need for reform seemed unnecessary, but race baiting always made good press among white Virginians. Some progressives blamed blacks for corrupt practices that ensured low black turnouts. Carter Glass developed a mechanism for ending once and for all a meaningful political role for blacks. Although many conservatives balked at bringing up the issue, several progressives jumped at the chance.

Under the reform provisions for elections, the state drew up two rolls, one prepared before 1 January 1904 and the other after that date. Local boards, appointed by the convention, would register Union and Confederate veterans and their sons, those who paid property taxes of at least $1, or those able to read and/or explain sections of the constitution, with local boards using a temporary understanding clause. Delegates presumed that this test would favor whites over blacks. Some Democrats thought this practice might lead to more corruption than currently existed, but they voted for the clause because of its expiration date.

The biggest weapon in the arsenal of those interested in reducing the potential black vote was the poll tax. Those who registered after 1 January 1904 had to present evidence that they had paid poll taxes ($1.50) for each of the previous three years. They also had to apply in their own writing, with no aid unless physically impaired, and supply their name, date and place of birth, residence, occupation, and previous voting record. No Civil War veteran had to meet these requirements. Black and white voting lists were kept separately.

Although registrars had difficulty meeting the letter of this law, the reformers achieved their objective of severely reducing the electorate. Other southern states protected white voters by not applying restrictions on anyone that could qualify to vote had he been living in 1860. Because all adult white males could vote at that time and blacks could not, restrictions applied only to blacks. Because this procedure directly violated the 15th Amendment, the Virginia convention chose not to employ it. After promising faithfully not to reduce the white vote, the delegates chose tactics that wiped out almost all the black vote and sharply reduced the number of poor white voters. The measures cut the number of votes cast in presidential elections by over half. Black wards in Norfolk and Richmond, which had up to 4,000 eligible to vote in 1902, ended up with numbers barely in the double digits a few years later, but the number of qualified whites also diminished, especially in the southwestern part of the state.

In respects other than race, the constitution followed the national trend toward regulation of big business. The year before the convention, the legislature required a western Virginia railroad to lower its passenger rates from four to three cents per mile, the state standard rate. But the right of the state to set rates remained an open question. A. Caperton Braxton, a lawyer and businessman from Staunton, headed the committee that recommended the formation of the State Corporation Commission, which would have power to set rates and otherwise control railroads and other organizations. Over strong objections of railroad attorneys and negative newspaper editorials paid for by railroad money, the convention adopted the Braxton plan. The constitution created supervisors chosen by the governor. Railroads would no longer be able to buy influence by issuing free passes to state or local officials. They could no longer demand discriminatory rates whereby a shorter haul cost more than a longer one. They, not their employees, were responsible for injuries to fellow workers.

Having solved its two most pressing problems, the convention then voted, though not with great enthusiasm, to promulgate the new document. The voters had approved all constitutions except the first one in 1776, but delegates did not want to allow those being deprived of the right to vote, whether black or white, to have a chance to reject the new constitution.

At the time the state eliminated the possibility of major black political participation, the Assembly and local governments moved to separate races in other ways. In 1900 the Assembly mandated that railroads and steamboats plying Virginia waters separate races on their facilities and four years later Pullman sleepers and dining cars could no longer be used by blacks. Because the first of these steps cost money, companies were not terribly keen about the idea. Nor were some of the passengers. One of Robert E. Lee's female descendants was arrested when she refused to separate from a black companion, apparently an old family retainer. Even before a law to segregate trolley cars took effect in 1906, one Richmond line implemented a modified form of segregation. In response, blacks boycotted the trolleys and drove it into bankruptcy, but the state later imposed segregation of all traction companies. Like the Constitution of 1902 these measures fit in with the progressive ideal of establishing a more orderly society.

In 1910 the state defined anyone with one-sixteenth African American blood as black, thus making it more difficult for blacks and whites to intermarry and promoting further separation of the races. In 1912, with rumors that blacks and whites were fighting each other for rental units in places like Richmond, cities were allowed to mandate that only members of the majority race could move into any particular block. A few years later the U.S. Supreme Court found these residency laws unconstitutional in a case involving Clifton Forge.

In a related matter, Woodrow Wilson separated federal workers by race in the District of Columbia. The new rules were in effect for Wilson's two terms in office and ended only when the Virginia-born president, stepped down from the office. Wilson, an advocate on the economic policy known as the "New Freedom," tried to prevent the circulation of a movie depicting the win of black boxer Jack Johnson over a so-called "Great White Hope," Jim Jeffries on the fourth of July 1910. Hearing about the outcome, whites in Norfolk attacked blacks leaving trolley cars. Fears that showing a film of the fight might cause a repeat riot persuaded local authorities to censor the movie.

Even though Governor Montague enjoyed a victory with the new constitution and persuading the legislature to agree to primaries, he did not advance to the U.S. Senate. In 1905 the "Red Fox" lost against incumbent Senator Martin in a contest that featured a lively debate, where Martin proved he could appeal directly to voters. An adroit politician, the Senator always responded to the individual needs of his constituents. He modified his conservative views when he had to, and he had the support of the courthouse clique. These several hundred rural officeholders and their cronies constituted the backbone of his organization. Outsiders like Montague had little chance of overcoming the organization on a statewide basis, but Glass, Montague, and William Jones, all dissenters, held congressional seats. Claude Swanson, with conservative help, became the new governor in 1906. As an activist, he supported many progressive ideas, but he remained on good terms with the conservatives. In 1911, with Martin's help, he replaced the deceased Daniel as U.S. senator, easily defeating Carter Glass in the primary.

Both conservatives and dissenters played roles on the national level. Glass became renowned as the "Father of the Federal Reserve." Conservative financier, Thomas Fortune Ryan, a wealthy Virginian who made money in New York trolleys, Virginia tobacco, and South African diamonds, tried to prevent Wilson from receiving the Democrat nomination in 1912. But Wilson's broad popularity in the Old Dominion allowed him to carry his native state. Nationally, Wilson received a plurality in the election over Teddy Roosevelt, the Progressive or Bull Moose Party, and the incumbent, Republican William H. Taft. The new president, who campaigned against the protective tariff and big business, called for the federal government to eliminate monopolies. Once in office, Wilson adopted Roosevelt's idea of creating a strong national government to supervise big business. On the banking issue Wilson insisted on a federal role in the proposed Federal Reserve System that was designed to permit flexibility in currency. Glass came around to Wilson's way of thinking, and helped get the legislation passed.

The Republican Party sank to second-rate status during these years. Whether a dissenter or conservative won the primary, Virginia Democrats usually won statewide contests. Indeed the Democratic primary became the real election in most of Virginia. The margin of victory in the regular election usually ran over 50,000 votes out of an electorate of less than 200,000. The only exception to Democrat rule was southwest Virginia, where Republicans, more often than not, won local and congressional office. Campbell Slemp, a Mahone man from Turkey Cove, Lee County, won a congressional race in 1902. When he died, after having been elected twice more, his son C. Bascom Slemp, became the Republican champion in the 9th District, or "Fighting Ninth." The younger Slemp then reeled off six more victories. Democrats pulled out all the stops to beat the hated Slemp in a race against Henry Stuart, who noted Slemp support for a protective tariff and claimed no Republican could be trusted on the race question. Slemp even invited Teddy Roosevelt, who had eaten lunch with Booker T. Washington to speak in the district. Because Slemp did not court the black vote and few blacks resided in the 9th District, the question of race carried little weight. Both sides bought votes and otherwise manipulated the polls, but Slemp eked out a win. Elections in this district were subject to a greater degree of corruption than occurred elsewhere, largely due to a vibrant two-party system.

The progressive impulse showed up in state affairs more gradually than on the federal level. During the early 20th century, the state set the foundations for the activist government of modern times. Those behind this movement wanted a more orderly society; some people hoped to harness the ideas of the scientists of the time. The drive brought together small businessmen, professors, and ministers, among a wide assortment of citizens.

Starting even before the Civil War, Virginians realized their oyster industry was in trouble due to depletion of their grounds. Immediately after the war, the state developed a policy of collecting revenues from both planting and taking oysters from various grounds. Certain areas, depending on the desires of local watermen, were put off limits. And a strong bias in state laws operated against dredgers, especially those from outside the state. Toward the end of the 19th century, the state regulated the fishing industry more tightly. Various laws were passed to restrict the use of special equipment to catch certain kinds of fish in designated rivers. Owners of dams had to provide fish ladders. Angling by hook was allowed, but the state also developed a concept of seasons for both fishing and hunting. The rules varied greatly from county to county (a law not to allow shooting fish in the Powell River was passed but then repealed), but nearly all the numerous acts were passed with the idea of protecting the species in question, and thereby qualify as conservation laws. In the 1890s Virginia also allowed the federal government to set up a tax-exempt fish hatchery in Wythe County. In the 1870s the state banned hunting waterfowl at night and the use of special guns that could kill dozens of ducks with one blast. By the 1890s state law protected homing pigeons, and after the turn of the century sportsmen could no longer kill any pigeons (1906).

As the 20th century progressed, so did the state in its efforts to subdue various diseases among animals. In 1915 the state government dealt effectively with an outbreak of hoof-and-mouth disease, something that would have caused far more damage had it appeared several years earlier. After 1906 state agents actively sought the eradication of the Texas tick. Twenty years later they killed the last cattle in the Dismal Swamp as part of that program. Progress was also being made against distemper and a form of pneumonia among cattle.

The state also had taken some steps on public health before 1900. A state board of health existed, though it had little power. In time, however, doctors and pharmacists had to pass tests unless they had a certain amount of experience. Thus newcomers to these professions had to qualify before they started their practices. Laws were on the books to prevent the sale of adulterated foods.

The state and private philanthropy also made some progress against human diseases in this era. Swanson got the General Assembly to budget for a revised Board of Health. The state built a sanitarium to treat patients with tuberculosis and a hospital for the blind, deaf, and mute. The Rockefeller Commission put private money into eliminating hookworm and malaria. The medical community sharply reduced pellagra. Better sewage disposal and water systems helped sharply reduce typhoid fever, especially in the Valley. Overall public medicine, with state and local help, made great strides during this era.

Montague, Swanson, and occasionally future governors called for better schools and roads, funding for various health programs, and commissions to deal with the dairies, insurance companies, and other commercial activities. The state even produced lime (a pet project of Governor Westmoreland Davis), over the objections of private interests, in an effort to help farmers.

At the outset of the era (1900), despite all the Readjuster efforts, Virginia had about half its school-age population in schools. These pupils attended less than 60% of the time. Male teachers received a little over $1 a day and females less than that. The numbers trailed the entire nation except the rest of the South. It was not a prescription for prosperity. Various national, regional, and local associations strove to change the situation. The Richmond Educational Association, led largely by elite women, convinced its city council to fund the impressive John Marshall High School. Montague worked with the Southern Education Board and other groups to upgrade the school systems. He also helped launch the "May Campaign of 1905," a massive private and public effort to improve education. The new president of the University of Virginia, Edwin Alderman, took an active role until Tom Martin, believing the movement was too closely associated with Montague, convinced him to desist, but officially Martin avoided direct opposition to the "Good Schools" movement. After hundreds of speeches, meetings, and newspaper articles, the state seemed ready to do something about the subject.

In 1905 voters selected Joseph Eggleston as the first elected superintendent of instruction, an office called for in the new constitution. The superintendent believed that the state needed to increase its funding of schools and to streamline its efforts. Under his lead, and with the backing of Governor Swanson, the Assembly made the College of William and Mary into a state school and gave it a mission in teacher education. The Mann Act called for state matching funds for high schools, which added agriculture and domestic science to their curriculum. Local school trustees could borrow from the Literary Fund for building schools and supplementing salaries for teachers. In 1908 the Assembly provided money for several new teachers' colleges for women (normal schools). These eventually became known as James Madison University, Radford University, and Mary Washington College. With the local governments cooperating, all the numbers concerning education grew from the length of the school year (over seven months by 1915) to per pupil expenditures, which more than doubled.

Despite all these efforts Virginia still lagged behind northern states in money for education. Still more discouraging, the new governor, William Hodges Mann, lost interest in education. And the state encouraged the localities to concentrate funds on white schools. Thus some heavily black counties, especially in the Southside, spent as much as $12 for the education of a white for every $1 spent on a black. Some whites thought even this paltry proportion was too much, because blacks paid a smaller share of taxes. Pay for black teachers fell well below that for their white counterparts.

The Good Schools movement was inextricably linked to one for "Good Roads." Public transport of schoolchildren, by wagon and increasingly by buses, became part of educational reform. And the schools played major roles as civic centers to end rural isolation. The drive for better roads started with a convention in 1894. Bicyclists and farmers both wanted improved highways. Railroad corporations even demonstrated new highway building techniques, cut freight rates for carrying equipment, and even promised to bring in convicts as workers for free. But rural legislators, not caring to pay for these improvements, preferred to keep the older system of having residents work so many days on the county roads or pay a $1.50 fine for not providing an adequate substitute. So the state continued to incorporate various toll companies to build and maintain bridges and roads. But this system had, according to a national expert on the subject, produced only one decent hard-surface road in rural Virginia—the old turnpike that coursed through the lower Valley of Virginia.

The coming of the automobile in the first decade of the new century put added pressure on the Assembly. The legislature called for Governor Swanson to authorize a state highway commission, which included civil engineering professors. Counties could now issue bonds and use convicts in construction under state supervision. The state made some $25,000 available to those counties not using prisoners. Auto owners paid license fees, and the state required each county to assess a 4% real estate and personal property tax for their roads. Counties could also borrow money for construction. In 1910 vehicle owners began to pay $5 and up annually for registration. The new rules fixed a 20 mph limit for driving in the country (8 mph in cities). Under this system nearly every county built some roads and bridges, but the number of vehicles registered in the state jumping from about 2,700 in 1910 to over 37,000 six years later kept the state from catching up with demand for roads. Moreover, counties put little into maintenance.

In 1916 the state developed a maintenance policy, and the federal government made available some aid under the guise of the need to deliver the mail or provide for the nation's defense. Upon receiving

$100,000 from the federal government, the state began a fairly active construction program, including a road at Moccasin Gap in the Southwest, the first such project. By 1918 Virginia had over 72,000 automobiles and several thousand miles of state and county highways, many of them little more than muddy paths. Road building became a priority in the next decade, but the state had created a foundation for such a program in the two preceding decades.

On a more negative note, the state also practiced eugenics to upgrade the quality of life. The thirteenth state to join this movement, Virginia passed a law in the mid-1920s that allowed medical people to sterilize patients deemed genetically inferior. The idea was loosely based on concepts connected to the idea of evolution of Charles Darwin, the famous English naturalist. Scientists figured out that genes had to exist (though no one had yet seen any). Some progressives believed mankind could be genetically improved through evolution. German scholars, with such ideas, greatly influenced American social scientists. A leading proponent of this point of view, Ivey Foreman Lewis, taught biology to hundreds of students at the University of Virginia from 1914 into the 1950s. Lewis and several other faculty members believed that mankind was subject to natural laws. Heredity made people what they were; the environment played but a minor role and the laws of heredity overrode Jefferson's ideal of equality. Like others, Lewis believed those from northern European descent were superior to people of other races and ethnic groups. The way to upgrade mankind, according to this thinking, was to prevent race and ethnic mixing. Exponents never could explain how traits of inferior people could overcome the characteristics of supposed superiors, but they considered themselves more scientific than others who studied culture. They also argued with traditional Christians who found Darwin's idea of evolution troublesome. Virginia had the unfortunate distinction of having its sterilization law the subject of a Supreme Court decision, *Buck v Bell*, which found that the state could officially have doctors tie the Fallopian tubes of an inmate at a facility that cared for epileptics and the feeble-minded. Defenders of the Nazis, on trial after World War II amid disclosures of the Holocaust, cited these laws as an example of hypocrisy, if nothing else. The Virginia legislature later expressed regret for the policy.

Most Virginians put their emphasis on improving mankind into prohibiting alcohol and gambling. These reforms clearly belonged to the Progressive Movement's goal of creating order in a chaotic world and bringing out the best in people. The idea of eliminating or drastically reducing alcohol production and consumption by state law dates from before the Civil War. Democrat politicians historically opposed such state interference. Postwar Democrats expressed little interest in the reform until it rose from the grassroots. At some point in the late 19th century, through a gradual process, many rural Virginians came to favor an idea that had historical roots in the North. Religious denominations, particularly the Baptists and Methodists, took steps to curb consumption among their congregations. Then they worked to reform the entire society. Presbyterians had long advocated such reform, but now the idea showed up throughout the southern tier of counties, the very area that had been the most resistant to this reform before the war.

The temperance movement made minimum legal headway before the Civil War, but likely convinced some inveterate drinkers to mend their ways. In 1862 the state banned alcohol as a war measure to save grain. Consumers evaded the law on a mass scale, as soldiers, whether in the field, in hospitals, or at home simply refused to obey it. Coming out of the war, with production and consumption running to high levels, the "drys" persuaded the Assembly to allow localities to outlaw saloons in 1886. By 1900 much of rural Virginia had no legal retail outlets, but those areas that had bar rooms catered to districts that did not and, lacking police enforcement, illegal operations also flourished. The Old Dominion had about 3,000 saloons and 800 distilleries at the time. Almost all the saloons were tiny and often disreputable. Residents of rural areas continued to complain about the behavior of the rowdies that frequented both the illegal and legal outlets. So contentious did the issue become that a Danville Democrat killed a minister for saying that he would prefer to have a sober black in political power than a drunken Democrat.

In 1901 Virginians organized the Anti-Saloon League as part of a national organization. Receiving support from various Protestant churches, the Anti-Saloon League first attacked the rural saloons, persuading judges not to issue licenses as the state kept passing more and more restrictions. The cause of prohibition received a big boost when a judge in Nottoway County bullwhipped one of the prohibition leaders. That man's lawyer, Senator Mann, had the judge removed from office. One of Mann's closest friends, the

Methodist minister and educator James Cannon, Jr., became the most powerful clergyman in Virginia since James Blair. Through higher taxes and license fees, the forces for temperance cut the number of saloons to less than one-third their former level. In 1908 the Assembly killed many of the remainder by prohibiting the sale of liquor except in jurisdictions with more than 500 residents, summer resorts, or in rural areas that had police. It also imposed tighter restrictions on distilleries. When citizens created fake private social clubs to evade the law, the Assembly controlled membership of the clubs. By 1910 local option ended saloons in at least nine of the smaller cities and over 140 towns, plus most of the rural areas. The number of distilleries fell to 50. By 1913 over 70% of Virginia's residents had no legal access to saloons in their localities.

Prohibitionists moved to eliminate saloons throughout the state. In 1909, Democratic Party leaders caved into prohibitionist pressure by backing Mann for governor. During the primary campaign Mann hedged on the issue of statewide prohibition but strongly endorsed local option, as did his opponent. Having eked out a narrow victory in the primary over one of the politicians outside the Martin machine, Mann then renewed his advocacy of statewide prohibition. As Martin and most of his Democratic hierarchy remained neutral on the issue, Cannon and his cohorts campaigned vigorously for the state legislature to take action. The House voted to take the matter to the people in 1912, but the Senate rejected the bill. In the campaign of 1913 Henry Stuart, a land and cattle baron from the southwestern part of the state that supported state prohibition, ran unopposed for the Democratic primary. Early the next year the lower house again easily passed the measure. When the Senate tried to water it down, a conference committee produced a bill that the Senate agreed to only when the lieutenant governor, well known for his drinking habits, cast the deciding vote in its favor. With much prayer and hymn singing, on 22 September 1914 the voters approved, with some 94,000 for and 63,000 opposed. Though the suburban interests in or near the bigger cities generally favored the idea, Richmond and Norfolk voted against prohibition, but rural Virginia imposed its will. At the same time eight of Virginia's congressional delegation voted for national prohibition.

Prohibition went into effect in November 1916, as the Mapp Act (named for Walter Mapp from the Eastern Shore) ended the production and sale of liquor in the state. A resident, however, could acquire a quart of whiskey, a gallon of wine, or three gallons of beer each month from outside the state. Post office officials noticed appreciably more business in the wake of this legislation, as customers waited in lines for their monthly allotment. During World War I the national government took steps against alcohol. And following the war, the 18th Amendment gave the Prohibitionists total victory. All of Virginia's congressmen voted for it, and Virginia became the second state to ratify the amendment. This draconian measure allowed no production or consumption of beverages of more than tiny alcohol levels. Both houses of the Assembly approved this amendment by immense margins, even though Bishop Cannon had reservations about the severity of the measure.

Governors Mann and Stuart responded to complaints about big-time gambling related to horse racing north of Norfolk. Those who complained labeled themselves progressives and were also active supporters of prohibition. Stuart finally used private detectives, designated as county court deputies, to stop the gambling, which also meant the end of big-time thoroughbred racing in Virginia.

Mann was also governor at the time of an incident at Hillsville in Carroll County. The event resulted from a feud between Democrat Floyd Allen and Republican members of a courthouse clique. When Floyd Allen was found guilty of obstructing justice, a gunfight erupted. Who fired the first shot will never be known, but members of the Allen clan were later found guilty of murdering several court people, including the presiding judge. Why the judge had failed to use a law to disarm those on trial remains a mystery. The governor used the same detective agency to track down members of the family that had fled outside the Commonwealth that he later hired to clamp down on gambling near Norfolk. Despite pleas for clemency, two of the Allen family died in one of the first uses of the electric chair in the state. In the 1920s Virginia tightened gun laws and required a high fee to obtain a license to carry a concealed weapon. Gun laws, the handling of the Allen case, and the general idea of law and order all reflect the spirit behind the progressive movement.

Compared to prohibition, the right of women to vote in the 19th Amendment met with a far chillier reception in the Old Dominion. Indeed, the Virginia legislature rejected the measure overwhelmingly, and resisted formal recognition of the idea even after the 19th Amendment became law. Despite differing attitudes toward the 18th and 19th amendments, the causes of prohibition and women's rights were linked. Governor Mann's wife once remarked that she wanted the right to vote only to be able to vote for prohibition. The role of women in Protestant denominations and the related move to prohibition gave considerable impetus to the drive for the right to vote.

Few Virginia women expressed interest in the subject at the time of the passage of the 15th Amendment, when national organizations started to pursue the matter. In 1870 Anna Bodeker organized the Virginia Woman Suffrage Association. Judge Underwood of Reconstruction fame and Elizabeth van Lew, a former union spy, did not help the cause when the two championed her reform, placing the movement on what was considered the lunatic fringe at the time. Over twenty years later Orra Langhorne organized another state suffrage association, but it experienced a short tenure. Lila Meade Valentine and many other prominent women, including novelists, Ellen Glasgow and Mary Johnston, formed the Equal Suffrage League in 1909. Although this organization made little headway, even among the majority of women, it printed periodicals, put on plays, talked to young women at colleges, occasionally petitioned the assembly, and wrote to congressmen. They usually emphasized their church, charity, and civic work as well as high educational attainments in an effort to persuade men that women merited the right to vote. They claimed special understanding about social needs. Suffragists combated the racist argument that black women would gain the right to vote by arguing that the literacy clauses and poll taxes would prevent any significant number of black women from voting. Despite all these efforts, on at least three separate occasions from 1912 through 1916, the Assembly rejected the idea of letting women vote.

Pauline Adams, the Irish-born and one-time president of the Norfolk chapter of the Equal Suffrage League, took a more radical stance. Having advanced her cause but little through conventional means, Adams called for picketing, considered by conservatives to be most unacceptable behavior and undermining their argument that women represented an unusually intelligent component of the community. Although Pauline Adams favored Teddy Roosevelt in 1912 and radicals marched in Woodrow Wilson's inaugural parade, most conservatives steered clear of partisanship. Adams also appealed to Norfolk's biggest labor union its annual Labor Day celebration, something a refined woman would never do. By 1915 the Virginia women's rights movement had split in two, but nearly all advocates supported progressive issues like education, health reform, and child labor laws. During World War I, Adams called for women to don uniforms and receive military training, as they actively campaigned for the right to vote. Her organization sold bonds and entertained members of the military, while conservative women dropped political activities and concentrated on charity and patriotism.

When Woodrow Wilson failed to take action on female suffrage, even though he favored the idea, Adams and others picketed a parade in the nation's capital in September 1917. Given a choice of sixty days in jail or a $25 fine, Adams chose the former and was remanded to the federal facility in Prince William County. Having spent some months there, she emerged with a long list of complaints about management of the place. As Virginia's conservative women strove unsuccessfully to persuade their legislature to change its attitude, the move on a national level proved successful.

In 1923 Sarah Fain, with the support of the powerful pilot's association, became one of the first two women (the other was Helen Henderson from southwest Virginia) elected to the General Assembly, as she won one of the extra seats given to Norfolk due to redistricting based on population gains noted in the census of 1920. As a former teacher who took summer courses at the University of Virginia for eleven years, she achieved a solid legislative record over six years, including legislation to turn over setting rates for pilot fees for ships plying Virginia waters from the state legislature to the State Corporation Commission. She called for an increase in the maximum vehicle speed from the current 30 miles per hour to 40 (the legislature in 1925 agreed to raise the rate to 35 miles per hour). In addition, she proposed reducing and flattening the income tax and ending inheritance taxes. Eventually Harry Byrd's program on taxes prevailed, but clearly this Norfolk representative knew a good bit about the subject. In fulfilling her role as a female delegate, she proposed an end to capital punishment, an idea that received serious consideration. She was so active that Democrats seriously considered running her for a congressional seat.

Local government also felt the effects of Progressivism. In Norfolk the old ward system, where saloon owners and other political bosses had undue influence, gave way to an at-large way of picking members of the council. "Good Government" people, often associated with anti-saloon interests, won temporary control of Norfolk in the mid-1890s, having elected a minister as mayor, but conservatives soon retook power. The reformers eventually managed to reduce the number of elected offices, council seats, and wards, and they also introduced civil service reform. They capped off their efforts by persuading the electorate to eliminate wards in 1917. Opponents argued that doing so would pave the way for the few eligible black voters to influence citywide elections. Reformers responded that race had no bearing on the issue. Under the new charter, eligible voters elected a five-man council at large without party labels. City charters called for recalls and referendums to make the more efficient governments responsive to the needs of the people. Councils selected a city manager to run the municipality. Indeed, Staunton in 1908 became the first city in the United States to have such a position. Richmond, however, failed to join the movement, the city retaining its ward system and a strong mayor until 1947.

On the national level the reform movement peaked during World War I and then lost momentum, as conservatives deregulated the economy, raised the tariff, and even used antitrust and federal trade laws to regulate unions not corporations. Ironically, just as the role of the federal government was about to diminish, the nation approved prohibition. After a few years, Congress and the people repealed the 18th Amendment, again ironically, as the federal government resumed regulating the economy. During all this, the state and municipalities remained committed to the idea of effective, responsive, and sometimes intrusive, government. Thus progressivism remained alive on the local and state level.

# Chapter 16

## The Era of Booms and Busts

World War I started in August of 1914, as the Central Powers lined up against the Allies, with Italy and Japan later joining the latter. As thousands died in trenches in France or in the more open fighting in Germany's eastern front against the Russians, the United States officially declared neutrality. The fact that Britain controlled the high seas meant that America's goods tended to help the Allies more than their enemies. German use of submarines to stop American goods from crossing the Atlantic brought the United States into the war in April 1917.

The Old Dominion sent 21 units as part of the American Expeditionary Force. Elements of the National Guard went in as the 116th Infantry (part of the 29th Division) and the 76th and 111th Field Artillery. The Norfolk Light Artillery Blues composed much of the latter, whereas the 2nd Virginia Infantry Band, home based in the Shenandoah Valley, belonged to the 116th. Camp Lee, constructed near Petersburg, provided for the training of thousands, especially the 80th Division. With Newport News serving as a port of embarkation, hundreds of thousands of "dough boys" passed through the City of Shipbuilders on their way to the front. After a prolonged buildup, Virginians became part of a massive effort to push the Germans out of France, starting with a battle just east of Paris in March 1918. Heroics at three major engagements, with the biggest loss of life occurring in October, brought victory in November. Virginians won their share of distinguished service crosses, navy crosses, and Congressional Medals. A sergeant from Richmond won a medal for his help in killing ten and capturing five Germans. A private won the Silver Star for saving his patients in driving an ambulance under heavy fire. An officer returned across an open area, raked by artillery and machine gun fire to retrieve a wounded comrade. No black Virginians received such medals, as Woodrow Wilson refused to permit them to fight as part of the national army. The war cost the lives of about 1,200 Virginians. Even members of the band died or suffered wounds from artillery blasts, and several suffered from gas attacks. A hospital unit started by the president of the Medical College of Virginia and trained at Camp Lee performed admirably near the front, tending to the wounded and the sick. Death from disease proved debilitating, as young men proved especially susceptible to the Spanish influenza that rocked the world as the war wound down. In the fall of 1917, marines at the new base at Quantico began to sicken and die. By the time the epidemic had run its course through two phases, some 140 marines died. In September 1918 at Camp Lee, near Hopewell and Petersburg, soldiers suddenly began to die of the flu, which probably came with soldiers returning from Europe. Over 500 died, and the disease quickly spread among the state's civilian population. Returning troop ships contained numerous patients. As occurred elsewhere, far more people died from the malady than in the trenches in France. Before ending the next spring, influenza carried off about 11,600 Virginians.

The military buildup transformed much of Southeastern Virginia. Norfolk's permanent population doubled. During the war, the Navy took over several buildings in downtown Norfolk for the Fifth Naval District and then moved to its permanent location at the new Navy Operating Base at Sewell's Point, the site of the Jamestown Exposition. At the outset of war, the Navy gave basic training to several thousand at its cramped grounds, opposite the navy yard (St. Helena). It then moved the training grounds to the new base. The navy base also sported a large supply center and numerous piers. The nearby Naval Air Station, along with Langley on the Peninsula, provided the facilities for pilot training. Just south of the navy base, the Army constructed a huge supply complex. During its construction phase, the facility had over fifty windows for those receiving pay on Saturdays. The navy yard in Portsmouth built and maintained hundreds of ships. Its peak employment reached over 11,000. After the fighting ended, it remained at maximum employment to convert a collier into the nation's first aircraft carrier. Also on the south side of Hampton Roads, Cape Henry became the site of artillery for coastal defense, the guns brought in by rail. After the war the site became known as Fort Story. On the Peninsula, the Newport News Shipbuilding and Drydock Co. hired over 11,000 at its peak to build battleships and many other ships, small and large. Fort Eustis became an important transportation facility for the Army. Yorktown ended up with a weapons station. In 1916 the DuPont Powder

Company began to produce nitrates a few miles from Williamsburg. The government added shell production and storage in 1918. Trainloads of material passed through the old capital daily. Other warehouses stood near Yorktown.

In some places, war totally transformed the landscape. With a demand for chemicals during the war, the DuPont de Nemours Co. created a huge plant at City Point (the Civil War depot). Hopewell, an entirely new community, emerged within months with over 20,000 people working at the plant, many commuting to nearby Petersburg. When Prince George County failed to control the area, Hopewell came to resemble a frontier town as prostitution, gambling, and illegal drinking prevailed along its waterfront. Much of the town burned in December 1915, but was quickly rebuilt. The population fell to about 2,000 shortly after the Armistice in 1918, but the city rebounded as a permanent chemical center.

The area near the District of Columbia also experienced increased activity. Fort Myer in Arlington, already operating as an airfield in 1908, when an accident killed an army officer testing one of the new aircraft, now experimented with dirigibles. Camp Humphries (later Fort Belvoir) in Fairfax County dates from this war, as does the Marine Base at Quantico. On a branch of the Potomac River, the government acquired over 5,000 acres of an area real estate developers had their eyes on near a shipyard. The Marines used an old brick hotel and dozens of temporary wooden huts to give advance training. Some 32,000 officers and others learned how to fly balloons, perform normal naval duties, and, most importantly, how to fight in the trenches in France.

The war stretched resources in many areas. Shortages showed up in nearly everything. With housing at a premium, the federal government funded several housing projects for civilian workers. Trolleys became so cramped and slow that passengers, both black and white, nearly rioted when forced to keep changing seats to make sure the state's segregation laws were not violated. Truck farmers could not even get crops out of the fields for lack of help, as blacks found higher paying jobs elsewhere. One city even ended up with dial phones due to the shortage of operators in 1919.

Women played active roles during the war. Many went to France to serve at Base Hospital 45 or in other places. There they encountered difficult conditions, including the notorious killer flu. On the home front, women purchased and encouraged others to buy war bonds, planted gardens, learned better ways to can goods, and collected and packaged supplies for relief in Europe and for soldiers. Marguerite Davis, wife of the governor, served as a volunteer at the Du Pont plant near Seven Pines, making silk bags and putting gunpowder in them. A special commission organized black women.

The war brought temporary gains for black workers. Coal trimmers and longshoremen made impressive gains in 1917 and 1918. Threatening a strike in 1917, the transportation union obtained a 31% pay raise. Late that year the War Shipping Board, a semipublic agency recognized the International Longshoremen's Association as bargaining agent. This multiracial national union ultimately affiliated with Norfolk coal trimmers, longshoremen, and others. One union even attempted to organize black women cigar makers and domestics. Faced with strikes threats and walkouts, the police chief began to arrest all "slackers" in a blatant effort to quell black workers. Once the war ended, most of the gains achieved by people of color disappeared. Management cut wages by 20% in one instance.

The end of the war ushered in an era of high prices and higher anxiety. The Bolshevik takeover in Russia convinced many that the Communists were about to do the same in Virginia. Agents looked for bombs in phonographs and perused all the Socialist opinions they could find. Employment levels remained steady through most of 1919 in Virginia, even in the face of thousands of returning veterans and a wave of strikes, including in Virginia's southwest among coal miners.. As leaders called for law and order, in what looked like a revolutionary situation, prices suddenly collapsed early in 1920. War work declined as the federal government canceled contracts for several destroyers. Newport News Shipbuilding, however, completed work on three battleships and two cruisers. A naval disarmament conference later cut off any more major construction. Work on a battleship ceased at the navy yard with about one-third of it complete, though workers finished an aircraft carrier. With new construction dropping, over 20,000 shipbuilders left Hampton

Roads. The price of cotton collapsed, leaving the Danville Mills with too much raw cotton and finished products. Management cut wages by 10%. It would take the better part of three years to stabilize the situation.

Folks supporting law and order faced the added problem of enforcing the new liquor laws. In some remote areas, such as in Franklin County, local residents had been avoiding the excise tax on whiskey since the Civil War. The county opted not to close its legal saloons and its residents later also voted against state prohibition. With the 18th Amendment, the county enhanced its reputation as a battleground over booze. During the era following the introduction of prohibition, authorities made almost 1,700 arrests, destroyed 131,000 gallons of liquor, broke up some 3,900 stills (over 10% of the state total) and confiscated over 700 automobiles in this county alone. Statewide, agents made some 186,000 arrests (many were arrested several times). The Dismal Swamp reputedly had many stills.

If that were not enough, illegal beverages made their way into nearly all parts of the state. On occasion agents caught up with one of the yachts and other craft employed in the business. Despite massive efforts, the liquor problem continued, though the number of incidents diminished as authorities eased their efforts to enforce the hated law. Police in many communities winked at the presence of "speakeasies," supposedly secret places where one could buy alcohol.

Westmoreland Davis served as governor during this tumultuous time. Elected in a three-way Democratic primary in 1917 as a wet against two prohibitionists, this reform governor improved the budgetary process, ended the convict-lease system, and increased medical care for penitentiary inmates. Davis saw the need for the state to find scientists, possibly at its colleges and universities, to provide the expert knowledge necessary to carry out progressive ideas. The legislature approved his proposal to create a State Industrial Commission to supervise the new workmen's compensation law. When Martin died in 1919, Davis appointed Glass an interim senator. Glass failed to return the favor, when he supported Claude Swanson for the other senate seat against Davis in 1922.

Virginia rolled into the Roaring Twenties trying to recover from the recession and with a dire need to build more roads, as thousands now had cars. With the temporary backing of the old Martin men, Lee Trinkle secured the nomination. His Republican rival advocated ending the poll tax, allowing labor to bargain collectively, and building better roads. Only the last of these resonated with most Virginia voters. Once elected, Trinkle, who had opposed borrowing money for road building, changed his mind. Harry Byrd, a member of the State Senate since 1916, originally favored changing the constitution to allow such borrowing, but in 1920 he opposed the idea, but the voters amended the constitution to allow road bonds. When Trinkle persuaded the Assembly to submit a referendum for an additional $50,000,000 in bonds, Byrd's opposition even convinced Trinkle to change his mind, and the people voted against it.

Many conservatives took the view that Virginia should develop a policy of "pay as you go," and ended up following Byrd as party leader. Not only did Byrd become the primary spokesman for the Democrats in preference to Trinkle, but he also outmaneuvered Senator Swanson. As a state senator and later as the governor elected in 1925, Byrd put his imprint on nearly all aspects of state governance. Under his leadership, in a policy known as "Pay as You Go," the state financed road construction through license and gasoline taxes to be spent as the money materialized and not before. Byrd liked the idea of a user tax, in part, because companies charged Virginians more than their neighbors for gasoline. Even before becoming governor, Byrd organized private efforts to force oil companies to lower prices. Gasoline taxes were also necessary because the treasury was running a deficit, as the economic slowdown reduced tax receipts.

With his star rising, Byrd bested Walter Mapp, the prohibitionist that received the backing of James Cannon, in the Democratic primary for governor by a sizable margin and then rolled to an easy victory in the general contest. Having campaigned for progress and efficiency, Byrd eliminated numerous duplicate positions and solidified over fifty departments into a dozen. Byrd also persuaded the legislature and, by a narrow margin, the electorate to change the constitution to reduce the number elected to statewide office to three positions, namely the governor, lieutenant governor, and attorney general. Members of the leading education association had serious doubts about making the superintendent of public instruction an appointed post, but the voters accepted the change in 1928.

Overall, public opinion backed Byrd's policies and actions, but on occasion criticism surfaced, such as when he sent troops into Gloucester County after someone shot at the state oyster navy boat in Mobjack Bay. In the seemingly unending fighting over the use of the state's oyster beds, some oystermen poached on grounds leased to one of the state's biggest oyster companies. The soldiers quickly withdrew as the company agreed to open up 2,000 acres.

As governor, Byrd also convinced the Assembly to stop collecting taxes on personal property or real estate. Only local governments could now collect such taxes. About half of Virginia counties responded by lowering taxes by some 25%, the full amount formerly collected by the state. Other communities reduced the burden by varying percentages over the years. The state made up the lost income, which amounted to about $3,500,000 by raising income taxes, cutting costs, and benefiting from a hugely expanded national economy.

In racial matters, segregation peaked at this time. As a state senator, Byrd did not vote on the 1924 Racial Purity Law that now defined anyone with any African ancestry as black. In 1926 the state enacted the Massenberg Law, named for a delegate from Elizabeth City County, who proposed the measure when the white wife of a prominent Newport News publisher complained about sitting next to a black man at a recital at Hampton Institute. Heavy fines were now imposed to separate the races at public assemblies. The measure took effect without the governor's signature. As governor, Byrd persuaded the assembly to pass a strong law against lynching in the wake of an incident in Wytheville, where a black man died at the hands of a mob. Some newspaper editors thought it ironic that a community named for one of Virginia's most famous experts in the law should experience such an effrontery as a lynching. Possibly they forgot that the very term came out of Bedford County, named for a local Judge Lynch, who vigorously assailed Loyalists during the American Revolution. Byrd's new law put the state well ahead of any other Southern state on this issue.

In a footnote in the census for 1930, assessors put an asterisk after the word "Indians" and noted, "includes a number of persons whose classifications as Indians has been questioned." At the time an agent of the state insisted on registering all those born to descendants of the first Virginians as Negro. Natives complained about the practice, which defined them as black under the segregation laws and also prevented them from marrying whites under the racial purity law of 1924. Many white Virginians proudly recalled their relationship to Pocahontas. It took several more legislative attempts to make the distinction between white and red. Meanwhile, bureaucrats labeled virtually all "Indians" as having black ancestry. The state agent bent on making all Native Virginians submit to the segregation ordinances belonged to one of the Anglo-Saxon clubs that urged tightening immigration laws to keep undesirables out of the country. They thought only people of northern European origins had value in a democracy and encouraged blacks to join the "back to Africa" movement.

As a progressive that for the most part encouraged business interests, Byrd attacked the gasoline and telephone companies for their excessive charges. He also championed conservation measures such as the development of the Shenandoah National Park and the formation of the State Conservation and Development Commission, an effort to preserve scenery and promote tourism. The commission placed hundreds of historic markers along the new roads. Hundreds of citizens donated money toward the purchase of the park.

Coincidentally, a minister in Williamsburg convinced John D. Rockefeller, Jr., to support the restoration of the historic community. The son of the famous oil tycoon saw the value of a restored capitol. Piecemeal efforts to save Williamsburg from the twin evils of decay and material decadence now gave way to an ambitious project to create an historic community. By 1934, several thousand people paid to visit the place. A preservation society founded in 1889 had been working for some time to save the ruins of the original church at Jamestown, burned in 1676. Virginia would soon have decent roads to its ruins as Virginia highlighted its past. As part of the progressive movement in 1906, Theodore Roosevelt approved an antiquities act, and Congress established a national park service in 1916. Under Herbert Hoover, the federal government acquired acreage in Jamestown and Yorktown (the latter included a golf course and country club) for a national park. A parkway soon connected the two facilities. The Petersburg battlefield also came under federal auspices. Thus conservation and historic preservation made major headway. Hoover, Franklin Roosevelt, and Byrd, proved pivotal in the reformation.

Byrd's reputation largely rested on fiscal matters. Another constitutional amendment made it much more difficult for the state to deviate from "pay as you go." The state turned a deficit of almost $1,400,000 into a surplus of $4,250,000 abetted by the booming economy. Tax receipts grew during Byrd's tenure because in 1926 the Assembly raised the income tax, first implemented in 1915. At that time Virginia adopted the first personal income tax, assessing single people a 1% charge on net income above $1,200 and married people the same on net incomes over $1,800, plus $200 for each child. In 1926 the Assembly created a system wherein those with a net income below $3,000 paid 1.5%, those who made $3,000 to $5,000 in wages or other earnings paid 2.5%. Those above that level of income paid 3%. Some critics complained that the common man bore more of a burden because the state reduced rates on intangible property and not collecting taxes on real property.

In national affairs in 1928 the national Democratic Party nominated New Yorker Al Smith, an opponent of prohibition and a Roman Catholic, for the presidency. For the first time since 1872 a majority of Virginians voted for a Republican (Herbert Hoover) for president. Hoover's strong credentials and the booming economy helped the Republicans; Smith's opposition to prohibition, and his Catholic religion convinced many Democrats to vote Republican. The anti-Catholic Ku Klux Klan had some influence in the state, originally presenting itself as advocating law and order. Members harassed a Roman Catholic priest for encouraging black education. Crowds of several thousand attended Klan functions in the Norfolk area in the early 1920s, but by 1928, poor publicity had severely reduced its ranks everywhere. Municipal governments passed ordinances against wearing masks in the mid-1920s to help curb the Klan. Nonetheless, many Virginians, especially in rural areas, harbored fears and resentments about the church in Rome. And even though many in the Old Dominion drank illegal liquor, the majority was still not willing to give up the "noble experiment." An unusually large number came to the polls in November to support the Republican candidate.

Cannon tried to parley the big turnout and Hoover victory to elect one of his own as governor. Breaking with the Democrats, he supported a third-party candidate who also received the nod from the Republicans. The Byrd organization easily repelled this effort by electing John Garland Pollard governor. Cannon disappeared from the political scene when he was charged with having hoarded flour during the word war and investing in illegal stock (a numbers racket) in New York. Although never proved, these assertions harmed his reputation, but Cannon had already lost his influence in breaking with Walter Mapp during the 1928 presidential election.

As Virginia stood poised to enter a new decade and what most assumed would be a time of even greater prosperity, the overall population now stood at over 2,400,000, with about 27% being black and almost 33% considered urban. The percentage of blacks continued to drop slowly. Virginia also became more urban, though the rate slowed down. Richmond now had almost 183,000 residents. Its biggest occupational group, aside from over 12,000 in the retail and wholesale trades, worked in the tobacco industry with over 3,000 men and 4,000 women. During the decade the number of Virginians in agriculture dropped, leaving the state with about 150,000 owners and tenants and around 120,000 agricultural laborers. The state now had almost 14,000 mining coal, twice that number making iron and steel and over 73,000 selling something other than automobiles. Richmond alone had almost 700 telegraphers and 960 telephone operators, mostly male in the first instance and female in the second. Norfolk had several hundred people at the new Ford factory, opened in 1925. In 1926 the Industrial Rayon Co. opened a large facility in Covington to go along with its machine shop, paper plant, and silk mill. By this point only about 10% of Alleghany County's population, a few years before an overwhelmingly rural place, remained engaged in agriculture. Hopewell had about 2,000 men and over 700 women producing chemicals. Over 880,000 Virginians were gainfully employed.

The new technology produced cloth made from synthetics. In 1917 the Viscose Co. built an artificial silk mill at Roanoke. Hiring hundreds of workers and using chemicals, it made rayon. A few years later, the DuPont Rayon Company set up a viscose process at Richmond and another plant using an acetate method at Waynesboro. Another firm at Hopewell used still a third method. An Ohio company put a silk mill in Covington. In 1930 the Viscose Corporation erected plants at Front Royal and at the Narrows (New River). These activities required the use of bleached pulp, often imported from other parts of the country.

All this progress meant that real incomes rose in Virginia faster than the national average in the first three decades of the new century, but Virginians had started far behind in this regard and would take additional decades to catch up. And despite all the progress in farming achieved in the recent past, Virginia still had numerous problems, compared to states in the Middle West.

A study comparing Prince Edward County with a counterpart in Illinois in the 1920s noted that Virginia had an advantageous climate with slightly hotter summers, somewhat warmer winters, longer springs and summers and a bit more rain spread evenly throughout the year, but Prince Edward in the Piedmont possessed undulating terrain where numerous streams had carved their way through the terrain, as compared to Illinois, with its flat and fertile land, not broken up by winding streams. By 1920 Prince Edward had but one-third of its land in improved farms, while the county in Illinois had almost 90% in that category. Woodlots covered at least 40% of Prince Edward. Every Virginia farm contained a pile of wood for kitchen stoves and small sheet iron airtight heaters for the home, none of which could be found in Illinois. Exceedingly crooked roads in Virginia followed the upland ridges between streams, where minor floods often carried away weak wooden bridges. A few paved highways could be found near towns but most roads were simply dirt or gravel trails. On a Saturday afternoon, people coming back home after shopping in town, walked, rode a horse or a mule, drove farm wagons often propelled by oxen, especially if they were black, or rode buggies. Few moved by automobiles, but in Illinois nearly all families had cars and drove on well-paved roads. In the Virginia Piedmont, red soil in advanced stages of weathering and unable to absorb rainfall because of underlying clay, exhibited various degrees of erosion. Years of leaching and erosion, along with sustained tobacco growing weakened the soil to a point where the land required huge quantities of commercial fertilizer. Virginia tobacco farmers needed to expend about $10 to every $1 spent by an Illinois producer, whereas land was worth in dollar value over 12 times as much in the western state. The per-acre yield of corn, the only crop both areas grew in volume, was three times as great in Illinois, where machines could maneuver with ease and farmers had the income to afford them. Not all Virginia rural counties were in such dire straits, but clearly most Virginia farmers were fighting a losing struggle to gain material prosperity. Even farmers of the Middle West were not doing particularly well in the 1920s, agriculture being one of the weak spots of the New Economy.

The Roaring Twenties came to a sudden end in the fall of 1929, when the New York stock market collapsed. Because only a few Virginians owned stocks, the Old Dominion felt little immediate impact from the crash, but the effects of the Depression eventually showed up. The Depression made its most devastating impact in the states with the largest industries, especially in steel, automobiles, and oil. With few steel plants and no oil, Virginia suffered a bit less from the full impact of the Depression.

The Depression hit lines of work that had been limping along in Virginia for some time, including coal mining, farming, and textiles. Farm and fabric prices fell. A severe drought in Virginia in 1930 compounded problems for agriculture. Textile workers in Danville struck at the very moment clothing prices declined. Competition from synthetics, like rayon factories in Roanoke and Covington, already kept cotton cloth prices low. Coal miners went on short time. The Ford plant in Norfolk, the only large auto factory in the state, also closed to retool.

In 1933, as over a quarter of the nation looked for work, Old Dominion levels of unemployment reached just under 20%. Industrial output fell by a third in Virginia and by a half in the nation. Pay for those that retained industrial jobs dropped, but at a rate less than experienced nationally. Many companies retained workers but used them only part of the time. Thus average workweeks dropped from the high forties to the mid-thirties. Many businesses outside service industries ended Saturday work. Coal flow, railroad traffic, and exports all dropped by a little less than half. Banks collapsed across the country, but currency capacity fell less in the part of the Federal Reserve that Virginia belonged to. Even so, banks failed (some failed in the 1920s), and many rural folk returned to bartering as a way of doing business. Robert Poterfield started his famous Barter Theater (named for the method of payment) in Abingdon at the time. Virginians faced the worst situation they had encountered since the Civil War.

Because people gave up new durable goods first, that kind of production felt the deepest impact of the Depression. Furniture makers in Martinsville and radiator makers in Newport News closed. Few people constructed homes; thus lumbermen, developers, and real estate agents struggled. Consumers also cut back on some discretionary items like paper; thus many paper mills went to short time or closed up. Clothing makers were supposed to be a bit shielded from the full effects of the Depression, but the large Viscose Corporation in Roanoke shut down for several months, throwing nearly 5,000 out of work in 1933. A Ford factory in Norfolk closed for retooling. Tobacco factories in Richmond continued to churn, as consumers refused to give up their smokes, although they often rolled their own cigarettes. Enough continued to bury the packaged variety, however, that Virginia factories made over a billion cigarettes in 1937. A second dry season also injured the tobacco crop, but the production and sale of illegal liquor likely suffered few ill effects from the downturn.

Only limited effects of the downturn could be seen in 1930, more in 1931, and then the bottom fell out in 1932 and 1933. Many middle-class whites gave up maid service, and thousands of black females now had no work. Black males who had entered nonagricultural careers, were the first fired. Unemployment among this group reached 50%, perhaps higher, in some cities.

Those out of work depended on private, municipal, and state charity. The system worked in the early stages of the Depression, as regular relief agencies and hundreds of churches extended charity, but as the Depression deepened, these agencies ran out of resources. Various municipal governments tried to help, but then found it necessary to eliminate kindergartens, cut back the school year, fire teachers, and reduce pay for educators, police, firemen, and other essential personnel. The state, hamstrung by an ideology against red ink and a constitution that prohibited heavy borrowing through bonds, could do little but cut expenses. On the national level, the government began to lend money for roads, local projects, and military needs. Congress also financed public works such as post offices. None of these steps sufficed to turn the economy around.

Franklin Roosevelt easily defeated Hoover in the 1932 presidential election in Virginia and nearly everywhere else. Campaigning for a "New Deal," the New York governor called for balanced budgets and a new approach to the economic troubles. Some Virginians backed Harry Byrd as a possible Democratic nominee at least for the vice presidency. When Roosevelt became president, he appointed Claude Swanson as Secretary of the Navy. Governor Pollard then sent Byrd to replace Swanson in the Senate. Swanson's delayed departure from the Senate cost Byrd some seniority.

Once in office, Roosevelt embarked on an ambitious program of alphabet agencies that amazed the nation. Through his New Deal, FDR persuaded Congress to pass a wide variety of relief and recovery programs. Instead of cutting the deficit, he increased it at first accidentally and later as a way to combat the Depression.

Both Glass and Byrd criticized essential parts of the New Deal as well as the philosophy behind it. The lynchpin of the First New Deal, the National Industrial Recovery Act, stopped federal anti-trust actions, set wages and prices through a system of codes, prohibited child labor, and called for collective bargaining for workers. With considerable hype, the administration started the "Blue Eagle" in 1933. Carter Glass, to whom Roosevelt had originally tended the post of treasurer, became a strong critic. The old progressive disliked the pro-business elements in the system and the strong-arm tactics of its administrators. Byrd did not like the Agricultural Adjustment Act, which paid farmers to withdraw fields from production and slaughter animals before they reached maturity. Over 20 years later people still complained about watching crops being destroyed as people starved in nearby cities. In 1935 the Supreme Court deemed both acts unconstitutional, and Roosevelt, who had developed doubts about the wisdom of the programs, turned to a more conservation-oriented agricultural program and direct help to labor unions with the Wagner Act, which set minimum pay in certain lines of work at 25 cents an hour. In 1938 Congress set minimum wages and maximum hours for most workers.

The Civilian Conservation Corps was the most popular First New Deal program in the Old Dominion. Under military officers and residing in camps, single and unemployed men between the ages of 18 and 25 worked on a variety of projects in Virginia's forests. Paid $30 a month, the men had to send all but $5 home.

Even though the work of the CCC resembled activities in Fascist Germany or the Soviet Union at the time, the Virginia government proportionately participated in this program more than in any of the other New Deal measures. With Governor Pollard's blessing, the government established some 80 camps, which at one point had close to 20,000 men enlisted. Starting in the George Washington National Forest, the camps spread across the commonwealth. The young men planted over 15 million trees, built nearly 1,000 bridges, cut out hundreds of miles of fire trails, strung telephone lines, and stocked fish, as they learned vocations and occasionally studied Virginia history. No state experienced more impact than Virginia from these programs.

As part of the Progressive Movement, the federal government acquired forestlands and developed national parks. In 1911 the federal government started to acquire eastern forests as a way to save rivers. These purchases included parts of a mountain ravaged by timber cutting. In 1930 President Hoover took administrative steps to create the George Washington National Forest in honor of the first president's 200th natal anniversary. Virginia and the nation, under Calvin Coolidge in 1926, had already created the Shenandoah National Park. Voluntary contributions, mostly from Virginians, plus about $1,000,000 of state funds paid for the project. By placing his presidential camp on the Rapidan River, president Hoover highlighted the ideas of establishing the park as well as constructing Skyline Drive, a road that ran along the crest of the Blue Ridge. In preparing to turn the property over to the federal government as a national park, the state forced most of the residents out of the park in an unprecedented use of eminent domain. In 1936 Roosevelt accepted the park as part of the national park system. Both Hoover and Roosevelt added to woodlands under federal jurisdiction. The Jefferson National Forest protected lands to the south of the first national forest. Although a chestnut blight forced the sale of lumber, federal policy and the low price of lumber during the Depression allowed for restoration of the mountain areas. The federal government, with Byrd's blessing and New Deal money, built the Blue Ridge Parkway, which started as a Public Works Administration program under the Interior Department and became part of the National Parks holdings.

Not only did the New Deal directly aid Shenandoah National Park and the roadways, it also assisted several new state parks, including Seashore State at Cape Henry and Hungry Mother near Marion, and others. In 1932, before Roosevelt took office, the State Assembly passed acts to secure acreage for sites in Fairfax County, at Cape Henry, and near Appomattox Court House. Some of these places held considerable historical interest. The CCC started four that were later turned over to the state and worked on seven others that belonged to the state at the time. The federal government pumped in about $5,000,000, to which the state contributed $100,000.

Under a congressional act designed to take marginal farmland out of circulation, the federal government secured control of over 20,000 acres in the Appomattox-Buckingham area, some 17,000 acres in Cumberland County, and smaller amounts in Chesterfield and Prince Edward. These were leased to the state in 1939 and deeded to it in 1954. The state acquired a 400-acre forest in Prince William County from a private donation in 1938.

During the New Deal, the state government and the two U.S. senators resisted some aspects of the relief measures for the destitute. Through the Federal Emergency Relief Agency (FERA), the national government for the first time took cared for the poor, usually by finding work. Virginia's leaders, insisting on expanding road building and maintenance projects as the primary way of offering relief, refused to participate in some programs. Because of this inaction and comparatively low unemployment levels, the Old Dominion received less federal relief aid than most states. State residents did benefit from the work of the Civil Works Administration. By 1934 over 80,000 Virginians were working on hundreds of little projects in parks, schools, airports, and the like. The state grudgingly contributed a minor part of a federal outlay of nearly $13,000,000 in the state before the larger Works Progress Administration (WPA) replaced the CWA.

Public building projects met with greater favor in the Old Dominion. Colleges and similar institutions received federal money under the Public Works Administration (PWA) to contract new structures. The University of Virginia soon had the Alderman Library, the Medical College a new hospital, and the Norfolk Division of the College of William and Mary a new all-purpose building. The state also acquired a new state library with the federal government, as in the other projects, absorbing about half the cost. The superintendent at VMI, General John Lejeune, used his ties to FDR to obtain several projects for his college.

How the Depression and the First New Deal affected the state can be seen in the experiences of Julian Meade of Danville. A college graduate and a teacher, he became a part-time reporter for the newspaper in his home city, where he watched scabs break a picket line in 1931. Police, many of them frequenters of pool halls given temporary power status, used tear gas and strong-arm tactics. The governor sent in the militia to restore order. Several prominent people, including a novelist, a socialist, and Governor Pollard, tried to mediate the differences. Management, however, insisted on maintaining its most recent pay cut and refused to recognize the textile union. Eventually, the strikers returned to their jobs, but only after state authorities intervened. The young reporter and teacher resigned from both occupations to seek an advanced degree in philosophy from the University of Virginia. After spending some time in Charlottesville, he went to Richmond, where he conversed, in an unfriendly fashion, with Ellen Glasgow. At Virginia Beach in the summer of 1933, a cast of young folks and some eccentric elderly held his interest, as he sunned, drank beer (soft liquor was legal by the end of summer), and wandered the boardwalk and beach. He likely often passed near the vacant buildings of a recently defunct private college, a victim of the Depression. Toward the end of the summer a huge storm roared in. Some visiting mountain people thought their end had come, as the hurricane raged for nearly 24 hours. Water poured under the doors, but the cottage held. The storm ruined or damaged nearly all the buildings and downed all the power lines. Nearby Norfolk became a virtual Venice. Having moved from one storm center to another, Meade made his way back to Danville, where he apprenticed at the mills for about $7 a week. By the time he returned to his hometown, the Dan River Mills had come under the National Recovery Administration, so Meade could read its posted code for cotton textiles that mandated a 40-hour workweek and minimum pay. Management also now had to accept a union, but Meade failed to mention such an organization. After a short time he took a job in one of the federal agencies (apparently under the CWA), and observed that many were giving up work in the private sector to take higher-paying federal jobs. In a somewhat critical vein, he commented that a number of these bureaucrats, who moved from job to job, had never qualified for any serious work before.

Meade also attended a meeting where an aging and weakened James Cannon criticized Hoover for cutting back federal money to enforce prohibition. Cannon expressed hope that FDR could be convinced to undo the pending repeal of the 18th Amendment. Such a scenario seemed unlikely since even before the 21st amendment had sufficient state approval, the president had opened up the sales of beer and wine after he took office. In December 1933, enough states voted to end the experiment in prohibition. As the amendment made its way through the ratification process, Governor Pollard, a "dry," under pressure from Byrd, called for a special session of the Assembly, which imposed state taxes on beer, as it submitted the issue of repeal to the voters. In October, Virginians joined the national movement by voting nearly 2 to 1 for repeal. The next year the Assembly created the Alcoholic Beverage Control Act. The state continued to permit the sale of beer and wine privately, but the state itself dispensed hard liquor. The state thereby obtained sorely needed revenues.

In 1935 Roosevelt put most of the relief and recovery projects under the Works Progress Administration. Funded at high levels, the WPA engaged the unemployed in nearly everything imaginable. Photographers scampered across the countryside with their cameras, locating scenes and people that in some way endorsed New Deal programs. Historians recorded the memories of the elderly, which told the stories of people, many with but limited education, struggling through hard times that often started long before the Depression. A New Deal writers program produced a guide for Virginia history as well as *The Negro in Virginia*. In 1935 workmen cleaned off used bricks in the construction of a football facility on the campus of the Norfolk Division of the College of William and Mary (Foreman Field). Some years later, black women left more pleasant jobs, which were turned over to white women, to reclaim a morass near the Norfolk airport for what became the Azalea Gardens (Botanical Gardens). Several artists found employment in another agency in painting murals, several showing scenes from Virginia history, for the many new post offices.

Interviews, mostly of ordinary folk, reveal how much Virginia had changed in the previous 60 or 70 years. Many accounts mention the difficulties and pleasures of living and working on farms or how people produced tobacco or gathered oysters, but they also tell us how viscose was made at a rayon plant. One need read but a few of these accounts to understand how the movement from farms to factories transformed Virginia, and not always in a positive way. The not entirely untypical case of Howard Reynolds must suffice to describe the fate of the working poor. Reynolds only received a few months of schooling before he had to nurse his invalid mother. After farming for a brief time when he was quite young, he mined in Botetourt County, after which he married at the age of 16. When the mines closed, he went to Iron Gate to work as a leather hanger. During World War I he split leather for gun carriages and harnesses. After working at a Harrisonburg tannery, he found employment in 1922 at a limekiln and then at Westvaco (West Virginia Pulp and Paper Co.) near Covington, making bleach. While engaged in this line of work, he inhaled gas fumes, the effects of which virtually ended his working career. For the six years before the interview, Reynolds had been trying unsuccessfully, including hearings before the State Compensation Commission, to obtain payments. He currently lived in little more than a shack.

The most important piece of Roosevelt's Second New Deal, the Social Security System, passed in 1935, and the government began to implement it in 1937. The idea of such a national program for the elderly met resistance in Virginia. Many business men liked neither the payroll tax nor unemployment insurance. Byrd did not like these ideas from principal; he also complained that the expected state contribution to the system would be too costly. The program's aid to the already retired seemed unfair. The measure also aided dependent children and provided unemployment insurance, which the states had to supervise. Byrd and Glass were among but six senators who opposed the measure. Four of the Virginia delegation joined 29 others in opposition to the 372 that voted for the idea. Virginia's representatives were clearly out of step with the views of the country and most Virginians on the issue. Democratic voters replaced Colgate Darden, one of the opponents of Social Security, as their nominee in the next election in the Second Congressional District. After sitting out a term, Darden returned to his congressional seat and became Virginia's governor in 1942. The Virginia the Assembly of 1936 failed to provide funds to implement the system. The House approved the pension for the already retired but the Senate refused to. The Senate narrowly approved unemployment insurance, but the House did not. After Roosevelt carried Virginia and the nation in the fall election that year, the Virginia Assembly overwhelmingly passed a bill to create a commission to handle unemployment insurance. In late 1937 a commission reported on the cost of pensions for the needy elderly. When the Supreme Court validated Social Security, a special assembly allowed the state to join the other 47 that had already entered the program.

The federal government actively promoted bringing electric power to Virginia farmers. Virginia felt the effects of the ambitious Tennessee Valley Authority, part of the First New Deal, only in the extreme southwestern part of the state, where the TVA tapped several rivers and supplied power and cheap fertilizers. The federal government developed and managed these enterprises over the objections of entrepreneurs that had been slowly moving into rural areas.

In Southwest Virginia, Appalachian Electric Power planned to build a large dam across the New River southwest of Radford. In 1931 the company's directors challenged the right of the Federal Power Commission to require it to secure a license to impede the river's flow. The attorneys general of several states, including Virginia, joined with the company in seeking to keep that power with the individual states. When the Supreme Court failed to exempt the company from the need to secure a federal license in 1934, Appalachian Power proceeded without the necessary paperwork to build one of the largest hydroelectric plants in the country. By 1939, when completed, Claytor Dam stood about 114 feet tall, equipped with some nine spillways. The lake it created covered over 200,000 acres and backed up the river some 21 miles. In 1940 the Supreme Court by a vote of 6 to 2 determined that the company had violated the 1920 law. During the 1930s, the company found itself under attack. The Federal Securities Exchange Commission, created in 1934, questioned the validity of stocks and bonds, especially after Congress took steps against holding companies in 1935. The federal government defended workers from company efforts to dismiss them. Despite it all, the dam still stands, and the state secured a portion of the new shoreline for a state park in 1946.

A federal agency (REA) did much to raise the percentage of Virginian farmers with access to electricity. With its help, the proportion tripled from 7 to 21% in the 1930s and rose to over 90% during the next decade. The private Virginia Electric Power Company (VEPCO) increased services, especially when rural folk formed cooperatives. In 1953 the Corps of Engineers completed the Kerr Dam along the Roanoke River, which Congress had called for to control flooding nine years earlier. Excess water could be used for generating electric power and siphoned off for municipal water supplies. Virginia Power (VEPCO) and a North Carolina power company purchased energy for times of heaviest demand. At about the same time Appalachian Power built a dam in Bedford County along the Roanoke and formed Smith Mountain Lake.

As a state with a large rural population, the Old Dominion had a deep interest in the agricultural New Deal measures. Under the Agricultural Adjustment Act (deemed unconstitutional in 1935), tobacco farmers reduced their output some 13 million pounds and saw prices double. In 1935 they also became beneficiaries of a federal system of tobacco inspection. Other designated crops such as cotton experienced higher prices. Those that participated directly in the aid program took in over $2,000,000 in benefits in less than a year. The ability to store produce in government granaries also helped farm income. In 1935, with some 87% under contract, farmers did even better, but the federal government collected more money from those that purchased and processed farm commodities than it distributed to local growers. Other states also far outranked the Old Dominion in receiving help. A few farmers thought Byrd's criticism of the program valid, but rising returns covered a host of evils, and Virginia farmers voted 30 to 1 to continue a part of the program to which Byrd objected. Byrd had fewer objections to a soil conservation program that paid farmers to shift to crops that restored fertility. It would be hard to overestimate the degree to which this program transformed farms in the state. In the first year farmers saved some 167,000 acres. It helped all farmers, not only those that produced staples. In 1938 the federal government passed a new agricultural adjustment act that expanded the use of federal warehouses, allowing farmers to receive part of the value of the crop at harvest time and the rest when prices rose. When enough farmers agreed, the government restricted production. When tobacco prices failed to increase, growers rejected the system, but when prices dropped to their lowest level in six years, they quickly accepted the established quotas.

Rural Virginians also made use of the Resettlement Administration, when mountain families, dispossessed by plans for the park, were relocated in pleasant homes on small farms in the Valley. Byrd objected about the cost of providing these people with indoor toilets and refrigerators. Several thousand residents of the Southside also received similar help from the Farm Security Administration. The FSA developed several communities, including one in Newport News called the Aberdeen Gardens. Built for black homesteaders, the project started under a division of the Department of the Interior and in 1935 came under the Resettlement Administration. Originally designed as a rural village with individual farm plots, it became a suburban enclave for blacks surrounded by white-owned farms. The final cost of the project produced heavy criticism, so much so that Governor Price, usually a strong proponent of New Deal measures, refused to participate in the opening ceremonies.

On the political front, Price campaigned for the nomination as governor in 1937. An advocate of most of the New Deal and an early entrant into the gubernatorial sweepstakes, the popular Price, a former lieutenant governor, received a reluctant endorsement from Byrd and his organization. Once in office, Price persuaded the legislature to approve Social Security, maximum hours for women to work, and aid to schools. But in replacing E.R. Combs, Byrd's right-hand man, as comptroller and chair of a compensation board, along with other Byrd stalwarts, he incurred the wrath of Virginia's junior senator. Despite the change, most all local government officeholders, from commissioners of the revenue to sheriffs, remained faithful to the organization. Roosevelt backed Price with some federal patronage, but the U.S. Senate turned down the governor's choice for a federal judgeship. The legislature remained in the hands of Byrd men, so Price obtained only part of his program.

By 1935, Virginia cut its unemployment rate by half, and the proportion remained at or below 10% for some time. A dip in growth in 1938 resulted from the collection of the payroll tax for Social Security and higher income taxes. By 1939 about 7.5% (about half the national level) of the potential workers were actively searching for a job. In the last half of the decade the Old Dominion enjoyed a degree of prosperity as its export volume, industrial production, coal tonnage, and agricultural output returned to or near pre-Depression levels. During the last half of the decade Hampton Roads benefited from federal contracts for ships. Not only did Newport News Shipbuilding and Drydock secure contracts for future famous carriers like the *Ranger*, *Yorktown*, *Enterprise*, and *Hornet*, but it also built several vessels for the U.S. Maritime Commission after 1936. Roosevelt and Congress agreed to a resumption of naval building as early as 1934. This decision enabled Newport News to bring its employment levels back to about half what they had been in 1919. The navy yard, which had become totally reliant on maintenance work for a peacetime navy, also increased its workforce, from about 2,400 to 6,500 in 1939.

The Second World War began in September 1939, as Germany invaded Poland, which forced Great Britain and France to declare war on Germany. Germany, having absorbed Austria a year earlier and with a rebuilt war machine, conquered France in the summer of 1940 and threatened Great Britain. The next year German armies moved east against the Soviet Union. The United States officially stayed out of the fighting, although the government sent materials to stymie the Nazi menace. Submarine attacks on American ships, including naval vessels escorting convoys, did not, as in the case of the First World War, bring a declaration of war from the United States. What did was a Japanese attack on Pearl Harbor on 7 December 1941. When the United States declared war on the imperial government of Japan, it also automatically went to war against Germany and Fascist Italy, both allies of Japan.

War preparations began in the United States and Virginia in earnest in 1940. The number of people building or repairing ships in the Hampton Roads area quickly soon surpassed the peak levels of the previous war. By the time of Pearl Harbor, Newport News Shipbuilding and Drydock and the Navy Yard employed over 40,000 workers. The Fifth Naval District purchased substantially more acreage to increase its base, including the size of the naval air station. The national government also resumed the selective service system. Because World War II dwarfed the previous war in length and degree of effort by a factor of at least four, nothing could prepare adequately for it. That it was a two-ocean war was in part responsible. In World War I the United States simply had to join the fray in France and help topple the Kaiser. In 1941 it would be necessary to beat Germany and Italy in North Africa, conquer Italy, and secure a foothold in Western Europe to be in a situation similar to the one in 1918. The Soviet Union stayed in the war, unlike the first war, and drained Germany of much of its military capacity, but France was effectively out of the war, but Japan occupied a good bit of British and American attention.

More than 300,000 Virginians served in the military during the Second World War, over three times the number of the Great War. About 9,000 lost their lives. Many National Guardsmen became part of the famous Blue/Gray Division (the 29th) composed of Virginians and Marylanders. This organization included a variety of battalions from the 629th (Tank Destroyer) to the 29th (Ranger). VMI graduate General Leonard Gerow commanded the landings at Omaha Beach in the Normandy Invasion on 6 June 1944, during which many Virginians died, including 21 young men from Bedford, members of the 116th Infantry. Because of the unusually high loss of life from this relatively small town, Bedford recently became the site of the special memorial for the D-Day landing. The 111th Field Artillery also served in the Second Front. General Lewis "Chesty" Puller, another VMI man and a marine, won several Navy crosses. General Lemuel C. Shepherd, a third one-time cadet, fought heroically in the Pacific. George C. Marshall, another VMI man, served as Army chief of staff and later became a most noteworthy secretary of state under President Harry Truman.

The second war put far more demands on Hampton Roads than the first one. Counting the buildup just before Pearl Harbor, the shipyard in Newport News constructed 11 carriers, 33 large warships, and 8 cruisers. At its peak in 1943, it hired over 31,000. Meanwhile Navy Yard employment soared to near 43,000 in the same year. Management at the Newport News facility claimed they could use thousands of additional workers, but many were siphoned off to work a nearby disembarkation center or elsewhere. Turnover proved to be a constant problem.

Once again, segregation laws came under attack. The Virginia Supreme Court, observing that whites sitting in black sections of a bus had not been told to move, overturned a lower court decision against a woman of color that refused to move to the back of a bus. Virginius Dabney, a Richmond editor, even called for white Virginians to consider ending this law, but Governor Colgate Darden did not wish to rock any racist boats (he, however, had earlier expressed interest in ending the poll tax). Meanwhile, the federal government's Fair Employment Practices Committee (FEPC) collected files on cases involving discrimination, even some by the federal government. Before Pearl Harbor, FDR, under coercion from the prospect of a black march on Washington D.C. ordered an end to bias in federal employment. Discrimination continued, but blacks broke into formerly restricted occupations. Women of color, however, had a very hard time finding the training necessary to secure skilled jobs.

As the number of civilian shipbuilders approached 75,000, the number of soldiers and sailors stationed in Hampton Roads grew from about 10,000 in 1939 to almost 169,000 late in 1943. The government activated the old bases, sometimes changing their purpose, and added to the list of facilities. The Navy added specialized camps for amphibious training, guard duty, and even a music school at Little Creek in Princess Anne County (now part of Norfolk and Virginia Beach). The Navy trained men in mine warfare in York County. Oceana and several smaller fields in Princess Anne (Virginia Beach) supplemented the main air station on Hampton Roads. Seabees, (construction workers) received their training at Camp Peary, just west of Williamsburg. The Army restocked its supply center, trained soldiers in coastal and harbor defense at Fort Monroe, armed Fort Story for coastal defense, stored ordnance in Nansemond County, gave antiaircraft training at Fort Eustis, and beefed up its artillery at Dam Neck, south of the resort strip in Virginia Beach. A midlevel command planned the attack on North Africa at the Nansemond Hotel at Ocean View.

The war came home in the summer of 1942, when sunbathers at Virginia Beach heard explosions and noticed columns of black smoke wafting offshore. German U-boats laid hundreds of mines and knocked out thousands of tons of Allied shipping along the coast. A coordinated effort eventually calmed the situation. Civilians in yachts and members of the Civilian Air Patrol, based at Parksley on the Eastern Shore of Virginia, helped locate the enemy subs. Bodies of German sailors were interred at a Hampton cemetery.

As Hampton Roads bristled with armament and manpower, other parts of Virginia also felt the impact of war, far more than they had in the first war. The army acquired two huge inland ranges—Fort A.P. Hill near Bowling Green and Fort Pickett near Blackstone. West of the Blue Ridge, the government contracted the Hercules Company to produce nitrates under army supervision, starting in 1940. At its peak the Radford Arsenal hired between 15,000 and 20,000. Around Richmond, the military took over the airport, used the terminal on the James, and built a supply center for chemicals, and a piece of Virginia became home to a huge defense center known as the Pentagon.

A hidden cost attended this war buildup. Long after the war, residents of a neighborhood near the Defense Supply Center in Richmond noticed contamination related to leaks at the facility. Those who want to convert the huge arsenal site near Radford to peacetime uses find such conversion especially difficult and costly. Even converting Fort Monroe and numerous other bases from military uses proves daunting, for no one knows for certain what lies underground

The presence of these bases and other facilities put strains on nearby communities during the war. Little housing existed anywhere near the arsenal across the New River from Radford, so workers rented where they could, with the government subsidizing housing. In Norfolk and Portsmouth, the situation became so tight that beds were rotated in eight-hour shifts. The experience of the previous war warned authorities about this possibility, but no one wanted to buck the local real estate people who feared a falloff after the war. Once again the government waited before moving ahead with public projects. Less than 3,000 units became available before 1943. Some 7,000 came on line after that date in the Norfolk/Portsmouth area. After much complaining, blacks finally secured two major parks. Unfortunately, neither water nor bus service was available. By that point the need for civilian workers diminished.

Colleges played an important role during the war as some of them had during the first war. Faced with declining enrollments, the administrations of these institutions opened their facilities to the military. Indeed, some of them would not have survived save for the government. The Army Specialized Training Personnel (ASTP) and the navy equivalent (V-12) opened up in 1942. Hampton Institute had a naval school, and the first black petty officer in the Navy received his training there. The Institute also trained cooks at the Chamberlin Hotel. Washington and Lee processed thousands of Waves and other noncombatants. The University of Virginia, the University of Richmond, Hampden-Sydney, and Emory and Henry had V-12 programs, while the College of William and Mary, Randolph-Macon, VMI, and VPI came under the ASTP umbrella. Manpower shortages forced the army to suspend its program well before the end of the conflict. The colleges integrated the servicemen and women into their sports and other social activities. The presence of the military, even though for short times in many cases, prepared the colleges for the huge influx of veterans under the G.I. Bill of Rights or Serviceman's Readjustment Act, passed toward the end of the war. And come to an end the war did, first in Germany in June 1945 and then, after two uses of the atom bomb, in Japan in August that year. Once again, Virginians had done their share and endured the hardships necessary to repel the threat to the American way of life.

The end of World War II also brought closure to a turbulent era of economic ups and downs. It had been a time of upheaval, but also one of considerable progress. In the interwar years, the state made considerable progress building roads, especially what appeared on maps as the blue highways, and after the war, a major road-building boom took place. State and national parks, both historical and recreational, came into being mostly in the 1930s. Hundreds of thousands of acres of forests now fell under federal regulation. Reforms in agriculture made headway and many farmers prospered, especially during the wars. Virginia's manufacturing base grew rapidly. Local governments were starting to treat sewage. On the other hand, damage to the environment, much of it unnoticed, continued apace.

# PART FIVE: THE RECENT PAST

The next 50 years or so brought even more change, though not in the fashion of a roller coaster. A number of important events and trends made life quite an adventure for those who experienced the time. Chapter 17 studies Virginia in the 1950s, chapter 18 discusses changes that took place in the 1960s and 1970s, while the last chapter carries the story through the end of the 20th century.

On the international front, a Cold War in 1947 divided the world between democracies and communist nations, with other nations not aligned to either side. Atom and later hydrogen bombs, with effective systems of delivery, made this a perilous period, indeed. The United States, as part of the United Nations, participated in the Korean conflict (1950–53) to stop communist advances. In 1962 a war scare occurred over the installation of Soviet missiles in Cuba, recently taken over by Communists. In 1965 the United States became fully involved in an effort to keep communist North Vietnam and the Viet Cong in South Vietnam from taking over the latter country. After heavy losses and the longest war in American history, Americans withdrew. After several "thaws" and "freezes" the American policy of containment announced in 1947 finally bore fruit as the old Soviet Union broke up and Eastern Europe fell from Russian and communist control.

On the domestic side, the economy experienced sustained prosperity in the 1950s (with two minor recessions) and in the early 1960s. The era of the Vietnam War slowed the real rate of growth, and, starting in 1973, with chronic inflation and an oil embargo, the economy faltered. Prosperity returned for the more privileged classes in the mid-1980s. A sustained boom benefited the state and nation during most of the 1990s but faded with the end of the millennium.

Changes in the economy brought numerous new products, led by televisions around 1949 with viable programming and later cable systems. Cumbersome computers, introduced shortly after the Second World War, gave way to effective personal computers. By the end of the century the way in which Americans communicated fundamentally changed with e-mail, cell phones, and other inventions. In the 1990s experts talked about the new technology and the "new economy," as if no other era had experienced change.

Attitudes toward race experienced a sea change in post-World War II America. Virginia's college students were not quite as rebellious as those found in many parts of the country during the Vietnam War, but the state experienced a sexual revolution, as divorce rates rose. Crime rates also rose as well, and finally in the mid-1990s they started to fall back to the levels of the 1960s (these were high compared to earlier decades).

# Chapter 17

## Virginia at Midcentury

At the midpoint of the 20th century the Old Dominion seemed somnolent, but under the surface the state was experiencing considerable change. The immediate post-World War II era brought changed attitudes in American culture that affected every state, Virginia being no exception.

With about 3,320,000 residents, Virginia ranked 15th of 48 states in population. Its density of 83 people per square mile ranked above that for the nation, about the same as in nearby states like Kentucky and West Virginia, but well below states to the north (Maryland had 237). Just as people tended to distribute themselves unevenly throughout the country, they also concentrated in parts of Virginia. Some of the mountainous southwest actually had more density than the state as a whole, as miners and others settled in the numerous valleys. The area farther north in the Alleghenies contained fewer vales and people, along with less coal. Sections of the Piedmont also had few residents as farms reverted to timber.

The urban trend, which slowed slightly in the 1920s and 1930s, rolled on in the 1940s. By 1950, some 40% (under the older definition) rated the urban label. About 1,560,000 Virginians lived in some 78 communities. Two cities (Richmond and Norfolk) had over 100,000; eight cities had between 25,000 and 100,000 whereas 34 contained between 5,000 and 25,000, and another 34 had above 2,500 to 5,000. Under a new definition of urban the census analyzers used that year, the state was 47% urban, whereas the national proportion stood at 64%. Four major metropolitan areas embraced some 40% of all Virginians. The biggest of these, Hampton Roads, held almost 570,000 (about 410,000 in 1940). Roanoke, the smallest, had about 133,000 (up some 19% since 1940).

Although blacks could be found in urban Virginia at about the same level as in the rural parts of the state, their overall proportion in the population continued to drop. Even though their number increased some 11% during the 1940s, their overall portion of the total population fell to 22% in 1950, as whites increased at a faster rate. Blacks tended to move north as Yankees came south.

By 1950 the suburbs of the District of Columbia were clearly on the move. Fairfax and Arlington Counties and the cities of Alexandria and Falls Church (established in 1948), with 448 square miles had over 300,000 residents. Only 8% of these were black. The area population about doubled during the previous decade. Less than 8,000 of its residents now lived on farms. Many breadwinners worked in the nation's capital. The residents of Fairfax drove far more than those in any other part of the state. The area contained few manufacturing plants, considering its population.

The metropolitan area near the James River, embracing Richmond, Hopewell, Petersburg, and part of Chesterfield County, had well over 300,000 residents (one definition placed it at 380,000). Richmond proper grew by almost 20% during the recent decade and its industries had more than tripled since 1930. Hopewell had about 10,000 people in 1950, roughly the same as in 1930. But its industries hired about that same number, suggesting that workers resided in nearby communities. Petersburg, with about 35,000, relied on tobacco, leather, and wood derivative plants. Its principal suburb, Colonial Heights, had about 6,000. Income levels in the whole area ran about half that of the suburbs of D.C.

The Hampton Roads metropolitan area approached a population of 600,000 in 1950, with the Lower Peninsula 150,000 of that number. Two years later the city of Warwick replaced the county by the same name and then merged with Newport News. Hampton soon absorbed all of what remained of Elizabeth City County. Norfolk passed the 200,000 mark during the war, with Portsmouth less than half that amount. Both cities stood poised to acquire parts of neighboring counties. In the early 1960s, however, the city of Virginia Beach materialized to prevent further annexation by Norfolk. South Norfolk and old Norfolk County combined to become the city of Chesapeake to thwart Portsmouth's ambitions. The area's economic lifeblood rested on the presence of the military and the vast tonnage that flowed through the ports. Hampton Roads ranked second in the nation (next to New York) in international tonnage. In export tonnage, with its reliance on coal, it exceeded all Atlantic Coast ports. Many of its residents came from other parts of Virginia or the United States.

Roanoke's core contained about 90,000 residents, with another 40,000 nearby. Its biggest employer, the Norfolk and Western Railway, had dominated affairs since the inception of the city in the early 1880s. But some 3,200 worked at the viscose plant and a textile company hired another 1,000 or so. Some 13.6% of its people were defined as Negro compared to about double that rate in the Richmond area. The prevalence of poor whites in the general area kept income levels below those of Richmond and well below those in Northern Virginia.

Defying Virginia's tradition as a staid place in the middle of the 20th century, many people seemed on the move. The proportion of residents born in the state dropped from close to 95% in the late 19th century to about 75% in 1950. New Englanders (about 33,000), Pennsylvanians (55,000), New Yorkers (43,000), and others showed up. Most importantly, whites were not fleeing from the state in droves as in the early 19th century nor at the more modest rates of the late 19th and early 20th centuries. Many blacks, especially women, moved out of the state, but others came from farther south. Whether from inside or outside the state, blacks tended to move from rural to urban, but whites congregated in suburbs, at least for residency. Virginia had few foreign born, with between 1% and 2% in that category.

Virginia had about 1,300,000 in the workforce, with over 100,000 in the military. Among civilians, government hired about 174,000. Almost 15% Virginians farmed and a little over 20% manufactured products (almost 8% made durable goods). The wholesale and retail trades had another 16%, transportation a bit less than 6%. Professional and personal services each carried another 7.5%. With such a small percentage in farming and manufacturing, Virginia ran well ahead of the national trend toward service sector employment. This phenomenon related to the number of government jobs and the tendency to hire maids. The number of persons engaged in making products increased from about 120,000 in 1929, to 180,000 in 1939, and to 240,000 in 1949. During that time Virginia industrialized at a faster pace than the nation as a whole. At some point in the 1940s, the number of Virginians involved in manufacturing exceeded those in agriculture (a condition achieved nationally in the first decade of the century).

Tobacco remained the mainstay of the southern Piedmont as producers continued to receive federal price supports. With acreage fixed, farmers increased yield per acre. On the whole, Virginians raised more cattle, hay, and barley. Irish potatoes fell back as soybeans increased. Truck farming shifted from the Norfolk area to the Eastern Shore of Virginia, as companies brought in migrant workers to help at harvest time. The area also developed significant poultry production, both raising and processing. Peanuts prevailed in parts of the lower Tidewater. Their popularity and price supports, developed by the federal government in the 1940s, made them too valuable especially during the war to allow their use for hogs (whether this practice degraded the Smithfield ham is a matter of some dispute). Apple orchards in the Valley fell back, as raising turkeys became more popular. The area near the nation's capital had some dairy farms and a fair number of gentlemen farmers (called "station wagon farming").

Despite a decline in farming, Virginia still had just over 150,000 farms in 1950. Total acreage was falling, but the average farm increased in size. Overall rural areas did not face decline. In a trend that had been underway for some time, rural residents developed more diversified occupations. Farming became a secondary line of work, as men and some women found their principal jobs away from their places of residence.

Wood processing industries could be found throughout the state and played major roles during these times. By 1950, roughly 20% of those employed in industry processed wood products. Only a few thousand procured the timber. The rest made pulp, paper, and synthetics from wood, much of which came from out of the state. Lumber production peaked between 1905 and 1915 and then dropped back. The Depression allowed some replenishment. In the 1930s the state acquired blocks of abandoned lands in the Piedmont to go along with the large tracts in national forests. In the late 1930s several hundred small sawmill operators increased production. After a surge following World War II, the industry reached a point of equilibrium, where natural reforestation and production stayed at similar levels. In the 1950s the state tried to educate the thousands of owners of timberlands on preservation techniques. Major corporations already had programs.

Virginia ranked eighth in coal production in 1950 with some 30,000 miners, mostly in coal. Although mines continued to extract a few thousand tons from the Montgomery County fields near the New River and Wise County produced vast quantities, Buchanan County became the single biggest coal county in the state, with about 25% of the annual yield of 20 million tons. Over the years miners had extracted about a billion tons from Virginia, but experts estimated that well over a billion more remained (these numbers proved conservative). Once the nation cleared the war economy, however, American markets for coal dropped back as foreign purchases made up for some of the reduced American demand. Even the Norfolk and Western shifted its locomotives to diesel in 1950. Coal workers were in a state of near crisis in the early 1950s, as unemployment rose.

Such industries concentrated, as one might expect, in urban areas. Tobacco processors frequented Richmond, Lynchburg, and Danville. That industry accounted for about a billion dollars in income in 1950, though it hired only about 15,000 workers. The biggest single business in Richmond was the DuPont chemical plant. The cotton mills in Danville hired about 12,000 workers. A somewhat higher number could be found building ships in Newport News. The statewide chemical industry kept about 40,000 busy making products that sold for about $750,000,000 at mid-century. It had big plants at Richmond and elsewhere. Roanoke had a variety of industries. The Waynesboro-Staunton area also now had several textile firms and would soon have a large General Electric plant.

But textiles and related chemical firms spread into parts of the Piedmont and the western part of the state, giving many small towns factories. The Burlington Mills, which entered Virginia in 1933 during the bottom of the Depression, developed a weaving plant at Altavista, a ribbon plant at South Hill, a nylon hosiery operation at Salem, along with firms at Radford, Galax, Chilhowie, and Marion. Another company made wool carpets at Glasgow. Indeed, several manufacturers ran small operations across the entire area. The Narrows had a Celanese plant and Front Royal a viscose operation. In what looked like a conscious effort to discourage labor unions, Virginia spread industrial workers over a large expanse, by putting much of its revenues from gasoline taxes into rural road construction, thus allowing people to live several miles from their place of work. Factories, dependent on limited rural labor, remained small.

Most of the politicians that ran the state at mid-century belonged to the party apparatus that U.S. Senator Harry Byrd Sr. ruled over. Conservative in fiscal policies on all levels of government, Byrd and his backers championed causes not substantially different from those of early 20th-century Democratic leaders, opposing high tariffs, federal taxes, and a strong federal government. Leaders like Carter Glass favored an international rather than an isolationist approach in foreign affairs, but he no longer championed progressive reforms.

The foundation of the organization rested on local politicians. Each county elected five constitutional officers—clerk of court, sheriff, commonwealth attorney, treasurer, and commissioner of revenue. Members of boards of supervisors represented magisterial districts in determining local policies, but real power resided with the constitutional officers plus the judge of the circuit court, appointed by the state assembly. City government differed somewhat, but it had many of the same positions. The State Corporation Board controlled the pay of these officers, whether rural or urban. Thus state officials had a great deal to say about local affairs. This symbiotic relationship allowed Democratic Party leaders to sustain power. Defenders of the organization argued that it was merely a disorganized band of like-minded folk (sharing the views of Harry Byrd) who were mostly interested in giving Virginia good government and capable public servants. One member said, "It's like a club, except it has no bylaws, constitution or dues."

Others contended that the system stifled dissent and drove people from political activity. Francis Pickens Miller, from the Valley, led the anti-Byrd sentiment and made a strong but losing bid for the governorship in the Democratic Party primary in 1949 (John Battle won that race). A liberal Democrat, Miller contended that Virginia fell somewhat short of being a free society, for a clique of men mired in the past retained power. Miller pointed out that Byrd governed the state long after serving as governor as an "absentee landlord" through E.R. Combs, chairman of the Compensation Board and Clerk of the State Senate. Miller believed the Byrd organization was as powerful as any political machine in the nation. Such control meant that only insiders had their needs met.

After analyzing the organization and the way the state did business, one political scientist, V.O. Key, labeled Virginia "a political museum piece," and in some measures of progress, the record did not look good. The percentage of people voting continued at low levels, though a burst of interest occurred right after World War II. One measurement suggested the state ranked 34 out of 48 in money for schools based on ability to pay. Virginia trailed even many other Southern states in that category. The 1950 census noted that the typical Virginian had barely started a high school education, putting put the state slightly ahead of Arkansas and behind Vermont. These numbers were largely a function of location, race, and sex. White females residing in a sizeable town or a city had 10.7 years of formal education, whereas black males living in an isolated rural area averaged but 6.1. Overall, people had about a year more schooling than they had at the beginning of the previous decade. In road construction, the record seemed better. In 1932 Byrd convinced the state to take over county roads. The rural sections of the state thus ended up with a fairly decent highway system. Virginia had the ability to provide other services. Whether it had the frame of mind was another matter.

As World War II was ending in 1945, Virginia elected burly Bill Tuck as governor. Tuck received Byrd's blessing and the support of the courthouse clique, though some people had some reservations about his flamboyancy, love for country music, and propensity to chew tobacco. Lieutenant Governor Tuck had a popular following in Southside, which rarely produced dissenters against the organization. On the day the crew of the *Enola Gay* dropped the atom bomb on Hiroshima, Tuck easily triumphed in the primary over his opponent, who came out against the poll tax and curried favor among the organized industrial workers. Tuck then won the *pro forma* contest against a Republican in the fall.

Tuck served as governor during a troubled time. With the Second World War at an end, Americans faced runaway inflation and feared a recession, as millions of military people returned to civilian life. A conservative backlash against elements of the New Deal surfaced. A fear of Communism mounted with the appearance of the Cold War. Race relations appeared on edge. The most immediate problem related to labor unions. A series of strikes swept the nation in 1946 as they had in 1919. Communists had infiltrated the maritime trades in the North, but it would have been next to impossible to find Reds in Virginia. Under a new law, no municipal officer could deal with any labor negotiator. Also any state employee that took part in a strike would be banned from public employment for a year. When 1,800 VEPCO (the suppliers of electric power) workers, as members of a powerful labor union, said they would strike in April, Tuck threatened to place them all in the Virginia State Guard, the inactive emergency militia unit. The union thereupon accepted the proposed wage increase. When coal miners walked out and national labor unions actively campaigned to unionize the entire state, Tuck had a special legislative session in January 1947 overwhelmingly pass a law to prevent strikes among public utility workers and another to make Virginia a "right to work" state, thus ending any possibility of "closed shops" or "union shops" in the state, under which a worker had to belong to a union. The Taft-Hartley Act, which passed later that year on the federal level over President Truman's veto, allowed states to have right to work laws. Although the United Mine Workers and the Congress of Industrial Organizations mounted a spirited campaign against these antiunion acts, Tuck tapped into a prevailing attitude among conservative Virginians. Even with about 12,000 miners, a few thousand textile workers, some longshoremen, and shipyard workers organized, Virginia had only about 13% of its workers in unions compared to double that level nationally. Many of these belonged to company-controlled unions. Even among factory workers, especially those in small towns and rural areas, unions with real power had only a few supporters.

When the labor situation calmed down, race relations heated up. Although considered safe on race issues, President Truman proposed a permanent commission on civil rights and employment practices. The courts had already opened up the Democratic primary to black voters, and now Truman wanted to protect their right to vote. A furious Tuck called for the legislature to revise the election laws to allow party insiders to determine the state's electoral vote to avoid support for Truman in the upcoming national election. The final legislation moderated the procedure somewhat and, indeed, made it easier for names to appear on the ballot.

When the Democrats nominated Truman for a new term at its summer convention in 1948 and went on record in favor of civil rights, dissident Democrats bolted the party, formed the Dixiecrats, and nominated Governor Strom Thurmond of South Carolina for president. The Southern Democrat received quite a bit of support in the Southside. Many urged Governor Tuck to join their ranks. A cartoon of the time depicted a rather sour-looking hag waving a flag for Truman competing with a luscious-looking lady bearing a banner for Thurmond, both vying for the affections of Governor Tuck. In the end Tuck and Byrd kept quiet, and only 13% of Virginia voters supported Thurmond. In a major upset Truman beat the Republican Thomas Dewey in the national race. In the Old Dominion, Truman won with almost 48% of the popular vote.

Forgotten in all the turmoil about labor and race relations was Tuck's contribution to state government. As a good organization man, Tuck adhered to the principal of "pay as you go," but he also convinced the Assembly to add a cent to the gasoline tax to help build more roads. The legislature, at his behest, also raised corporate taxes on net income and elevated personal income taxes. Revenues derived from these taxes allowed future governors and legislatures to fund services at higher levels. Byrd was not entirely pleased with elevating taxes, but the plan passed. Also like Byrd before him, Tuck reduced the number of state agencies but added an agency to deal with water pollution.

Matters relating to race were not destined to disappear. In 1948 Richmond voters elected Oliver Hill as the first black candidate on its council in some 52 years. Even though only a few hundred blacks were qualified to vote in the city, they could occasionally elect one of their own, with virtually no white help as long as they voted for only one candidate (called "single-shot voting"). In this fashion blacks slipped their candidate into ninth place in a field of 29 and thus secured the last council seat. The same technique failed to work in Norfolk in the 1950s, but in time increased number of blacks in the electorate dramatically changed the political situation.

John Battle, elected in 1949 after a bitter three-way Democratic primary, served as governor when the state executed the infamous "Martinsville Seven," a group of young black men and boys who raped a white woman. The victim survived the gruesome crime. Battle could not bring himself to exempt even the youngest of the criminals. No one could remember when a white man of any age had ever been executed for rape. During Battle's time in office the movement toward integration gained momentum, though the governor and the legislature had little to do with it. Battle said he stood ready to defend against efforts to integrate the state parks. State leaders watched the courts end segregation on interstate buses. In 1951 the Danville Leafs, suffering late-season doldrums, played a local black to boost minority attendance. They thereby broke the professional baseball color line in Virginia for the first time. Also that year Wendell Scott, a black stock car driver, competed in a race near Danville and then throughout the state. Some competitors tried to run him off the tracks, but others befriended him. He eventually participated in major league runs at Martinsville, a track recently established by the National Association of Stock Car Racing. At about the same time a black boy played Little League baseball for a team from Norton. When teams in other parts of Virginia refused to play them, the Norton boys represented the state in national competition.

Although Virginians might reluctantly accept integration in certain circumstances, they would stoutly resist ending segregation in public schools. The story began in 1951, when black high school students in Prince Edward County boycotted classes to protest inferior conditions. Their complaints ultimately became part of the famous *Brown v Board of Topeka* case (*Davis v Prince Edward County*) decided in 1954. In it, the U.S. Supreme Court decided that the "separate but equal" doctrine violated the 14th Amendment and mandated the integration of public schools "with all deliberate speed." Thomas Stanley, another resident of Southside Virginia, had just taken office as governor, when the decision came down. Stanley had barely bested Theodore Roosevelt Dalton, a Republican in the race in the fall. Only Byrd's direct intervention and claims that Dalton wanted to sack "pay as you go" (he backed highway bonds redeemed from gasoline revenues) allowed Stanley to survive. Some anti-Byrd Democrats likely voted for Dalton as fissures began to appear in the Byrd organization.

In 1954 a group of "Young Turks," including Armistead Boothe, George Cochran, Stuart Carter, and Walter Page attempted to repeal a law recently sponsored by Harry Byrd, Jr., that automatically returned surplus revenues to the taxpayers. Although the young legislators forced a compromise in having a few million dollars diverted to services, they paid for it by losing status in the organization. Unlike most Democrats, the dissidents wanted to work out a compromise on integration.

In the wake of the Brown decision, 12,000 Virginians, including Congressman Bill Tuck and many in Southside organized the Defenders of State Sovereignty. That organization conducted a vigorous campaign against any integration. When the court first announced its rejection of segregation of public education, Governor Stanley urged Virginians to remain to use cool judgment, but he then announced that ending the constitutional mandate for free public education might be a way around the crisis. Liberals responded in disgust, one even saying that he had no problems sending his own children to school with blacks. After backing off the idea of ending all public education, Stanley called into being a commission, composed exclusively of legislators, mostly from the Southside, to find legal ways of evading the courts. No blacks served on the commission. The chairman of the commission, Garland Gray, held a hearing in the fall of 1954 and listened to over 100 speakers. The Gray Commission advised the state to let localities accept limited integration where only a small number of blacks might be involved. It also urged the state to control assigning children to schools on the basis of individual welfare and to grant funds for tuition payments for parents that wished to send their children to private, nonreligious schools or other public schools. State law would be modified so that no child had to go to a school where races mixed.

A special session of the General Assembly took up the recommendations of the Gray Commission. Over the objections of practically the entire black community and some white dissidents, the legislature proposed an amendment that endorsed tuition payments. On 9 January 1956 voters accepted the amendment in principle, though the fate of local option remained unclear. The legislature later enacted a version of Madison's old idea of "Interposition," or the "principles of '98." James Kilpatrick editorialized on the subject in the *Richmond News Leader* in the fall of 1955 and convinced legislators that they could block integration with this doctrine. That Virginians repaired to their past in these circumstances could be predicted. As in 1798, the state rejected outright nullification, but it resolved to interpose itself between its people and the federal government. Because such an idea seemed to belong in a political museum, the federal courts paid no attention to this device. Madison's idea in 1798 showed concern for freedom of speech or protecting civil liberties from federal power. Kilpatrick seemed unconcerned that resisting federal power seriously harmed the civil rights of a large minority of Virginians. During the fracas, E. Blackburn Moore, the powerful speaker of the house introduced a resolution to reject local option. His measure passed easily in the House but died in committee in the Senate. However, a constitutional convention, meeting in Richmond in March 1956 to put into effect the work of the 9 January referendum, failed to endorse local option. In an August special session, the General Assembly approved the Stanley Plan, which required the governor to shut down any school under court edict to integrate and end all state funds from any school that dared to reopen in response to a court order. Emboldened by the support of other Southern conservative politicians that issued a manifesto and Virginia public opinion, Byrd spoke of the need for "Massive Resistance." In 1956 the state took away Arlington County's right to elect its own school board (the only place allowed to vote for members) when that body tried to phase in integration.

In 1957 J. Lindsay Almond, who as the attorney general had been at the center of the storm over integration, beat Republican Ted Dalton. The race was not even close, as it occurred about the time Republican president Dwight Eisenhower sent in the 101st Airborne to force the integration of schools in Little Rock, Arkansas over the objections of the governor of that state. Almond ended up being the governor that would enforce the Stanley Plan in Virginia. In September 1958, the federal courts mandated the integration of schools in Front Royal, Charlottesville, Arlington, and Norfolk. The governor accordingly closed the affected schools. In Norfolk some 10,000 students in three high schools and three junior highs now had no public schools. As the lockout continued, some children went to schools in other cities and others attended ad hoc facilities. The Norfolk School Board tried to get around the state mandate, but voters rejected a proposal to reopen the public schools without state aid. The embittered Norfolk city council voted, with one abstention, to close the city's only black high school. Even Governor Almond thought such action unwarranted. Editor Lenoir Chambers of the Norfolk morning paper received a Pulitzer Prize for his efforts to reopen the schools.

On the same day in January both the state and federal courts decided in favor of reopening schools. The Virginia Court of Appeals based its decision in *Harrison v Day* on the state constitution's requiring public education. The federal district court in Norfolk, with local Walter Hoffman one of the three judges, declared in *James v Almond* that the state's actions violated the 14th Amendment. On 2 February 17 black youngsters entered the reopened schools, without major incident, but so many white rising seniors failed to graduate the following spring that they became known as the "Lost Class of 1959." The next fall two schools in Charlottesville opened with black students in attendance, Judge Paul of that area's district court having granted permission to run segregated schools until that time.

Although both state and federal courts had spoken, Almond appeared ready to resist the possibility of "sadism, sex immorality, and juvenile pregnancy" in the schools. In the end he incurred the wrath of resisters like Harry Byrd by suggesting the legislature accept some integration but minimize its impact by repealing the compulsory education law and by forming a new commission. The commission reported back with a plan for "Freedom of Choice." That proposal returned the power of assigning pupils to the local school boards. Over serious opposition from die-hard Massive Resisters the measure passed by a narrow margin.

When the Supreme Court, as a follow-up of the Brown case, ordered the integration of the schools of Prince Edward County in September 1959, the supervisors cut off funding for public education. White children went to private schools, built with private funds but using state-funded tuition grants. Blacks had no schools until a private association, with the help of Attorney General Robert Kennedy, secured federal aid. The state finally allowed the school buildings to be used. In 1964 the Board of Supervisors reopened the public schools consequent to a Supreme Court mandate. Few whites attended these schools for many years, preferring Prince Edward Academy.

In trying to find Virginia's collective personality around the midpoint of the 20th century, Jean Gottmann, a French geographer, decided that the Old Dominion stood out as a unique state because of its dwelling on the past. A rural background encouraged conservatism and cautiousness. The past made Virginians proud, a bit resistant to change, and respectful of tradition and social order, but change was in the air. The nation to which the state belonged forged ahead to economic hegemony and world power. Try as they might, traditional-minded Virginians would not be able to avoid the trend.

The Frenchman said little about the crisis over integration, but in a sense the partial solution to that problem reflected other changes as well. Unlike other places, Virginia did not need national guardsmen to achieve social justice, because the conservative nature of the people did not lend itself to violence. Virginians proved surprisingly agile in coping with the many changes then underway and others that would ensue.

# Chapter 18

## The Winds of Political Change

As Virginia abandoned Massive Resistance and the civil rights movement gained momentum, the state experienced sustained demographic changes and a shift in party alignment. As liberals played larger roles in the state Democratic Party, Republicans made headway in creating a viable two-party system. With blacks voting in substantial numbers, conservative whites, especially in the Southside, shifted party allegiances, starting a trend that continued in the next decade. Some members of the Byrd organization adapted to the new situation, but the organization's resistance to integration greatly damaged its status, and in the era that followed it simply ceased to be a major political factor.

On a return trip to Virginia in 1968, Jean Gottmann detected change. Population grew rapidly after 1950, mostly due to a "Baby Boom." Now about 75% of the residents lived in urban areas. By 1967, only 8% of the overall number resided on farms, still a bit above the national average, but only just over 90,000 of 1,635,000 worked in agriculture. The number of miners also fell, as those in manufacturing increased. Containerization in the ports increased both imports and exports without adding to the number of longshoremen. Increases could be detected in a wide variety of in white-collar (professionals) and other service positions, which rose from 54% of the workforce in 1950, when Virginia was already running ahead of the nation in this respect, to above 60% in 1967. Personal income also increased faster than the nationally as Virginia edged toward parity. Although Virginia held its own in preserving forests, Gottmann identified problems like urban sprawl and water pollution.

The state's road system also made remarkable strides during this era, due mostly to the Interstate Highway Act passed in the mid-1950s under President Eisenhower. The state authorized agencies to build toll tunnels. Two linked Portsmouth and Norfolk, another one connected south and north Hampton Roads, and the mammoth 17-mile long bridge-tunnel, completed in 1964, joined the Eastern Shore of Virginia with Virginia Beach. By the early 1970s Route 81, the north-south road through the Valley of Virginia, and Route 64, the east-west highway, along with Route 495 circumnavigating the nation's capital and Route 95, hugging close to the Fall Line, were completed.

As the economic pace quickened, political change followed. Richard Nixon, the Republican candidate for president in 1960, narrowly bested the charismatic John Kennedy in the Virginia vote but lost the national election by a narrow margin, as Byrd formally announced his policy of "golden silence," not taking any public position on presidential candidates and Governor Almond favored Kennedy. A Byrd man, Albertis Harrison, was elected governor in 1961, with limited Republican opposition. The Republicans failed to gain any additional seats despite making a solid showing, but they did make credible gains in Assembly races the next year. Midway in Harrison's term in office the winds of change began to blow. In 1964, following the assassination of President Kennedy, the new president Lyndon Johnson, a Democrat from Texas and once thought trustworthy by Virginia conservatives, strongly supported the federal Civil Rights Act of 1964. That act called for equal access to public accommodations, prevented discrimination in public contracts, and promoted integration in schools. Conservative Howard Smith of Virginia added a clause that called for an end to discrimination against women in hiring and employment. Despite filibusters and other maneuvers, the bill passed as amended. In January of that year the 24th Amendment outlawed the poll tax in federal elections. One of the few states with a poll tax, Virginia's substitute residency requirement also failed to pass judicial muster. With the end of the tax, the number of black registered voters jumped by thousands. Over 1,000,000 citizens cast their votes in the 1964 presidential election, over a one-third increase over any previous election. Johnson handily defeated his conservative Republican rival, Barry Goldwater, in Virginia as well as nationally. The Civil Rights Act of 1965 provided for federal supervision of the registration process. And in 1966 the federal courts invalidated the poll tax in state and local elections. A case brought by Evelyn T. Butts of Norfolk, with the help of liberal politician Henry Howell, ended the poll tax for good in *Butt v Harrison*.

Having defeated Goldwater in a landslide, President Johnson launched his Great Society. In addition to civil rights, Congress approved an education act that, under Title I, funneled over a billion dollars for books and special programs for the poor. Related acts protected the wilderness. Medicare and Medicaid rendered medical aid to the elderly and poor respectively. As part of Johnson's program Congress also aided poor preschoolers, helped low-income high school students get ready for college, and assisted the poor in Appalachia. Grants went to cities for various projects. An ambitious program, the War on Poverty reduced, but failed to eradicate, poverty. It stirred up considerable opposition in Virginia. Needless to say, Byrd had grave doubts about the whole business.

The winds of change struck full force in 1966. Having been elected governor in 1965, Mills Godwin staked out a progressive agenda. A member in good standing with Byrd, the lieutenant governor, nonetheless, strongly backed Johnson's reelection in 1964. As governor, Godwin embraced ideas that Harry Byrd once opposed, such as a sales tax. With many municipalities creating their own, Godwin persuaded the General Assembly to pass a 3% tax with 1% returned to the localities. In 1968 the state added another 1%. The resulting increase in revenues allowed for advances in higher education. Four-year colleges and universities received help, and the legislature created the community college system. Within four years 38,000 students attended some 16 new two-year vocational and general education colleges. An educational conference in the fall of 1966 eventually led to the end of "pay as you go." Governor Godwin called for a commission to study constitutional changes, which recommended an easing of restrictions on future borrowing. In a 1968 referendum the electorate approved $81,000,000 in bonds for a variety of projects. In 1969 the Assembly accepted several major changes in the state's constitution, which once approved by the voters in 1970 were made effective on 1 July 1971. The new constitution also prohibited closure of the state's public schools, and in Article XI prioritized the conservation of resources, including clean air and pure water, as well as the development of recreational facilities and the preservation of historical sites. Oyster grounds, long considered public property, could neither be sold nor leased.

The late 1960s also brought renewed interest in the outdoors. In 1966 the state developed a plan under which it added some 36 parks to its system. Within four years the state subscribed over $9,500,000 to acquire Natural Tunnel, Mason's Neck, Smith Mountain Lake, and at least four other sites. Private gifts netted the state Chippokes and three other locations. With earth days and clean air and water legislation, Americans and Virginians reflected a renewed interest in conservation and preservation, including historic sites. In the early 1970s the Assembly took steps to save portions of scenic rivers, and eventually designated over 300 miles out of the thousands of miles in the state.

Over the years the state also materially added to areas designated for the preservation of animal life. Virginia started as early as 1930, when Game and Inland Fisheries acquired a site in Roanoke County, but nothing further happened until the 1950s, when the state acquired several major sites, especially late in that decade. Then in the 1960s and 1970s it added several wildlife management sites and "natural areas." Then the pace of acquisition considerably slackened, except for the work of the Nature Conservancy. In the mid-1970s the Camp Corporation gave conservation a big boost by turning over about 100,000 acres (about half in Virginia) of the Great Dismal Swamp to the Nature Conservancy, land that later became part of the federal domain. In addition, the General Assembly in 1966 passed a law that required owners of strip mines to restore the land under which seams of coal had been extracted, leaving a scarred landscape. A reclamation board eventually regulated these activities.

The Byrd era ended in 1965, when the senior senator, having been reelected in 1964, resigned due to ill health. Although Harrison chose Harry Byrd, Jr., to succeed his father and the young Byrd narrowly beat Armistead Boothe in the Democratic primary the next year, the organization could not survive. William Spong bested the aged Senator A. Willis Robertson that year, and a liberal knocked off conservative Howard Smith in the 8th District Democratic primary. Republicans then won that seat as well as another in the always contentious "Fighting 9th," thus doubling its congressional delegation. In 1968, they added a fifth congressman in the person of G. William Whitehurst, from the second district, and held half the House seats.

As Johnson pushed his domestic program, the situation in Vietnam heated up. Determined to defeat Communist efforts to take over South Vietnam, the president sent in thousands of American troops. By January 1968, it became clear that not all was going well, as people, especially the young, rebelled against the war. Johnson imposed a special tax, but he insisted on carrying on both his Great Society and a war in Southeast Asia. After creating a surge of inflation, he did not run for another term.

The election of 1968 proved to be one of the most divisive in American history. Vice President Hubert Humphrey received the nomination of a fractured Democratic Party and Republicans nominated Richard Nixon. Running as an independent, George Wallace, an Alabama segregationist, carried over 13% of the popular national vote (almost double that percentage in Virginia). He drew many votes as expected in the Southside, the center of Strom Thurmond's strength 20 years earlier, but he also made inroads in normally liberal precincts in the cities, among construction workers and others that were upset about antiwar rhetoric and changing mores among the young. The Democrat ticket garnered only a third of the vote, as Nixon carried the state with less than 44%.

In the wake of their presidential victory, gubernatorial candidate Linwood Holton, a traditional Republican from Big Stone Gap running a campaign of inclusion, beat the Democrats, who were split into three factions as a result of a bitter primary. Moderate William Battle, son of a governor, narrowly defeated liberal Henry Howell in a runoff. Even the normally Democratic AFL-CIO endorsed Holton, who also received an unusually high minority vote. Not all was darkness for the Democrats, however, as they won the race for lieutenant governor with the charismatic J. Sargeant Reynolds and that for attorney general with Andrew Miller, but Reynolds soon died of a brain tumor, depriving the party of a potential unifier. When Holton took office in January 1970, precisely a century had lapsed since the inauguration of the last Republican governor Gilbert Walker. Holton built on the Godwin initiatives and secured small increases in taxes on gasoline and alcohol. Extra money went to schools, mental health centers, and the ports of Hampton Roads. Some Republicans criticized him for finding jobs for minorities and women and not for party regulars. His failure to find a post for Richard Obenshain, a party organizer that had lost in the race for attorney general, irritated conservatives.

After waiting for some time for true integration of the public schools, the courts finally called for busing children out of their neighborhoods to mix the races. In Norfolk, authorities used federal funds to wipe out residential areas that showed signs of integration, a tactic that also minimized the possibilities for integration of the schools. The situation in Richmond became especially troublesome. Conservatives assumed Governor Holton would stand with them against busing. But the governor, who personally opposed busing, took his daughter to her newly assigned Richmond school. Busing would not subside as an issue in Richmond, and thousands of whites fled with their children to live outside the city. When a federal judge decided to create one school district out of the city and its adjacent counties, near panic ensued. Eventually higher courts reversed that ruling.

In 1970 Harry Byrd, Jr., made clear his disenchantment with the Democratic Party by resigning from it and running as an independent. When he refused all overtures to join the Republican Party, Governor Holton called for a convention to nominate a candidate to run against the incumbent and his Democrat rival. In so doing, the governor ran afoul of conservatives in his own party as well as President Nixon. In the election most Republicans and many conservative Democrats gave Byrd an easy victory in the three-way contest. Republicans picked up another seat in the House of Representatives, where they now outnumbered Democrats. In 1972, in the Democratic defeat in the presidential race, moderate Senator William Spong lost to William Scott, whom Democrats had gerrymandered out of a congressional district. Spong, running a lackluster campaign, fell before a media blitz. Both Scott and Nixon rolled to victory in the fall. Scott proved to be a weak senator, but no Virginia Democrats now served in the U.S. Senate, a condition that had not existed since the 1880s. Richard Nixon prepared to enter his second term as president.

The next major achievement for the Republicans occurred in the gubernatorial race in 1973. Mills Godwin, concerned about the liberal tendencies in his party and by the possibility that Henry Howell would be the nominee of that party in the race for governor, entered the lists as a Republican. After the death of

Reynolds in 1971, the liberal Howell had become lieutenant governor as an independent. In 1973 he retained his status as an independent, but the Democratic Party, which his supporters controlled, ran no candidate. "Howlin' Henry" sustained his long-running populist attack on Virginia Electric Power Company and other corporations. He also called for an end to the sales tax on food and nonprescription drugs in part because his opponent had sired the tax in his first administration. Nearly everyone assumed Howell had little chance, but when a poll disclosed the Lieutenant Governor had moved ahead in the race, conservatives rallied with money and media to move Godwin slightly ahead at the end. That a liberal of Howell's stature could garner 49.3% of the vote in conservative Virginia against a former successful governor seemed strange, particularly because he received 90% of the black vote but also did well in precincts generally viewed as Wallace strongholds.

Part of the explanation for Howell's strong showing rests with the Watergate disclosures and with the earlier forced resignation of the Republican vice president, a "carping critic" of liberals, for tax evasion. A one-time losing Republican candidate for Congress and now federal judge, Walter Hoffman, the same judge who handled the federal integration case in 1959, accepted the resignation. Nixon's handling of the Vietnam situation also incurred some disfavor, but his forced resignation in the face of impeachment over obstruction of justice in the Watergate matter gave the Democrats renewed vigor. An oil embargo resulting from war in the Mideast created an energy crisis compounded by inflation in the midst of a recession. Republicans soon lost two congressional seats from Virginia.

Godwin's second term as governor turned out to be one of reaction to a whole set of problems over which the governor had little control. The recession, with its accompanying inflation, put a serious crimp in the state budget, negating pay raises and forcing the legislature to do imaginative financing. The energy crisis produced long gas lines and high electric bills. Fuel stored at the Cheatham Annex (a naval site on the Peninsula) deteriorated and had to be moved. The governor allowed individual purchases of gasoline only on alternative days and agreed to the federally mandated maximum speed of 55 mph. The State Corporation Commission allowed VEPCO price increases, a policy the public constantly complained about. All the governor could do was to observe that Virginia had several nuclear facilities either built or coming on line at Surry and North Anna and that the future lay with nuclear power. Godwin also disputed with the federal Department of Health, Education, and Welfare over numerical goals and quotas in integrating higher education and differing wages paid for building Route 66 from the new Dulles Airport to the District of Columbia.

In the midst of all these problems, Hopewell's sewage system broke down because of a pesticide known as Kepone, produced by a company under contract to Allied Chemical. The state tore down the plant and tested workers, nearby residents, and fish in the James River. Federal authorities found unacceptable levels of the chemical, and the governor closed the river for fin or shell fishing. Later, when shad proved toxic, netting them was also banned. The governor directed the State Department of Agriculture and Commerce to inspect bluefish and other species from the waters of the river and the Chesapeake Bay. The state never did find a way to dredge the river of this contaminant, but in time the levels of toxicity in the fish fell, allowing a partial revival of the fishing industry. In 1977 the federal government declared Virginia to be declared a disaster area twice, first for heavy rain and then for drought, but the entire time might be considered a disaster. Watergate and its attendant crises brought crosswinds, but careful navigation brought Virginians through the storm.

As the nation approached its bicentennial in 1976, it seemed caught in a negative frame of mind. People found something wrong with nearly every sector: the military, medicine, education, business, government at all levels, and religion. Poll after superficial poll showed a high level of discontent. Governor Godwin took this "Crisis of Spirit" seriously, assuming that it came from the weakness of leaders and not institutional failings. That year Jimmy Carter, a peanut producer from Georgia, bested Republican Gerald Ford for the presidency. A moderate, Carter took much of the South, losing Virginia by a narrow margin. As a southern Baptist and farmer, he did better than recent Democrat presidential candidates in rural areas. In office Carter discovered Americans were suffering from "malaise," whose symptoms sounded a lot like the disease Godwin had detected a bit earlier.

In the election for governor in 1977 John Dalton, the son of Ted Dalton, easily defeated Democrat Howell, who raised conflict of interest charges against the lieutenant governor, which proved suspicious but largely groundless. Republican charges about Howell proved even more spurious. It probably made little difference, for the public had tired of the indefatigable Howell. During Dalton's time in office, conditions calmed a bit, though the nation experienced another energy crisis, this time related to a revolution in Iran. Southwest Virginia and the nation experienced one of the longest coal strikes in history, idling some 13,000 Virginians and starting just as Godwin was about to leave office. On a more positive note, Dalton helped form the foundation for northern Virginia's future foray into new technology, with special funding for George Mason University. He also resolved problems with the federal government over integration of higher education.

In 1978 the Republicans nominated Obenshain, one of the architects of the modern Republican Party, Over Secretary of the Navy John Warner in the race for the U.S. Senate seat, but when Obenshain died in an airplane crash, the party's central committee reluctantly turned to Warner, who narrowly defeated Democrat Miller in the fall election. Well-known actress Elizabeth Taylor, Warner's wife at the time, attracted more attention than the issues. Warner was not as committed a conservative as party leaders wanted, but he retained the seat through several more elections. As a member a military committee, he assured Hampton Roads and national defense a prime position over the years. In 1982 Congressman Paul Trible triumphed over a moderate Democrat in gaining the seat vacated by the one-time independent Harry Byrd, Jr. With Ronald Reagan's victory over Jimmy Carter in 1980, during which Virginia voted solidly for the former governor of California, Virginia Republicans, one might assume, would be ready to achieve their objective of a total takeover of the Old Dominion.

# Chapter 19

# Currents and Crosscurrents

The last two decades of the 20th century brought some relief from the turmoil of the 1960s and 1970s. On the whole, conditions materially improved along with the confidence of the people. Americans and Virginians rode a strong current toward a better society, as negative crosscurrents continued to buffet the people and the ships of state.

During the 1980s and 1990s, despite some rockiness, the economy grew, with a proportional decline in non-service employment and the appearance of new lines of work. Mines produced over 46,000,000 tons of coal in 1990, but the industry needed considerably fewer miners, as mechanization and strip mining allowed considerable growth. The United Mine Workers made a comeback to represent some 13,000 out of 23,000 coal miners in the state by 1977, but in the 1980s membership fell as the number of miners decreased. By 1988 there were only about 11,000 miners. Those working with wood products remained at relatively high levels. Newport News secured a Canon plant, whose workforce rose to near 2,000, and the giant shipbuilder in that city still made carriers for the Navy. The Ford plant in Norfolk, now making trucks, provided several thousand jobs. Norfolk Southern (a merger of two major railways) controlled thousands of miles of track across much of the nation from its headquarters in Norfolk. In 1985 two businessmen created America Online, based in Northern Virginia, and changed communication. As the new technology took over, older industries, such as textiles and furniture making, faded away, victims of a global economy.

The number of large corporations and their workers dropped. In Richmond, Philip Morris cut its workforce by about 40% during the 1990s, but in 2005 it planned a large research park in the city. Alcoa took over Reynolds Metals and closed part of the local operation. A larger corporation took over A.H. Robins Pharmaceuticals, a mainstay of the local economy. Local firms have become part of larger national or even international organizations, especially so in banking and other financial industries. On the other hand, several smaller companies emerged in a wide variety of fields, including telecommunications. Overall Richmond's unemployment rate flutters at about half the national rate.

During Ronald Reagan's two terms in the presidency, starting in 1981, the economy overcame high interest rates and a recession to ride a crest of apparent prosperity. The energy troubles of 1974 and 1979 did not recur for the rest of the 20th century. The destructive inflation of the earlier time also came under control despite large federal deficits. During the early 1980s, many businesses streamlined management. Unemployment ran to 11% in late 1982, but once the economy stabilized, workers found new careers, though often at lower-paying jobs. Reagan and Congress downsized the nonmilitary side of the federal government and curtailed some of the War on Poverty, but Democrats prevented a complete undoing of the Great Society. Those in poverty rose from about 11% to over 14%, but costly entitlements like Medicare and Medicaid kept most of the elderly out of poverty.

Under Reagan, Congress also lowered taxes and the military received a boost. Revenues grew, but not anywhere near the rate of increased federal spending, resulting in annual deficits of over $200 billion, not counting Social Security surpluses. Tax cuts helped the rich amass even greater fortunes while people of middling income held on. Relaxation of federal rules on financial institutions under Carter and Reagan led to a crisis in the savings and loan industry in the latter's second term. A rising stock market dropped suddenly in 1987, but did not signal a declining economy.

Virginia did fairly well during the Reagan years. Although Congress held the line on social spending, Virginia benefited from defense expenditures. The Old Dominion had more defense contracts and military in proportion to its population than any state in the union. Virginia's senators and congressmen from northern Virginia and Hampton Roads made sure their constituents retained a big stake in the defense budget. The military buildup under Reagan ultimately paid off when reformers took over the Soviet Union. Unable to compete with the United States militarily, the Soviets ended the Cold War by sharply reducing offensive missiles. Reagan's successor, George Bush, and the world watched as the old Soviet Union and its empire disintegrated.

Bush, who had been elected over a liberal Democrat in 1988, took office as the economy slowed. He scored a popular success in leading a coalition against Iraq to force its withdrawal from Kuwait. Thousands of military from Hampton Roads participated in this successful effort. Despite a pledge not to raise taxes, Bush agreed to an increase in the marginal rates on the wealthy and an unpopular tax on income on Social Security. Despite a high popularity rating at the time of the Kuwait crisis, Bush lost the election to William Clinton, the governor of Arkansas, in 1992, thus ending a 12-year reign of Republicans in the White House.

During the 1980s political currents carried Virginia in two directions at the same time. The year after the nation and Virginia elected the Republican Reagan to be president Virginia picked Lieutenant Governor Charles Robb, a moderate Democrat, over Attorney General J. Marshall Coleman. Running a centrist campaign, Robb separated himself from the liberal wing of the party without alienating the old Howell people. Coleman labored under his acceptance of numerical objectives for integrating the races in higher education. The religious right, traditional Republicans, Democrats for Reagan, and others were unable to unify to beat back the Democrat challenge.

Moreover, the process continued in the next two elections for governor. After overwhelmingly favoring Reagan's reelection in 1984, Virginia voted for Democrat Gerald Baliles for governor the next year. Even more remarkably, the Democrats managed to elect Doug Wilder the first black governor in 1989, a year after voting for Republican George Bush for president. The Democrats also kept working margins in both houses of the Assembly and usually held other statewide elected posts. Eventually Robb took one of the U.S. Senate seats. The congressional delegation remained evenly split.

Moral issues came to the forefront during these times. A religious agenda appeared at earlier times in the state's history, as, for example, when the largest Protestant denominations banded together to support laws against alcohol, gambling, prize fighting, and the end to Blue Laws. The end of prohibition, the creation of a state boxing commission, and a state court of appeals decision to allow professional baseball and other forms of entertainment in 1933 and 1934 during the Great Depression proved to be major setbacks for these organized religious efforts.

In more recent times, Virginia spawned two prominent religious organizations with political agendas. Pat Robertson, the nearly destitute son of a U.S. senator, started a television ministry in Portsmouth with the help of donations from some 700 supporters ("the 700 Club"). His Christian network and Regent University, based in Virginia Beach, carried religious programs and provided higher education. He sought freedom of choice in education and tuition vouchers. Many of his supporters concentrated on the issue of abortion that attained attention in the wake of a 1973 Supreme Court decision. In the mid-1980s Robertson ran for the Republican nomination in 1988. Failing to find the necessary support, he later formed the Christian Coalition to carry on his political platform.

Jerry Falwell, the minister of Thomas Road Baptist Church in Lynchburg with over 800 members, also founded Liberty University and the Moral Majority, which sought to re-instill moral values in Americans. People of this persuasion showed up at conventions and primaries of both parties. Falwell and his followers sought to end abortion and pass an amendment to allow school-sponsored prayer. By the early 1980s, with Reagan as president, they found a home in the Republican organization. Falwell found free enterprise sanctioned in scripture, paving the way for his forces to join with economic conservatives. While Democrats worried about a polluted environment, Falwell and others expressed concern about polluted minds

The "religious right" lamented the drift away from two-parent families, feminism, the lax code regarding sex and drugs, gay rights, liquor by the drink (passed in the early 1970s), and the demise of Sunday blue laws (passed by a combination of popular votes under local option and court action). Religious interests also took a blow when in 1988 the legislature, with Republican support, approved pari-mutuel horse racing with betting parlors under local option. Residents of Roanoke stymied efforts to place parlors in their jurisdiction. Although investors established a track in New Kent County, the kind of interest in traditional horse racing that flourished among urban Virginians a century ago has thus far failed to materialize. The state itself went into the gambling business by creating a lottery, the profits from which were supposed to aid schools. Voters approved a constitutional amendment in 1970 to allow state lotteries and ratified legislation passed in 1987. By the end of the century, the lottery returns to the state averaged about $350,000,000 annually. In November 2000 a referendum required all funds so derived to be disbursed to the localities for education.

In 1983 Virginia joined several other states as well as the District of Columbia to coordinate efforts to combat pollution in the Chesapeake Bay. Citizens had created the Chesapeake Bay Foundation in 1964, with about 2,000 members in its formative years. By the end of the century it had over 80,000 members. Its efforts to "Save the Bay" convinced the federal Environmental Protection Agency to advise several governors to support the Chesapeake Bay Preservation Act. Governor Baliles also set goals of reducing phosphorus and nitrogen levels as well as preventing oil spills. The Assembly also created a secretary of natural resources. As of this writing, alien oysters are being introduced to act as water filters. Few Virginians object to the idea of saving the ecology, but how much they will be willing to pay for a sustained effort remains to be seen.

Baliles called for the legislature to raise the gasoline tax in order to finance a bond issue for road construction. Rejecting a bond issue, the Assembly raised the gasoline tax 2.5 cents and the sales tax, along with other incidental taxes, to finance over $400,000,000 annually. Despite all this, traffic jams afflicted Northern Virginia and Hampton Roads well into the next century. Efforts to persuade people to accept alternative transportation systems found little support. The governor and the legislature struck a blow against drunk driving by lowering the tolerable level for blood alcohol from .15 to .10 (later it would be lowered to .08). Drivers and passengers had to wear seat belts.

Most governors and state legislators, both Republican and Democrat, favored spending state funds to court businesses. Governor Baliles expanded international trade. Aid to ports began as early as the 1920s with the Hampton Roads Port Commission (renamed the Virginia Port Authority in 1925). The governor's numerous trade missions increased Virginia exports. Even the state's contribution to museums and other cultural entities may be seen as not only a promotion for tourism, but also as a drawing card for industries.

Funding all these projects fared fairly well in times of prosperity. Without any major increase in taxes since the 1960s (and, indeed, with piecemeal reductions) the Old Dominion, like most states, collected more and more revenue. Governors and legislators directed funds into education, transportation, tourism, and a host of activities. Problems arose only when the national, and therefore, the state economy sagged or when politicians overreached.

The first happened just after Wilder, the state's first black governor, won the election in 1989 over Republican Marshall Coleman. Some years earlier when asked when a black would be elected to statewide office in the commonwealth, Dr. Larry Sabato, the state's premier pundit, jokingly replied "when hell freezes over." Sometime later, reporter Dwayne Yancey wrote *When Hell Froze Over*, which covered Wilder's election as lieutenant governor. Still later the voters picked Wilder to be governor. Winning in an election closer than polls anticipated, Wilder proved to be conservative in dealing with the recession that accompanied George Bush's term as president. Wilder had a running feud with senator Robb, who eked out reelection to the U.S. Senate in a three-way contest in 1994 with his principal opponent, Republican candidate Oliver North, deeply implicated in a deal that used money obtained from Iranians to fund anticommunist rebels in Nicaragua. Robb then met his political Waterloo in the 2000 U.S. Senate election against George Allen.

Republican George Allen, elected governor in 1993 over Democrat candidate Attorney General Mary Sue Terry, encountered less difficulty in his term because the national and state economies experienced low unemployment and solid growth. Allen could, therefore, direct money at state prisons to control the crime wave sweeping the nation and state. Starting in the 1960s, crime rates rose swiftly due to the greater use of mind-altering drugs. The spread of crack cocaine in the late 1980s accounted for another sharp rise in crime, as Richmond gained infamy as a "murder capital." The legislature increased jail time and built two "super max" prisons. By century's end the state had so many cells that it rented out space for criminals from other states. Some critics complained that far too many of the inmates, a disproportionate number being black, had not committed violent acts, but had been caught up in the war on drugs. The relative absence of career criminals on the streets, the availability to find work in the growing economy, enforcement of laws against carrying unauthorized guns in Richmond, restrictions on the number of weapons purchased on the state level and federal efforts to keep guns out of the hands of felons helped reduce the number of murders and other serious crimes. Capital punishment remained a central issue. For a time the Supreme Court forbade executions for murder. In the late 1970s Virginia and other states satisfied the federal court with their procedures, and in 1982 the state reactivated its electric chair (later it employed lethal injections). Over the next two decades the state killed prisoners at a pace close to that of the states leading in that category. In 2000 the state retained some of the toughest restraints on appeals in the country.

In other matters, the booming economy helped, with heavy Republican prompting, to reform the welfare system. States now had more control over the matter, and Virginia, like many states, toughened work requirements, limited pay outs, and pursued "deadbeat dads." Allen also expanded the recruitment of high tech businesses. The amount of new capitalization in the state in the 1990s paled beside anything seen before. It was especially noticeable in Northern Virginia and around Richmond. But fiber optics companies also spun from proximity to Virginia Tech. The economy benefited from increasing incomes and tax revenues as a result. In education, the Allen administration secured major changes in lower and higher levels. Prior governors had worked on upgrading collegiate education for teachers. Allen secured Standards of Learning tests for several levels of primary and secondary education to be implemented over the next several years. And he imposed a freeze on tuition hikes at public colleges and universities, as the state increased funding for 300,000 students.

The Allen administration confronted a problem in coeducation. The federal Fourth Circuit Court of Appeals found VMI in violation of the 14th Amendment in not admitting women. VMI and the state claimed that women would have difficulty with the "rat line" and other practices designed to promote camaraderie. The state underwrote a special school of leadership for women at Mary Baldwin College in an attempt to satisfy the court but to no avail. Because carrying on as a private entity meant no state or federal aid, the school's board of trustees accepted women. By this time all public colleges in Virginia were coeducational, a process that commenced in 1918 with the College of William and Mary and reached a peak in the late 1960s and early 1970s, as the teachers' colleges admitted males. Athletic programs at these coed institutions also became subject to Title IX, part of a 1972 amendment to the Civil Rights Act of 1964. Though not enforced immediately, this measure ultimately required both lower and higher education to prorate support for sports to each sex. With increased funding, women's sports grew rapidly.

The governor enthusiastically endorsed a proposal by the Disney Corporation to develop an historic theme park near Manassas, which would give Virginia a third major tourist theme park to go along with Kings Dominion, north of Richmond, and Busch Gardens near Williamsburg. The Assembly considered an aid package (somehow a defeated proposal for riverboat gambling became entwined in the tale), but residents, some of them quite wealthy, grumbled about the possible influx of traffic and other undesirable changes. Historians and other preservationists worried that the project might endanger the famed battlefield. The state of Virginia as conservator of the past ran directly into the Old Dominion as economic developer. Disney pulled the plug on the proposal.

The second Republican to be elected governor in the 1990s, James Gilmore easily beat Democrat opposition in 1997 by calling for a rolling back of the local property tax on vehicles. During his term, Republicans gained control of both houses of the Assembly. Everything went smoothly until the stock markets declined in 2000. As a state heavily dependent on the income tax, revenues fell short. Gilmore had underestimated the amount of state money needed to pay back the localities for removing the car tax. Late in his term he faced an impasse with the State Senate (including fellow Republicans) over further reduction of car tax, resulting in the Assembly's failure to adopt a budget. Under Gilmore, for the first time since the 1880s, representation on some of the boards of visitors of the public universities became a matter of party preference. Governor Gilmore even made partisan the Chesapeake Bay Tunnel Commission, as those that hoped to develop the Eastern Shore vied against those who saw the move as an invasion of their area.

That project, considered one of the major manmade wonders of the world, opened in 1964 under the auspices of a state-run commission, which issued some $200,000,000 in bonds, with no government funds involved. It required the construction of two long tunnels as well as one high bridge along with the main bridge, all covering some seventeen miles. Engineers planned for some 2,500 piles for the bridge, all of which had to be properly aligned. In the construction phase, builders used a huge pile driver, the "Big D." An Ash Wednesday storm in 1962, however, destroyed that machine, delaying the project. A "Two-headed Monster" helped workers cut the piles to proper heights. Huge slab setters then created the bed for the roadway. Two large manmade islands had to be created so that 30 some tubes, each roughly three hundred feet long, made of steel and covered with concrete, could create each tunnel. During this phase another storm damaged the work site.

After overcoming all sorts of obstacles, the Chesapeake Bay Bridge Tunnel opened in April 1964, thereby vastly improving transportation along the East Coast and linking more closely the Eastern Shore to mainland Virginia. Although once severely damaged by a U.S. Navy ship, the facility proved a valuable resource. Having proved to be a financial success, the commission built parallel bridges in the 1990s. Some argue that lowering the $10 toll (factoring in inflation means that the effective rate has dropped some over the years) would increase traffic and help development.

Virginia experienced a growth of real income throughout the entire century. Starting out well behind the nation, Virginians increased individual wealth by a factor of five between 1900 and 1930, as the per capita national wealth quadrupled. In 1981 income of Virginians finally exceeded the national average and soon rose to 14th place. Pay in Hampton Roads and much of the rural part of the state, remains low, but high incomes in northern Virginia account for the state's relatively high standing.

Some experts argue that the state needs to put more money into education, noting that neighboring North Carolina is now paying its teachers more than the same receive in the Old Dominion. Critics point to a research center in North Carolina. Several studies show that Virginia taxes are comparatively low considering income levels of its residents (state revenues from taxes amount to about 10% of income compared to a national average of about 14%). Some say the state could lure more corporate headquarters by providing more amenities to residents. Others think low taxes encourage vital businesses to locate in the state.

Census data for 2000 reflects overall growth and a degree of stability. The state's population now exceeds some 7,000,000. Virginia has roughly the same share of the nation's people as it had in 1990. Thus its number of congressmen recently remains at 11, the number based on the 1990 census. Virginia also pursues the national trend toward diversity. While the percent of blacks remained essentially the same, the number and percentage of Hispanics, Asians, and others rose. Although blacks have a majority in several core cities, the proportion of nonwhites in the suburbs grew. Whites still comprise nearly five of every seven residents of the state. Well over half the total population of the state may be considered suburban. Fairfax County has nearly 970,000 people and Prince William County around 280,000. Nearby Loudoun County had a 97% increase, as northern Virginia passed the million and a half mark. Virginia Beach now tops 425,000, and fast-rising Chesapeake had almost 200,000. Henrico and Chesterfield counties have about 260,000 each. Meanwhile, the older core cities slid, with Norfolk at not quite 235,000 and Richmond falling below 200,000. Recent data suggests a continuation of this trend into the 21st century. Between April 2000 and July 2001, northern Virginia gained close to 60% of a state increase of about 110,000 people. About half of the increase in Northern Virginia took place in Loudoun County, the second most rapidly growing county in the country.

Virginians are concentrated in three main areas. Northern Virginia has about 1,500,000, a considerably higher number than in 1990. Richmond and its three most immediate suburban counties have about 700,000, also an appreciably greater number than ten years earlier, but not as big as the increase in northern Virginia. The eight cities of Hampton Roads have about 1,500,000, reflecting only a slight rise from 1990. Over half of the state's population resides in these three areas, which covers but a fraction of the total landmass of the state. Moreover, the growth of the Richmond area and Northern Virginia accounts for much of the increase in population for the whole state. Big percentage increases showed up in Stafford and Spotsylvania, nearly 40 miles south of the Potomac and in Hanover and Powhatan counties near Richmond.

New Kent County also picked up population, as the settled portions between Richmond and Hampton Roads moved closer to each other. Newcomers are taking up residence in numbers across the York River.

As Northern Virginia, Richmond, and Hampton Roads move towards each other, the state will ultimately come to possess a "Suburban Corridor." Geographers detected a movement toward an "Urban Corridor" over thirty years ago, but substantial rural gaps remain between the major population centers. Now suburbia blankets once rural areas with residents, as core cities lose the number of residents per square mile. The overall density of population for the state has risen, but only a few areas are materially affected by the increase.

In the late 1970s the city of Virginia Beach drew an imaginary "Green Line," below which development would be discouraged. Special tax incentives helped slow growth, but suburban pressures continue. The city also struggles to create a downtown and thus an identity as something other than a suburb. The Beach improved its chances for more development when, at considerable cost, it overcame legal hurdles thrown up by North Carolina and some Virginia localities to tap water at Lake Gaston. In the 1950s and 1960s Virginia Power built two dams along the Roanoke River in North Carolina. One of these created Lake Gaston, on a small arm that branched into Virginia. The construction of the pipeline to that branch gave the city opportunities for development that did not depend on Norfolk's water or require desalinization. Virginia Beach also pioneered in finding innovative uses of old dumps. When the city came into being in 1963, it inherited a huge trash pile in what had been Princess Anne County. Leaders planned for an unusual sanitary landfill that would not only be covered with the proper amount of soil but also produced a park of some 165 acres in 1971, including a lake, with fishing and boating, plus tennis courts, picnic grounds, and parking. So successful was Mount Trashmore that the city currently is working on another site for a second mountain of trash.

The story of one site suffices to encapsulate Virginia's peculiar way of preserving history in a changing environment. In 1613 Englishmen settled a community on the James River, later labeled Shirley Hundred. This corporate tobacco plantation soon lost most of its residents to the Indian Massacre of 1622, but in the 18th century one of the famous Carters built the still-existing mansion, where in the next century Robert E. Lee (whose mother was a Carter) spent considerable time. The plantation, of course, relied heavily on slave labor, leading a Carter that opposed slavery to yield control of the estate to other members of the family. When intensive tobacco production wore out the soil early in the 19th century, the owner shifted to more diversified farming. After the Civil War, which caused considerable damage, the Carter family kept control of much of their acreage, unlike many neighbors that sold to Northerners, and opened their home to the public to supplement income from farming. The most recent Carter to own and manage the place had sludge dumped on part of his estate to create a field that can be rented for playing polo. In addition, scows, loaded with New York garbage, unload on the riverfront to distribute their cargoes at another place in Charles City County—all to attain further revenue to keep this historic home open.

One factor that tends to slow down change in Virginia is the presence of a strong desire to preserve the state's heritage. No state has more historic estates and battlefield sites in proportion to its population. The blending of preservation with tourism that first developed in a major way in the 1920s continues to play a major role in public policy and in other aspects of life in the Old Dominion.

Where once a few thousand native peoples hunted and farmed a wilderness, Europeans harnessed the land for greater production. Tobacco, field corn, sweet corn in the 20th century, cotton, peanuts, and soybeans (introduced well into the 20th century) can be seen in the Southside. Hay still grows in the Valley and tomatoes on the Eastern Shore, but much of central Virginia is now in forest (Route 60 west of Richmond), and even in agricultural areas, much land remains fallow or forested. Coal still comes from the mountains, in varying amounts. Richmond still makes millions of cigarettes, but many growers have stopped producing the weed. Lynnhaven oysters ceased for a time but are making comeback. Princess Anne turkeys seem extinct, but Smithfield hams are still tasty.

In some cases, sites have been returned to their more natural state. Early in the 20th century, private and semipublic interests constructed dams across the state, mostly to create electric power. In 1915 a power company built a dam at Balcony Falls along the James as it passes through the Blue Ridge. After years of service, the facility shut down and in 1969, after Hurricane Camille backed several feet of water into Glasgow, the company destroyed the dam. More recently, the dam that once stood above Fredericksburg on the Rappahannock was removed.

One has but to look at any recent detailed map of the state to note changes regarding in land use by various levels of government. Interstates and urban roads such as 195, 264, 464, 495, 564, 581, and 664 (all colored blue on the map). Several bridges and tunnels, all now part of the interstate system move traffic (albeit sometimes slowly), with most tolls removed in the 1970s. Electric trolleys disappeared just after World War II and railroad passenger service is now quite restricted.

One state map uses green to designate federal forests and state and national parks. Big green blotches can be seen, especially in the west, denoting a national park and two huge national forests. National parks honor the Jamestown settlement, the victory of Yorktown, and the dead of the Civil War. The latter has the National Military Park on the outskirts of Petersburg, smaller parks southeast and east of Richmond, and at least four sizeable parks in the Fredericksburg area. In the extreme southeastern part of the state, a national wildlife refuge occupies about 50,000 acres on all sides of Lake Drummond in the Dismal Swamp. Thousands of birdwatchers and other naturalists visit the site every year. Federal wildlife refugees can also be found near Chincoteague in Accomac County on the Eastern Shore and in the lower part of Virginia Beach.

Since the 1930s Virginia has added substantially to its recreational park sites. In the late 1960s Occoneechee State Park appeared on the banks of the giant Kerr Reservoir, created by the damming of the Roanoke River below Clarksville. Even though the waters now cover the once-existing island where a tribe was nearly exterminated by Bacon and his men in 1676, residents of modern Virginia can enjoy nature as modified by man as they recall that natives once roamed these lands. More recently, the defenders of the park blocked an effort to turn part of the park into a golf course. A few miles to the west, marked on maps as another spot of green, the state also runs the Staunton River State Park. Buggs Island Lake, another product of a dam built by the U.S. Army Corps of Engineers, lacks a state park, but as in the case of the Kerr Reservoir, its construction covered sites used by a native culture that possibly dated as far back as 15,000 years.

Also in the early 1970s, the state permitted what is now Dominion Power to create Lake Anna on the North Anna River, which separates Spotsylvania and Louisa counties, to act as a cooling reservoir for its nuclear reactors. As part of this arrangement, the state ended up with a park on the manmade lake on the north shore opposite the power plant. As of this writing, Dominion Power is considering adding more reactors.

Virginia contains about 100 federal military facilities, also usually depicted in green on maps. When the government recently considered closing bases as a cost-cutting measure, a Virginia newspaper produced a map showing some eighteen installations in the Hampton Roads area and another twelve in the rest of the state, all potentially on the closure list. Of the twelve, half of them were situated in northern Virginia.

The state also has dozens of parks that provide a variety of recreational uses from camping to water sports. Many of these came on line during the Depression, but Virginia added facilities over the years until it now has the best park system in the country given the small amount of money the state invests in them. As noted earlier, Virginia has numerous wildlife management preserves, all also marked in green on the map of the state. Every city and several counties also have lands set aside for parks. Richmond, for example has several hundred acres spread along the James River.

As a diverse state, Virginia reflects many cultural trends, including those in entertainment. The Appalachian part of the state contributed to country music (the Carter family) and bluegrass (Bill Stanley). In the 1930s A.P. Carter roamed the mountains, tracking down ballads and indigenous tunes. This haunting music, often with strong religious roots mixing optimism and occasional deep sadness, reflected the overall culture and the struggles experienced by its people. Patsy Cline from Winchester in the Valley of Virginia became the biggest celebrity in the 1950s, singing numerous songs that focused on the implicit turmoil of relations between the sexes. Virginia also produced famous black musicians and dancers, such as Bill

Robinson (Bojangles), from Richmond, and Pearl Bailey and Ella Fitzgerald out of Newport News, but they developed their careers in other parts of the nation.

The state has produced a lengthy list of sports stars. High school and college programs trained dozens of professional baseball, basketball, and football celebrities, despite the absence of any major professional teams. The geography of Virginia, along with the political decision to stop annexation in the 1960s, prevented the rise of any unified major city that possessed the ability to finance such teams.

Virginia has come a long way since the Spanish first set foot on these shores in the 16th century. Over 400 years ago the English implanted Anglican culture. As Native American life waned, English characteristics, especially those of the English West Country influenced life in Virginia around the middle of the 17th century, but the climate and soil encouraged residents to produce a unique society. Africans slaves, Scots-Irish, and Germans came by the thousands, along with a few hundred Huguenots. Still later, in the middle of the 19th century, Irish and another wave of Germans made their way into Virginia, followed later by Eastern and Southern Europeans and other ethnic groups in the early 20th century. Later in the 20th century Asians and Hispanic people brought elements of their culture. All have contributed to the overall culture, but in large measure the foundation for Virginia's political system came from English culture, altered by the physical characteristics nature provided.

The relationship of mankind and nature has been playing out in Virginia for some time. The first Virginians lived close to nature and modified the physical landscape and the natural resources only minimally due to comparatively small numbers and a primitive lifestyle. With over ten times as many residents as occupied the same area at the time of the founding of the nation, current residents put tremendous pressure on the land and its bountiful resources. The end of the 20th century found Virginia, like much of the civilized world, trying to balance environmental concerns, prosperity, and even human rights. Despite all these changes, the land and its people survive, now facing threats from terrorists, climate change, and other potential dangers.

In 2007, Virginia celebrated its 400th anniversary of the English implantation on these shores as well as the centennial of the exposition that commemorated the 300th birthday of that English settlement. One can only hope that the present generation possesses the resolve and the capacity to adapt exhibited by our forbearers to allow future Virginians to celebrate the 500th anniversary of this noted event.

# INDEX

Jeffries, Jim, 145
Jesuits, 10, 36
Johnson, Andrew, 121–23
Johnson, Chapman, 79
Johnson, Jack, 145
Johnson, Lyndon, 174–76
Johnston, Joseph, 114
Johnston, Mary, 133, 150
Jones, John Paul, 59
Jones, William, 145
*Journey to the Land of Eden* (Byrd II), 42
*Journey to the Mines* (Byrd II), 42
Jouett, Jack, 61
Judiciary Act, 70
June Laws, 22, 26

Kaskaskia, 58
Kemper, James L., 125
Kemp's Landing, 55
Kendall, George, 12
Kennedy, John F., 174
Kennedy, John P., 93
Kennedy, Robert, 173
Kent Island, 17, 18
*The Kentuckian in New York* (Caruthers), 93
Kentucky Resolution, 69
Kepone, 177
Kerr Dam, 162
Kerr Reservoir, 185
Key, Elizabeth, 33
Key, V.O., 170
King William's War, 34
Kings Dominion, 182
Knights of Labor, 128
Knights of Pythias, 139
"Knights of the Golden Horseshoe," 37
*Knights of the Golden Horseshoe* (Kennedy), 93
Know-Nothing(ism), 109
Ku Klux Klan, 122, 156

Ladies Benevolent Society, 139
Lafayette, Marquis de, 61
*laissez faire*, 49
Lake Drummond, 5, 185
Lake Gaston, 184
Lamb, William, 134
Lancastrian School, 89
Lane, Ralph, 11
Langhorne, Nancy, 127, 141
Langhorne, Orra, 133, 141, 150
Langley, 152
Langston, John Mercer, 128
"Last Gathering of Giants," 78
*Lawes, Divine, Morall and Martiall*, 13
Layden, John, 27
Lederer, John, 20
Lee, Charles, 58
Lee County, 145
Lee, Fitzhugh, 128, 142
Lee, Francis Lightfoot, 57
Lee, Henry "Light Horse Harry," 67
Lee, Richard Henry, 57, 67
Lee, Robert E., 69, 112–21, 145, 184

Leesburg, 95
Leesburg and Alexandria Turnpike, 137
Leesburg Pike, 97
Lejeune, John, 160
Letcher, John, 110–11
*Letters of a British Spy* (Wirt), 92
Lewis, Andrew, 53, 56
Lewis County, 80
Lewis, Ivey Foreman, 148
Lewis, John, 41
Lewis, Meriwether, 70
Lexington, Virginia, 55, 88, 91, 92, 93, 97, 110, 118, 138
Liberia, 101, 103, 106
*Liberty* (Virginia naval ship), 59
Liberty Hall Academy, 65
Liberty University, 180
Lincoln, Abraham, 99, 110–16, 118, 119–22
Lindsay, Lewis, 123
literacy, 63, 90, 121, 130, 131, 141, 150
Literary Fund, 89, 126, 147
literature, 90, 92, 93, 102–104, 141, 142
Little Round Top, 115
Locke, John, 35, 48, 79
Long Assembly, 22
Longstreet, James, 115
Longwood College, 127
Loudoun and Hampshire railroad, 95
Loudoun County, 78, 89, 97, 111, 112, 117, 183
Louisiana Purchase, 70, 73
Louis XIV, 23
Louisa County, 128, 185
Louveste, Mary, 113
Low Moor Iron Co., 136
Lower Norfolk County, 19, 21, 23, 27, 28
Lower Valley of Virginia (northern), 6, 29, 58, 114, 120, 121, 147
Loyalists, 19, 20, 53, 55–61, 64, 65, 101, 155
Ludwell, Philip, 20, 21, 23, 37, 38
Luther, Martin, 11
Lunenburg County, 40
Lynchburg, 77, 82, 92, 96, 97, 104, 107, 109, 111, 116, 118, 125, 127, 128, 136, 139, 140, 141, 143, 169, 180
Lynch, Judge, 155
Lynnhaven, 59, 133
Lynnhaven Bay, 72
Lynnhaven oysters, 184

Macabees, 139
Macon's Bill #2, 71
Madison, Dolley, 72
Madison, James, 42, 43, 49, 50, 57, 58, 63–73, 75, 78, 172
"Magic City," 135, 138, 140
Magruder, John, 114
Mahone, William, 82, 118, 124–28, 134, 145
Makamie, Francis, 35
Malvern Hill, 114
Manakin Town, 23
Manassas, 118, 182
Manassas Junction, 115
Manassas Rail Road, 96, 112
Manchester, 95
manitou, 10
Mann, William Hodges, 147–50; Mann Act, 147

Manteo, 11
Mapp, Walter, 149, 154, 156; Mapp Act, 149
Marbury, William, 70; *Marbury v Madison*, 70
Marion, 159, 169
maritime rights, 40, 72
Marshall, George C., 163
Marshall, John, 67, 70, 71, 73, 74, 78, 79, 109
Martha Washingtonians, 88
Martin-Brandon Hundred, 14
Martin, Thomas Staples, 143, 145, 147, 149, 154
Martin's Hundred, 14, 15
Martinsburg, 97
Martinsville, 158, 171
Martinsville Seven, 171
*Martin v Hunter Lessee*, 73
Mary, Queen of England, 23
Mason, George, 43, 53, 57, 63, 66, 67
Mason, James M, 108
Mason, John M., 108, 109
Mason, John Y., 77
Mason's Neck (park), 175
Massacre of 1622, 184
Massacre of 1644, 18
Massenberg Law, 155
Massanutten, 114
Massey, John, 126
Massive Resistance, 172–74
Matoax. *See* Pocahontas.
Mattaponi River, 6, 37, 59
Mattaponi (tribe), 15, 19
Matthews, Samuel, Jr., 19
Maynard, Robert, 37
Maury River, 138
McClellan, George C., 113–15, 118
McCormick, Cyrus, 85
McDowell, Irwin, 114
McDowell, James, 103–4, 108
McGuffey, William, 90
Meade, George, 116
Meade, Julian, 160
Meherrin River, 37
Mennonites, 41
mercantilism, 49, 51, 53, 65, 94
Mercer, Charles, 79, 89, 101
Methodists, 50, 77, 88, 92, 101, 105, 148, 149
Mexican War, 108
Middle Peninsula, 6
Middle Plantation, 21, 36
Miller, Adam, 41
Miller, Andrew, 176, 178
Miller, Francis Pickens, 169–70
Mingoes, 53
Missouri Compromise, 109
Mitchell, John, 128
Modern Puritans, 139
Mobjack Bay, 155
molasses, 46, 51, 56
Monacans, 15, 23
Monroe, James, 67, 70–73, 78, 100, 101
Monroe Doctrine, 73
Montague, Andrew Jackson, 143, 145–47
Monticello, 42, 61, 63, 78
Montpelier, 42

Moore, E. Blackburn, 172
Moral Majority, 180
Morgan, Daniel, 58
Mosby, John Singleton, 117, 121, 140
Mount Trashmore, 184
"Mr. Madison's War," 72
Muhlenberg, Peter, 58, 61
Myers, Moses, 74

Nansemond County, 56, 86, 164
Nansemond Hotel (Ocean View), 164
Nansemond River, 6, 59, 95, 132
Nansemond (tribe), 13, 15
National Industrial Recovery Act, 158
National Park Service, 155, 159
National Republicans, 74–75, 89
Natural Tunnel (park), 175
Nature Conservancy, 175
Navigation Acts, 20
*The Negro in Virginia*, 160
Nelson County, 7
Nelson, Thomas, Jr., 54, 57, 61, 62
Neolithic (New Stone Age), 9
"New American Woman," 142
New Bern, 92, 93
New Deal, 130, 158–62, 170
"New Freedom," 145
New Kent County, 17, 21, 65, 181, 184
New Lights, 49
New Market, 97, 117
Newport, Christopher, 12–14
Newport News, 135, 139, 152, 155, 158, 162, 163, 167, 169, 179, 186
Newport News Shipbuilding and Drydock Co., 135, 152, 153, 162, 163
Nicholson, Francis, 35–36
Nixon, Richard, 174, 176, 177
Nomini Hall, 42, 100
Non-Intercourse Act, 71
Norfolk Association for the Improvement of the Poor, 95
Norfolk and Petersburg Rail Road, 82, 92, 95, 124
Norfolk and Western Railway, 134–36, 168–69
Norfolk County, 23, 55, 59, 132, 142, 167
Norfolk Division (of the College of William and Mary), 159, 160
Norfolk, Franklin and Danville rail, 135
Norfolk Light Artillery Blues, 152
Norfolk Navy Yard, 72, 114
*Norfolk Revenge*, 59
Norfolk Southern Railroad, 136 179
Normal and Collegiate Institute, 126, 128
Northampton County, 26
Northern Neck, 6, 20, 23, 38, 42, 49, 100, 135
Northwest Territory, 65, 102
Nottoway County, 148
Nottoway River, 59, 134
Nottoways (tribe), 18, 37

Obenshain, Richard, 176, 178
Obici, Amedeo, 136
Oceana (Naval Air Station), 164
Occoneechee State Park, 185
Occoneechees, 21

"Urban Corridor," 184

V-12 (World War II), 164
Vagrancy Act, 121
Valentine, Lila Meade, 150
*Valley of the Shenandoah* (Tucker), 93
Valley of Virginia, 5, 6, 8, 29, 41, 50, 51, 53, 60, 77, 85, 107, 110, 114, 117, 119, 132, 147, 174, 185
Van Buren, Martin, 73, 75, 76
Van Lew, Elizabeth, 150
vestries, 18, 22, 25, 36
Vietnam War, 166
Vincennes, 58
"Virgin Queen," 11
Virginia Agricultural and Mechanical College, 126
Virginia and Tennessee Rail Road, 82, 94, 96, 97, 112, 134, 135
Virginia Beach, 160, 164, 167, 174, 180, 183–85
Virginia Central Rail Road, 82, 83
Virginia Company, 11, 12, 14
Virginia Constitution of 1776, 62
Virginia Doctrine (Resolves of 1798), 52, 69, 74
"Virginia Dynasty," 47, 73
Virginia Electric Power Company (VEPCO), 161, 162, 170, 177, 184
Virginia Iron, Coal and Coke Co., 135
Virginia Military Institute (VMI), 90, 91, 110, 117, 124, 160, 163, 164, 182
Virginia Normal and Collegiate Institute, 128
"Virginia Plan," 66
Virginia Resolves. *See* Virginia Doctrine.
Virginia Supreme Court, 163
Virginia Tech, 132, 182
Virginia Woman Suffrage Association, 150
*Voice of the People* (Glasgow), 133

Wagner Act, 158
Wakefield, 92
Walker, Gilbert, 123–25, 176
Walker, Maggie, 139
Wallace, George, 176, 177
Walpole, Robert, 41
Walton Act, 128
Wanchese, 11
Warner, John, 178
War of 1812, 70, 81, 94–96, 101, 102, 105
War Shipping Board, 153
Ward, Jackson, 128
War of Jenkin's Ear, 40
Warrenton, 97, 137
Washington and Lee, 65, 164
Washington and Ohio, 137
Washington, Booker T., 146
Washington, Bushrod, 101
Washington County, 97
Washington, George, 43, 45, 50, 53, 55, 58–61, 65–69, 87, 100, 101
Washington, Martha, 60
Washingtonians, 88
water closets, 140
Wayne, "Mad" Anthony, 61, 69
Waynesboro, 97, 156, 169
*Wealth of Nations* (Adam Smith), 48

weather, 6, 7, 45, 62
Webster, Daniel, 74, 76, 77
Weems, Mason Locke, 87
Wells, H.H., 123
werowance (weroance), 10
Werowocomoco, 12
Wesley, John, 50
West Country, 19, 25, 42, 43, 186
Westham Foundry, 61, 65
Western State Asylum, 91
West Indies, 13, 30–32, 46, 50, 51, 54–56, 61, 62, 72, 74, 94, 101
Westover (estate). 3-. 42
Westvaco Co., 161
West Virginia, 5, 9, 41, 53, 86, 112, 117, 120, 121, 123–25, 134–36, 167
Wharton, Gabriel, 135
"What think ye of Christ" (Whitefield), 34
wheat, 16, 64, 84–87, 94–97, 112, 132
Wheeling, 72, 76, 82, 85, 96, 97, 108, 109, 120
*When Hell Froze Over* (Yancey), 181
Whig Party, 75–77, 88, 89, 91, 93, 108–10, 120, 121, 123, 124
whiskey tax, 68
White, John, 11
White Sulphur Springs, 93, 141
Whitefield, George, 32, 34
Whitehurst, G. William, 175
Wilder, Doug, 180, 181
Wilderness Road, 88, 93, 97
William (King), 34, 35
Williamsburg, 21, 29, 34, 36, 42, 43, 50, 51, 54, 55, 60, 61, 65, 91, 114, 142, 153, 155, 164, 182
Willoughby Spit, 6, 114
Wilson, Woodrow, 143, 145, 150, 152
Winchester, 29, 41, 50, 51, 59, 76, 85, 89, 97, 98, 108, 115, 185
Windsor, 92
Wingfield, Edward, 12
Wirt, William, 74, 75, 92
Wise County, 134, 135, 169
Wise, Henry, 81, 88, 90, 109, 110, 113, 114, 122
Wise, John, 126, 128
witchcraft, 26, 32
Wood, Abraham, 18, 20
Woodstock, 97
Works Progress Administration (WPA), 159, 160
World War I, 130, 131, 149–52, 161, 163
World War II, 130, 140, 148, 163, 165–68, 170, 185
Wright, Robert, 101
Wyatt, Sir Francis, 17
Wythe County, 146
Wythe, George, 51, 57, 62, 64, 67
Wytheville, 97, 155

Yancey, Dwayne, 181
Yeardley, George, 14
"Ye Bear and Ye Cub," 19
Yellow Fever (Norfolk 1855), 93–95
York River, 6, 12, 55, 62, 82, 184
Yorktown, 29, 53, 61, 114, 142, 152, 153, 155
Young Men's Christian Association (YMCA), 140
"Young Turks," 172